NURSING
YOUR BABY

For personal counselling in breast feeding, or to secure printed information on practical breast feeding suggestions, contact:

La Leche League International
9616 Minneapolis Avenue
Franklin Park, Illinois 60131

NURSING YOUR BABY

Karen Pryor

A WALLABY BOOK
PUBLISHED BY POCKET BOOKS NEW YORK

POCKET BOOKS, a Simon & Schuster division of
GULF & WESTERN CORPORATION
1230 Avenue of the Americas, New York, N.Y. 10020

Copyright © 1963, 1973 by Karen Wylie Pryor

Published by arrangement with Harper & Row, Publishers, Inc.
Library of Congress Catalog Card Number: 62-20132

ISBN: 0-671-79113-3

First Wallaby printing February, 1980

10 9 8 7 6 5 4 3 2 1

WALLABY and colophon are trademarks of Simon & Schuster.

Printed in the U.S.A.

Acknowledgments

This book is a thank you note to my husband, Tap, and our children, Ted and Mike, Barracudas both, and Gale, a Gourmet. My thanks also go especially to Dr. Sidney Townsley, of the University of Hawaii. A good teacher teaches more than his subject matter; in a course on the taxonomy of marine invertebrates Dr. Townsley taught the art of tracing information, and, more important, of evaluating one's finds, in the trackless forests of scientific literature. I am grateful also to Dr. Michael Newton and his wife, Niles Newton, the eminent psychologist, for the outstanding quality of the research they have done and are doing on human lactation. Their published papers are basic to this book. In addition I would like to thank the staffs of the Sinclair Library of the University of Hawaii, the Honolulu County Medical Library, and the Rare Book Collection at the New York Academy of Medicine.

Many other people helped me greatly. Ginger MacKaye and Joan Potter contributed not only their own experiences as nursing mothers, but extensive interviews with friends. Other mothers who contributed include Eleanor Cody, Lynn Cowan, Mary Ellen Doherty, Pat Greer, Frances Haws, Elise La Taille, Mimi Martin, Moana Morris, Alice Nelson, Marianne Pryor, Gwen Stevens, Mary Townsley, Lucinda Webb, Ann Zapotocky, and the members of La Leche League.

The following people read all or part of the manuscript, and their comments were astute and helpful: Mr. and Mrs. Paul Breese; Elizabeth Christman; Dr. George Ewing; Edwina Froehlich; Dr. Bruce Alspach; Dr. James Lancaster; Taylor Pryor; Dr. and Mrs. Ernest Reese; Dr. Paula Selinsky; Mary Ann Shallenberger; Marian Tompson; Ricky Wylie and the editors of Harper & Row.

Through interviews and correspondence, many authorities contributed valuable information and suggestions, for which I am grateful, including: Dr. Louise Ames of the Gesell Institute; Mrs. Glenn Aiken, editor of *Child-Family Digest,* who provided me with a complete back file of this now out-of-print magazine; Dr. David Danforth; Dr. Irenous Ibele-Eibesfelt; Dr. Paul Gyory; Mildred Hatch; Dr. D. B. Jelliffe; Dr. E. R. Kimball; Margaret Mead; Agnes Fay Morgan; Niles Newton; Dr. Frank Howard Richardson; Dr. R. Y. Sakimoto; Dr. Robert A. Semsch; Dr. Henry Silva; Dr. Rene Spitz; and Dr. Robert Wyatt. I would also like to thank Mr. Horace Hughes and the staff of the Maternity Center of New York; Miss Margaret MacPherson of the Boston Directory for Mother's Milk; Mrs. Allen Hill of the Wilmington Mothers' Milk Bank; Mrs. Robert Jessee and Mrs. A. E. Grauptner of the San Francisco Mothers' Milk Bank; Edwina Froehlich, Marian Tompson, Dee Hoder, and Betty White of La Leche League; and the members of the Evanston Jr. League Premature Babies' Milk Bank, with special thanks to chairman Marja Newton, who not only corresponded with me at length, but baby-sat with my children while I toured the milk bank.

This book could not have been written had it not been for the friends and family who acted as baby sitters at various times: the grandparents, Mr. and Mrs. Samuel Pryor, Mr. and Mrs. Philip Wylie, and Mrs. Sally Ondeck; Koa Adolpho; Marlee Breese; Rachel Johnson; Ella Nee; and Mary Ann Shallenberger.

For the revisions in this new edition I am deeply grateful to La Leche League International, for including me on the program of the 1971 Convention. There I met many doctors, nurses, and mothers who provided me with new and exciting information and much-appreciated encouragement. I am especially in debt to R. M. Appleyard, M.D., Hugh Riordan, M.D., Frank Countryman, M.D., and Betty Ann Countryman, R.N., Gregory White, M.D., and Mary White, and Herbert Ratner, M.D.

I could not possibly have garnered so much information in so short a time without the help, support, and friendship of Carol Gholson and Faye Young. I am grateful too to Skipp Rapp, Linda Batchelor, Karen Ostergaard, Jimmie Avery, Kathy Beaudette, and Doris Haire, and to the many others who took time to write or tell me their thoughts and feelings.

Karen Pryor
Kaneohe, Hawaii
January 1973

Contents

PART ONE

Part One

1·The Nursing Couple

The oneness of the nursing mother and her baby has always fascinated mankind. Like lovers, they are united both physically and spiritually. Unlike lovers, their union lacks the ambivalence and tensions of sexuality. Christianity is not the only religion that reveres the image of mother and infant as a symbol of pure love. The Egyptians always portrayed their chief goddess Isis with the infant Horus nursing at her breast. Mother goddesses in the Near East preceded Isis, the Madonnas of past and present art follow her. Almost every great artist, from the unknown sculptors of the Hittites to Michelangelo, Renoir, and Picasso, has used as a subject the nursing mother and her child, trying to convey in stone or clay or paint their rapport, the sense of being two people and yet one.

It is brief, this unity. Within a year or two, the baby is weaned and his world expands far beyond his mother's arms. She then becomes a part of his life, rather than its center. But this is an intense relationship, for all its brevity. Mother and child share a rapport so complete that it can exert a profound effect on both partners. Without this

1

mutual understanding, breast feeding does not proceed successfully; it is as much a part of breast feeding as is the giving and taking of milk. Nursing a baby is an art; a domestic art, perhaps, but one which like cooking or gardening brings to a woman the release and satisfaction that only creative work can give. Anne Morrow Lindbergh, the poet, writes, "When I cannot write a poem, I bake biscuits and feel just as pleased." Nursing gives this same sort of satisfaction and joy. Successful nursing mothers, who have enjoyed a long, happy nursing relationship with their babies, often find it hard to understand why others refuse to breast feed. They may not be able to express in words what they themselves like about nursing. For one mother, nursing the baby may be an intense, joyful experience, while for another mother it is as casually routine as pouring a cup of coffee. But all successful nursing mothers unite in regarding the bottle-feeding mother with pity—the same pity a happily married woman feels for a frigid wife. She just doesn't know what she's missing.

THE START OF THE NURSING RELATIONSHIP

The relationship between the nursing mother and her baby begins with physical compatibility. When the mother's milk starts to flow easily, and the baby starts sucking consistently, they can become what psychiatrist M. P. Middlemore named the nursing couple, rather than two strangers. This can happen from the very first feeding, a few minutes after the baby is born. Then the nursing relationship seems to arise spontaneously, like love at first sight. This is probably the biologically normal situation. In our culture, however, the first nursing is often delayed, and both mother and baby may be under many physical or emotional handicaps. So the nursing relationship begins with a courtship, which may last for days or even weeks. If personalities clash, the courtship may be a stormy one. An occasional truly neurotic mother, breast feeding against her real wishes, cannot give herself to the baby at all. There are, after all, frigid breast feeders just as there are frigid wives. In such a case, the physical aspects of motherhood are a source of distress to both partners, and bottle feeding is gladly substituted. An occasional baby suffers from a difficult birth or other problems and does not respond normally to the breast, so that the start of breast feeding is complicated or delayed. But usually mother and baby come gradually to an understanding. They enjoy their experiences together more and more, and successful feedings become the rule. Thus a happy nursing relationship begins to grow.

THE BABY'S ROLE

Doctors, nurses and people who do not breast feed often seem to assume that the chief reward for the nursing mother is a sense of virtue, the knowledge that in breast feeding she is doing the right thing for her baby; in short, the same reward the doctor feels when he prescribes a particularly satisfactory formula. Actually, of course, while the mother is proud that the baby thrives, her reward lies in the physical satisfaction of nursing, and in her baby's response to her.

Because of the tremendous adjustments a mother needs to make in our culture, not only to the often unfamiliar job of motherhood and presence of the infant, but to learning this job under biologically bizarre circumstances, we tend to think of the mother as making all the effort in breast feeding. In reality, the effort is equally the baby's. The baby must learn that milk is what he needs, and that his mother's breast is the place to get it. If the nipple is hard to grasp he must learn how to get hold of it. If the milk is slow to start flowing he may have to acquire more patience and perseverance than he was born with. He must cope with the way his mother handles him and with the way he is dressed or wrapped, whether that suits his preference or not. Simply feeding at the breast is an effort. A baby can take milk from a bottle almost without trying, but he must work, and work hard, to milk the breast. The British novelist Angela Thirkell has described this:

"Edith was sitting in a low chair, her baby in her arms,

4 NURSING YOUR BABY

horrible greed. Her face became bright red, her few dark
hairs were dank with perspiration, one starfish hand was
clenched on a bit of her nightgown . . . she was victualling
herself as far as her adoring grandmother could make out
for a six weeks' siege at least."

When a baby contributes such hearty effort, the mother
can't help but feel grateful. Feeding is not her job alone;
the baby is an equal partner, a member of the team. And
this equality and mutual effort is the essence of the nursing
relationship.

CONTAGIOUS EMOTIONS

As Dr. Sibylle Escalona has pointed out, emotions are
contagious. Even tiny babies can "catch" emotions from
their mothers; and, as parents of high-strung, colicky babies can testify, infant emotions are contagious too. Sometimes this creates difficulties at the start of the nursing
relationship. A tense, nervous mother makes her baby so
tense that feedings are difficult or vice versa. However,
contagion of emotions can also work in favor of mother
and baby. The father's satisfaction with his wife can
soothe her immeasurably. An experienced, relaxed mother
can sometimes calm a frantic baby simply by being near
him. And when a baby settles down and begins nursing
well, his evident enjoyment and relief can convey themselves to the mother, so that she begins to enjoy the feeding too. Some trained nurses have a remarkable ability to
convey their own emotional state to others, so that everyone around them, mothers and babies alike, begins to feel
calm and cheerful. Such a nurse often has phenomenal
success in helping mothers and infants to become happy
nursing couples.

THE BONDS OF LOVE

Once the nursing relationship is established, it is not
lightly broken. Mother and baby need each other both
physically and emotionally. The baby, of course, has a

physical need for milk. His emotional need is also great: a need for contact with his mother, and for the love and reassurance he gets through all his senses while nursing, but especially through his highly sensitive mouth. The mother, in turn, has a physical need for the baby to take the milk from her breasts. Moderate fullness is not a discomfort; nevertheless, emptying the breast is relieving, satisfying, like a drink of water when one is thirsty. So a sensation of fullness makes a mother yearn for her baby, and for the satisfaction of feeding him. Many mothers learn to expect and look forward to the physical relaxation of nursing, in part an effect of the hormone oxytocin. But most of all, perhaps, the mother, like the baby, needs to be shown that she is loved; and the behavior of even a tiny baby at the breast is proof positive of that. His greed is flattering, his blissful enjoyment is contagious, his drunken satiety is a comical compliment. As he grows older, his love of his mother becomes conscious and intense. The baby of three months stares and stares at his mother's face as he nurses, looking into her eyes, and loving her with all his soul. At five or six months he plays at the breast, fiddling with a ribbon or button on his mother's dress, patting her lovingly. He smiles out of the corner of his mouth, or puts a hand up to her lips to be kissed, showing her at every feeding how much he loves her. It is quite an experience. Life is not so full of true love that one regards it as commonplace in any circumstances. It surprises no nursing mother to learn that women who breast feed have, on the whole, larger families than women who do not.

I do not wish to imply that the mother and baby who do not breast feed don't love each other; of course they do. But happy nursing couples feel differently about each other. Mothers who have bottle fed one or two children and then found that they could breast feed subsequent babies are poignantly aware of this difference. The physical intimacy of breast feeding dispels the barriers that always exist between individuals in a way that no amount of conscientious mothering can do. The nursing couple have learned to work together as a team at feedings, and this mutual understanding extends to all the other contacts they make. So mothers say a nursing baby is "easier." The ease lies not only in being free of the annoying chores of bottle feeding, but in feeling companionable and agreeable with the baby. The nursing baby is often taken along with his mother wherever she goes, not only because he needs his mother's milk, but because he is "no trouble," and mainly because she misses him when they are apart even for a few hours. This rapport can continue to be a part of the relationship of mother and child long after weaning.

It is not just in his relationship to his mother that the nursing baby enjoys a casual intimacy that the bottle-fed baby may miss. A happy nursing baby is easier on the whole household. He is always around, but seldom in the way. The nursing couple fit into the family as one individual, the baby simply an extension of the mother, nursing while she reads to other children, nursing while she has a martini with her husband, or naps, or talks on the phone, or sits down to her own dinner. It seems as if the breast-fed baby gets so much bodily attention that he requires less social attention. He is the least demanding or trouble-some member of the family, and he gets a full share of love and approval from all.

The strength of the bonds that join a nursing couple is most evident, perhaps, when those bonds are broken. It is customary at present for pediatricians to take babies off the breast for a great variety of trivial and often quite erroneous reasons. While an occasional bottle in the mother's absence does the nursing baby no harm, the infant who has been nursing at his mother's breasts for several weeks and is abruptly and totally weaned sometimes takes very unkindly to artificial feeding, has trouble digesting formula, or develops allergies. He may in fact refuse to feed altogether. One authority on infant nutrition refers to these annoying infants as "breast-milk addicts"; and the tendency among medical men is to give every baby at least an occasional bottle from birth, rather than risk his objecting to sudden weaning. As yet there seems to be little medical interest in minimizing the likelihood of sudden weaning.

It is not only the babies who object to weaning. Doctors

are often aghast at the violent reaction of nursing mothers when they are told that they must stop nursing. The mother who has been part of a happy nursing couple may burst into tears on the spot; she may even cry for days. Tell her she is still a good mother, that the baby will thrive on formula, that she has already completed a good job of breast feeding; it makes no difference. She admits her distress is foolish, but she "just can't help it." More aggravating still, it is not necessarily the nervous or childish mothers who break down; it is often the most stable and reliable women. Some doctors actually discourage women from breast feeding at all in order to avoid risking this unpredictable traumatic response when breast feeding is ordered stopped.

The mother who is told she has to stop nursing does not feel guilty or inadequate, as is often assumed. She feels grief-stricken. She feels as if her nursing baby were being taken away from her, to be returned as a stranger who needs her no longer. Of course, the woman who rejects her role as wife or mother can relinquish breast feeding easily. It is the deeply feminine woman, the truly maternal mother, who is seriously deprived when the nursing relationship is broken. That is why doctors have trouble predicting which woman will be upset by orders to wean and which will not. In this case the apparently hysterical response does not come from the hysterical woman, but from the normal mother, who feels a totally normal grief. The resourceful person will try to argue or cajole her doctor out of making her stop nursing. She may change doctors. She may beg, sometimes quite reasonably, to be allowed to resume nursing after stopping temporarily. She will, indeed, take any precaution to postpone or avoid weaning.

For example, one mother who developed a breast infection while nursing was told that she would have to wean her baby, not because her breast was infected (although this is often taken as cause for weaning), but because the antibiotic she was being given would harm the baby, through her milk. (Not true.) As a result, when she developed pneumonia while nursing a second baby, she refused any and all medication, enduring serious illness for herself rather than risking weaning the baby. Her determination was foolhardy, perhaps; it was also courageous.

Many such mothers have nursed their babies in the face of hostile critics, unsympathetic doctors, pain, and disapproval, with incredible courage and devotion. Many a grandmother who was forced unnecessarily to wean her own babies still gets tears in her eyes as she remembers how she felt. This strength of feeling, this unreasoning determination, does not arise from guilt, or neurosis, or fears of failure as a mother. It is not stubborn selfishness in the face of medical wisdom. It is love, the brief but intense love of the nursing couple.

THE BRIDGE TO INDEPENDENCE

What effect, if any, does this nursing relationship have upon the emotions and personality of the child? Many authorities (anthropologist Ashley Montagu, Dr. John Bowlby and Dr. M. Bevan-Brown among others) believe that a good nursing relationship is valuable, perhaps essential, for the emotional growth of the infant, and possibly of the mother as well. Dr. Montagu suggests that the human infant is delivered at nine months because the rapidly growing brain cannot pass through the birth canal much later than that, but that it is not a "mature" product until about nine months later, when it has teeth and a fair amount of mobility. Consequently, the species is adapted to about nine months of extrauterine gestation which ought to provide as fully for the infant's needs as did his complete protection within the womb during the nine months of pregnancy. Perhaps it is relevant that some babies wean themselves rather abruptly and spontaneously at or around the age of nine months, from breast or bottle. While nursing is often continued far beyond the nine-month point, this seems to be the earliest point at which weaning naturally occurs.

The separation of mother and child at birth is a physical and emotional shock to them both. Lactation permits this separation to be accomplished gradually, over at least a second nine-month period. Only gradually is the child parted from his old, uterine existence. When his mother feeds him long and often at her breast, this world still consists mainly of her warmth, support, and movements, her pulse, her voice, her body chemistry. He can acquire understanding of his new world of temperatures, textures, lights and sounds—"a vast, booming, blooming confusion"—from the familiar home base of her body. And it is gradually, rather than abruptly, that the mother is separated from this extension of herself, her baby. Psychologist Sîyvia Brodie, in her book *Patterns of Mothering,* describes final weaning from the breast, at nine months or more, as a kind of second birth, in which mother and child are severed spiritually as they were severed physically by delivery.

It seems reasonable to suppose that the gradual transitions provided by breast feeding are truly beneficial to the infant. Dr. Herbert Ratner says "the quickest way to make your child independent is to take care of his needs when he is dependent." It is worth noting that modern programs of infant care imitate more and more closely the natural environment and interaction of the nursing couple.

ARE BREAST-FED BABIES HAPPIER?

Breast-fed babies are indubitably *healthier* than bottle-fed babies, as we shall see in following chapters. But are breast-fed babies happier? Do they grow up to be "better adjusted?" No, say the bottle feeders. Yes, say the breast feeders. In Japan, the first question a school asks when a child is entered is how long the child was breast fed. Practical experience has indicated that the child who wasn't breast fed has a harder time getting used to school. But surveys in this country, trying to find differences between breast- and bottled-raised children at school age, have had very mixed results, and even those which have shown some advantages for breast feeding can be challenged on the ground that those children were happier because they had more affectionate mothers who were naturally more apt to breast feed.

We tend to think of breast feeding as something that involves small infants only. But human babies throughout most of the world remain nursing babies for at least one year, and often two or more. And the older baby derives obvious and perhaps important reassurance from being able to nurse. This is true of other species as well. Cornell University scientists point out that when a person enters a field of goats or sheep, all the babies run in fear to their mothers and immediately begin to nurse. Explorers have noted the same thing when a stranger enters an African village; children even of five or six immediately run to their mothers for a reassuring swig of milk. The experienced nursing mother knows that when a toddler is weaning himself he may cease to want the breast for nourishment, but still need it very much when he is frightened or has somehow hurt himself. The older bottle-fed baby gets this kind of comfort from his bottle; how adequate this is as a substitute for his mothers' lap and bosom would be hard to say.

The psychoanalytical viewpoint holds that repeated and unrelieved frustrations or unpleasant experiences in infancy, such as occur in poorly managed or unsuccessful breast feeding, are at the basis of some personality disorders in adult life. Some doctors for this reason do not encourage breast feeding, lest some patient who breast feeds hostilely or half-heartedly will do harm to her infant's psyche. But hostile or rigid bottle feeding is harmful too. It might be better to teach the mother the art of relaxed, normal breast feeding than to abandon her completely to her own nervous ways. Because of this general misunderstanding of breast feeding, it is customary to tell mothers who do not wish to nurse that bottle feeding is just as good, if it is combined with plenty of loving care, and if the baby is held and cuddled as if he were drinking from the breast. The trouble is that cuddling a baby who is taking a bottle is rather like talking to someone who is reading a newspaper. The baby is interested in the bottle, not in the mother. The mother's tendency is to begin propping bottles within a few weeks of birth; the baby is more fun to be with at other times. Perhaps this doesn't matter to the newborn. And perhaps the very affectionate mother, who enjoys giving the bottle, can "fool" the baby by holding him close and smiling and talking to him while he drinks from a bottle, so that feedings are pleasant for them both. Nevertheless the relation is platonic for her at least. It does not involve her body, her hormones, her nervous system. Her response to the baby cannot be the same. And even the most conscientious mother doesn't hold her baby once he is big enough to lie on his back and hold the bottle for himself. Again, it is hard to say what effect this has on the baby. One could speculate that this transfer of the baby's attentions from the mother to the bottle and her inevitable abandonment of him at mealtimes, whether it occurs at two months or five, make the bottle more important than ever as a token of comforting, and that this is at the root of our American admiration of material things at the expense of the spiritual. Or perhaps this widespread substitution of food for love in the American infant's life explains why we tend to be overweight and overeaters. Or perhaps, as some psychiatrists maintain, such grown-up habits as smoking, drinking, and even talking, are but substitutes for the suckling at our mother's breast that was denied us in infancy. In fact, most scientists in the field of infant behavior are beginning to agree that the fantastically high level of mental illness in this country is due, at least in part, to the systematic frustration of normal mother-infant relationships, from standardized surgical deliveries to the hospital isolation of infants, rigid child-care systems, and the almost universal failure of lactation.

WHAT ABOUT THE MOTHER?

The nursing relationship (or lack of it) may well have profound effects upon the personality of the infant. Is the mother helped in any way by the experience of nursing? Unfortunately, in this country few mothers get a chance to find out. Most Americans today know nothing about normal breast feeding. The physical events of lactation, and the emotions which are its essence, are so misunderstood, overlooked, hampered, and tampered with, by doctors, hospitals, families, friends, and nursing mothers themselves, that most of the young mothers who do try to nurse their babies never establish a normal nursing relationship. They nurse for a few weeks, augmenting their milk with formula and "solid" food, and the experience, such as it is, is over almost before it is begun. This limits the professional observer's understanding of breast feeding, as well as the mother's. The psychiatric literature therefore is not, at present, concerned with the long-range effect of nursing upon the mother, but almost entirely with her unconscious motivations as she begins lactation. The layman's impression from reading this literature is that to refuse to breast feed is neurotic, to try and fail is not normal, and to be excessively determined to succeed is suspect too.

Mothers who have experienced a normal nursing relationship, in which mother and baby are a happy nursing couple for many months, are often well aware of the emotional maturity that the experience brought them. The doctor who understands the management of breast feeding, and who in consequence sees a great many happy nursing mothers, will concur. Successful lactation seems to have a permanent and valuable effect on the mother.

Lactation is the final chapter of a woman's biological functioning. It is an oversight to consider (as Kinsey did) that sexual intercourse and its variations are the only significant form of female sexual behavior. Men, indeed, have only one biological function related to their sex: intercourse. Women have five: the ovarian cycle, intercourse, pregnancy, childbirth, and lactation. Each of these events has a powerful effect on the woman's life.

We are quite aware of the physical and emotional changes that take place when a girl reaches puberty and begins the ovarian cycle. The emotional significance and maturing effects of intercourse are reasonably well understood. Pregnancy has become a field of considerable interest to students of human emotions. Nowadays the emotional repercussions of a poorly managed childbirth and the mental and physical rewards of a well conducted labor and delivery are sufficiently recognized for natural childbirth associations to have sprung up all over the country.

But we are generally unaware of the psychological effects of experiencing a normal lactation.

When a woman breast feeds, she must give herself to the baby. She must let the baby set the pace, make the decisions, do the work. Many mothers cannot do this at first, especially if they have been handed (or have asked for) a fixed set of rules. But the normal girl eventually gets "lazy" and slips into the feminine role. She forgets to look at the clock, she doesn't bother to interrupt the baby for her own reasons, she doesn't worry about when or why he wants to eat. She actively gives the baby her milk and her love, whenever he seems to want it. She lets him move around, start and stop, nurse at his own rate, interrupt his meals, or, when she has leisure, prolong them. She learns to participate in feedings without dominating or deciding anything, to be deeply interested but quite casual about the whole matter. This is the natural result of successful breast feeding, no matter what kind of personality the mother has. The woman who cannot develop this completely casual approach with the first baby often adopts it with her second; that is one reason why many nursing mothers "have more milk" the second time around. And even the most managing of women can often learn how to breast feed in a natural, relaxed way from contact with other mothers who are nursing successfully.

This kind of cooperation is the essence of the female role, in this or any other mammalian species. It is rather foreign to our culture. For many American girls, prolonged breast feeding constitutes their first experience of being truly feminine, of the receptive female role which is in a sense as active as any masculine decisiveness. The experience of true biological femininity, over a year or so of breast feeding, can teach a mother how to go about being womanly. Her relationship with her husband may change for the better. Her attitude toward the rest of her children may improve; by being more womanly she becomes a better mother to all of them.

THE FATHER AND THE NURSING COUPLE

A man usually derives great satisfaction from the pretty sight of his wife nursing his child. Dr. Hugh Smith, the Dr. Spock of eighteenth-century London, wrote, to urge mothers to nurse their babies:

Oh, that I could prevail upon my fair countrywomen to become still more lovely in the sight of men. I speak from the feelings of a man . . . rest assured, when he beholds the object of his soul cherishing and supporting in her arms the propitious reward of wedlock . . . it recalls a thousand delicate sensations to a generous mind.

For a mother, then or now, one of the happiest rewards of nursing is the glow of approval on her husband's face when he first sees the baby at her breast.

Becoming a father changes a man's position somewhat. He becomes the head of a household of three rather than the companion or mate of courting days. And in no place is his paternal guidance and strength more valuable than in the nursing relationship. The mother's ability to give her milk, and her love, to her baby is built upon the love and security that her husband gives to her. He is the foundation of the family. A new nursing mother, totally involved with her new condition of being two people instead of one, is in many ways extremely dependent. She needs to be guarded and cared for, so that she is free to grow gradually into motherhood, without outside problems. Her husband provides this buffer against the outside world. A husband can often be far more clear-sighted about minor nursing problems than his wife could be. Many a nursing mother is aware that she has nursed her baby successfully entirely because her husband thought she *should* and knew she *could,* whatever the neighbors said. On the other hand, if a husband does not support his wife in breast feeding she will almost certainly fail. For example, Muriel McClure, R.N., professional lactation consultant who guarantees breast feeding success for her patients, will not accept a case if the husband disapproves of breast feeding, no matter what his reasons. Even husbandly indifference is ominous; in her experience, indifference or lack of enthusiasm conceals a disapproval which is enough to insure that the wife will not be able to nurse successfully.

In our culture, perhaps more than any other, the father's role in encouraging the nursing mother is vital. The American bride is totally ignorant of the skills of breast feeding. Any little girl in Bali or Beirut grows up with ample experience of observing successful nursing couples, starting with seeing a sibling at the breast shortly after she herself is weaned. A new American mother may never have seen a baby nursing, even once, and she may never have held a new baby until she first holds her own. In the trial-and-error process of learning about breast feeding she needs the help and support of her husband very much. And because doctors, hospitals, and relatives may be as ignorant of nursing as she is, the new father has the vital task of shielding her from her culture, of defending his wife's right to be a true mother and his infant's inalienable right to its mother's milk.

2·How the Breasts Function*

MAKING MILK

Any woman can nurse a baby. Most women could nurse twins. Medical science has never recorded a case of a woman who gave birth and did not subsequently have milk in her breasts. There is no medical reason, save dangerous infectious disease, mortal illness, or insanity, for

* This chapter, "How the Breasts Function," stands as reference material to the rest of the book. I suggest browsing through it quickly, to understand the basis of the chapters that follow, and then returning to it later for detailed explanations if desired. In the interests of readability, I have used the terms "breast milk," "human milk," and "mother's milk" interchangeably. The term "fully breast fed" refers to the infant who is getting no sustenance other than breast milk, and is getting that in adequate quantity. I have used the term "formula" for all milks (other than breast milk) or milk mixtures or milk substitutes which are fed to babies in bottles. Formula is no longer considered an adequately scientific term but it is the one which mothers use, and which doctors use in speaking to mothers. I have used "bottle feeding" and "artificial feeding" interchangeably. "Breast" refers only to the human mammary gland. The general term "mammary gland" includes all species. "Weaning" refers to the complete cessation of breast feeding, unless otherwise specified as in "weaning from the bottle."

preventing a mother from nursing. If you are fit to have a baby you are fit to nurse it.

When milk is present, it needs only to be removed for the body to make more milk. The more removed, the more will be made. Thus the supply increases as the demand increases. This system is so automatic that it is possible for a woman who has not had a baby in years to develop a bountiful milk supply simply by putting an infant to her breasts. Many mothers in the United States are discovering that they can nurse an adopted baby long after having weaned their own youngest. It is the custom, in some African tribes, for grandmothers and mothers alike to suckle the babies, thus assuring ample milk in times of hardship. It is possible for a mother who did not nurse her baby during its first weeks of life to start putting it to the breast at the age of a month, or two months, or three, and by letting demand increase her supply, build up enough secretion to maintain the baby entirely on her own milk. The problem of feeding a baby who is allergic to formula has recently been solved in this way by several American mothers.

This remarkable function, the ability to produce ample and excellent food for the newborn young, is what separates us mammals from the lower creatures. Lactation probably arose early in the evolution of living creatures. In a sense, it is older than pregnancy. The monotremes, those ancient but still living forms such as the duck-billed platypus, lay eggs like reptiles. But the young, once hatched, drink their mother's milk. The platypus has no nipples. Milk simply oozes through the pores of the skin on the abdomen, and the babies lick it off. The next step, as shown in marsupials such as the opossum, was the development of the nipple, which serves to collect the milk in one spot, gives the young something to grasp, and prevents accidental separation from their milk supply. In mammals, internal gestation was the final step in protecting and nourishing the young.

How the Breasts Develop

The mammary glands, from which the word "mammal" is taken, appear early in the development of the embryo in the form of two thickened bands, the mammary ridges or milk lines, running down the center of the body. In the human species these milk lines are discernible when the embryo is six weeks old. By the time it is five months along, the nipple, areola, or darkened area around the nipple, and the duct system beneath the nipple are all developed. In humans, of course, the mammary glands develop relatively high on the embryonic milk lines, in the chest region. In other species, the glands may develop low on the milk line, as in hoofed animals, or in serial pairs, as in dogs and cats. The existence of auxiliary pairs of nipples in human beings, either below or above the usual pair, is not too uncommon—occurring about twice as often as the birth of triplets. These supernumerary nipples usually (but not always) are non-functioning during lactation.

When a human baby is born, its breasts are usually enlarged, due to the presence of lactation hormones received from the placenta. Regardless of the sex of the child, the glands may actually secrete drops of milk during the first days after birth—what nurses and midwives sometimes call witches' milk. Once this activity ceases, the mammary glands remain inactive, simply growing along with the rest of the body, until a year or two before puberty. Then, in girls, the ovaries begin to release increasing quantities of estrogen into the bloodstream, causing the nipples and areolas to enlarge.

When the menstrual cycles begin, the ovaries give off increased estrogen in amounts which wax and wane cyclically. When estrogen levels are highest, around the midpoint of each menstrual cycle, the major part of breast development takes place. The ducts continue to ramify and branch away from the nipples like tributaries of a river or branches of a tree, and fat is laid down around the duct system giving the breast its size and shape. (Buxomness or the lack of it is not a good indication of potential ability to lactate; it is mostly a result of the quantity of nonfunctional fatty tissue in the breast.) The development of the breasts depends not only upon estrogen, but also upon pituitary hormones which govern general body growth. Once the body is mature and growth has ceased, in the late teens or early twenties, breast growth is not noticeable until and unless the individual becomes pregnant.

BREAST CHANGES IN PREGNANCY

Everyone who ever got pregnant is aware of the changes that pregnancy produces in the breasts, often in the very first weeks. Some women have sensations of fullness and soreness which normally occur for a day or two before each menstrual period. When these sensations suddenly seem to be going on day after day, the experienced mother goes flying to her calendar to figure out when the new baby might be expected. By the time the first period is overdue the glands of Montgomery, which lie in the areola in a ring around the nipple, have become prominent. (Montgomery described them in a famous medical hyperbole as "a constellation of miniature nipples scattered over a milky way.") By the fifth month the mother is out buying larger bras. Nipple and areola become larger and darker; in a brunette, the whole breast may become darker. By the ninth month even the new bras may seem a little tight. These changes reflect the preparation of the breasts for lactation, and are caused by hormones circulating in the bloodstream. With elegant economy, nature uses the same set of hormones for milk production that are used to govern the menstrual cycle.

The menstrual cycle is maintained by a sort of hormonal round robin, in which the pituitary gland and the ovaries stimulate each other to produce a series of hormones which in the first half of the cycle develop and release an egg, and in the second half of the cycle prepare the uterus for possible pregnancy, should that egg become fertilized. The ovarian hormone progesterone (pro-gestation) which predominates in the second half of the cycle, causes the uterine lining to thicken. It is apparently progesterone also which produces premenstrual changes in the breasts: the feeling of tenderness and fullness, and sometimes an actual temporary increase in size. If no pregnancy takes place progesterone production ceases and the uterine lining is sloughed away in the menstrual flow. If conception takes place, however, the fertilized egg itself produces a hormone which keeps the ovaries producing progesterone; the uterine lining remains to support the embryo.

After about six weeks the placenta develops and begins to take over the hormone production job. The placenta releases very high levels of estrogen, as well as some progesterone, into the body. This combination stimulates tremendous changes in the breasts. Up to now, growth has taken place only in the duct system, which will transport the milk down to the nipples. Once the placenta has developed, a whole new system is added. This is the secretory system which actually makes the milk. The end of every duct branches and rebranches and buds off into little sacs, called the alveoli, which are lined with milk-secreting cells. The increase in breast size during pregnancy is a result mainly of the addition of alveoli to the mammary structure.

In the second half of pregnancy the placenta begins producing prolactin, the pro-lactation hormone. This stimulates further growth of the alveoli, and also causes them to secrete milk. There is milk in the breasts from the fifth or sixth month of pregnancy; miscarriage or premature delivery from this time on is followed by lactation.

If prolactin, which causes milk secretion, is present and the alveoli are capable of producing milk, why don't pregnant women lactate? Apparently because the very high levels of estrogen (and progesterone) produced by the placenta stimulate breast growth but inhibit the secretion of milk. Once the baby is born and the placenta, with its hormones, is gone, normal milk secretion can start. How soon it starts depends on sucking stimulation.

How Lactation Begins

It is customary in this country to tell mothers that the milk will "come in" three to five days after delivery. It is also customary not to put the baby to the breast for the first time until twelve or twenty-four or even thirty-six hours after birth. Feedings thereafter are limited to six a day, or five, if a night feeding is omitted. Sucking may be restricted to five minutes a side until the milk comes in. Under these restrictions the early secretion of the breast, a yellowish fluid called colostrum, does not give way to true milk for several days, sometimes a week or more. As true milk production begins, the repeated long intervals between feedings allow the breast to fill up, and then overfill. The milk is said to have "come in," and what is actually a gradual affair may seem very sudden; the mother who was not conscious of any milk production on the third day may wake up on the fourth day, after an eight-hour sleep, to find herself bursting and dripping with milk. She may swiftly become so full that it becomes difficult to withdraw the milk by any means. This engorgement is a common problem in American maternity wards. High prolactin levels after delivery cause a high rate of milk secretion, greater perhaps than will be experienced again, once supply is adjusted to demand, for many months. As one doctor tells his patients, "Nature doesn't know you didn't have twins." With milk secretion proceeding at such a pace it is no wonder that the mother overfills when the hospital routine keeps the baby away from her four or even eight hours.

Infant Weight Loss and Gain

If the baby is not fed on formula he loses weight during this long waiting period before the milk comes in, and while engorgement is making feedings difficult. He may lose a pound or more. This weight loss has long puzzled doctors. A baby is born with extra fluids in its tissues; it is to be expected that it would lose a few ounces as its fluids balance becomes normal and as the bowels are evacuated. But why should nature routinely delay the advent of the mother's milk, and allow the baby to lose more weight than he can afford to lose?

A team of researchers working with village women in India found that under conditions more normal, biologically speaking, than ours it would appear that nature does *not* delay the milk, and the baby does *not* lose an excessive amount of weight. If the baby is nursed at the hour of birth, and long and often thereafter without restriction, colostrum gives way to true milk about twenty-four hours after delivery instead of the three to five days Western hospitals have come to expect. While secretion may be over-abundant at first, so that the breasts are often full, the baby is always available to reduce the overload, the supply soon adjusts to demand, and there is no painful engorgement. The baby loses a few ounces in the first day, as he excretes surplus fluid and as the slightly laxative colostrum cleans out his digestive tract, but he turns the corner and begins to gain weight within thirty-six to forty-eight hours after birth.

"DRYING UP" THE MILK

Doctors who wish to dry up a mother's milk generally prescribe Stilbestrol. This is a synthetic form of estrogen. By maintaining estrogen levels in the mother's body at the pre-delivery high, milk secretion is inhibited. Sometimes it is possible to get through the "drying up" period without having the breasts overfill painfully by inhibiting secretion in this way. Stilbestrol suppresses lactation but it does not terminate secretion; milk secretion stops because milk is not removed from the breast. So lactation is actually terminated by the mother's failure to nurse her baby. The mother who has been given Stilbestrol by mistake can still lactate if she continues to let the baby nurse. Stilbestrol is also used in some hospitals to inhibit secretion, even in nursing mothers, with the intention of preventing overfilling and engorgement. In India, folk medicine prescribes garlic for the newly lactating mother. Garlic contains plant estrogens, and may possibly have some effect in reducing overfilling.

In the last few years various other drugs have been coming into use to prevent lactation. Some of these can be administered during labor or even before labor. One is supposed to be effective not only in suppressing milk secretion, but in reducing the mother's desire to nurse.

Breast Feeding, Menstruation, and Conception

Throughout pregnancy, the menstrual cycle can be thought of as being suspended at a point just before menstruation would have taken place, had conception not occurred. Once the baby and hormone-producing placenta are removed, the menstrual cycle in effect takes up at the point where it left off. Progesterone production falls off, the uterine lining is discarded through menstruation, and the cycle resumes.

However, if the mother nurses her baby, this event may be postponed. Prolactin is the pituitary hormone which triggers the production of progesterone in the menstrual cycle. Its role in the menstrual cycle is brief; it appears as a result of high estrogen levels caused by the release of an egg from the ovaries, and disappears as those estrogen levels fall. But prolactin can be produced in two cases: when estrogen levels are high, or when the breasts are stimulated by the sucking of a baby. When a mother nurses her baby this very action produces the prolactin which keeps her ovaries secreting progesterone. The menstrual cycle continues to be suspended and ovulation does not take place. Breast feeding therefore tends to provide a natural contraceptive. (Progesterone is also the main constituent, in synthetic form, of birth-control pills such as Enovid, which act to bypass the ovulation half of the menstrual cycle.)

It takes a lot of sucking stimulation to hold the menstrual cycles at bay, especially in the first months. The baby who is nursed frequently, and is maintained exclusively on his mother's milk, provides this ample stimulation. Throughout most of the world, because babies are nursed this way for six months or more, the menstrual cycles of their mothers are suspended for six to eighteen months after delivery, the length of time in individual cases depending, probably, on the baby's avidity for the breast, the feeding customs of the area, and the mother's general health. Thus babies tend to arrive at roughly two year intervals. It has been suggested recently by some doctors that repeated menstrual periods, year in, year out, are neither good nor normal, and that perhaps nature intended mature women to have one pregnancy plus one lactation, followed by another pregnancy and lactation, and so on, with only a few menstrual periods in between.

If nursing of the newborn is restricted during the first few weeks, by a four-hour schedule for example, the menstrual cycles may resume shortly after delivery. If the baby is given copious quantities of solid foods or formula, he will spend less time at the breast and the mother's menstruation will resume.

The younger the baby, the more the solid foods will interfere with his appetite and digestion, and the more likely they are to reduce nursing and allow menstruation to resume. However, a mother who was giving her baby a lot of supplementary food in the first two or three months, and then becomes more confident, builds up her milk supply, and begins breast feeding fully, may find that she has one or two periods and then no more for many months, because full lactation is suppressing them.

When the fully breast-fed baby reaches the age of six months or so, and is ready and eager for finger and spoon feeding, he is about twice the size and weight he was at birth. He may continue to make substantial demands on the breast, even though he is beginning to eat other foods, and this may continue to suppress menstruation. His demand may dwindle with almost imperceptible gradualness, from five or six nursings a day at six months to one nursing a day at eighteen months. At some point, whether it occurs at the three-feedings-a-day-level or the one-feeding-every-other-day level, his mother's menstrual cycles will resume. (Of course menstruation will resume promptly if the baby is abruptly and entirely weaned.) The resumption of the menstrual cycle is a by-product of lactation events. In itself it has no effect on milk production, and a woman may and often does continue to feed her baby at the breast long after her periods have started up again.

It is thought that the menstrual cycle usually resumes with menstruation rather than with ovulation, and that usually two or three periods take place before the mother ovulates. The chances are good that a woman will not conceive again before she has had at least one period. For the nursing mother who is interested in the contraceptive value of breast feeding a fuller discussion is available in "Breast Feeding and Natural Child Spacing," by Sheila K. Kippley (see Selected References).

But suppose the menstrual cycle in a mother who is still lactating is interrupted by another pregnancy? What happens to the mother and her milk? For the first few weeks, very little. Then as the placenta develops and produces high estrogen levels, milk production is once again suppressed. Golopan and Belevady's studies in India, where village mothers may nurse the "old" baby until the arrival of the new one, show that the quantity of milk diminishes greatly as pregnancy advances, no matter how much the baby nurses, but that such milk as is produced is extremely rich in fats and vitamins and may continue to form an important source of nutrition for the older baby.

How long a pregnant mother should continue to nurse the previous baby is dictated on the whole by custom. In some cultures the baby is weaned as soon as the mother realizes she is pregnant again. If other good food is available the older baby may spontaneously wean himself as the breast becomes less productive. In other cultures the mother may nurse the older infant through her pregnancy and right along with the new one afterwards.

There is no doubt that lactating, especially during the second half of pregnancy, is a drag on the mother. In each six months or so of lactation a mother may produce a hundred pounds or more of milk, which makes greater demands on her bodily reserves than the six or eight pounds of baby produced and nourished during the nine months of pregnancy. Where living conditions are poor and diet is inadequate, the mother's health suffers more severely when she is breast feeding a baby than when she is pregnant with one. If she is doing both at once the developing fetus is likely to suffer too.

Human Production Capacity

The power of natural selection, though it has not produced such extreme production capacity as man has bred in the modern dairy cow, has nevertheless made all female mammals relatively good producers of milk. The number of young a mammalian female can feed is limited not by ability to produce milk but by the number of nipples available. Peak production capacity is well above normal peak demand. This seems to be just as true for humans as for other species. Hospital milk banks, which collect and store human milk for premature and sick babies, have found that almost any woman who cares to be a donor can produce surplus milk beyond her own baby's needs. Many women can produce at least twice as much milk as is needed by the average baby; experienced nursing mothers generally have no trouble breast feeding twins. Such individual variations as exist seem to be entirely within the mammalian safety margin. A woman with a supernormal ability to lactate might be able to nurse three or four babies. Such women were often on the staffs of foundling hospitals in previous centuries. (There is a record of a woman in a French orphanage who for a short time maintained seven babies on her own milk.) A woman with a subnormal inherited potential can probably produce enough milk for at least *one* baby. One often hears it suggested that because we in the United States raise so many babies on the bottle, allowing the survival of offspring of mothers with subnormal lactating ability, we are becoming in truth what the Russians call us in jest: a nation of milkless women. Fortunately, evolution does not work that quickly. The ancient mammalian equipment cannot be rendered nonfunctional in the random breeding of a few generations.

The existence of the hypogalactic woman, that is, the woman who cannot make enough milk for any baby because she does not have enough alveoli in her breasts, has been often postulated but never very clearly demonstrated. What *has* been clearly demonstrated is that alveoli can be developed in the presence of prolactin and possibly other lactation hormones even without the high estrogen levels of pregnancy. The sucking stimulus alone, by triggering hormone production, is able to cause the development of sufficient alveoli to maintain full lactation. Perhaps the fact that breast feeding itself makes the breasts function is what makes it possible for the mother who can give her newborn baby but a few ounces of milk per day to produce a quart or more daily after a few months of lactation. Poor lactation in our society is due to a multitude of cultural interferences rather than to physical incapacities. In natural populations of animals, and in human societies all over the world, virtually every female normal enough to bear offspring is able to give adequate milk. By and large the only naturally occurring physical causes which interrupt lactation are: the extreme illness or death of mother or baby; birth of a baby to a mother so young that her breasts have not developed; or the birth of a hare-lipped or otherwise abnormal baby which cannot suck.

GIVING MILK

THE LET-DOWN REFLEX

Despite normal equipment, a great many civilized women "cannot" nurse a baby. They just don't seem to have enough milk. If prolactin causes milk secretion, why can't we solve the problems of the modern woman who "doesn't have enough milk" by giving her prolactin injections? This has been tried, but it is generally not a success. Almost always, the factor which is limiting the amount of milk a mother has for her baby is not prolactin production; in fact, it has nothing whatsoever to do with how much milk she is making.

Making milk, so simple and automatic when enough sucking stimulation is provided, and the milk which has been made already is removed, is only half of lactation. *Giving* milk is the other and equally important half. The nursing baby cannot get his mother's milk by himself. Even the powerful mechanical suction of a breast pump can remove no more than about a third of the milk, that milk which lies in the large collecting ducts or milk sinuses right under the nipple. The milk in the smaller ducts and alveoli themselves cannot be withdrawn by outside forces.

To make all the milk available to the baby requires the functioning of a reflex within the breast which, because dairymen have always spoken of cows "letting down" their milk, is called the let-down reflex. (In England it is sometimes termed "the draught." The name "milk ejection reflex" is also used.) In the milk-secreting lobes of the breast and along the walls of the ducts lie octopus-shaped cells called basket cells, which reach their thread-like arms around the alveoli and duct walls. When the let-down reflex operates, all these cells contract. The alveoli are compressed and the ducts are widened. Milk is quickly pushed down into the main milk sinuses under the nipple. It may even be pushed out of the duct openings to drip or spray from the nipples.

When the baby nurses, he does not actually remove milk by suction. Such suction as he exerts is merely sufficient to keep the nipple in place in the back of his mouth. Then with tongue and jaws he compresses the areola and the large milk sinuses beneath, and presses the milk that is in the sinuses into his mouth. In this way he milks the breast; and this is the way all mammals (except of course, the platypus) get their milk. When the baby starts to nurse, he usually empties the milk sinuses fairly quickly. Meanwhile, the tactile sensations received by the mother from the highly senstive nipple trigger the release of the hormone that causes the basket cells to contract. The milk lets down. The sinuses refill immediately, as fast as the baby can empty them. He need hardly make the effort to milk the breast; the milk comes pouring into his throat of its own accord. Even a very tiny or weak baby can thus get plenty of milk, almost effortlessly. In fact a newborn baby can be quite overcome by the sudden abundance from a strong let-down reflex. He may choke, gasp, sputter, get milk up his nose, and have to let go and catch his breath while the milk goes to waste, spraying all over the bedclothes and his face. Fortunately, most babies are excited rather than upset by this misadventure, and come back to the breast with avid greed.

A functioning let-down reflex is crucial to the nourishing of the baby, not only because the baby receives but a third of the milk without the let-down, but because he can receive the fat content of the milk *only* if the milk is let down. It has long been known that the last few swallows of milk are the richest; dairymen distinguish between the thin "fore milk" and the fat-filled "hind milk." Dr. F. E. Hytten of the University of Aberdeen in Scotland has shown in an ingenious demonstration with sponges that the fat particles, being sticky, tend to cling to the walls of the alveoli and ducts and to be drawn off only as the alveoli are emptied. As we have seen, the alveoli are never emptied if the milk doesn't let down. Since in human milk 50 per cent of the calories come from the fat content, an inhibited let-down reflex means a hungry baby even if a fair amount of fluid is being taken in.

If the milk is let down then the fat content of the milk rises throughout the feeding, reaching a peak at the end. Although the first milk looks thin and bluish, the last drops are creamy and white. (In the breast that the baby is *not* nursing from the fat mixes into the milk as the let-down occurs, and the difference is less noticeable.) Even a weak let-down reflex results in both more and richer milk being available. (Measurement of fat content before and after a feeding has been suggested as a simple hospital test for let-down function.)

The let-down reflex is a simple physical response to a physical stimulus. It is supposed to work like clockwork. Why then is failure of the let-down reflex the basic cause of almost every breast-feeding failure? Because this reflex is greatly affected by the mother's emotions. Any disturbance, particularly in the early days of lactation, can cause inhibition of the let-down reflex. Such stresses as embarrassment, irritation, or anxiety actually prevent the pituitary from secreting oxytocin. Thus the woman who dislikes breast-feeding or is very much afraid she will fail may actually give less milk than the mother who is interested and hopeful of success. A strong disturbance, such as real anger or fear, sends adrenalin through the system, which causes the small blood vessels to contract, so that oxytocin, even if released, does not reach the basket cells which make the milk let down. This is what is happening to the girl whose milk stops flowing and baby starts crying when a critical relative walks in the room.

Fatigue; interruptions; embarrassment; fear and pain; anxiety about money, about children at home, about breast feeding itself; brusque doctors and disagreeable nurses; these and similar disturbances are almost unavoidable features of hospitalization for childbirth. Many mothers do not even begin letting down their milk until they leave the hospital, by which time they may have been told they cannot breast feed because of the baby's excessive weight loss. Others do all right in the hospital but "lose their milk" on going home, when household responsibilities and family stresses inhibit their let-down reflex. Even the mother who gives her baby a fair amount of milk and who seems to be making a success of breast feeding may have a weak or unreliable let-down reflex for the first six weeks or longer.

When the let-down reflex is poorly established, any minor disturbance, such as company, a late evening, a cold, a quarrel, is enough to tip the balance, to inhibit the reflex so that milk is left in the breast. Furthermore the fatty particles in the milk remain in the secretory cells, so that what milk the baby does receive is low-calorie. Consequently the baby is hungry and must be given a bottle. Soon milk secretion is diminished because less milk is being removed. Unfortunately this is usually regarded by both mother and doctor as the beginning of the end of lactation, rather than as a temporary and remediable situation.

Physical repercussions of a poor let-down reflex: The

inhibited let-down reflex is at the root of many of the apparently purely physical problems common in modern hospitals.

Engorgement due to feeding delay can be relieved simply by nursing the baby; but when the let-down reflex is not working, engorgement grows worse even when the baby is fed, because he cannot take the milk out of the breast. An injection of oxytocin, followed by pumping with a breast pump, may relieve the breast of prodigious quantities of milk, unless the overloading has progressed to the point where the surplus milk presses on the milk ducts, keeping them shut so that no milk can pass.

A faulty let-down reflex also increases the chance of cracked or injured nipples, because the baby chews and sucks fruitlessly, creating strong negative pressures and causing abrasion by alternately sucking and spitting the nipple out.

Mastitis, or bacterial infection within the breast, is almost always a result of faulty let-down. A bacterial infection can start only if stasis exists, that is, if milk flow in all or part of the breast has stopped. Women who are just starting to lactate are probably especially vulnerable, since their let-down reflex may not yet work with any efficiency. Mastitis in later lactation is often associated with some emotional crisis. A nursing mother's husband or child is injured; the shock interrupts her let-down reflex so that temporary stasis sets in, and an infection starts. In Great Britain during the Second World War it was noticed that the rate of mastitis among nursing mothers rose considerably during periods of bombing raids.

The medical treatments of these ailments of the nursing mother are many; if would be much simpler to avoid the ailments by treating their principal cause, the inhibited let-down reflex itself. And it is only by improving the let-down reflex that we can even hope to treat the major problem of lactation: failure to give enough milk.

Encouraging the let-down reflex: How can we treat the faulty let-down reflex? Of course we cannot psychoanalyze every new mother to remove deep emotional blocks to breast feeding. Chances are that few mothers have any

serious problems along those lines anyway. But this is no
reason to overlook ways to encourage a good let-down reflex, starting with alteration of hospital routines to permit
adequate time for breast feeding, and with removal of at
least some of the hospital disturbances which inhibit the
let-down reflex. Medication can help, too. Tranquilizers
help some mothers in letting down their milk despite disturbances in the hospital or at home; for most mothers, a
mild alcoholic beverage will do the same trick. One famous obstetrician prescribes a small glass of wine for
nursing mothers just before feeding time. This has the
double benefit of relaxing the mother and relieving discomfort from sore nipples, "stitches," or cramps, discomfort which may in itself hamper the let-down reflex.

When a mother's circumstances or anxiety make her
particularly slow to let down her milk, some doctors prescribe 0.5 to 1.0 cc. of oxytocin, to be administered in a
nasal spray just before each feeding. The oxytocin is
quickly absorbed through the nasal membranes and the
milk lets down unfailingly. The effect of emotional inter-
ference is bypassed, and the mother's self-produced let-
down is conditioned. (One mother reported that by the
second week her milk began to let down when she picked
up the nasal spray bottle.) Simple manual expression of
milk (by compressing the areola and the large ducts with
the fingers) before the baby feeds can also make the milk
let down, and is sometimes used to save a weak or reluctant baby the effort of pre-let-down sucking, or to spare a
cracked or sore nipple from the extra stress of being
nursed before the milk flow starts. In some hospitals massage is used to promote the let-down reflex. A light,
fingertip massage of the breast can stimulate the reflex.
(Firm massage of the whole breast, from the perimeter towards the nipple, followed by manual expression, can
move milk down into the main sinuses and out of the duct
openings simply by mechanical pressure. However, if the
breast is at all engorged, firm massage is painful and can
lead to bruising and further difficulties.)

Perhaps the easiest tool at mother's or doctor's disposal
for encouraging a good let-down reflex is the nature of the

reflex itself. It is very easily conditioned. By exposing the mother to some other constant stimulus, it is possible to "teach" the let-down reflex to operate when needed, even if inhibiting factors are present. Some hospitals go so far as to ring a bell when the babies are about to be brought from the nursery. The mothers' milk soon begins to flow, like the saliva of Pavlov's dog, at the sound of the bell. Any routine that is customarily followed before nursing, such as drinking a glass of milk, or bathing the breasts, or simply sitting down and unbuttoning, can be a conditioning stimulus for the let-down reflex. This reflex can be conditioned to a time interval; after the first few weeks, when some babies settle down to a fairly predictable feeding pattern, the milk may let down automatically when mealtime rolls around. It's often quite a surprise for a new mother, out at a party for the first time since the baby arrived, to find herself suddenly drenched with milk at 10 P.M. As the reflex begins to be conditioned, the milk may let down when the mother sees the baby, or hears it cry, or even when she simply thinks of the baby. The let-down reflex can even become conditioned to the mother's emotion as she starts to nurse, letting down whenever she feels a sense of pleasurable anticipation: one mother's milk lets down when she sits down to a good dinner; another's when she steps into a hot tub. Making love can make the milk let down.

The early symptoms of irregular let-down, such as uncontrolled leaking, milk letting down at the wrong time or not at all, and marked fluctuations in milk production, decrease as the reflex becomes really well conditioned and established. In the American mother nursing for the first time, the let-down may not even be strong enough to be felt (as a pins-and-needles or pressured sensation) for six weeks or more. Leaking and spraying and other symptoms of incomplete conditioning may continue for months, even throughout the nursing period. In mothers in other cultures, or in the experienced mother with her second or third or fourth nursing baby, the let-down reflex feels very strong from the first week or even from the first feeding. It operates without fail at every feeding. Leaking and spraying soon stop, perhaps because the sphincter muscles within the nipples begin to function. Presumably these sphincter muscles, like a closed drawstring, hold the milk in the breast until the baby relaxes the nipple by sucking. In this case, after the milk lets down, the filled milk sinuses may stand out in visible ridges under the areola, but no dripping or leaking out occurs.

The well-conditioned let-down reflex of the experienced nursing mother is the secret of her ample, steady milk production, day in, day out, and of her satisfied baby. She hardly thinks of it; she may not even be aware of the prickling or swelling sensation as the milk lets down. Her baby wants to nurse, she gives him the breast, and the milk comes; it is infallible. Only when the baby himself begins to lose interest in the breast, which will not occur for at least nine months, does her milk supply diminish and her let-down reflex appear later and later in the feeding, and finally fade away. If the baby were to get sick at this point and want the breast more often, or if, as in the old custom of wet nursing, another baby were adopted, both milk secretion and let-down reflex would return.

When the let-down reflex is truly secure, even a real emotional shock may not shake it. And the normal extra efforts that occur in every woman's life—sitting up all night with a sick child, or cooking a Thanksgiving dinner for twenty, or catching the flu,—can be withstood. Milk supply and nursing baby flourish.

MILK TENSION

One additional cause of a fluctuating milk supply, especially in the early months, is overfilling of the breasts. Increasing milk tension, or pressure within the breast as milk accumulates, mechanically inhibits the secretory cells so that they may slow down or cease production, temporarily. The inexperienced mother who postpones feedings or sleeps through feedings despite her own increasing discomfort, may mechanically reduce her milk supply for following feedings.

The storage capacity of the breast increases over the

months of nursing. Here a small-breasted woman may be at an initial disadvantage. Her breasts may fill to the point of undesirably high milk tension in two or three hours, necessitating frequent feedings during the first weeks, until storage capacity improves. In general, if the full breast feels lumpy, there is some back pressure occurring and the baby should be fed.

MILK ABUNDANCE

Making milk and giving milk; secretion and let-down; these are the two halves of lactation. We are beginning to understand how it is that the body performs these functions. But many mysteries remain. How do the mammary tissues take sugar, protein, and fat molecules out of the bloodstream and convert them into the entirely different sugars, proteins, and fats found in milk? Biochemists are just beginning to study this involved problem. Perhaps even more puzzling, what is the mechanism that controls the abundance of milk?

On a practical level, any nursing mother can answer that. The amount of milk produced is a direct result of the amount the baby removes. Ordinarily, researchers have found, a baby removes about 80 per cent of the milk in the breast. When hunger makes him nurse longer or more frequently, so that he removes almost 100 per cent, production is increased until the breasts are again meeting his demands, and also producing the 20 per cent surplus. When he is less hungry for milk, and leaves more than 20 per cent within the breast, production is correspondingly diminished.

The mechanism works; but what hormones or neurological reactions make it work, we don't know. The growth hormone, somatotrophin, which plays some part in mammary gland development, may have a role in maintaining milk abundance. Perhaps the thyroid gland, which controls the rate of metabolism, is a factor too. Many women are slightly deficient in thyroid during lactation. Administering thyroid to such mothers has been observed not only to relieve such symptoms as excessive fatigue, but also in some cases to increase the amount of milk produced.

NUTRITION

All over the world, women produce abundant milk on very inadequate diets. With anything approaching an adequate diet, women in most primitive cultures not only produce plenty of milk but do so without physical detriment to themselves. Yet in 1958 F. E. Hytten and others found that in civilized England, among women on presumably ample diets, "breast feeding is by no means usually associated with maternal well-being." Hytten found that 44 per cent of a group of one hundred lactating women lost weight, felt excessively tired, and suffered from repeated minor infections. In India, researchers who compared the diet and health during lactation of a group of poor village women with those of a similar group of relatively well-off urban women suspected that over-nutrition, the result of a diet too rich in fats and sugars, might be more of a threat to lactation than under-nutrition.

It may be that the complaints of fatigue and barely adequate milk supply which are sometimes made by American nursing mothers are not psychosomatic, as is generally assumed, but the result of unsuitable diet. Despite the wide availability of good food in this country, some women select very poorly balanced diets; subclinical vitamin deficiencies are common among pregnant American women. Surveys indicate that the most poorly nourished member of the household is apt to be the mother. Even though she fixes big breakfasts for her family, substantial lunchboxes for her children, and big dinners each night, by the time she has cooked and served the evening meal, she is too tired to eat. Her own diet consists of coffee, pastry, and sandwiches.

Whatever the origins of the "nursing mother's syndrome," the lactating woman who feels tired, loses weight, and is fearful, irritable, and blue may be dramatically improved by better nutrition and especially by taking a good vitamin B complex supplement. She cheers up, gets her appetite back, and may well find that her milk supply simultaneously increases from mere adequacy to abundance. This may account for the continued popularity, despite medical scorn, of B vitamin-rich substances such as brewer's yeast, beer (especially imported beer), ale, and stout as tonics for lactating mothers.

Of course, many mothers can maintain abundant milk production over an indefinite period without any dietary help. Some wet nurses have continued to give copious quantities of milk for years. According to physiologist S. J. Folley, lactation is the natural state of the mammary gland. The human breast is designed to give milk continuously, except when inhibited by the hormones of late pregnancy, throughout the childbearing years. Under simpler conditions than our own, it usually does so.

PHYSICAL BENEFITS OF LACTATION

The physical benefits which breast feeding can give to the mother begin in the hour her child is born. Under primitive conditions, a newly delivered mother usually picks up her baby and puts it to her breast as soon as it is born, sometimes even before the placenta is delivered. The sucking of the infant makes the let-down reflex operate, and the let-down hormone oxytocin also causes a powerful contraction of the uterus. This causes the expulsion of the placenta, if that has not already taken place. Because the uterus is firmly contracted, danger of hemorrhage is greatly reduced.

In our hospitals it is not customary to allow a baby to nurse in the delivery room; and heavy anesthesia often affects both mother and baby so that nursing would be impossible. Pitocin, a synthetic form of oxytocin, is sometimes administered to make the uterus contract and reduce hemorrhage.

As lactation gets under way, oxytocin released at each feeding causes mild uterine contractions. At first, these contractions can be uncomfortable; however, personnel in hospitals which allow mothers to nurse in the delivery room feel that the procedure of nursing in the hour of

birth contracts the still-active uterus so well that it prevents the spasmodic cramping contractions or after-pains
which are common when the first nursing is delayed.
Throughout the time a mother is nursing, her uterus contracts during and after each feeding. Thus it involutes, or
returns to normal size, more rapidly than that of the mother who doesn't nurse.

Far from harming the shape of the breasts, lactation
may actually improve them. If lactation is ended abruptly
the breasts may be flat and empty for a period of weeks, as
the alveoli degenerate. By six months after weaning, the
breasts have usually regained their former shape, whatever
that might have been, but are apt to be slightly smaller,
presumably due to reduction in the amount of fatty tissue.
In the normally flat-chested girl this makes little difference, since she didn't have much fatty tissue to begin
with. The overly buxom girl often finds her figure improved by lactation. Breast tissue which has functioned is
said to retain its shape over a longer period of years than
breast tissue which has not. Some doctors think that
breasts that have never lactated may be subject to atrophy,
and are more likely to be prematurely pendulous or shape-
less.

Lactation may also combat the cumulative effects on
the figure of several pregnancies. Some of the weight
gained in pregnancy represents nutrients such as calcium,
which are stored in the mother's body, to be withdrawn
during lactation. When lactation is suppressed, it is possible that these stored nutrients remain in the body; each
pregnancy therefore tends to make the mother a little
heavier, and this accumulated weight is very difficult to
lose.

BREAST FEEDING AND EROTIC RESPONSE

Doctors, psychiatrists, and other (chiefly male) obser-
vers sometimes regard breast feeding as an important
source of sexual satisfaction to nursing mothers. However,
in reality sustained sexual pleasure in nursing is not the
usual experience. Although the nipple itself is erogenous,

during lactation it becomes relatively desensitized. During feedings most sensations fall upon the areola, which is always quite insensitive to touch. Mild erotic sensations may be felt briefly at the start or end of feedings. Intense or constant stimulation would constitute a distraction rather than an asset as, once the milk has let down, the mother should and does feel patient and tranquil rather than excited or anticipatory. An occasional mother finds an occasional feeding sexually stimulating, even to the point of orgasm, but this effect is usually transitory.

As we have noted the release of oxytocin makes the uterus contract during the feeding and often for many minutes thereafter. In the first days after delivery, these contractions may be painful. Later on they cannot be felt by most women but they could conceivably contribute some sort of subliminal satisfaction to nursing.

CANCER

In America four out of every hundred women develop breast cancer. In areas where women have several children and nurse them each for a year or more, breast cancer is almost unheard of. Apparently breast cancer is primarily a result of failure of the breast to perform their natural function. Even a little breast feeding seems to go a long way toward protecting the breasts against cancer. According to one team of investigators, the risk of getting cancer of the breast diminishes from one in twenty-five chances to one in a hundred and twenty-five when a baby is nursed for six months. It is difficult to understand why this simple method of reducing breast cancer is ignored while methods of detecting breast cancer receive such wide publicity.

It is, of course, highly unlikely that a woman who is lactating will develop a breast cancer. However, the breast is apt to be full of strange lumps and bumps during nursing, especially in the first weeks. National promotion of early breast cancer detection has almost every mother nervously probing her breasts, so persistent lumpiness can be very alarming. Usually such lumps are simply enlarged lobes of alveoli, which swell and dwindle as the breast fills and empties, and which may feel very hard and distinct when the milk has just let down. A lump which does not change in any way is often a lactal cyst, or milk-filled pocket within the breast. These cysts are harmless. However, the nursing mother who finds a lump in the breast is much better off to have the obstetrician check it, even though he may think her a hypochondriac, than to ignore it or lie awake worrying without doing anything about it. A word of caution: Such cases should be examined by a doctor who is really familiar with lactating women. He is the only one who has the experience necessary to tell good from bad in these matters. Both the obstetrician whose patients do not usually breast feed and the general surgeon have been know to recommend surgery for "abnormal" conditions which are actually part of the normal range of breast changes during lactation.

Other factors than breast feeding also contribute to protection against breast cancer; early pregnancy, before the age of twenty, seems to be one such factor. There is also evidence that a tendency toward breast cancer may be inherited. A mother with a history of breast cancer in her family would be especially well advised to breast feed, to protect herself.

Some years ago it was discovered that by line-breeding tumor-prone mice a strain of mice could be developed in which the females almost inevitably developed breast cancer. Interestingly enough, the virus causing the particular mouse cancer was not inherited but was passed to the next generation in the mother's milk. This discovery led to some speculation in the press that human mothers with a history of breast cancer should not nurse their daughters. Research at the Michigan Cancer Foundation demonstrated that human mothers with a family history of breast cancer sometimes have viruslike particles in their milk which are not usually present in the normal population. This does not mean that the disease is passed through the milk; people are not mice, and the particles exist elsewhere in the bodies of both mother and baby. What it does suggest is that it might be possible, by study of these particles, to work toward a vaccine against breast cancer.

Due to the low incidence of breast feeding in this country, it has been difficult for researchers to obtain enough milk samples to keep their work going. A nursing mother who has had breast cancer or whose mother, sisters, aunts, or other blood relatives have had the disease might wish to aid this study by contributing milk samples; write to Michael J. Brennan M.D., Michigan Cancer Foundation, 4811 John R. Street, Detroit, Michigan 48201.

The Breasts and the Baby

To accomplish breast feeding successfully takes two people: the mother and the baby. The mother's breasts, efficient as they are at making and giving milk, still cannot function well unless the baby plays his part. The baby is born with specialized physical equipment for breast feeding. In his cheeks are two round pads of fat, sometimes called the sucking pads. It is these pads which make a baby's face so round and his cheeks so plump. When he is feeding, the presence of the sucking pads keeps his cheeks firm; they cannot "collapse" inward no matter how hard he sucks. A baby's nose is short and flat, which helps him to breathe while nursing (just as the bulldog's "pushed-in" nose enables him to breathe while taking a grip with his jaws). The baby's gums, usually toothless at birth, are provided instead with a ridged edge which helps to compress the milk sinuses behind the nipple.

When the baby nurses, he protrudes his tongue to make a trough which, with the lower lip, forms a seal around the outer edge of the areola. The upper lip, like an inverted U, completes the airtight seal. The baby has to learn to keep his upper lip down while nursing; at first the breast may push it up against his nostrils, obstructing his breathing. When he learns to hold his head away a little, and to keep a stiff upper lip, a "sucking blister" usually forms in the center of the upper lip, and may persist for weeks. This blister is not an injury but an adaptation to the job of nursing.

During feedings, the throat and base of the tongue form a ring through which suction can be exerted. The tongue also keeps the nipple in place against the roof of the mouth, which is arched to receive it. Some dentists feel that the normal development of an infant's jaw and palate depends upon this combination of pressure and suction: that the child who was breast fed has more adequate palatal development than the one who was not, and that some malocclusions, requiring braces in later years, are a direct result of bottle feeding. A mechanical device designed to offset this effect of bottle feeding is now on the market. This, the Nuk-Sauger nipple, has a soft, bulbous base, with a short, fat, flat-topped nipple that is supposed to reproduce the shape of the human nipple in the baby's mouth. It forces the baby to chew and milk the nipple, as he would when nursing at the breast, and is intended to eliminate the strong suction, the pressures of a long, rigid bottle nipple, and the abnormal tongue placement which accompanies bottle feeding. A Nuk-Sauger pacifier (called an "exerciser") has also been designed. It is intended to correct certain orthodontic problems in small children who were bottle fed.

The normal infant has a strong urge to suck, and can suck efficiently once the urge is triggered. However, some babies are very hard to stimulate into normal sucking, and it has recently been shown that this can be due to medication given to the mother during late pregnancy and labor. Barbiturates in particular, given during the last days of pregnancy, seem to be concentrated by the fetus and can inhibit the sucking reflex in the infant for five days or more after birth, both at breast and bottle.

By the time a baby is six months old, adaptations for breast feeding are beginning to be replaced by adaptations for eating solid foods. The sucking pads diminish, to be largely gone by the end of the first year. Incoming teeth (rather than the gum ridge) form the "leading edge" of the jaws, although the gum ridge may persist below and in front of the lower teeth for a while. The tongue becomes more mobile, less protrusive; the baby no longer shoves solid food out of his mouth in an effort to swallow it. As the baby's hands come under control enough so that he can pick up a cracker or a piece of meat his eating equipment develops enough to make use of such items. Although he loses his infantile breast feeding specializations, he can of course continue to feed at the breast. By six months he has considerable know-how; he does not need special equipment to nurse efficiently and comfortably. His incoming teeth do not interfere with his feeding, nor do they constitute a hazard for his mother; during feedings his tongue protrudes over the lower jaw so that he cannot bite and nurse at the same time. In humans, breast feeding continues to be nutritionally advantageous for many months. As the baby grows, his throat, tongue, jaws, and lips can still work very efficiently to milk the mother's breast; and as long as he nurses, the breasts can function too.

3·Milk

Human Milk vs. Cow's Milk.

The remarkable thing about human milk is not that it is so different from the milk of other animals, but that it is so similar. Huge whales, shrews weighing less than an ounce, fast-growing rabbits and slow-growing elephants, herbivores, carnivores, insectivores, all give milk that is really very much the same. Whatever kind of mother a sample of milk comes from, it still looks like milk, smells like milk, tastes like milk. It is still made of four basic ingredients: water, fat, special milk proteins, and milk sugars. It will contain at least some of each important vitamin and mineral. If it is left to stand the cream will rise. Be it the milk of a human, cow, or rabbit it is capable of being made into cheese or butter and will go sour in the same way. Whatever the source, milk is milk.

Probably milk, like any other product of evolution, is not perfect: Some milks may contain useless ingredients, just as our bodies contain an appendix which no longer has a function. Some milks may be inadequate in some ways. The milks of rats, cows, and humans are all low in iron, and they produce anemia in the young that are maintained on milk alone for too long a time. On the whole, however, it is safe to assume that the milk of each species is more suited to it than the milk of any other species, and, if present in sufficient quantity, is better for the infant than any other diet could possibly be.

In what ways does human milk especially suit the human baby? In many, particularly as compared with the usual substitute, cow's milk. The milk of cows, and of ruminants generally, is designed for a very different animal, and is far more remote from our own than the milk of the wolf that is said to have nourished Romulus and Remus.

PROTEIN

Cow's milk has twice as much protein as human milk and must be diluted before a newborn human can tolerate it. This is why newborn infant formulas add water to cow's milk. Because of the kind of proteins which it contains cow's milk in its natural state forms a large, tough curd when it is mixed with digestive juices. The infant with a stomach full of the solid curds of raw cow's milk can be in real trouble. Diluting the milk helps; heating also makes the curds smaller and softer. But they still tend to linger in the infant's stomach, so that he feels full for about four hours after a feeding. The curd of human milk, on the other hand, produced from a different balance of proteins, is soft and fine, almost liquid. The stomach of the breast-fed baby empties rapidly and easily. Consequently he wants to eat more often, usually every two or three hours during the daytime, for the first two or three months of life. This in turn stimulates his mother's milk supply.

The protein in cow's milk is mostly casein. In human milk, casein forms only about a third of the protein content, and the remaining proteins are easier for the human baby to digest. Human milk also contains a significant proportion of essential amino acids, the "building blocks" of protein, which can be absorbed and used by the infant just as they are. Colostrum, the specialized milk which is secreted in the first few days after birth, is especially high in amino acids. According to Drs. Icie Macy and Harriet Kelly, well-known authorities on infant nutrition, this bonus of nutrients probably forms a splendid basis for the rapid growth and profound changes taking place in the body of the newborn human.

The human infant uses the protein in breast milk with nearly 100 per cent efficiency. After the first few days of life, virtually all the protein in breast milk becomes part of the baby; little or none is excreted. The baby fed on cow's milk, on the other hand, uses protein with about 50 per cent efficiency, and must waste about half the protein in his diet. Some of it passes undigested through his system and is excreted in the feces. Some is digested, but cannot be utilized by the cells of his body, and is excreted in the urine. Thus to get the benefit of one gram of protein in cow's milk, he must take in two. He cannot drink "straight" cow's milk, at least in the first months of life; the strain on his system is too great. So to get enough protein that is usable he must take in a much larger volume of milk than the breast-fed baby. The mother who has bottle fed one baby, and watched him tuck away eight or ten ounces or even more, on occasion, may worry because her subsequent and breast-fed baby couldn't possibly be getting a similar volume of milk. But, because he absorbs nearly all of every drop from the breast, the breast-fed baby doesn't need to take in as large a volume of milk. The formula-fed baby, in taking aboard extra milk to get the protein he needs, also gets extra carbohydrate, which may make him obese.

WATER

Eliminating unusable protein is largely the job of the kidneys. This may place quite a strain on a function which is as yet immature. For years it was widely believed that premature babies gained better on certain formulas than they did on breast milk. Finally investigators found that the weight gain was due not to growth but to retention of fluid in the tissues. This is the result of strain on the imma-

ture kidneys which are not yet properly equipped to eliminate unsuitable proteins and mineral salts.

Human infants get plenty of water for their metabolic
needs in their mother's milk. During hot weather, it is the
mother who needs extra water, not her breast-fed baby,
although an occasional baby seems to enjoy drinking
water. The baby fed on cow's milk, on the other hand,
needs water not only for his own metabolism but to enable
his kidneys to eliminate the unusable proteins and salts.
Thus he needs water by bottle in addition to the water in
his formula, especially in hot weater.

FAT

The total fat content of human milk is about the same
as or higher than that of undiluted cow's milk. (In diluted
cow's milk formulas, the fat content is drastically reduced,
and consequently so is the amount of fat-soluble vitamins.) But human milk is much lower in saturated fats
than is cow's milk; the possible long-term benefits of this
are now being studied. Most of the fat in human milk is
passed out towards the end of a feeding. When lactation is
in full flow, the mid-morning meal usually has the highest
fat content. This is because the breast accumulates more
milk overnight than the infant can consume at the early
morning feeding. So the next feeding begins not with the
thin fore milk but with the fat-filled hind milk left over
from breakfast, and includes a second amount of hind-
milk as the breast is emptied.

If both breasts are used at a feeding, hind milk and fore
milk will mix, during let-down, in the second breast, resulting in rather high-calorie milk being quickly available
to the infant. Thus it is wise to offer both breasts at each
feeding, especially if the infant is ill or weak or gaining
slowly.

At one time the idea that a mother's milk should be
measured for fat content was very popular. Doctors did
not realize the difference between fore milk and hind milk
in each feeding. They did not take into account that there
might also be variations in the overall fat content of feed-

ings during the course of the day. Many women were told, on the basis of one sample of an ounce or two of milk drawn off in the doctor's office, that their milk was "too thin."

Dr. Richard Applebaum states that in an individual mother, fore milk may have 1.5 calories per ounce and hind milk 30 calories per ounce, with some mothers averaging out to 25 calories per ounce, or about the equivalent of the light cream sold in supermarkets as "half and half." He points out that an experienced nursing mother whose let-down reflex is well-conditioned might be a valuable asset in a premature infant nursery, as she could get some of that digestible yet high-calorie milk into tiny infants who might only be able to take an ounce or two a day.

While overall fat content does vary slightly from woman to woman it is not enough to make any difference to a baby; he simply takes a little more or a little less milk. And the variation between individuals is far less than the variation during feedings or from one feeding to another in any nursing mother.

SUGAR

Breast milk contains about twice as much sugar as whole cow's milk. That is why some kind of carbohydrate is generally added to cow's milk formulas. Also, because cow's milk must be diluted to reduce the protein level, even more carbohydrate must be added, to raise the calorie level. Otherwise the infant, like eighteenth century babis who were fed bread-and-water pap, would have to swallow liquid by the quart to get enough nourishment to subsist on. The sugar in human milk is largely lactose, whereas that in cow's milk includes galactose, glucose, and other compounds. It is thought that lactose is easier for the infant to digest, and that its presence also makes it easier for the infant to utilize proteins; this may contribute to the fact that the breast-fed baby eliminates almost no protein. Macy and Kelly report that a high lactose concentration is also believed to help the absorption of calcium. One important contribution of human milk sugar is its effect on the bacteria which grow in the baby's intestines. The process of digesting lactose creates an acid medium in the baby's intestinal tract, whereas other sugars result in an alkaline medium. Many bacteria cannot survive in an acid medium; a favorite formula of the past, used to combat diarrhea, was based on buttermilk or sour milk. The intestinal tract of the artificially fed baby, on the other hand, with its alkaline contents, supports the growth of many organisms, including harmful and putrefactive bacteria. That is why the stool of the artificially fed baby has the usual fecal stench, while the stool of the breast-fed baby has no unpleasant odor. The intestinal contents of the breast-fed baby are practically a pure culture of one beneficial organism, *Lactobacillus bifidus*. By-products of *bifidus* metabolism make the infant's intestinal tract even more resistant to the growth of other, invading organisms.

Dr. Paul Gyorgy, discoverer of the vitamin B_6 and pioneering researcher into human milk and nutrition, found that human milk contains a sugary compound, the *bifidus* factor, which is not found in the milk of cows, and which is essential for the growth of many varieties of *L. bifidus*. The *bifidus* factor and the acid medium resulting from the digestion of lactose in breast milk promote the establishment of a safe and protective bacteria in the newborn, and thus offers him real protection against invading organisms.

VITAMINS

The vitamin content of any kind of milk varies somewhat according to maternal diet. But generally speaking human milk contains from two to ten times as much of the essential vitamins as does cow's milk. This difference is doubled when cow's milk is diluted, as it must be for human infants. And the vitamin content of cow's milk (and of all formulas) is again reduced when the formula is sterilized, since many vitamins are destroyed by heating.

This is the major reason why formula-fed infants must have not only vitamin drops but supplementary feeding of liquified "solid" foods, as early in life as can be managed. The pureed vegetables and meats, the fruits and juices and cereals, all contain at least some of the needed vitamins that are so poorly supplied in sterile, diluted, cow's milk formulas. Breast-fed babies, on the other hand, do not need any outside source of food until around the age of five or six months. Even then, breast milk continues to be a good source of the vitamins they need.

Vitamins can be divided into two groups: those that dissolve in fat, which can be stored in the body, and those that dissolve in water, which must be supplied daily by the diet. Except in very peculiar circumstances, breast milk contains plenty of the fat-soluble vitamins A and E, which are supplied from the liver and other storehouses in the mother's body even when they are low or absent in her diet. Both of these vitamins are especially plentiful in colostrum, where they are undoubtedly valuable to the newborn, who at birth has very low supplies of them. At the age of one week, the breast-fed newborn has more than five times the amount of vitamin E in his system than does his bottle-fed counterpart.

The third fat-soluble vitamin, vitamin D, does not normally come from diet, except in northern and Arctic climates where a diet rich in fish oils and fish liver is eaten. In the rest of the world, vitamin D is synthesized in the body upon exposure to sunlight. Both breast-fed babies and nursing mothers synthesize their own vitamin D. Some vitamin D is also supplied to the baby through his mother's milk.

Vitamin D controls the body's ability to absorb calcium. When it is not provided by the diet and if exposure to sunlight is curtailed, as in Moslem cities where women are confined or veiled, children have rickets and the nursing mother may develop osteomalacia or brittle-bone, due to failure to absorb calcium. However, her breast-fed baby apparently has first claim to whatever vitamin D is available in the mother's body, since he is unlikely to develop rickets until he is weaned.

The water-soluble vitamins, vitamin C and the B complex, must be supplied in the diet. Cow's milk contains almost no vitamin C, since calves can manufacture their own. Human milk, on the other hand, contains quite a lot, and if the mother is eating plenty of vitamin C-bearing foods, her milk may have ten times as much vitamin C as whole cow's milk. The vitamin C content of her milk increases immediately the vitamin is added to her diet.

Again, the nursing baby has first claim to whatever vitamin C is present. Dr. F. E. Hytten found that, immediately after a feeding, when milk production is presumably at its peak, there is a sharp drop in the maternal serum levels of vitamin C as the active mammary glands corral all the available supply. This mechanism is so effective that scurvy, the disease caused by lack of vitamin C, has never been seen in a breast-fed baby, even in parts of the world where it is common among adults, including nursing mothers.

The B complex vitamins, a mysterious and extensive group, play a role in human and animal nutrition that is not yet entirely understood. Some are supplied by the diet. Some are synthesized in the body. The most thoroughly studied B vitamins, including thiamine and riboflavin, are about twice as plentiful in undiluted raw cow's milk as they are in human milk; some of the others are more plentiful in human milk.

In most parts of the world, at least enough B complex vitamins for survival are supplied to breast-fed babies by their mothers, whatever the diet. The notable exception is Malaya, where polished rice is the main item of food. Polishing removes the thiamine, and whole populations may be deficient in the B vitamin, with many breast-fed babies dying of beri-beri, the thiamine deficiency disease. Dr. D. B. Jelliffe comments that it is almost the only disease that we know how to prevent but which is nevertheless increasing. Polished rice has more snob appeal than unpolished rice, and unpolished rice cannot be stored as long in warm climates; it is difficult to persuade manufacturers not to polish rice when polishing is to their economic advantage.

Deficiency of other B vitamins in breast-fed babies has not been seen, even under poor dietary conditions. However, all B-vitamin needs may not be supplied by cow's milk formulas. For example, some babies have been found to have convulsions caused by insufficient vitamin B when they were fed sterilized cow's milk formulas in which this vitamin is destroyed by heating. Such babies may have a more-than-average need for the B vitamin. But human milk usually supplies enough of this and the other B vitamins, even under poor conditions, to compensate for such individual variation.

CALCIUM

The adequacy of the mineral content of human milk is still a matter of opinion. Human milk contains less than a quarter as much calcium as cow's milk, and babies on cow's milk formulas grow larger and heavier skeletons than breast-fed babies, in the first year of life. However, they also have to excrete a lot of unused calcium and phosphorus, whereas breast-fed babies excrete very little. At present our understanding of calcium needs, in babies or adults, is inadequate. One authority sees a need to investigate the "poor calcification" of the breast-fed baby, to see what long-term or immediate disadvantages result. Another accepts the breast-fed baby as normal, and deplores the distorted growth curve of the baby on "too highly mineralized" cow's milk.

IRON

Stress is often laid on the fact that human milk contains "no" iron. As a matter of fact it contains more iron than cow's milk, but there is no doubt that this is not enough to support the needs of the baby indefinitely. Iron is needed to make red-blood cells. The baby is born with a good store of iron in its liver, and with a high concentration of red blood cells, which is presumably diluted to normal over a period of growth. If the mother is not anemic during pregnancy the baby's stores of iron are probably adequate for the first year of life, even on an exclusively milk diet. Augmenting the baby's diet with solid food after six months or so automatically prevents any iron deficiency from occurring. While eggs, liver, and other rich sources of iron are not available to most human babies, there is iron in grains and some plants, and the iron content of food can be vastly increased simply by cooking it in an iron pot. Thus the breast-fed baby is not normally anemic. High levels of vitamins C and E in breast milk function in making iron available to the baby's system. A breast-fed baby may actually absorb more iron than a bottle-fed baby getting an iron supplement.

If the mother is extremely anemic during pregnancy, as is the case in many parts of the world, fetal stores of iron may become inadequate within two or three months, and suckling anemia results. Suckling anemia is seen even in the children of healthy mothers when solid foods are withheld for an unusually long time. In Renaissance Italy it was customary to give babies nothing but breast milk for a year and sometimes two years. The results are illustrated in many paintings of the period. Representations of the Madonna and Child frequently show the Infant Christ as a fat, pasty-white, anemic baby.

Babies on cow's milk formulas receive even less iron from their diet than do breast-fed babies. They are more subject to anemia, so an effort is usually made to have them eating iron-rich foods, such as egg yolks, as soon as possible. However, this early exposure to eggs and other such foods may cause allergic reactions. The eventual necessity of adding iron to the diet and the desirability, around the middle of the first year, of introducing the baby to new foods ("A little bagel, a piece salami, he should know what good food tastes like"), should not be used as an argument to promote feeding solids to the already well nourished breast-fed baby at the age of two months, or two weeks, or, as is fashionable in at least one American city, two days.

TRACE ELEMENTS

The minute but essential trace elements also occur in human milk. Human milk is much higher in copper than is cow's milk; copper seems to be associated with iron metabolism. The baby shares the benefits when his mother drinks fluoridated water. The human mammary gland tends to concentrate iodine. This means that radioactive iodine must never be used as a diagnostic tool in the nursing mother; real harm to the infant's thyroid gland can result.

RH FACTORS; JAUNDICE

Doctors sometimes think that mothers whose babies have an Rh factor problem should not breast feed; their fear is that the mother's antibodies, which are harmful to the baby's blood, will occur in her milk as well as in her blood. In fact, any Rh antibodies that occur in breast milk are destroyed in the baby's intestinal tract and do not harm the baby. Nowadays in the case of an Rh conflict the mother can and should be given medical treatment directly after the birth of her first child (or a first miscarriage or abortion) which will prevent future Rh difficulties.

Many doctors were alarmed by the publication of research indicating that a compound in the milk of some mothers produced jaundice in their infants. The liver is the body's filter for foreign substances in the blood; jaundice is a yellowing of eyes and skin which indicates that the liver is working overtime. Newborn babies are often slightly jaundiced, especially if the mother received many drugs during late pregnancy and labor which the baby's liver now has to clear out of its system. So-called "breast milk jaundice," occurring in the first to eighth weeks of the baby's life, is a rare medical curiosity; in fact, some researchers contend that it does not exist; if and when it occurs it is, to quote the discoverer of the syndrome, "thoroughly benign." That is, it is harmless and no cause for weaning. In the event that breast milk jaundice is diagnosed, it can be treated by removing the baby from the breast for three or four days only, while the mother pumps her milk, and then returning to breast feeding. The most solid reason to do this may be that it sets the physician's mind at rest.

STRONTIUM 90

Strontium is an element resembling calcium and sometimes picked up by the body in its place. Radioactive strontium, or strontium 90, occurs in the atmosphere as a result of nuclear tests, and has been found to be about ten times more abundant in cow's milk than in human milk. Furthermore, fully breast-fed babies actually excrete more strontium 90 than they take in, suggesting that the chemical balance of human milk is such that it enables the baby to get rid of some of the potentially harmful mineral salts laid down in its bones before birth.

DDT AND OTHER CONTAMINANTS

The discovery that breast milk sometimes contains DDT caused alarmists to suggest that cow's milk might therefore be preferable infant food. Cow's milk, of course, contains some DDT too, and the "baby food" supplements which generally are added to a cow's milk or other formula diet contain a host of preservatives, dyes, emulsifiers, stabilizers, and other substances, including high levels of salt and dextrose, which are certainly not found in breast milk.

DDT and other pesticides now occur in the ground, the air, the rain, the oceans, and the fatty tissues of most animals. The nursing mother can minimize the effects of this pollution upon her own body by avoiding the use of insect sprays herself, by limiting her intake of animal fats (pork, butter, etc.), and by avoiding areas where pesticides are being used. She should also avoid contact with "permanently moth-proofed" garments, which have been treated with dieldrin, an insecticide that can be absorbed through the skin. And she should remember that tobacco plants are sprayed with pesticides, and smoking is thought to be a major source of ingested DDT.

MEDICATION, ALCOHOL, AND DRUGS

Anything a mother puts into her system which gets into her bloodstream can pass into her milk. In general, this occurs in such small quantities that its effect on the baby is clinically unimportant; a nursing mother can take antibiotics, for example, without any effect on her infant. Barbiturates and laxatives may affect the baby; perhaps a nursing mother who takes these medications should try fresh air and exercise instead.

What is not generally realized is that drugs taken by a pregnant woman pass through the placenta with far higher efficiency than they will ever pass into her milk. Many an infant is born with his kidneys and liver working overtime to get rid of medications given his mother before or during labor, or with his behavior altered and his sucking reflexes reduced for several days after birth. The effects of barbiturates given to a mother as long as four or five days before giving birth may be seen in the subdued responses of her newborn. Aspirin, over-the-counter sleep preparations, cold pills, and other drugs which we swallow without a thought may affect the fetus. Doctors are right when they beg pregnant women to take only what has been predescribed for them.

Some pediatricians feel that nursing mothers should avoid antihistamines, including Dramamine, which is given for seasickness, and most of the hay fever, sinus, and allergy remedies, whether prescription or not. At least some of these, in drying up nasal passages and secretions, also temporarily dry up the milk. Diuretics are also suspect. A nursing mother who is seeing a doctor for some medical problem unrelated to obstetrics should remind him that she is lactating, so that he can adjust his treatments accordingly. However, while some medications may briefly affect the milk supply, most medications do not affect the baby and should not be considered cause for weaning. An exception are some drugs prescribed for epilepsy.

Alcohol in moderate quantities is probably good for

most nursing mothers, especially in the first weeks; it is analgesic and tranquillizing. It will appear in the milk only if drunk in enormous quantities. The classic case is of a mother who drank a quart of port at a sitting: Both she and her baby passed out.

If a mother smokes, there will be nicotine in her milk. It is possible that some babies do react to nicotine. One nursing mother who smoked heavily found that her baby was not gaining well. She recalled that she herself never gained weight while smoking, so she quit, and the baby began gaining at once. Mothers should be aware that smoking is definitely one of those things which has an effect upon the baby before birth. On the average, babies born to smokers are smaller at birth than babies born to nonsmokers.

Marijuana probably behaves rather like alcohol, except that it stays in the system for several days rather than several hours. Getting stoned on grass may not harm your milk or your baby; it may, however, affect your mothering. This of course is true of alcohol, too. No mother who has read it could ever forget the scene in John Updike's *Rabbit, Run* in which a young mother absentmindedly drinks too much scotch and lets the baby slip under the bath water.

The stronger psychedelic drugs such as LSD may powerfully affect a mother's behavior and will reach the baby in utero and, if taken in sufficient quantities, the nursing baby. The same goes for amphetamines and barbiturates (uppers and downers) and for all the grotesque mixtures of hash and strychnine, Sparine (animal tranquillizer) and other chemicals that are available on the streets of every major city. Opium, heroin, and similar drugs pass through the placenta and through the mother's milk. The baby of a mother who is addicted to morphine or heroin is born an addict; playwright Eugene O'Neill is supposed to have been a victim of this misfortune. Standard treatment for such babies, to reduce the agony of withdrawal symptoms following birth, is to have them breast fed by the mother. Then as they are gradually weaned from the drug-laced breast milk they are gradually cured of their addiction. This presumably would be the recommended course also for an infant whose mother is taking Methadone.

The Pill

Birth control pills prevent ovulation by tinkering with the body's hormonal system. Some women who have taken birth control pills during lactation find that their milk supply is definitely reduced. Others notice no effects; lactation is maintained normally by suckling, even in the presence of hormones sometimes used to "dry up" the milk.

We do not yet fully understand the effects and possible hazards of routine use of birth control pills and other hormones. It would seem wise to be conservative, if possible, during lactation, and to use contraceptive methods which do not have an effect on the mother's whole system. Therefore, because of the unknown factor of future effect on the baby, mothers ought to seriously consider another form of contraception while they are lactating.

The Mother's Diet

There are no special foods that harm the milk supply. One often hears that chocolate is "binding" or that fruit has the opposite effect on the baby, but as one doctor caustically points out, these notions may be perpetuated by hospital nurses because they thereby become the recipients of gifts of fruit or candy sent to new mothers. Likewise there seems to be no specific article of diet that increases the milk supply in a healthy mother, although every culture has its own pet lactogogue, ranging from the powdered earthworms prescribed by Avicenna to innumerable herbal concoctions. Probably all these owe any effectiveness they may have to the power of suggestion, which relaxes the anxious mother, relieves her doubts, and thus enables the let-down reflex to work better.

Volatile oils, which give most spices their characteristic

odors and flavors, pass through milk unchanged. This does not mean, however, that a nursing mother has to avoid spicy foods. While we adults may object to drinking the odorous milk of a cow that has been eating wild onions, there is no evidence that the breast-fed baby objects in the slightest to garlic- or curry-flavored mother's milk.

If the mother is undernourished or malnourished, the effects will be felt by her long before they will be felt by the baby. U. N. investigators in India have found that a mother can breast feed, and have a healthy baby and normal milk, even when she herself is going hungry. Crucial ingredients like vitamins and calcium and protein will be robbed from the mother's body without declining in her milk; the old superstition, "you lose a tooth for every baby," reflected dietary conditions in which the mother was not receiving enough calcium.

Good all-around maternal nutrition is important for the nursing mother's own health. It is surprising how many American mothers with adequate incomes are malnourished; you can't nurse a baby and thrive, yourself, on a diet of Cokes and potato chips. Fad or fashionable diets should be treated with suspicion. The vegetarian or low-meat diet many young families espouse is perfectly satisfactory provided it contains a truly wide variety of foods, and protein in some form, whether cheese or eggs or a variety of vegetable proteins. A strict macrobiotic diet, with its limited choice of foods, is probably inadequate for most nursing mothers. It's important to realize that humans, like all other living things, come from varying genetic backgrounds, and that biochemical needs are highly individual; an Eskimo who could not tolerate a high-fat, low-starch diet would not have been a very good genetic risk; people of oriental diet may be well adapted to a diet largely of rice and greens which would not at all suit the personal chemistry of people of Scandinavian, seafaring extraction.

In general, we all have the same nutritional needs, but specifically some of us need more or can thrive on less of one or another diet element. The nursing mother with common sense eats a varied diet of nutritious, basic foods, for her own sake as much as the baby's.

IMMUNITY FACTORS IN BREAST MILK AND COLOSTRUM

It is beginning to be apparent that human milk is not only a well-balanced all-inclusive ration which is cleaner, more nourishing, much better flavored, and easier than formula; it also offers the human infant some definite immunity against disease. Dr. Paul Gyorgy has studied in detail several cases of formula-fed babies who developed acute, intractable diarrhea due to bacterial infections of the intestinal tract, and who recovered with dramatic suddenness after receiving breast milk, sometimes improving after only *one* feeding. It would seem that the infecting organism, usually *Escherichia coli* which is common in the adult intestine, gets such a foothold that the baby's own powers of resistance are overcome. The single feeding of breast milk, however, apparently transforms the intestinal environment to such an extent that the infecting organism is suppressed, and the baby can get well. These babies have no adverse response to cow's milk itself, but have simply been overcome by infection. Once they begin to gain, they can be put on a cow's milk diet again.

In addition, it can be demonstrated in the laboratory that breast milk itself is antibacterial. While staphylococcus and streptococcus organisms can be found in milk within the breast, these and other infecting organisms do not seem to reach dangerous levels in the presence of fresh breast milk; only when stasis sets in is infection a danger. The presence of fresh breast milk acts as a natural protection against bacterial infection within the breast, on the mother's nipple, in the baby's mouth, and probably in the baby's stomach as well.

Breast milk, like human tears, contains the enzyme lysozyme, which has the ability to dissolve some kinds of bacteria. In human tears lysozyme may have value in protecting eye and lid tissues against infection, particularly when the tissues are inflamed from crying. It is possible that lysozyme also contributes to the antibacterial effects of breast milk. These protective aspects, combined with the relative cleanliness of human milk, must account for the fact that, even in tropical slums where dysentery can debilitate almost all the population, the breast-fed baby under six months is usually strong and healthy and free of infection.

Colostrum, the thick, yellowish liquid which is present in the breasts before birth and for a day or more thereafter, plays a particularly vital role in protecting the infant against disease. Colostrum contains disease antibodies, and particularly viral disease antibodies, which have now been found to be utilized by human babies and to protect them against specific diseases throughout the first six months of life, whether or not breast feeding is continued after the first few days. Some of the pathogens for which colostrum provides protection are polio, Coxsackie B virus, several staphlococci, and *E. coli,* the adult intestinal bacteria which can cause particularly vicious intestinal, urinary, and other infections in newborns. These antibodies are not received through the placenta. They are present in colostrum in much higher concentrations than they are in the mother's blood serum. One doctor feels that the immunological value of colostrum is such that the day will come when all newborns are started off with a "colostrum cocktail" whether or not their mothers plan to breast feed. Of course dairy farmers have been doing this for years; all new calves are given colostrum for their first feeding, not milk. The immunological advantages of colostrum have been long known in animals, but only recently demonstrated in humans.

Colostrum is an interesting substance; it resembles blood more than it resembles milk, because it contains many living cells, particularly lymphocytes and macrophages, blood serum corpuscles which can attack and digest disease organisms and foreign material. The first feedings of colostrum may in effect sweep the infant's gastro-intestinal tract clean of infectious organisms, giving the baby a real running start.

Colostrum may also function in humans, as it has been demonstrated to do in some animals, in a phenomenon known as gut closure, in which the walls of the infant's intestine become impermeable to large molecules, thus making the subject less susceptible to invasion of disease organisms. Rapid gut closure may also be a factor in protection against allergy due to the absorption of whole protein molecules through the bowel. A single feeding of colostrum may reduce intestinal permeability and render the infant capable of digesting such molecules rather than absorbing them unchanged. The bottle-fed infant, on the other hand, may continue to absorb whole proteins, and develop reactions to them, well into the second year of life.

BREAST-FED VS. FORMULA-FED BABIES

There are many obvious differences between the healthy breast-fed baby and the healthy bottle-fed baby; one can learn to tell them apart at a glance. The bottle-fed baby is apt to be bigger, plumper, and paler. The breast-fed baby has a warm sun-tanned color. The bottle-fed baby grows faster and gains more; the breast-fed baby follows a slow but steady growth curve which extends further into childhood.

The exception to the normal picture of the healthy breast-fed baby is the breast-fed baby who is not getting enough milk. In the United States this is almost without exception due to the mismanagement of lactation. This hungry baby is pale, and lacks the snap and cheeriness of the satisfied nursling. He may be fretful and cry often, or he may be lethargic, sleeping for longer and longer periods. His stool is scanty and green. Supplementing the diet with formula produces an immediate change for the better. Meanwhile, improvement of the mother's milk supply and let-down reflex can be attempted, with gradual reduction of the supplement as natural conditions are restored.

LONG-TERM BENEFITS OF BREAST FEEDING

Several researchers are beginning to find sound evidence that breast feeding confers long-term health benefits

that have hitherto been unsuspected. It has been thought
for some time that the overall health of children and adults
who have been breast fed may be higher than that of people fed cows' milk or artificial formulae in infancy. Dr. E.
Robbins Kimball of the Northwestern University School
of Medicine compared the illness rates in 178 patients between birth and ten years of age, and found that the
bottle-fed children had, when compared to children fully
breast fed for six months or longer, four times as many ear
infections, four times as many colds, eleven times as many
tonsillectomies, twenty times as many diarrheal infections,
and from eight to twenty-seven times as many allergic
conditions requiring a doctor's care.

A study at Oregon State University of dental caries in
two well-matched communities, one with fluoridated water
and one without, turned up a surprising side issue. As it
happened, both towns had unusually high percentages of
breast-fed children, so there were many in the study. Children who had been breast-fed for three months or longer
had 45 percent fewer cavities than their bottle-fed coun-
terparts in the nonfluoridated community, and 59 percent
fewer cavities in the fluoridated community.

Incidentally, the three-month period seemed to be a significant factor; children who had only been breast fed two
months showed lessened protection (10 percent and 20
percent less cavities, respectively).

A British study has demonstrated that ulcerative colitis
in adults is 100 percent more common in patients whose
medical history includes weaning from the breast before
two weeks than in patients who were breast fed for longer
periods during infancy.

One well-recognized possibly harmful effect of bottle
feeding as opposed to breast feeding is the bottle-caused
distortion of the infant's use of the facial muscles and the
pressure on his mouth, jaws, and palate. This is interestingly diagrammed in R. M. Applebaum's "The Modern
Management of Successful Breast-Feeding" and is considered to be a major cause of malocclusions and many other
dental and facial development problems in some children.

The uncovering of even a few preventative effects of

breast feeding reaching far into adult life has occurred largely by accident; in the case of the Oregon dental caries investigation and the British study of ulcerative colitis, the investigators had no idea in advance that any such correlation would show up. One wonders how many "modern" diseases, thought to be by-products of the tensions of civilized life, are in fact physiologically related to our widespread unnatural systems for feeding infants.

ALLERGIES

A conspicuous difference between breast-fed and formula-fed infants is that breast-fed babies have far fewer allergies. Allergies are thought to be caused primarily by proteins which are unfamiliar to the body's chemistry. Most authorities think that new babies are more intolerant of alien protein than are older babies; too early supplementation with solid foods may set off allergic reactions, especially when the supplement contains complex proteins such as those in eggs. The protein in cow's milk is among the worst offenders in causing allergic reactions. A switch to goat's milk may be called for, to try to avoid the offending protein; or a formula may be used in which the protein fraction comes not from milk but from meat or soybeans. However the breast-fed baby has no such problems. The proteins in breast milk do not cause allergic reactions in the human infant.

A tendency to allergy is inheritable, and more and more doctors are urging mothers to breast feed if there is a family history of allergy or asthma. Breast feeding is the best way of preventing severe allergic illnesses in the children of allergy-prone parents.

In some cases substances which no longer trouble the mother may disturb the baby through her milk. Cow's milk, again, is high on the list; one mother found that her baby developed an allergic reaction if she herself drank too much cow's milk in a day. By experimenting she narrowed it down: incredibly, if she drank twelve ounces of cow's milk the baby showed no discomfort; if she drank thirteen ounces or more the baby was upset and developed diarrhea and a rash.

Babies who might become allergic should be kept on a diet of solely breast milk for five or six months. The tendency to develop allergic reactions decreases with age. By the time nature intended a baby to be sampling new foods he is passing the danger point when allergic reactions become established.

INTOLERANCE OF COW'S MILK

The human baby is remarkably adaptable. Most babies do well on almost any kind of diet that is anywhere near adequate; it is quite possible to raise a human baby on a diet of ripe banana and green coconut and water. However, while most babies do get along well on formulas, there are many who without being actually allergic are never entirely suited by them. The gradient of intolerance probably runs all the way from "normal" crankiness to the obvious cases of convulsions and the progressive emaciation called marasmus. There is the baby with rashes, and the baby with gas, and the baby who vomits sour milk all over the house, and the baby who cries inconsolably by the hour. There is the baby who screams as he evacuates his bowels. There is the "colicky" baby. There is the baby who perpetually has a runny stool and diaper rash. These symptoms are seldom seen in the breast-fed baby. Most of these imperfect adjustments to an imperfect diet are not in themselves harmful. The babies gain well and are not sick. And in most cases these maladjustments are eventually outgrown. But while they exist they may be distinctly unpleasant for the parents and they are no doubt unpleasant for the baby.

There are a few babies, even today, who can tolerate no diet save human milk. These babies, if put on formula, do badly from birth, and eventually are back in the hospital receiving fluids intravenously while one formula after another is tried in the hope of finding something the baby will tolerate. Sometimes the missing factor or the intolerable ingredient can be pinpointed. The baby cannot use cow's milk proteins, so a soybean formula is substituted; or it is the sugar, or the lack of some particular vitamin, that the baby cannot adjust to. Sometimes the fact that a particular baby is more sensitive than the average does not appear at first, because he is breast fed; he thrives until a routine supplement is introduced, or until he is prematurely weaned, at three or four months perhaps, when mother and doctor have serious difficulty in finding a formula that the baby can take without ill effects. All such babies, however, can tolerate human milk, and in some cases when no formula can be found that seems to fill the bill for a particular infant, the baby's life is saved only when a source of human milk is located.

As far as infant nutrition goes, all we can say with complete certainty is that breast milk is the only completely adequate food for the first six months, and forms a splendid addition to the diet thereafter. In a reasonably healthy mother breast milk has all the needed nutrients. Unless lactation is inhibited so that the baby does not get enough milk, he will thrive. Such individual variations as occur are easily adapted to by the baby, and the marvelous flexibility of lactation almost always insures a good and abundant supply of milk, whatever the vicissitudes of the mother's physical environment. There are still many questions to be answered about human milk. The one question that we can answer empirically now is whether or not the best food for a human baby is its mother's milk: It is.

4 · What Happened to Mother Instinct?

MOTHER DOESN'T KNOW BEST

In 1850 a new mother learning to take care of her first baby may have felt nervous, but she was bolstered by the firm conviction that whatever she did was right; that only a mother knew what to do for an infant; and she, by the grace of God, having become a mother, would be able to feed and care for her infant, thanks to her "mother instinct." Then, in the 1900's, along came the psychiatrists to tell mothers that whatever they did molded their offspring's future neuroses, and the doctors to tell mothers that they were killing their children with bad feeding practices, and the child psychologists to say that love and laxness spoiled children, and that what they needed were schedules, deprivation, and discipline. In the twenties and thirties babies seemed to go out of fashion entirely and the "only child" was commonplace. In the 1940's psychologists swung to permissiveness. Now they seem to be heading back towards discipline.

This has left the average mother with nothing to go on.

She can no longer trust herself and her instincts. Whatever *her* mother did was all wrong, so she can't go on memories of her own childhood. And the specialists contradict each other so often that they are not very successful at giving a mother confidence.

So today's mother, face to face with her new infant, has little cultural help to bolster her confidence; her own inexperience is frightening, at least to her, and good old Mother Nature seems to have let her down too. It's infuriating that any cat or rabbit can raise fine babies with every appearance of knowing exactly what she is doing from the start, while human mothers, with all their advantages of brainpower, are helpless.

But are they? Do animals have a real advantage over us? The truth is that animals do not have the clear-cut inborn guidance that they seem to have. The biological aids that bring a mare and her foal together, that enable a dog to care for her pups, or a mouse for her little mice, are available to human beings too. Perhaps if we understood how it is that other mammals arrive at motherhood so successfully we would be aware of instinctive aids when they exist in our own situation; and we would be able to use them, as animals do, to learn to be mothers.

HOW ANIMALS LEARN MOTHERING

With animals, as with people, past experience is a factor in successful mothering. Every person who has raised horses or dogs or any other animal knows that mammal mothers do not do a perfect job the first time. Some horses are so nervous with their first foal that they must be restrained by force before they will let it nurse. Some dogs neglect their first litter. Some pet rabbits, and many zoo animals, are so rattled that, in licking and cleaning themselves during and after giving birth, they lick up and finally devour their newborn babies; no "instinct" tells them not to. Laboratory rats, which have been studied in great detail, may lose some or all of their first litter through inexperience—letting the babies get chilled, or go hungry too long, or stray from the nest. Even birds, ruled by instinct as they seem to be, become better parents through practice.

We now know that animals have a chance to practice some aspects of baby care before the babies arrive. If a female rat is made to wear a collar throughout life, so that she cannot reach her body and never has a chance to lick herself, she does not know how to lick her babies as they are born. Then they have a hard time functioning normally and making contact with her, and generally they do not survive. If a rat is deprived of the experience of carrying things in her mouth she will not know how to build a proper nest, nor how to retrieve the babies if they stray. It is possible that some house cats arrive at maturity without good carrying experience: a new mother cat, for all her aplomb, may not know how to pick up a kitten. She may spend half an hour taking it by a paw, by the nose, by the tail, before she discovers the scruff-of-the-neck hold. The cat that has had a chance to hunt and kill and carry mice will pick up a kitten properly on the first try.

Observation can be important too. A chimpanzee which was reared in the London Zoo and had never seen a baby of her own species was so horrified at the sudden appearance of her first baby in her nice, safe, and hitherto private cage that she leapt backwards with a shriek of terror, and could never thereafter be persuaded to have anything to do with her offspring. Her second, born a year later, she only accepted after her friend the keeper demonstrated its harmlessness and showed her how to hold it. Apparently some primates, including ourselves, learn mothering by mimicry of their own kind, and cannot manage well without this kind of vicarious experience.

Anxiety caused by inexperience is widespread in the animal kingdom, even in birds. Zoologist W. Craig writes:

When a male dove performs some instinctive act for the first time, it generally shows some surprise, hesitation, bewilderment, or even fear; and the first performance is in a mechanical, reflex style, whereas the same act after much experience is performed with ease, skill, and intelligent adaptation.

He is speaking of a dove building a nest; but the description fits the new nursing human mother just as well. The innate elements of the behavior are merely a rough framework. Experience provides the details and finesse. How much of the behavior is innate may vary from species to species; the dismaying sense of ignorance seems to be universal.

HORMONES AND MOTHERLINESS

It is likely that at least one hormone of lactation, prolactin, which causes the secretion of milk, gives a mother an inclination to be motherly. Unless she is experienced in mothering, however, she feels this inclination only as undirected restlessness and anxiety. This has been demonstrated in a number of animals. A human mother may find herself blaming these restless, anxious feelings on the baby. It takes time and experience, particularly the experience of giving milk, to learn that mothering the offspring will soothe that vague craving which lactation hormones cause.

Another hormone, oxytocin, which causes the let-down of milk, is soothing in itself. The nervous mare or highstrung bitch that becomes noticeably calmer after the first successful feeding of her young is probably responding to the tranquilizing effect of this hormone. Experienced human nursing mothers may be quite conscious of a flooding sense of peace and joy as their milk lets down. As one mother describes it, "It's much more relaxing than a cigarette, and just as habit-forming." This rewarding aspect of lactation helps a mother, animal or human, to take a personal and growing interest in her newborn.

INFANT INSTINCTS

Among lower mammals the mother may be, at first, totally ignorant of her job, so it is the baby and not the mother who must take the initiative in establishing contact. No matter how blind and helpless the newborn mammal may be, he can perform a few instinctive actions which will almost guarantee that he winds up attached to his milk supply. These include crawling or walking, groping with the mouth when the face is touched, and sucking.

In the hoofed animals, the baby gets to its feet soon after birth, and moves toward the nearest large object, which, of course, is its mother. Provided the mother holds still, pretty soon the baby bumps into her, and continues to move along her side until he is stopped by her leg. If it is a hind leg that stopped him, then his nose is not very far from his breakfast, and accidental contact of his muzzle and her flank will elicit a reflexive head-neck gesture of reaching for the udder, producing the first successful feeding. If he gets stuck under a front leg his shoving will provoke his mother into moving away from him entirely, and he must start over again.

Animals which bear litters usually give birth in a nest. Again the babies move toward the nearest large object; warmth is an important feature that attracts them. When their noses make contact with fur, they grope around until they eventually find the nipples. An inexperienced mother may get up and down a lot at first, giving the babies no chance to start sucking. As one kennel owner put it, "It looks as though the bitch is puzzled. There they are, ten babies, and she thinks she ought to do something about them, but she isn't sure what. Finally she gives up, and lies down to rest—and it happens!"

Human infants also have a number of innate actions which help them to find food and which may help to make up for the mother's inexperience, inattentiveness, or clumsiness. Most conspicuous of these, of course, is sucking, a rather complicated activity which the baby can carry on very efficiently, once he gets started. In order to get the nipple into his mouth he has a "grope reflex" which he shares with all young mammals. In the newborn human it consists of turning his head and "reaching" with his mouth in the direction of any touch on his cheek. When the mother picks him up, his head is apt to fall into the crook of her arm, bringing her breast near his cheek. When the nipple touches his cheek he swivels his head toward the touch, and grasps the nipple in his mouth. If the whole breast bumps his cheek, providing generalized stimulation, he may shake his head back and forth very fast as if to "home in" on the stimulus. Once he has grasped the nipple, he draws it back into his mouth with his tongue, and presto! he's nursing. Misunderstanding of the grope reflex often leads to difficulties in the hospital. A nurse may try to force the baby's mouth open by pinching both cheeks; a sensitive baby will become frantic trying to respond both ways at once. Or the nurse may try to put a baby to the mother's breast by pushing his face toward the nipple; the baby valiantly gropes away from the breast, in the direction of the pushing fingers, and the nurse writes on the chart, "Baby refuses breast!"

A newborn human baby shares with the great apes the habit of clenching his fist when hungry and releasing the grip when satisfied, and of shoving his feet in a "neonate crawl." When a baby chimpanzee is born, he immediately grasps whatever he can with his hand, and starts to crawl. Since he usually grasps the hair on his mother's abdomen, his crawl takes him up her body, with or without her help, to her breasts. The newborn human is not as able a climber, but his neonate crawl serves him rather well if he is sleeping at his mother's side or on her stomach. If he shoves himself along he is likely to progress until he is stopped by his mother's chin or arm. Now groping and seeking with his head may well produce milk. Like his distant relative the baby chimp, he grasps tightly in his fists any part of his mother's clothes or anatomy he may come in contact with. This further insures that he will not lose contact with the breast. Many a newborn baby seems to nurse more steadily and happily if he is holding something —his mother's finger, perhaps—in his fist.

In addition to a need for food and the reflexes which enable him to get it, the human infant displays a need for the presence of his mother. He needs warmth, skin contact, and the feeling of being firmly contained; infants cry less in nurseries if they are wrapped snugly, in simulation of being held closely. It has also been found that a low tone, broadcast at a rate of about eighty beats per minute, is soothing to babies in hospital nurseries; the tone simulates the maternal heartbeat, which has dominated each infant's experience for nine months, and which would still be present were he lying next to or near his mother.

THRESHOLDS

The strength of responses and the ease with which they are produced both vary. A hungry baby will respond to a touch on the cheek far more vigorously than a full one. Psychologists say that his "threshold" to the stimulus of touch has been lowered. A really hungry and vigorous baby may suck anything that touches his lips, even his mother's arm or the side of her breast. There are also individual differences in the strength of the reflex, which is subject to the same variations as are all the other hereditary features of living creatures. One baby never gropes very strongly, and the mother has to put the nipple in his mouth for him. As he grows, the grope reflex disappears entirely. Another baby gropes towards the slightest touch, from birth, and has problems with his bedclothes touching him on the cheek. An accidental, unnoticed light touch on the cheek may continue to provide a groping response in such a child for years. On a recent comedy television show movies were shown of a pretty woman "accidentally" annoying a man sitting next to her by letting the long feathers on her hat brush his face. The man was trying to be polite, and to ignore the tickling feathers and make conversation; but every time a feather brushed his cheek, he unconsciously opened his mouth and turned his head toward the touch. It was the grope reflex, still operative in the grown man.

HUMAN NIPPLES AND BOTTLE NIPPLES

Sucking in the human infant is not spontaneous; it is triggered by one particular stimulus, probably the pressure of the nipple when it reaches a position well inside the baby's jaws, up against the roof of his mouth. When a baby does not receive this normal stimulus he acts as if he doesn't know how to suck. A poorly shaped or partially

retracted nipple may not be an adequate stimulus to release sucking behavior. The English physician Mavis
Gunther suggests that Western mothers without other
nursing women to mimic sometimes hold their babies in
poor positions, making it difficult for the baby to get a
good hold and thus to experience the proper releasing
stimulus.

After the baby has experienced just once the proper
stimulus of a firm shape in his mouth (it may be a bottle
nipple or even his mother's finger) he will usually suck in
a practiced manner and seek the breast and feed actively.
The change from apathetic feeder to active, strongly sucking feeder is permanent. However, the nipple of the bottle
may be a much stronger stimulus than the nipples of the
mother's breasts. This is called a supernormal stimulus
and it can distract the baby from the normal stimulus. Dr.
M. Gunther says, "The baby's mouth response may then
rapidly become altered and suited only to receiving the
thrust of the bottle teat." In some British hospitals supplementary formula is given to breast-fed babies only by
spoon, to prevent this inhibition of the infant's ability to
nurse at the breast. Just by making this change the incidence of successful breast feeding is said to have been increased up to 50 per cent in some hospitals.

THE CRITICAL PERIOD

The sooner the first feeding takes place after birth, the
more likely it is to be successful. If it is delayed too long
there may never be a successful feeding. How long it takes
for this crucial feeding to be achieved varies from one species to another. Among cats, the first kittens may be nursing before the last are born. Thus the feline mother is
rapidly initiated into the mysteries and rewards of motherhood. In cattle, it may be an hour or more before the baby
calf gets to its feet and finds its mother's teats. Both the
baby's urge to nurse and the mother's interest in the baby
are strongest immediately after birth. This is the optimum
period for establishing a maternal relationship. At Cornell
University, Dr. Helen Blauvelt separated mother and baby

goats for varying intervals during this critical period, and found that their chances of getting together could be reduced or destroyed completely even by short separations. Postponing the initial contacts beyond the first few hours of life generally resulted in an abandoned baby.

In human beings, we also find signs of the existence of an optimum period in which both mother and child are best equipped to make their first successful contact. As with animals, this period is in the first hour or two after birth. Hospital nurses have often noted that a newborn baby (unless he suffers from the effects of anesthetics given to his mother) is both lively and wakeful in this first hour, and that he makes strong groping motions with his mouth. If put to the breast he will "latch on" at once and with vigor, in marked contrast to the behavior of many babies having their first sucking experience twelve or twenty-four hours after birth. Failure to take advantage of this extremely receptive period may account for some of those hospital-born babies who are lethargic, apathetic, difficult feeders at the breast for days, or even weeks.

The human mother who has just given birth, provided she is not drugged or otherwise incapacitated, is also in a highly sensitive, receptive state. She is eager to see her baby and yearns to touch and hold him. If permitted she will try immediately to feed him. Unless outsiders interfere, this first feeding may last half an hour or longer.

This immediate feeding is deeply rewarding to the mother, as well as being physically beneficial. The firm contraction of the uterus which results suggests that her intense emotional response to this immediate feeding sets into operation a very strong let-down reflex. The weak and unreliable let-down reflex so typical of many new nursing mothers in the United States may be at least in part a result of delaying the first feeding beyond the critical period.

Immediate feeding may benefit the infant physically too. All he gets is a teaspoonful or two of colostrum; but some nurses observe that this helps to reduce the troublesome tendency of newborn babies to regurgitate and aspirate the mucus that is in their stomachs at birth. The taste of something sweet and the experience of sucking and swallowing seem to get the whole digestive tract working in the right direction.

The human mother's keenness to interact with her baby continues to be at a peak in the first days after birth. An example of the power of this urge is the almost irresistible tendency mothers have to unwrap their new baby and look at it all over when it is first brought from the nursery. If the nurses, in the interests of asepsis, are particularly fierce about not permitting this, the mother may do it secretively, and try to wrap the baby up again exactly as it was, but do it she will, with the inevitability with which a little girl of two or three will strip the clothes off a new doll.

The hospital system in our culture of keeping mother and baby separate as much as possible and of frustrating their interaction when they are together may not only inhibit the establishment of lactation but the development of normal behavior patterns in mother as well as child. The anxiety and depression which new mothers sometimes feel, the "baby blues," may be an expression of unrecognized distress due to deprivation. The human mother, in the first few days after birth, may, like other mammals, need the touch, the sound, the smell, the presence of her infant as badly as the infant needs hers.

LANGUAGE WITHOUT WORDS

Once the mammalian mother has learned to be maternal, she will continue to care for her young as long as she is giving milk. Wild horses may nurse a colt throughout another pregnancy, and then allow the yearling to nurse to the accidental detriment of the newcomer. But ordinarily as the young animal begins to take adult food, its need for milk decreases; and as the mother's milk supply wanes, so does maternal behavior. When the milk has gone, the love of the mother for her baby may go with it. She may regard her offspring at last simply as an acquaintance, or even an intruder to be driven from her territory.

It seems to be lactation that keeps the mother caring for and, presumably, loving her baby. Yet animals sometimes display maternal behavior without lactation. Male mice will retrieve and "cuddle" baby mice. An old barren horse may adopt an orphaned colt. Furthermore, as we all know perfectly well, a human mother can be a good mother, and love her baby dearly, without lactating at all. Does this kind of mothering arise consciously and deliberately? Or are there instinctive aids to mothering that do not depend on the mechanism of lactation?

We know that animals respond with reflex physical actions to stimuli presented by other animals. An example we have seen is the sign stimulus of nipple shape which elicits the sucking reflex in the human infant. But parental love is a social attitude and far more complicated than a mere reflex. Without benefit of language, how does the infant make the mother like him, and make her feel that he likes her? He uses the language of gesture, cry, and facial expression—the automatic by-products of his own emotional state. These signals comprise a language more primitive than any word, and yet understood by any adult.

All higher animals have such a language. "Get off my hunting grounds!" "Don't hurt me, I'm only a baby." "Look out! Danger!" "Hey, I found something to eat!" "Shall we dance?" Animals convey this kind of message to each other by means of the "social releaser," a stimulus or signal automatically supplied by one animal, which triggers or releases a specific mood or emotion, often leading to action, on the part of other animals in the same species. When a male duck sees a female in the breeding season his parade before her with head bobbing and wings fanning is a social releaser. So are the raised back hairs and low growl of a male dog or wolf, responded to in kind by another male. A social releaser can be a sound, such as the wailing cry given by a chicken when a hawk passes overhead, making every chicken within earshot run for cover. It can be a scent—the odor of the urine of a female fox, mink, or dog in heat, which arouses mating behavior in the male. It can be a gesture—the way a puppy rolls on its back, exposing its vulnerable throat and belly, to plead for mercy. It can be a pattern, such as the black, fluttering outline of a jackdaw's wings or the phosphorescen array of lights on the sides of some deep sea fishes, conveying the message, to others of the species, "Come with me, we are the same kind."

The most easily observed social releaser stimulus presented by young animals is the infant distress call. This is the cheep, cheep, cheep of a hungry chick, the ear-splitting ki-yi-yi of a puppy caught in a fence, the bawling of a strayed calf, the wail of a newborn child. The infant distress call is usually loud, rhythmical, and distinctive. It is not easily ignored. All animals, including humans, react to the distress call of their own species by exhibiting anxiety and distress of their own. As Dr. Spock has said, "The cry of a young baby is like no other sound. It makes parents want to come to the rescue—fast!" It does indeed. That is what it is meant to do; and to get on your nerves, to make you feel distracted and upset, until you can put a stop to it.

Human infants present many social releaser stimuli to their parents besides the distress call. Dr. Konrad Lorenz, the brilliant German zoologist, has suggested that the whole appearance of a baby is a releaser for parental affection—the rounded features, large eyes, soft cuddly contours, that make us say, "Oh, isn't he cute?" when we see a baby. The sign stimulus features of an infant's face, the short button nose, round cheeks, and chinlessness, are often exaggerated to make the "adorable" faces of many children's dolls and cartoon characters.

An interesting social releaser in very small babies is sound other than crying. From the first weeks of life, breast-fed babies murmur as they nurse. Little coos and hums which seem to express pleasure and relaxation can be heard throughout the feeding. A toddler may make the same little singing sounds when he is playing enjoyably by himself, and one can hear the same class of sound—little sighs and murmurs of comfort—from an adult who is enjoying, for example, a good back rub.

Dr. Richard Applebaum has made the striking observation that bottle-fed babies do not vocalize during feedings, or, if they do, that the sound is apt to be sputtering and grunting rather than cooing and melodious murmuring.

Furthermore, a breast-fed baby who is switched to the bottle will stop cooing within a few feedings. If he is switched back to the breast, the vocalizing begins again. Probably the artificial configuration of mouth and throat during bottle feeding hampers the baby's ability to vocalize and eat at the same time. Possibly however the baby does not feel the same sublime enjoyment at the bottle as he did at the breast, and so has no emotions of comfort and pleasure to be expressed in pleasant sighs and murmurs. Certainly the nursing baby's little song is received by the mother as a message of comfort, contentment, and love, even if she is not consciously aware of it, and thus serves to strengthen the nursing bond.

It is possible that the smell of the infant may be a releaser. Mothers who breast feed are apt to comment on how good their babies smell, a scent which has nothing to do with baby powder. And the exclamation, "Baby smells so sweet!" is usually accompanied by a hug and a kiss and a nuzzle for the baby: socially desirable behavior triggered by a releasing stimulus. The formula-fed baby, on the other hand, may have an unpleasant odor, due to the chemical nature of his sweat, urine, stools, or spit-up stomach contents. Some nursing mothers dislike picking up a bottle-fed baby because of the smell.

The baby's grasp reflex, besides helping him hang on to the mother, serves as a social releaser. At the Yerkes Laboratory in Florida, where chimpanzees have been carefully raised and studied for years, it has been noted that a female who has just given birth is apparently very impressed when her baby reaches out with its little hands and takes hold of her. It is this touch of hands which tells her the baby is one of her own kind. In humans, touching of hands conveys friendship in a simple, universal—and therefore instinctive—way. The firm, responsive way a newborn baby grasps your finger is therefore a useful releaser for affectionate behavior from mothers and fathers.

Smiling is a social releaser. A newborn baby, when its stomach is full, often smiles, a fleeting grimace, as it falls asleep. This is called the smile of satiety, and it is an automatic response to the comfort of a full stomach. The onlooker may dismiss it as gas but to the mother it means something. It means her baby is happy; and that makes her feel happy too. While the baby is still very small, four to eight weeks old, this smile of satiety becomes a true social smile. At first the releasing stimulus for this smile is a pair of human eyes. When the baby sees you looking at him, he smiles. Later he smiles at the sight of a face, and soon only at special, familiar faces. Smiling as he catches your eye is a very valuable instinctive response, and it in turn acts as a releaser for social behavior from the parent, or indeed from almost any human, even another child or a grouchy old man.

It is apparent that these tools of instinct, the sign stimuli and social releasers, are present in all mammals, even to some extent in that elegant and advanced mammal, the human being. We perhaps are less automatic about the giving of and responding to releasing stimuli than our lower brethren. We can conceal the frown of anger, or hold back the unsuitable laugh (sometimes, at least). We can learn to ignore releasers for social behavior—an invitation to courtship, the face of rage, even outstretched hands pleading for mercy. It would be futile, after all, if we had to be aware of, and to respond to, the emotional states of all the people we pass in the street or do business with. But in the relationship of mother to child, the universal language of instinct can still serve as the foundation for months of nursing and mothering.

BABIES NEED LOVE TO SURVIVE

Social attention is life itself to the human baby. The baby who does not receive extra handling and attention beyond what he needs for physical survival does not develop normally. Institutionalized babies who receive splendid physical and medical care but who have no social contact with other people begin to show altered development before two months of age. They are listless and underweight. They do not smile or babble or crawl at the appropriate ages; by six months they are visibly retarded, both mentally and physically. They have fevers for no apparent reason, and are extremely susceptible to infection. Frequently they die before the age of two or three.

In *Child Care and the Growth of Love,* Dr. John Bowlby points out that these symptoms of abnormality disappear with amazing speed if the infant is placed in a home and receives maternal care. However, there appear to be critical periods in the development of social responses which, once past, cannot be recaptured. Complete deprivation of social contact during the first or second six months of life produces a permanently abnormal personality. Deprivation for periods during the next two years may or may not result in permanent harm.

INNATE SOCIAL RESPONSES IN INFANTS

The human infant, as well as his mother, responds to social releasers; these stimuli trigger social behavior just as the physical stimulus of the nipple triggers sucking behavior. For example, Dr. René Spitz, who is world-famous for his studies of emotional deprivation in infancy, has found that even young babies with no previous experience show a predictable response to the sight of a nodding "yes" head, which pleases them, and a shaking "no" head, which produces only apathy; these gestures may be part of the basic repertoire of human social releasers.

THE SENSE OF TOUCH

By far the most important releasing stimulus to the human infant is the sense of touch. The skin of a new baby is far more sensitive than that of an adult. It flushes and mottles at every sensation. It is through his kinesthetic awareness, through being touched and moved and handled, and through the things that touch his sensitive mouth, that a baby first locates himself and makes contact with reality. The continued experience of being touched and held is an important part of his development.

This is true of every mammal. Rats that are unhandled from infancy become savage, while rats that are handled daily are placid and tame, even when the daily handling is followed by an electric shock. Baby monkeys have been experimentally raised with surrogate mothers. The monkey raised with a "mother" made of chicken wire goes to "her" for food, but spends the rest of his time cowering in a corner, and screams with fear at any change in his environment. The monkey raised with a "mother" made of padded chicken wire clings to the soft padding, like any baby monkey to his mother, investigates new objects with normal monkey curiosity, and shows fairly normal development. The only difference is in stimulus to the sense of touch.

It may be that the need for physical contact is especially acute during the critical period of the first hours and days after birth, when we customarily isolate babies. If postponing the sucking experience beyond this time contributes to the apathy of some newborns, perhaps eliminating body contact is a factor in producing both apathetic and overexcited babies. Though it appears that the baby a few hours old is asleep except when hungry, actually his periods of quiescence alternate with periods of awareness in which he scans his environment with all his senses. The same thing has been described in newborn goats, who are alternately inactive and actively searching. In the natural situation, a newborn baby remains by his mother after birth, close to her body. Tired from exertion, the mother sleeps for most of a day or two; in her waking periods she becomes adjusted to the presence of the baby, through feeding and playing with him. Awake or asleep the baby is surrounded by the stimuli of her warmth, heartbeat, and touch. It is no wonder that a baby may not respond correctly when he is isolated in a crib as soon as he is born, and thirty-six hours later is handed into the arms of an apprehensive mother with nervous grip and racing heart. It is no wonder that this mother, coping with a difficult baby, may be less than normally aware of her own maternal instincts.

BODY CONTACT AND PERSONALITY

Body contact may not only be vital to the newborn in adjusting to extrauterine existence; it may be more important than we know in personality development through the first two years. Dr. James Clark Moloney has written at length of the contrast between the Okinawan culture and ours, and of the confidence and serenity apparent not only in the Okinawan adult but in the infant and toddler. Okinawan children are breast fed for two years or so. Breast feeding of course necessitates a great deal of simple physical contact between mother and child. Also, the babies are carried on their mother's back for much of the time during the first and second years. Subjective evidence from American mothers indicates that this kind of prolonged, impersonal contact has a profoundly calming effect on babies. It would appear, as is indicated by the raising of baby monkeys with surrogate mothers, that physical contact with the mother is even more important than social attention; that the baby who gets plenty of breast feeding and carrying about develops more normally, and becomes a more secure individual, than the baby who gets plenty of social attention but less physical contact. Possibly the anxiety that marks our culture is in part due to the custom of depriving our infants of body contact, leaving them in firm-surfaced cribs, feeding them with a cool, rigid rubber nipple and glass bottle, picking them up as little as possible, and even carrying them about in a plastic chair rather than against the mother's body.

PATTERNS OF MOTHERHOOD

Parturition and lactation are not just physical events. They are part of a pattern of social behavior, a pattern that is partly innate, partly physiological, and partly, in humans, dictated by the society in which we live. During childbirth, women are usually receptive and suggestible. If they experience inappropriate emotions during labor and delivery, their biologically desirable maternal behavior patterns may be adversely affected. Mothers anesthetized during the birth may hesitate to believe the baby is theirs; animals experimentally rendered unconscious during birth almost always reject their young. Dr. J. C. Moloney suggests that the phenomenon of post-partum depression is a response to the frustrations experienced in typical Western-style childbirth. Newton and Newton, in observations of more than six hundred mothers, found that disruption of the biologically normal pattern of labor and delivery was the major factor contributing to a mother's rejection of her newborn baby. For example the mothers who were given friendly attendants throughout their labor were twice as likely to be pleased at the first sight of their baby than mothers who were left alone or treated coldly. In most primitive cultures, babies are delivered with the mother squatting or kneeling; in the Newtons' observations, mothers delivered with the aid of a back rest enabling them to approach the primitive squatting position were much more likely to complete the normal pattern by showing strong interest in the baby than were mothers delivered in the standard Western way, lying on their backs. The actual events of delivery, even when the delivery was difficult, had no harmful effect on the mother's response. The maintenance of an encouraging, relaxed environment during labor and delivery had more effect on the mother's response than did her personality and background.

But even when labor and delivery have taken place in a supportive environment, the relationship of mother and child can still be distorted. Breast feeding may be made impossible by formula supplements in the nursery. Or a mother may become frantic and give up the idea of breast feeding when her baby, reacting to an abnormal environment, repeatedly screams and rejects the breast. The frustration and unhappiness which both mother and baby feel when breast feeding goes badly and is finally abandoned can be followed by an endless series of misunderstandings between them, as this disruption of the normal pattern is followed by further distortion of the mother-child relationship.

Mother Instinct in Humans

We are coming to understand that instinct is not a blind, inflexible force but a series of nudges, of small reflexive responses to internal or external stimuli which, added together, tend to produce certain patterns of behavior. There is room for individuality, for adaptation to circumstance; the higher the animal the more room there is. And the basic actions, the little pieces of the pattern, cannot easily be elicited in the laboratory under artificial circumstances, as one can elicit a flinch from an electric shock, or salivation at the smell of food. Responses do not operate infallibly, in every animal, every time; even ants have been found to display individuality in their behavior. It is by long and careful observation of animals in their natural environment that the patterns of instinct can be seen, and the little reflexive responses which create the basis for those patterns can be isolated.

It is very likely that this kind of observation of humans would show us that even as adults we demonstrate many instinctive behavior elements. The nursing relationship is a fertile field for observation. How much of a mother's behavior is part of the innate pattern? In the light of the fact that babies are soothed by the maternal heartbeat, consider the startling observation made in 1960 by researcher Dr. I. Salk: Out of 287 newly delivered mothers the great majority, regardless of past experience or right- and left-handedness, held their babies on the left side, over the heart. What unrecognized feeling in the mother, what releasing stimulus offered by the baby, precipitates *that* visible part of the maternal pattern of behavior? And how many other maternal and infant instincts do we inadvertently frustrate, with our logic and rules, and with what results?

Perhaps, as we come to learn more about instinctive patterns in humans, we can remove some of the strict rules that our society imposes on such functions as childbirth and child care, and give the natural patterns freedom in which to emerge, so that one part of the pattern can lead smoothly to another as nature intended. Then biologically normal labor can result in appropriate maternal response to the baby; successful early contacts can result in successful lactation; prolonged successful lactation can result in continued good mothering and emotionally stable children.

5·Doctors Who Don't Help

Apathy. Incredible apathy. This is the attitude of the medical profession in America toward breast feeding. Almost all doctors will give lip service to the idea that breast feeding is the best way to feed a baby. Yet in their own practice most of them continue to discourage or prevent women from breast feeding. Obstetricians ignore the need to prepare inexperienced mothers. Pediatricians order their favorite formulas for every patient whether the mother wishes to breast feed or not.

Some doctors, those who personally find breast feeding an unpleasant idea, use every trick in the book to discourage mothers from trying it. Hospital routines often prevent successful lactation entirely. Nurses with no training in lactation techniques are allowed to criticize and interfere with breast-feeding mothers. In many hospitals drugs that suppress lactation are routinely administered to new mothers without even consulting them. Of the few babies in this country that do start out at their mothers' breasts, most are needlessly weaned within a few days or weeks.

Some forward-looking doctors are taking a backward

glance at breast feeding and are beginning to try to understand and encourage it once more. But most are slow to change their attitudes. And in the face of spoken or unspoken opposition from the medical world a mother who wishes to breast feed must have real fortitude if she is to succeed.

MEDICAL NO-MAN'S-LAND

In this day of specialists, the nursing mother is in a medical no-man's-land. Her breasts are the concern of the obstetrician. The milk within them is the concern of the pediatrician. The pediatrician prescribes for cracked nipples; the obstetrician treats the infected breast. If the milk supply should be increased, call the pediatrician. If the milk supply should be dried up, that's the obstetrician's job. Many a nursing mother has spent a worried day just wondering which doctor she ought to be calling this time.

No matter which she calls, she stands a good chance of being hindered rather than helped by the doctor's advice. What he tells her may not even be true. It is a common complaint of doctors that foolish women will listen to any sort of nonsense from their friends and relatives rather than to the wisdom of their doctor. But almost every woman who has breast fed or tried to breast feed a baby can quote half-truths or out-and-out old wives' tales told to her by a qualified physician: "You're too flat-chested to breast feed." "Your milk doesn't agree with the baby." "Breast feeding is going to ruin your figure." "You southern women (or northern, or white, or oriental, or whatever the doctor is not) are too nervous to nurse a baby." "Your milk is too thin." "Most women nowadays *have* to give complementary feedings." "You can't nurse a baby if you have another child to look after." "Breast feeding will make you tired and run down." "You're not the nursing type."

SABOTAGE

The woman who disregards this propaganda and starts breast feeding may be ordered to wean her baby for trivial or even nonexistent reasons. Although rigidity is inappropriate to the management of the nursing couple, breast feeding is often terminated needlessly because it is not proceeding according to the doctor's rigid rules. Babies have been weaned because they insisted on taking both breasts at a feeding, or because they refused to take more than one; because they couldn't give up night feedings at some specific age; or because they were "too playful" at mealtimes. Sometimes a conscientious doctor orders a baby weaned because he is so unfamiliar with anything but formula-fed babies that he does not recognize that the baby is normal. Perhaps the baby is naturally a slow gainer (he could be stuffed like a goose with formula, but you can't force-feed breast milk); perhaps he likes to eat every two or three hours instead of on the bottle-fed baby's four hour schedule; perhaps he spits up a lot or can't be made to burp at all; perhaps the baby has some normal infant ailment such as colic or a diaper rash. The doctor may respond to all these events by ordering the child weaned from breast to bottle, as casually as if he were suggesting a minor formula change. As Dr. H. F. Meyer points out in *Infant Foods and Feeding Practice,* many a doctor has interpreted the normal breast-fed baby's stool as diarrhea, or the normal tendency of older breast-fed babies to empty their bowels once every three or four days as some kind of constipation. In each case he has weaned the baby. Babies are frequently weaned on the basis of such inadequate tests as the appearance of the mother's milk (normally thin and bluish), or the baby's weight gain in a few hours, or the measured fat content of one small sample of milk. It is not physical inability in the mother which causes most women to give up breast feeding; it is sabotage.

A great many potentially successful nursing mothers are sabotaged right from the beginning. Some women have retracted nipples, a condition which makes nursing difficult and painful, but which can be easily corrected during pregnancy. Many are victims of hospital regulations which curtail nursing time to such an extent that adequate milk production is impossible. A mother whose milk doesn't come in until the fourth or fifth day may find that some high-handed nurse, seeing that the baby was losing weight, has been stuffing him with formula. Just when the mother is suddenly loaded with a huge, gushing milk supply, the baby, instead of being ravenous, has no appetite at all. The breasts become engorged, feedings become very difficult, and lactation fails. Other mothers are simply frightened out of nursing successfully. The hospital situation and the behavior of the nurses are such that the mother can never relax enough to let down her milk. The milk is there, but the baby isn't getting it. Instead of understanding and correcting the situation, the doctor usually uses it as an excuse to talk the mother out of breast feeding.

THE DECLINE OF BREAST FEEDING IN THE UNITED STATES

The result of this widespread neglect and ignorance is that the United States has the lowest percentage of breast-fed babies in the world. Fewer than 25 per cent of the babies born in this country are nursed even for the five days of the usual hospital stay. In far too many hospitals no babies are breast fed at all. This situation does not disturb or even interest most American doctors despite the fact that half a dozen countries in which breast feeding is customary have lower infant mortality rates than we do. In Great Britain, in contrast, the medical profession expresses general and public concern because, while almost every baby is breast fed for a while, only 50 per cent are breast fed for six months or more. In America any sign of lactation trouble is adequate reason for weaning to a bottle. In New Zealand and some other parts of the British Commonwealth a mother whose milk supply falters may be hospitalized with her baby until lactation is reestablished. In America thousands upon thousands of papers have been published on the scientific aspects of artificial feeding. But almost all of the comparatively scanty published scientific research on breast feeding comes from Europe, and especially from Sweden, where even illegitimate babies are breast fed for six months to a year or more. We Americans are a backward nation in this respect. We know far less and care far less about human lactation than about lactation in dairy cows.

INERTIA IN ACCEPTING FACTS

The American physician by and large behaves as if breast feeding no longer had important nutritional advantages over bottle feeding. What little support he gives to breast feeding is in recognition of its emotional benefits. If the mother is having any difficulty in breast feeding then the doctor presumes that neither she nor the baby is reaping those emotional benefits, so there is no good reason not to switch to a bottle.

Why does a doctor give up so easily when he runs into lactation problems? Usually because he has no idea of how to solve them, or even that they can be solved. Medical school has taught him next to nothing on this point. He probably has no personal experience with lactation in any species. Fifty or sixty years ago many families kept a cow, and almost every household had puppies or kittens in it now and then. Today's young doctor is much more likely to have been raised in a city apartment than on a farm. Lactation to him is not a fact of life but something unknown and rather peculiar.

Such research as has been done on human lactation, most of it within the past thirty years, is generally ignored. Statistics demonstrating increased resistance to disease in the breast-fed baby don't affect in the slightest the widespread tendency to bottle feed all babies. Almost every technique now proven to be harmful to lactation is still widely practiced. In the nineteen forties it was demonstrated that giving babies formula in the hospital nursery is always "a practice associated with lactation failure" and a major contributing factor to inadequate breast milk.

This is still nearly universal practice. Likewise it was proven that to induce successful lactation a baby should be fed at both breasts at every feeding. But many doctors and hospitals today still insist on one breast at a feeding only. By 1950 Dr. Michael Newton and his wife, Niles Newton, demonstrated that the widespread practice of limiting sucking to five minutes a side, to prevent sore nipples, not only harmed the chances of successful lactation (which depends on liberal, unrestricted sucking during the first weeks) but increased the nipple damage. They also showed that most of the ointments and medications that doctors and hospitals use to treat sore nipples actually made them worse. Nevertheless, the first thing any mother hears in almost any American hospital is that she must not nurse her baby more than five minutes on a side or her nipples will get sore, while alcohol, soap, tincture of benzoin, and other harmful substances continue to be applied routinely to the breasts of nursing mothers.

Why does this inertia exist? The doctors, of course, make haste to blame it on the laity: "Husbands today don't like their wives to breast feed." "The modern woman doesn't have the leisure for breast feeding." "Breast feeding only works in a primitive society." "I'd like to recommend breast feeding but mothers seem to get so upset and depressed when they fail that I don't dare encourage it." Rather than re-educate themselves and the public, and investigate the problem of making lactation a success, they prefer to give it up altogether.

In reality, the maternal reluctance to breast feed is at least as much a reflection of the medical attitude as a contribution to it. A Harvard study on patterns of incidence of breast feeding, reported in the *New England Journal of Medicine* in 1958, sums up its findings with this conclusion:

The attitude of medical practitioners, who are responsible for most of the antenatal supervision in the U.S., probably accounts both for the regional variation in amount of breast feeding and its general low prevalence. Where individual doctors are themselves convinced of the value of breast feeding more of their patients feel this way notwithstanding the prevailing mode.

WHAT MEDICAL SCHOOLS DON'T TEACH

Medical schools do a fine job of ignoring breast feeding. A common problem in the daily routine of medical practice for a G.P. or a pediatrician is that of teaching mothers the art of breast feeding. But it may come as quite a surprise to the young doctor that he is called upon for help in this department, because he has been taught nothing about it. A prominent doctor writes that he completed his medical training, including specialization in obstetrics, without ever once seeing a nursing mother in action. At present, medical-school education about breast-feeding is apt to consist of a paragraph in the anatomy text about the structure of the breast, another about the hormones of lactation, and a lecture or two based on the professor's experiences and prejudices about breast feeding, with emphasis on the "contra-indications" to nursing. The many methods by which a canny doctor can help his nursing mothers to succeed are not taught at all. The doctors who use them have either re-invented them for themselves, or picked them up via the grapevine.

While virtually ignoring breast feeding, the medical student puts in a great deal of time on the complicated subject of artificial formulas. Thus he starts his professional career with the inevitable impression that artificial feeding is important but that breast feeding is not. Breast feeding, like wood stoves and kerosene lamps, is a relic of the past; charming, perhaps, but not really practical, and if not spontaneously successful, to be bypassed for the more interesting and reliable methods of artificial feeding which one has just learned about in such detail. Of course there have always been a few doctors crusading for better understanding of breast feeding but most remain apathetic, and the arguments of the crusaders are lost in a deluge of fresh technical information about this or that variety of artificial feeding.

Propaganda for Formula Feeding

Technical or scientific interest in artificial feeding grows and flourishes today under an economic stimulus. Breast feeding is of economic advantage to no one (except, of course, parents). But a great deal of money is made by a great many companies who manufacture and sell baby foods. It is to their conspicuous advantage to propagandize artificial feeding in every way possible. Doctors are peculiarly susceptible to Madison Avenue. The individual doctor has no time to review all new research for himself, and must take his opinions at least to some extent from others. And the physician's need to rely on responsible outside sources lays him wide open to propaganda. If a company has sufficient prestige and dignity, if it presents the advantages of its product in such a way that they seem to be entirely confirmed by good scientific research, and if its product is endorsed by enough brilliant names, a doctor will probably accept it as reliable. There has recently been a lot of publicity concerning drug companies which took advantage of this fact to sell doctors on an unnecessary variety of antibiotics and "wonder drugs," and even on unsafe drugs such as Thalidomide. It is a successful way to sell infant formulas too. For instance, some companies manufacture milkless formulas for infants allergic to cow's milk. They have propagandized their product so successfully that some pediatricians, anxious to avoid having allergic patients, order these formulas for almost every baby under their care, from birth. They even presuppose, on the evidence offered them by the formula manufacturer, that a baby might be allergic to his own mother's milk. So such a man may instruct all his patients not to breast feed but to give soybean "milk" or some such invention instead.

Baby Food Fads

This kind of misdirection can spread fast. Infant feeding fads sweep the medical profession and mothers alike, to the benefit of the businessmen. One example is the early feeding of solids to infants. When Gerber and Heinz first came out with a line of canned, puréed fruits, vegetables, and meats for infants, these were not commonly offered to babies younger than four or five months. But the easy availability of such foods, and of funds for research into their value, has produced reports on the virtues of giving fruit, cereal, and meat to babies right from the first few weeks. Naturally the baby food companies make sure that any such research reaches the attention of every pediatrician possible, and at the same time, through store displays and advertising campaigns (including direct mail to new mothers), they educate mothers into asking about solid foods early. Today a doctor may start his infant patients on a regimen of "solid" foods practically from birth, despite the fact that *truly* independent scientific research now indicates that this spoon feeding, to which some babies violently object, is not good for them in the least. Solid food given in the first few months of life is merely a substitute for the nutritionally superior milk, "worsening the nutritional state of the infant rather than bettering it;" allergies to food substances are increased; spoon feeding alters infant oral responses, and frightens and frustrates many infants—"and that isn't any too pleasant for the experimenting mother," as Dr. F. H. Richardson points out. The practice of feeding solids early, concludes the Committee on Nutrition of the American Academy of Pediatrics, merely "attests the adaptability of the baby to the whim of his caretakers."

THE PEDIATRICIAN'S WIFE

A recent survey of pediatricians indicates that the physician's attitude towards breast feeding does not depend primarily on medical research, advertising, or indeed any conscious source, but simply on whether or not his own wife breast fed their children. If she tried and failed he is going to expect lactation to be full of difficulties, and will concentrate his efforts in his own practice on reassuring the mother who fails as expected. He may even unconsciously resent the woman who succeeds. If his wife is the kind who wouldn't *dream* of breast feeding, the doctor is unlikely to regard breast feeding as important, and will be indifferent to the point of callousness towards any mothers who insist on nursing. He may even sabotage nursing mothers by some method such as suggesting that at least one-bottle be given daily to every baby—a procedure almost guaranteed to suppress lactation.

THE BIASED OBSTETRICIAN

Given a private lack of enthusiasm for breast feeding, some doctors turn up so many medical reasons against the process that they feel honestly justified in interfering even with totally successful lactation. Without a thought for the happiness of the nursing couple, they employ any means to bring about weaning.

Obstetricians are the worst sinners in this respect. Once an obstetrician has delivered a baby his responsibility ends, as far as the baby is concerned. He is possibly more susceptible than any pediatrician to persuasions of excellence on the part of the formula purveyors because he does not see the babies who provide evidence to the contrary. Having recommended a good pediatrician, he dismisses the infant and his needs from his mind and concentrates on the well-being of the mother. Unfortunately, he may not understand that this well-being is more than merely physical; if he has had no personal experience with nursing couples, he may not realize the strength of the nursing relationship, the powerful bonds of love that it establishes, and the grief and distress that normal mothers feel when those bonds are shattered by premature weaning.

The principal ailment the doctor wishes to avoid is the abscessed breast. Mild breast infections, which are not uncommon, can be cleared up easily if antibiotics are administered within a few hours after the symptoms start, and if the baby, gentlest of breast pumps, is put to the infected breast often, keeping it relatively empty of milk. This was demonstrated by Dr. E. Robbins Kimball of Northwestern University Medical School, who treated one hundred nursing mothers suffering from mastitis with antibiotics and frequent nursing. All one hundred recovered completely within a few days. Another thirty mothers were treated with antibiotics but their babies were weaned immediately from the breast. All thirty developed abscesses, fifteen required surgery, and none recovered in less than sixty days.

Unfortunately most American obstetricians persist in the old-fashioned treatment of weaning the baby at once from the infected breast. The result is engorgement and total stasis, the rapid spread of infection through static milk and swollen tissues, and the surgery which may be necessary not once but many times. Any doctor would be anxious to spare his patients this ordeal.

Mastitis is probably as common, even more common, among mothers who have their milk "dried up" than among mothers who nurse, since it is a result of stasis. But many doctors persist in regarding breast feeding as a cause of mastitis. For this reason an obstetrician may, without a twinge of conscience, discourage mothers who wish to breast feed and scold mothers who are already breast feeding. And some hospital staffs prohibit breast feeding entirely in an attempt to reduce mastitis epidemics which actually come from overcrowded babies in contaminated nurseries.

The happily nursing mother who does happen to develop a breast infection may be shocked by the violence of the obstetrician's efforts to make her stop. A doctor who wouldn't dream of telling a bride unpleasant things about marital sex, or frightening a pregnant woman with details of abnormal childbirth, may have no moral compunctions at all about telling a nursing mother anything that comes into his head. Being of the opinion that nursing is a cause of mastitis, and that treatment for mastitis starts with immediate weaning, he is doubly insistent because he has found that mothers are unreliable about weaning their babies. So if he really wants a woman to wean her baby immediately he has to shame her or else scare her thoroughly. Whether the lecture that he hands out is biased or even full of nonsense is not important if it achieves his objective: the cessation of breast feeding.

The Defeatists

Some doctors discourage breast feeding simply out of defeatism. Their breast-feeding patients always have difficulties, and usually fail. The constant repetition of this pattern is so discouraging to the doctor that he turns against breast feeding altogether. One such doctor wrote to La Leche League, a group of nursing mothers, that he wished the mothers in his area would breast feed in the calm, happy way La Leche mothers do, instead of getting nervous and upset about it. Another doctor, an internationally famous pediatrician, once lectured on infant feeding to a large audience of doctors and specialists in New York. At the close of his learned lecture, one doctor inquired why he had not mentioned breast feeding. The pediatrician answered that he never recommended breast feeding because it was far too complicated.

What these doctors fail to realize, of course, is that the complications and failures of breast feeding that they see in their own practices may be caused by their own behavior. Perhaps they show dubious or critical attitudes which destroy a mother's all-important self-confidence. Almost always they try to make their patient follow one or more inappropriate rules which make breast feeding difficult or impossible. What makes the mothers frantic is not the breast feeding but the constant conflict between what the baby wants and what the doctor has told them to do. Human nature is such that the more trouble a doctor has with nursing couples the more he insists on his pet rules. Thus the loudest voices in support of harmful rules are the voices of doctors with conspicuously few successful nursing mothers to their credit.

Exporting Our Errors

It is depressing to regard the effect of the American medical attitude towards breast feeding on nursing mothers in this country. But it is appalling to see the tragedy that results when this attitude is exported.

The medical men who spread our enlightened civilization into the far, hot, germy corners of the earth take their destructive attitude toward breast feeding with them. Doctors in underdeveloped areas usually assume that mothers take to artificial feeding because they think it is sophisticated. The implication is that all women, even primitive or uneducated females, think being fashionable is more important than anything else, and the doctor must go along with the trend. Actually, it is usually the doctor or medical worker who has the feeling that bottle feeding is more sophisticated than breast feeding. Fear is the real motive of the primitive mother who offers her baby a bottle. From doctor and health worker, with their talk of vitamins and orange juice, and from the ubiquitous milk company advertisements which plaster buildings in Johannesburg, and hang in village general stores in Luzon, and decorate roadsides from Guam to Guatemala, she has gained the impression that breast milk is not good enough. If educated Western women can succumb to this suggestion, how much more easily the innocent primitive mother can lose her confidence. How natural, how unavoidable, is the pang of fear she feels if the baby is taken ill or doesn't seem happy. Her milk! Something must be wrong with her milk. She prepares a bottle—perhaps with the advice of a health worker—and gives it to the baby. The baby does not improve. He gets diarrhea. Another bottle is given, unavoidably a fine solution of milk and bacteria. As bottles replace feeding at the breast, the mother's milk supply decreases. Perhaps anxiety inhibits her let-down response. The baby frets at the once so abundant breast. He gets more contaminated bottles, and so he begins the downward spiral which ends in death.

As Jelliffe, Welbourn, and other World Health Organization medical workers emphasize, this combination of events is occurring all over the world, and with ever increasing frequency. A survey made in Uganda in 1952 showed that infectious gastroenteritis was almost never seen in infants there. It ranked a low tenth on the list of causes for infant hospitalizations. Today it is the first by a long shot, affecting the majority of babies in Uganda hospitals. In almost every part of the world where Western medical care has become available, clinics and hospitals are proud to display a new phenomenon: recently built, modern "rehydration centers." These are outpatient facilities designed to treat the hospital's ever-growing overflow of infants dangerously dehydrated by diarrhea. But the tremendous and recent rise in these death-dealing intestinal infections is almost never linked to the corresponding rise in the use of dietary supplements and bottles. Under primitive conditions, vitamins, fruit juices, formula and semisolid foods present a dangerous source of infection for infants under six months of age. This far outweighs their potential values as sources of nourishment. Breast-fed babies don't need these things anyway. Yet this kind of supplementing of infant diets (necessary for formula-fed babies, and taught in medical schools) is prescribed by transplanted Western medical workers as routinely as vaccinations and vermifuges. Whenever a mother is found with a remotely serious ailment she is ordered to wean her baby. A mother who fears that she does not have enough milk is told how to fix artificial feedings just as if she were a housewife in the United States instead of in a jungle hut or sewage-strewn slum. Thus early weaning is promoted, despite the fact that abandoning breast feeding before two years means, in most tropical countries, that the child will probably develop an overt case of the dreaded kwashiorkor, or protein deficiency disease, in addition to frequent bouts of gastroenteritis. It would be far easier to understand and promote lactation here and abroad than to make every village in every country as sanitary as our own home towns. But the medical world, aided and prompted by commercial advertisers, sticking to precedent, would rather attempt the second than accomplish the first. Sanitation here and abroad may be improving, thanks to medical help; lactation certainly is not.

6 · Doctors Who Understand

HOW THE DOCTOR LEARNS

"My doctor really believes in breast feeding."

"I could never have nursed my baby without my wonderful doctor."

"My pediatrician talked me into trying breast feeding, and am I glad he did!"

"My doctor has six breast-fed children of his own, and *all* his patients breast feed."

These mothers have found the kind of doctor a nursing mother needs: one who not only shows enthusiasm for breast feeding but also understands its management. Usually both the enthusiasm and understanding have been acquired through shrewd observation over years of practice. Any general practitioner or pediatrician who does not actually forbid mothers to breast feed is going to have some breast-fed babies among his patients. The attentive doctor who gives his nursing mothers a sufficiently free hand cannot help but be enlightened by their experiences. He may see a mother whose milk supply seems to be dwindling but who rejects the complementary bottle and, through rest and increased feedings, redevelops an abundant supply. He may see nursing mothers successfully weather breast infections or influenza without giving up breast feeding, or mothers who breast feed easily despite having several small children to care for, in addition to the baby. These object lessons encourage him to help and advise other mothers in the same circumstances, rather than just prescribing formula at each sign of difficulty. The doctor may see a mother breast feed twins successfully, even against his advice. Next time he won't advise against it. He may see the mother of a premature baby keep her milk supply going by pumping or manual expression for six weeks or more until her baby can leave the hospital. Then he knows at first hand that it is possible for mothers of premature babies to breast feed.

As a pediatrician's understanding of breast feeding improves, he is able to help more and more mothers. And with a larger sample of breast-fed babies to observe, he cannot help but be impressed by the sparkling good health of the average breast-fed baby. The doctor's appreciation of this is a tacit compliment to the nursing mother. She and the doctor both feel rewarded when he can say, "It's a joy to see a baby doing as well as yours."

THE MOTHER-DOCTOR TEAM

A doctor comes to respect the successful nursing mother for her ability as a mother, just as she respects him for his medical skill. This often leads to a highly workable relationship between them; mother and doctor can deal jointly with the child as self-respecting members of a team rather than as master and servant. Some doctors believe that there is a perceptible difference between mothers who have breast fed successfully and those who have not. The doctor who has had the experience of caring for many breast-fed babies may come to prefer working with mothers who have "made the team" to such an extent that, like Dr. E. Robbins Kimball of Northwestern University, he refuses to accept a baby as his patient unless the mother is prepared to make "a dedicated, determined effort to learn to breast feed."

The physician who knows how to help mothers through the difficulties of learning to breast feed is not afraid to encourage new mothers to try. He knows that there are certain women who could never be persuaded to nurse a baby as long as an alternative exists. But he has found that most women, even today, even in America, will breast feed willingly and eagerly once their misconceptions and fears about this unfamiliar process have been cleared away.

HOW THE OBSTETRICIAN CAN HELP

Clearing away such misconceptions is not the pediatrician's job; he may not even meet the mother until after the baby is born—too late to begin re-education. It is the conscientious obstetrician who takes the time, during a woman's pregnancy, first to plant the notion that he expects she will breast feed, and then, as delivery draws near, to discuss the advantages of breast feeding for both mother and baby, to settle the doubts and fears the mother may have, and to correct any detrimental physical conditions that may exist. If physical problems such as mastitis should arise during lactation, he treats them with an eye to maintaining breast feeding rather than abandoning it, as long as that is the mother's desire.

Some physicians who are breast feeding enthusiasts have more zeal than knowledge. It does not always help a mother to urge her to breast feed without being able to offer her practical assistance. Fortunately, an excellent pamphlet is now available to physicians, containing reprints of Drs. Michael and Niles Newton's "The Normal Course and Management of Lactation" and Dr. R. M. Applebaum's "The Modern Management of Successful Breast-Feeding." It may be ordered from *Child and Family,* Box 508, Oak Park, Illinois 60303, at fifty cents a copy, with quantity discounts available.

The Crusading Doctor

The obstetrician or pediatrician who is successful in establishing breast feeding finds it discouraging to have a mother willing and eager to breast feed but unable to do so because she was not prepared during pregnancy, or because her milk was arbitrarily suppressed in the hospital. It's frustrating for him to hear of babies with illnesses that might have been avoided by breast feeding; so he is apt to become something of a crusader. One dedicated man may start by passing on his own techniques to his colleagues. He may be able to alter local hospital procedures to make breast feeding more feasible. The pediatrician who is convinced of the advantages of breast feeding may find support from obstetricians interested in natural childbirth and spontaneous deliveries. He will certainly find support from the mothers themselves. Dr. Frank Howard Richardson, a national authority on breast feeding, has supervised widespread demonstrations resulting in the breast feeding of 85 per cent or more of the babies born in various communities. Writing of the success of these demonstrations he says:

Whereas the participation of many physicians in a community is desirable, it usually happens that it is due to the energy and efforts of some *one man* in a town that the work is actually prosecuted with the zeal that alone will make it "go."

This zeal on the part of individual obstetricians and pediatricians reflects a growing awareness among astute medical men that physical care alone, however superior it may be, is not enough, especially during childbirth and the postpartum period. The introduction of modern obstetrical techniques and hospital deliveries have reduced turn-of-the-century maternal and newborn mortality rates tremendously. But since the initial plunge, these mortality rates have not dropped much more, despite additional medical improvements. It was the psychologists who first recommended maternity care which provided emotional as well as physical support; the result has been ever-widening acceptance of classes for expectant parents, natural childbirth programs, rooming-in, and the encouragement of breast feeding. The expected goal of these programs was happier parents and babies; the unexpected dividend has been further reduction in the rate of deaths, injuries, and illnesses among mothers and new babies.

NATURAL CHILDBIRTH

The obstetricians who are dubious of spontaneous, conscious deliveries, or who feel that catering to the "whims" of the mother is mere sentimentality, are limited to those who have not had or have not taken the opportunity to observe natural or trained deliveries for themselves. If the mother knows what to expect beforehand; if she is given privacy and a trusted companion (usually in this country her husband) to coach her through labor; if she is treated kindly by the nurses and without condescension by her doctor; if she is allowed to deliver by her own efforts, at her own rate of speed, possibly even in her own choice of comfortable position, and with no more analgesia than she herself feels she wants; then childbirth is a triumphant, rewarding experience. The old-fashioned G. P. delivered most babies this way. He didn't call it natural childbirth, but common sense. A naturally delivered mother, even if she has never considered breast feeding before, is likely to feel after delivery that it is the logical next step, and to proceed about it happily and easily. This is not to say that a woman who has had a Caesarean section or a high forceps delivery cannot breast feed easily: It is maintenance of the biologically normal, supportive emotional environment that is important rather than the actual physical events of the birth. Breast feeding is usually considered a desirable adjunct to the natural childbirth program; the experience of "natural" childbirth is also the normal prelude to successful breast feeding.

ROOMING-IN

Once the baby is born, whether or not it is breast fed
may well depend on whether or not the hospital continues
to provide a reasonably normal environment for mother
and baby. This, of course, means keeping the pair together. Rooming-in, once an unquestioned custom but now a
radical innovation, is the name given to any kind of hospital arrangement in which the mother has her baby at her
side all the time, and assumes responsibility for at least
part of its care. It was pioneered in this country at Grace
New Haven Hospital in Connecticut, and at Duke University in North Carolina. It has become routine procedure in
military hospitals, and is gradually gaining acceptance
throughout the country.

Although most of us have come to think of the central
nursery as a standard or even a necessary part of the hospital care of newborns, history will probably show it to
have been a transient fad. From a biological standpoint,
separation of mother and newborn is completely unrealistic. Both of them need the emotional reassurance of each
other's presence. The infant needs to nurse more or less
constantly; the mother's breasts need frequent stimulation
to function normally. On a practical level the mother
needs a few days of constant, peaceful contact with her
baby in which to get acquainted with her new task of
mothering.

There are serious medical disadvantages to the central
nursery. Chief among these is the way in which it increases
the danger of staphylococcal infections. Even rigidly aseptic nursery technique is not enough to reduce such infections to a negligible level. Hospital personnel carry germs
to the babies, and from baby to baby. Infants contaminate
their mothers and the rest of their families. Often infant
deaths attributed simply to pneumonia are actually a result of staphylococcal infection; and much of the maternal
mastitis and infant infections that originate in hospital
nurseries go unreported as such, because they do not appear until the patient has gone home. A hospital that

states that it has no staphylococcal problem is usually a hospital that does not keep records of such things.

Crowding susceptible infants into a central nursery provides for rapid transmission of intestinal and other diseases as well. The whole problem is solved by separating the babies from each other and putting them into the care of their individual mothers. Some hospitals have adopted rooming-in simply because it offered the only good solution to control of such nursery epidemics.

Rooming-in insures better general care for the baby. No hospital has enough nurses to give each baby the constant high-quality care his mother can give. Dr. C. A. Aldritch and others found that even in an excellent hospital nursery the babies cried on the average of almost two hours a day. They commented, "One would question the nursing care on any floor where the average adult patient found it necessary to ring the service bell two hours out of every day." Where all the babies are rooming-in, no baby cries. Each infant's needs are met by the mother promptly and fully. Crying may be "good exercise"; if so it is an exercise rooming-in babies do not indulge in. One researcher commented on the difference between the central nursery in one hospital, with piercing screams issuing round the clock, and the "almost church-like hush" in another hospital where rooming-in was routine. Routine rooming-in for healthy babies allows hospital nurses to devote more time and care to the sick or premature babies who must be kept in the nursery. It frees nurses from the routine chores of diapering and bottle feeding, and from the time-consuming task of taking babies out to their mothers six or eight times a day. A certain amount of time must be spent the first day or so in teaching new mothers the skills involved; this is more than made up for by later savings in time.

Most authorities feel that rooming-in should not be optional. The patient who is asked to choose between rooming-in and central nursery care may have doubts or misunderstandings; but the patient who finds herself rooming-in routinely, just like all the other mothers around her, almost always enjoys it tremendously. She is about twice as likely to breast feed successfully as with central nursery arrangements. Even the few mothers who are at first reluctant and hostile, not only about rooming-in but about motherhood in general, may soon be giving truly excellent and affectionate care to their babies. The stimulation of the baby's presence, the example of other nursing mothers, the encouragement of the medical staff, and above all the experience of breast feeding may work wonders. As Plutarch said of nursing mothers in the first century, A.D., "They are likely to be better disposed and more loving to their children, and, by Jove, not unnaturally, for the close association of suckling makes a bond of good feeling."

Dr. David Danforth, chairman of the Department of Obstetrics and Gynecology at Evanston Hospital, Evanston, Illinois, feels that rooming-in is imperative for the sake of the baby, no matter how the mother feels about it. Originally against the idea, he made a tour of eastern hospitals to gather material to combat Evanston's plans for a rooming-in unit. He returned a confirmed advocate of rooming-in: "The baby has to make a great many adjustments to the nursery situation. It is far more humane to give the baby the advantage, and let the mother make the adjustments." Evanston Hospital now has excellent rooming-in facilities for every mother.

Rooming-in is not as workable when it occurs only as a concession to the occasional mother. When only one or two mothers have their babies with them on the maternity floor, the lessening of work for the central nursery is negligible but the disruption of normal staff routines is hard on the nurses. This may lead to resentment which is felt by the mother. Furthermore, unless some attempt is made to relax normal hospital routine for the rooming-in mother, the constant procession of scheduled baths, medication, temperature taking, doctors' rounds, students, mop ladies, and so on, added to the care of the baby, may well be exhausting. One mother, who had arranged to have her baby with her in a private room at a hospital which ordinarily did not encourage rooming-in, counted the number of times that doctors, nurses, or other hospital personnel came into her room, often awakening her from a nap.

During her five-day stay she was disturbed from fifty to seventy times a day. Ordinarily, however, with hospital routine relaxed for rooming-in mothers, rooming-in is fully as restful as the usual arrangements. Because of the mental relief it affords, and because night feedings "on demand" are snug, sleepy interludes compared to the usual full-scale, lights-on 2 A.M. visitation from the nursery, rooming-in mothers with few exceptions complain far less of lack of rest than do breast feeding ward mothers. Researchers report that those who do complain are often doctors' wives.

HOME DELIVERIES

The main drawback of rooming-in is that it takes place in the hospital. No matter how elegant the bath fixtures, or how pleasant the room is made with chintz curtains and piped music, it is still the hospital. Most new mothers miss their home and husbands terribly. If they have other children at home they miss them more than they imagined they could. Many a mother has surprised herself by bursting into tears at the sight of her two- or three-year-old waving towards her hospital window from the pavement below.

A nationwide reaction against the mechanistic, dehumanizing aspects of our society has led since 1960 to an increase in the numbers of mothers who really want to deliver their babies at home, and also to a resurgence of the profession of midwifery, common in Europe but rare in the United States.

The midwife, whose business is the management of normal deliveries, functions easily in the patient's home. She is usually associated with a physician, and her knowledge of when things are going wrong and when more help is needed is crucial to her patients. Home deliveries are only safe if such an experienced eye is available, and if an emergency system exists in the community whereby the mother can be transferred to a nearby hospital if difficulties arise.

Some doctors, whose practice includes many "street

people," communal families, or others whose choice of life-style is a rejection of "establishment" values, find that their patients refuse to have anything but home deliveries. In such practices, one or more midwives are invaluable aides. A few doctors make a practice of permitting home deliveries for any of their patients, usually provided that this is not the first baby the woman has had, and that no complications are expected.

The Chicago Maternity Center exists to provide home deliveries and family-centered prenatal and postnatal care; it is also a teaching center. Chicago Maternity Center staff members deliver about three thousand babies a year at home. Mothers who have had home deliveries with the Maternity Center seem to love it: "I dreamed so much of having my baby beside me instead of him being taken away like in a hospital"; "I got more attention at my home delivery than in the hospital"; "When labor slowed down, they were right there, they tried everything and had everything when they came to my home"; "My children and my husband were so near."

Mothers who have had the experience of a home delivery extol the peace and joy of giving birth in familiar surroundings, at your own pace, and with your dear ones nearby; and of having and keeping your baby, and sharing him with the rest of the family, from the moment of birth. Perhaps eventually the emotional rewards of home delivery and the medical protection of hospital delivery can be combined in some way for everyone, to make childbirth as safe as it can be and as joyful as it was meant to be.

THE LACTATION NURSE

Once a mother has been sent home, no matter how easily things may have gone in the hospital, she may feel her inexperience; then she turns to her doctor. The doctor whose experience with breast feeding has led him to appreciate the importance of emotional support as an accompaniment to physical care is neither resentful of the mother's frantic telephone calls nor quick to brush her off with a glib reassurance. On the other hand, he does not want to waste his precious working hours on totally non-medical problems. The very workable solution is to refer breast-feeding problems to a nurse who is especially interested in lactation. The natural teacher of new nursing mothers is the nurse who has breast fed her own babies. Such a woman is interested and sympathetic as only another nursing mother can be. True medical problems, such as cracked nipples or a colicky baby, she will of course pass on to the doctor. But most of the problems that panic inexperienced nursing mothers—a fussy, greedy baby, leaking milk, a critical grandmother—she can advise on herself. Many of them she has experienced personally—any nursing mother has. That fact alone can be vastly reassuring to a new mother.

Even the amateur can help. One doctor keeps a file of volunteer breast-feeding mothers in his city to whom he refers new mothers for coaching and encouragement. Others make good use of the nursing mothers' circles such as La Leche League. Dr. Caroline Rawlins, of Hammond, Indiana, frequently holds a "kaffee klatsch" for old, new, and prospective nursing mothers, in her own home. The exchange of ideas and experiences helps her patients to breast feed with remarkable success.

A RELACTATION CLINIC

In Uganda, Dr. D. B. Jelliffe has founded a relactation clinic to re-establish breast feeding in mothers who come to the hospital with sick artificially fed babies. His system is simple. He puts the mothers to bed (with their babies, of course) to provide adequate rest. He takes the bottle away. ("Bottle is a dirty word in our hospital.") He orders the mother to nurse her baby every two hours. He gives the mother plenty of milk to drink, both to keep her fluid intake up and to suggest that what goes in must come out ("sympathetic magic"). He gives her a therapeutic dose of Chlorpromazine (100 mgm. three times daily), which may or may not have any effect on lactation, but he *tells* the mother, "It will make the milk flow like the waters of the Nile." For the first day or two, he also administers an oxytocin nasal spray just before each feeding.

The mother usually finds that by the third day of Dr. Jelliffe's regimen she has ample milk once more. However, as he points out, it is not the medication that has produced this miracle. Adequate rest, adequate fluid, liberal, frequent, unrestricted nursing, and above all the firm conviction that the method will work are all that is needed.

HOME HELP

For many American mothers the first few weeks at home, without adequate help, are the hardest part of having a baby. Having servants is by and large a custom of the past. Practical nurses for the baby, though they are available, are not the answer. Ideally, in Dr. Benjamin Spock's words, "The mother takes care of the baby, and the household takes care of the mother." In actuality, the mother usually finds herself taking care of the baby and the household, and nobody, including herself, takes care of her. Her convalescence may be miserably prolonged because of the necessity of doing too much too soon. Lactation may fail because constant irritation and fatigue inhibit her let-down reflex.

The new mother is not adequately cared for by a doctor who simply feels the fundus, looks at her episiotomy, and turns her loose with instructions to "take it easy" and "come back in six weeks." The doctor who is skilled at helping nursing mothers instructs his mothers before delivery to arrange for help at home: a cleaning woman, a relative, a husband on vacation; and he checks up before he sends them home from the hospital, to see that they have done so. He may find it advisable to expressly forbid any washing, cooking, or cleaning, for a week or two.

In Denmark, Sweden, and Finland, the problem of home help is solved by the existence of a state-supported home helpers' agency. Trained women are available to go into the homes of invalids or new mothers for a few hours daily, to do the work that would normally be done by the mother of the household. In this country, the state of New

Jersey has established a similar and very successful agency: the Visiting Homemakers of New Jersey. This agency hires women who are experienced mothers and housekeepers, but whose families have grown up; the women are often referred to the agency by their own doctors, who feel that they need a challenging occupation. They are given a six weeks' intensive training course in everything from marketing to physical therapy and child psychology, and then are sent out on call, not to anyone who happens to want them, but at a doctor's request only. The state pays most of the Visiting Homemaker's salary; patients pay one dollar an hour, or get the service free if necessary. The homemaker markets, cooks, cleans, and entertains children, following the mother's own systems and preferences as much as possible, for three hours daily. This can make a remarkable difference to a newly-delivered mother's well-being, and to the speed with which she recovers from childbirth. Doctors in New Jersey, far from considering home conditions as being out of their province, are delighted to be able to do as their colleagues in Scandinavian countries do, and write a prescription for skilled, friendly home help for new nursing mothers. Other states now have plans for similar programs under consideration.

ENLIGHTENED MEDICAL CARE

Some authorities have suggested that the whole pattern of medical care for mothers and children needs to be changed. Dr. James Clark Moloney, a founder of the experimental Cornelian Corner in Detroit, feels that medical, psychiatric, and maternal care of children should coincide, and that parents and professionals should be able to meet on a common ground and work jointly, as they do at the Cornelian Corner. Dr. H. F. Meyer, in *Infant Foods and Feeding Practice,* points out that the current separation between the doctor and the parents of an infant patient leads to misunderstandings on both sides. He warns young doctors:

The questions asked by parents are rarely motivated by crit-

icism but rather from a desire to know the current truths. . . .
When a mother plaintively (or aggressively) asks when her infant will have a certain solid food added . . . she is usually
seeking information rather than voicing a censure; or she may
be seeking a plausible argument to refute her neighbor whose
own doctor is engaging in a kind of gastronomic race in adding "strained cucumbers" at the sixth week . . . by such questions the physician is either exhausted or challenged. All of
these varied questions are born of a curiosity which is homely
and personal, rather than to doubt the practitioner's authority.

It has been suggested that the physician should not have
to be burdened with routine cares, and with the mother's
nonmedical questions—that his skill and intensive training
should be reserved for when they are needed. This is
where a lactation nurse can help. The same holds true in
obstetrics, where such time-consuming matters as classes
for expectant mothers, giving emotional support during
the first stage of labor, and allaying the anxieties of pregnant women, make little use of a highly-trained specialist's
medical skills. Some obstetricians here, and many abroad,
maintain on their staffs a "labor nurse." Dr. Niles Newton
writes:

They save the physician untold work and at the same time
it is easier for them to do the work because that is their chief
interest. For instance, sitting with a woman throughout a long,
normal labor can be emotionally satisfying to such women;
whereas it may frankly be a nuisance to a man who has been
trained for more intricate and complicated things.

Modern childbirth is all too often what Dr. Helene
Deutsch dryly calls "a miracle of masculine efficiency."
The masculine technical viewpoint can be counter-
balanced simply by using these feminine helpers. The formula feeding of infants, with its accurate methods, is also
a typically male, technical procedure, not easily transferred to the ultra feminine techniques of successful breast
feeding. Again, women helpers are the natural answer.

For example, Margaret O'Keefe, R.N., a professional lactation consultant who nursed all of her own family of seven, suggests that there are a few simple changes any hospital staff could adopt to make breast feeding possible:

Every maternity floor in the land could make sure that on every shift there was at least one nurse who was experienced in helping mothers to breast feed and had the enthusiasm to back it up. Part of her job would be to talk over the advantages of breast feeding with every new mother—and I'm sure mothers will put aside their comic books to listen.

Mrs. O'Keefe also suggests use of a demand schedule for all babies, even where rooming-in is not feasible:

It takes no longer to return a crying baby to his mother than it does to sterilize and heat a bottle for him, even if the baby is carried in arms, as most hospitals insist. But with wheeled cribs, any hospital—even one with an outmoded floor plan—should be able to provide the flexible, frequent feeding arrangements so necessary to establish a new mother's flow of milk.

Niles Newton writes, in her book, *Maternal Emotions:*

Unfortunately it seems easier to help a woman express negative feelings than to re-educate her. It seems easier to suppress lactation than to teach the mother how to breast feed successfully. It seems easier to separate the mother and the baby at birth in the hospital than to teach her how to care for the baby. It seems easier to drug the woman into unconsciousness rather than to teach her the techniques that make birth a more welcome experience.

If the medical care of the future follows the trends exemplified by the best of current practices, where mother and infant receive the help and consideration they need both from trained medical specialists and from a constellation of helpers, at home or in a peaceful, homelike atmosphere, medicine may well become a potent force in making all aspects of the job of motherhood more enjoyable, and consequently in making the American woman more successful at that job.

7 · Women Who Share

THE NEED FOR MOTHER'S MILK

In a hospital in Fresno, California, a baby girl was dying. She was not sick; she was starving. The baby's doctor wrote, "We had tried everything in the dietary and nothing was tolerated by the baby . . . it seemed likely that we might lose the baby if we did not soon find a food that this infant could gain weight on." The doctor knew that there is one diet almost any baby can tolerate: human milk. But where could he get any? A few ounces might come from the hospital maternity ward, where an occasional new mother might be breast feeding. But this baby needed a steady supply, and fast.

Then he heard of the Mother's Milk Bank of San Francisco. He called them. Hours later, frozen, pasteurized human milk, packed in dry ice, was on an airliner. More shipments followed. In a few days a relieved doctor could write the Mother's Milk Bank, "Since starting the breast milk she has gained over a pound in weight and should be able to leave the hospital in the next few days . . . thank you very much for the timely help in a very trying case."

The San Francisco milk bank, one of the few in this country, came into existence to supply this kind of need. As a Gerber's researcher has remarked, formula manufacturers cannot yet compete with God. Mother's milk is the only food some babies can thrive on; if the baby's own mother is not supplying it, some outside source must be found. Modern milk banks are organizations which collect milk from mothers who are nursing their own babies, sterilize it, and keep it frozen for emergency use for other babies, usually by doctor's prescription only.

The greatest use of such milk is for premature babies. In hospitals which have their own milk banks, such as the Evanston Hospital in Illinois, every premature baby is entitled to mother's milk. The next most important use is in cases like that of the Fresno baby who could not assimilate any formula, or of babies, such as those studied by Dr. Gyorgy, who have violent intestinal infections which a breast milk diet successfully combats. Mother's milk is also used for the extra protection it gives to babies who must undergo surgery.

WET NURSES AND MILK BANKS

Buying and selling human milk is not a new idea. In previous centuries, when sanitary precautions were unknown and when the differences between human milk and the raw milk of other animals were not understood, animal milk was generally fatal to human babies. The only successful substitute for a mother's milk was the milk of another human mother. In ancient Rome, nursing mothers gathered each morning near the Colonna Lactaria to sell their surplus milk by the pitcher, or, for a price, to feed a hungry baby on the spot. Wherever urban civilizations arose, some women of leisure declined to breast feed and hired wet nurses instead. Doctors in ancient Greece, medieval Europe, and even Victorian England, devised dozens of tests for telling a good wet nurse from a bad one, ranging from the color of her hair to the behavior of her milk when dripped onto a polished metal surface.

Unfortunately, until recent times there were no tests for the detection of tuberculosis or syphilis. Thus a wet nurse could infect both her unfortunate infant charge and his parents. And the parents were apt to compound the misfortune by firing the nurse and putting the ill baby to the breast of a new wet nurse who became infected in turn.

Because the wet nurse was indispensable she commanded a higher price than any other servant, and was free to tyrannize the household. In the sixteenth century an irritated father, Luigi Tansillo, wrote, concerning wet nurses, "To greater insults must you daily stoop than from the invasion of a hostile troop." It was a seller's market. An unscrupulous girl could bear an illegitimate child, send it to die at a baby farm, and make her fortune by hiring out as a respected and well-paid wet nurse. (An eighteenth-century pastor in a village outside London wrote despairingly that the death bell tolled there continually day and night, to mark the passing of farmed-out babies.) The nurse who loved her baby might substitute her own child for that of her employer. The plot of Gilbert and Sullivan's *H.M.S. Pinafore* revolves around such a wet nurse's swap, as does Mark Twain's *Pudd'nhead Wilson*. No one will ever know how often it was the heir who died at the baby farm, while the wet nurse's baby was brought up in comfort.

Wet nursing was never really in fashion in the United States. Since colonial days, American women have been too independent to take on such a job for someone else. A noted infant feeding authority of the 1920's deplored not only the general scarcity of wet nurses in America but their tendency, when hired, to regard themselves as equals of the rest of the household. Only in the South, where slavery had flourished, were wet nurses commonly available.

In the 1900's, as pasteurization was developed, one American city after another began setting up safe milk stations where clean cow's milk could be bought for babies. As more and more dairies began inspecting their cows and keeping their herds disease-free, and as aseptic techniques were developed so that babies could be bottle fed without developing the feared "summer flux," the demand for wet nurses slackened.

But there have continued to be a few babies who need mother's milk and are not getting it. One answer has been the establishment of breast milk banks. Although the modern milk bank is invariably a charitable organization, supported by donations, most existing banks do charge for the milk baby gets, depending on the parents' ability to pay. Charges range from one cent to thirty cents an ounce and can be quite a consideration when a premature baby may receive a thousand or more ounces of mother's milk before being put on formula. (In at least one state, Blue Cross insurance will pay for the first thirty days of milk.) Most of the milk banks also pay the donor mother from seven to ten cents an ounce. One of the most successful milk banks, the Premature Babies' Milk Bank at Evanston, neither charges nor pays for its milk, on the ground that parents cannot afford it, and that mothers are glad to be helping others by giving their milk and don't want to be paid. On the other hand, Mrs. Allan Hill, director of the Wilmington Mothers' Milk Bank, insists on paying donors, and tells the mother who tries to refuse payment to put the money into savings for the baby. She feels that mothers donate longer, whatever their financial status, when they are being paid for their milk.

Organizing a Milk Bank

The most successful milk banks are those that have been started and run, not by hospitals or doctors, but by mothers themselves. In 1956 an Evanston mother whose premature baby desperately needed mother's milk organized a milk route among friends of hers who were nursing their babies. She rented electric breast pumps from a drug company, supplied each mother with sterile bottles, and each day drove from house to house collecting the milk her baby had to have. As one mother on the route weaned her baby, another was added until the premature baby was old enough to transfer smoothly to formula feeding.

From this grew the Evanston Premature Babies' Milk Bank, which is run, with guidance from local pediatricians, by the Evanston Junior League. The Evanston Hospital contributes laboratory space, a technician to process the milk, and sufficient sterilizing equipment. The Junior League raises the money for bottles, electric breast pumps, and a freezer. Junior League volunteers pass out the pamphlet explaining the milk bank to new mothers at the hospital, keep the necessary records, teach mothers how to use the breast pumps, wash and wrap bottles for sterilizing, and, in pairs, drive the collecting routes to distribute sterile empty bottles and collect full frozen bottles of milk from donating mothers. Most of the Junior League volunteers have small children themselves; many have been donors to the milk bank, as well as volunteer workers. Visiting along the route, chatting about babies and nursing, is pleasant for volunteer and donor alike; and mothers seem to profit from this community approval of the fact that they are nursing their babies.

The Wilmington Mothers' Milk Bank was also started by a mother, one whose baby could not tolerate anything but human milk. Her child was saved by milk brought in by Railway Express daily, on ice, from the Boston milk bank. Obviously Wilmington needed its own milk bank; with the enthusiastic assistance of local doctors, a volunteer-run milk bank was organized at the Delaware Hospital.

A milk bank must be run day in, day out, without fail. But the Christmas rush, summer vacations, and other civic duties cut into Wilmington's supply of volunteer workers, so in 1952 Mrs. Allan Hill, R.N., was hired to manage the Wilmington milk bank. As in Evanston, the hospital supplies lab space, an autoclave, and a technician. Soliciting of donors, record keeping, preparation of bottles, and delivering and collecting milk are all done by Mrs. Hill. "Every day is different," she says. "I don't know when I've had such a satisfying experience. Rich or poor, black or white, the mothers are all so nice, and I've made so many good friends among them." Mrs. Hill, who nursed three babies of her own, is on call to donor mothers twenty-four hours a day. Her practical help and cheerful advice have probably accounted for the breast feeding success of many a Wilmington mother.

Other milk banks have had varying success with other systems. In Phoenix, Arizona, a mother's milk bank was at one time operated as part of the Blood Bank of Arizona. Some hospitals maintain small milk banks for their own use, with milk coming from mothers in the maternity wards, and from the occasional outside donors who are willing to come to the hospital once or twice a day to give milk. Milk banks tend to come into existence, and to thrive, in those areas where family centered maternity care is practiced, and where, in consequence, the value of human milk is recognized by doctors, and there are plenty of mothers who are breast feeding. The milk bank succeeds best when the interests and needs of donor mothers are met, and when the operation seems warm-hearted, rather than civic-minded.

DONATING MILK

At least one milk bank still relies on teaching donors the technique of manual expression to collect milk. However, some mothers find this technique uncomfortable or tedious, and it is not always easy to keep the milk uncontaminated, since it tends to run over one's hands. Most milk banks supply mothers with electric breast pumps, despite the initial cost of about $125 per pump. The breast pumps are oblong chrome boxes containing a motor, connected by tube to a glass gadget that fits over the nipple and areola and exerts a gentle, repeated suction, safely and comfortably withdrawing the milk. Removing a little milk after each feeding quickly increases production. Once production is increased, most mothers pump two or three times a day, after or between feedings.

Pumping milk provides a wonderful buffer for the mother's own supply. If she is tired or catches cold, and her milk supply is temporarily reduced, there may be less milk for the milk bank, but her own baby still gets plenty. The breast pump is a blessing when the baby begins to sleep through the night feedings, so that the mother wakes up simply bursting with milk at four in the morning. It's a consolation when one worries that the baby is not getting anything; nothing could be more reassuring than seeing a bottle fill up with four ounces of milk beyond what the baby wanted. "As long as I had a pump I never let myself become convinced that my milk supply was low. It is grand to have this confidence," writes one mother. The pump is a great convenience for a mother with a demanding social life. She can pump enough milk before she goes out so that the baby can have a bottle of his favorite nourishment while she is gone; she can pump when she gets back to relieve the pressure of milk held over in the breasts. One mother wrote that when she began to wean her baby, and started by sending back the breast pump, "I felt as if I were losing a friend!"

Some milk banks also lend pumps to mothers who need them, even when they cannot donate to the milk bank. Julianne King, an Evanston mother who has been chairman of the milk bank as well as a volunteer driver and a donor, writes, "We have been especially pleased to help out mothers who must leave premature or sick babies behind at the hospital, by sending them home with a pump. This is a real boost to these girls who feel they are doing something for their babies. A surprising number of these girls have been able through daily pumping to keep their milk until their babies come home."

COST OF OPERATING A MILK BANK

The cost of running a milk bank can vary widely. The Evanston milk bank costs about $600 yearly, mostly for glassware and printing. Extra funds are raised for the purchase of breast pumps; the bank began with six, and now keeps thirty or more in constant use. The Wilmington bank, with Mrs. Hill's salary to pay, and with a policy of paying donor mothers for their milk, costs more. Some of the costs are met by charging for the milk; the difference, about $2,000, must be made up by donations and fund-raising, through charity raffles and the like. A similar situation exists at the Boston Directory for Mothers' Milk.

Raising funds calls for vigorous efforts from volunteer groups. One of the largest efforts is extended on behalf of the San Francisco Mothers' Milk Bank, which was founded in 1948. This bank is conducted independently of a hospital, and must maintain a building, its own laboratory, its own paid technicians, and a salaried registered nurse to teach mothers manual expression and see that health regulations are observed. Donors are paid for milk, but recipients receive the milk free; costs run as high as $2,000 a month. A huge staff of volunteer workers must labor to keep up with these expenses, and the elaborate fund-raising efforts necessitate the services of a full-time secretary. The donor mother has become somewhat lost in the shuffle. She is given a strict list of instructions, and her milk is collected anonymously from the doorstep.

Nevertheless, the state of California has reason to be thankful to the San Francisco Mothers' Milk Bank, for the emergencies in which it has helped over the last fourteen years, for the thousand smiling children pictured in its scrapbooks who might have been only memories. Other states are not as lucky. In New York City, for instance, the milk bank that operated in the forties no longer exists. A prominent pediatrician in New York fought for funds for a new milk bank, and even though he was successful in collecting the money, it lay idle as he tried to find a suitable staff, while other equally prominent physicians teased him about his pointless dream and hoped out loud that he'd never get it going. The decline in physicians' support for breast feeding has led to widespread disregard for the medical irreplaceability of breast milk. Milk banks are an amenity of the past, and probably of the future, but a rarity at present.

LA LECHE LEAGUE

How La Leche League Began

Of course the best way to get more babies raised on the milk they were meant to have is to get more mothers to breast feed their babies. But how? Mothers say that doctors should help more. Doctors seem to feel that mothers don't need help, that they all could breast feed "if they really wanted to." Where should the revolution begin?

In 1956 two nursing mothers in Franklin Park, a suburb of Chicago, took their babies to a picnic. They were ordinary young mothers, the kind you might meet in church or pass in any supermarket. They were unusual only in that they were successfully breast feeding. As often happens when a nursing mother takes her baby out in public, other mothers at the picnic began to talk about their own attempts and failures to breast feed. The nursing mothers were very sympathetic. Like many nursing mothers in this country, they had each had real difficulty in nursing their first babies, and had not been truly successful until their third or fourth babies came along. Both agreed that it would have been much easier if they had known, at the start, what they knew about breast feeding after three or four babies. Both agreed that they might have been successful from the beginning if they had known another more experienced nursing mother to go to for encouragement and advice.

From that picnic conversation came the idea for an organization to enable nursing mothers to get together and help each other: a sort of AA for breast-feeding mothers. Its name, La Leche League, was taken from a poetic Spanish title for the Madonna: *Nuestra Senora de la Leche y Buen Parto* ("Our Lady of Bountiful Milk and Easy Delivery").

Seven nursing mothers made up the original board of La Leche League. They started out by reading all they could find about lactation, and by discussing breast feed-

ing with interested doctors. Then, armed with facts and
the experience of nursing their own babies, they held a
series of four meetings for those friends of theirs who were
expecting babies. Discussions were led by nursing mothers
on such subjects as: the advantages of breast feeding; the
art of breast feeding and overcoming difficulties; childbirth; the family and the breast-fed baby; and nutrition
and weaning. By the time the first series was over so many
mothers were coming that La Leche League split into two
groups to handle the crowds. Dr. Herbert Ratner, nationally known authority on marriage and the family, contributed his services as medical adviser and also offered to
conduct a fifth meeting for fathers only. This meeting, in
which the men could discuss from their own point of view
all aspects of pregnancy, delivery, breast feeding, and so
on, proved immensely popular, and usually lasted until
past midnight, at which point many of the men would go
home and wake up their wives to continue the discussion.

By the time the third series of meetings was under way,
and La Leche League was a year old, there were three
groups. Local doctors were beginning to attend meetings.
One woman obstetrician filled her car with expectant patients and drove sixty miles for the monthly meetings.
Grandparents, doctors, and nurses were valued guests, and
so, above all, were the nursing babies, for some expectant
mothers were beginning to return with their blooming
nurslings, to show off their success and to share their enthusiasm. Often it was not a specific question answered or
problem solved that made nursing so much easier. It was
the knowledge that other young mothers have the same
worries; that you can nurse a baby in spite of the worries;
that you need not face them alone. Success came from
being able to get the encouragement that a mother needed
when her breasts appeared empty and the baby was crying. It came from the chance for a young mother to chat
with a whole roomful of other mothers who were nursing,
or who hoped to nurse, and who admired her for doing so
too.

The women whose gratitude was greatest, and who
were most inspiring to La Leche Leaguers themselves,

were those who had tried and failed, over and over again, to breast feed; and who now, for the first time, were knowing the joy of the nursing relationship, the joy they had always sensed and struggled for without success. By the end of the first year, a mother who had failed with two was happily nursing a third. Another mother who had given supplements to her first three, until the supplement replaced her own milk, now nursed her fourth all by herself. She kept it up for a full year. Another, after five bottle-fed babies, was breast feeding number six.

The young organization began receiving national publicity. Dr. Grantly Dick-Read, famous British crusader for natural childbirth, agreed to give a lecture under the auspices of La Leche League. The suburban high school auditorium was packed, and hundreds were turned away. Inquiries from nursing mothers flooded in; soon there were more than three hundred phone calls a month, some from anxious and lonely nursing mothers as far away as California and Florida. Letters arrived at the rate of four hundred a month, each to be answered, with enthusiasm, encouragement, and practical pointers for nursing success, by a La Leche League mother.

THE BORMET STORY

Sometimes it took a lot of work to help a mother. And sometimes that help was vital. One morning La Leche League president Marian Tompson received a phone call from a truly desperate young mother, Lorraine Bormet. Lorraine's three-month-old baby David, her fifth child, was dying. His doctor could find no formula the baby could tolerate; to each change he reacted with continuous diarrhea, eczema, and convulsive seizures. He was skin and bones. The doctor had suggested that breast milk might save him. Lorraine had tried and failed to nurse each previous baby, so she had not even tried to nurse David. She had gotten the LLL phone number from a pamphlet in her doctor's office. Did Marian think it was possible for her to get her milk back, after nearly three months?

Marian knew it was possible. La Leche League researchers had come across several such instances in medical literature. If the baby could be induced to nurse long and often enough, the breasts would respond. Another nursing mother was found, not too far from the Bormets' home, who agreed to nurse David while his mother's milk was coming in. When he was put to this woman's breast David sucked, his mother said, "as if his life depended upon it— which it did." Then, for the first time in his life, he slept through the night. On the neighbor's milk, all David's reactions cleared up, and he began gaining weight.

Several La Leche League mothers helped Lorraine manage the first difficult days of starting her own milk supply. She was advised to nurse David as often as possible, between the five daily trips to her neighboring nursing mother. Despite the tranquilizers prescribed by her doctor, and the relaxing beer or two she drank in the evening, Lorraine was extremely nervous. For long hours she rocked and patted David, coaxing him to nurse at the empty breast, first on one side, then the other, while the baby would suck momentarily, then wrench away and cry.

It was eight days before the first milk appeared; just eight or nine drops. Still, it was an encouraging sight. Every day there seemed to be a few drops more, as the nursing continued. La Leche League mothers called and wrote Lorraine, wishing her success. Her husband did not object to the neglected housework, and even helped with the other children. On the seventeenth day, Lorraine woke to find her milk spilling forth of its own accord—the first sign of a let-down reflex starting to work. By the twenty-fourth day, Lorraine was nursing David eight times a day on each breast, the milk was letting down at each feeding, and it was time for her to start managing on her own.

Throughout these weeks, Lorraine's family and friends naturally took every opportunity to tell her that what she was trying was impossible, that they had never heard of its being done, that she was too nervous anyway, and so on. But six weeks after she had started, Lorraine had enough milk to maintain David entirely by herself. He was no longer skin and bones, but a plump, happy, healthy, bright-eyed nursing baby.

He continued to be nursed for many months. Mrs. Bormet wrote to La Leche League:

Some days I would doubt that the milk would ever come in, and what would our poor little David do? How would I ever get breast milk enough to feed him if I didn't nurse him myself? And then I would talk to you and you would tell me, "Of course it will come in. You would have to be a very weird kind of person if it didn't come in. Your body is designed to function in this particular way." And I would be bound and determined then NOT to be that weird kind of person. Having had five problem babies, I wanted to be a whole mother—and my spirits would rise and I would pick up baby again even if he was sound asleep and put him to suck. Thanks again, and to Mrs. White too for her encouragement . . . and to Mrs. Froehlich for her letter that boosted me when she said, "God gave you the tools, now use them." But nothing I could ever say would really express our thanks.

Sincerely,
Lorraine Bormet

Mrs. Bormet is now herself a valued La Leche League member. Her experience has been repeated by a number of mothers who had decided not to nurse and then found themselves with highly allergic babies. La Leche League provides the kind of help and support that these mothers really need.

"THE WOMANLY ART OF BREAST FEEDING"

In the second year of La Leche League's existence, Edwina Froehlich and other board members began putting together a manual, to convey in their own way some of the things they had learned about breast feeding. This manual, *The Womanly Art of Breast Feeding,** brought the con-

---

* *The Womanly Art of Breast Feeding,* La Leche League International, 9616 Minneapolis Avenue, Franklin Park, Ill., 60131. Soft cover $3.00, hardbound $4.00; in French or Spanish, $3.00. Include $.25 for postage.

tent of the meetings to women who lived too far away to attend. Because the founders know that it is not always facts that a mother needs, but the confidence that comes from personal contact with another nursing mother, they assign every woman who orders their manual to a board member with whom she can correspond. In the foreword of the manual they explain:

The mother assigned to you hopes to share with you the "spirit" of nursing that comes from experiencing the quick, strong, love ties so natural between a nursing mother and her baby; from her sure understanding of the baby's needs and her joy and confidence in herself to satisfy them; and from seeing the happy dividends from this good relationship as the baby grows up. It is a spirit first sensed, then gradually understood and absorbed, and finally realized by a mother as she nurses her own new baby.

THE NEED TO SHARE

La Leche League groups have as a basis for factual information *The Womanly Art of Breast Feeding,* this book, *Nursing Your Baby,* and a constantly growing collection of well-researched information sheets on special topics such as breast feeding and diabetes, breast feeding and drugs, and so on. Most groups also maintain a lending library of books and medical reprints that have been found helpful. Some have enthusiastic support from local doctors. Some do not; for those groups the occasional problem that is truly medical, rather than emotional or due to circumstances, must be referred by long distance to the original league group's medical advisers.

It is not only the fact that La Leche League fills the needs of the new nursing mother that makes this group strong. It is the satisfaction that it brings, the need that it fills, for the experienced nursing mother who finds herself teaching others. She is a mother who has enjoyed a true nursing relationship, who has breast fed her own baby freely and affectionately for many months. And her attitude, whether she is rich or poor, a farmer's wife or a city

The classic nursing pose, with the infant supported on the mother's raised knee. Egypt, about fifteenth century B. C.

The classic nursing pose, Germany, sixteenth century A. D.

The classic nursing pose, France, about 1780.

The classic nursing pose, France, about 1820.

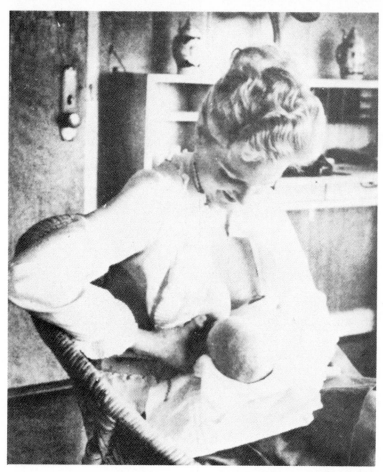

FRANCIS HAAR PHOTOGRAPH

Nursing the newborn baby. The mother holds her full breast away from the baby's nose so he can breathe freely.

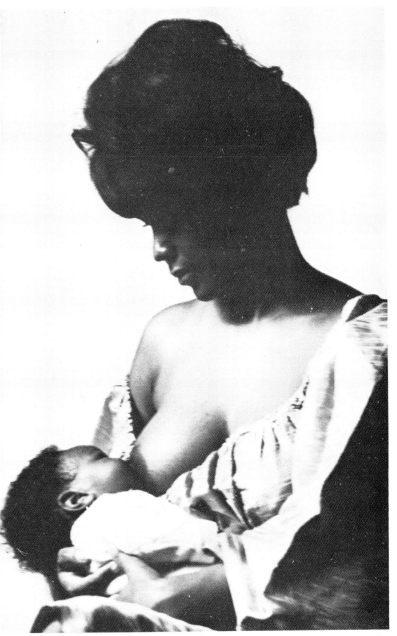

Three months old.

VAN GOGH PHOTOGRAPH

Nursing twins. Judy and Jill, at four months, are thriving on mother's milk alone.

Toddler. Eighteen months old. For mother and baby both, nursing provides a reassuring moment of peace in a busy day.

A La Leche League meeting. Experienced nursing mothers offer advice and encouragement about breast feeding to new and first mothers.

La Leche League International convention, Chicago, 1971.
More than 1.400 mothers attended.

Princess Grace Kelly of Monaco is greeted by members after her speech at the La Leche League convention.

girl, a Californian or a New Yorker, is this: She feels very sympathetic towards mothers who try and fail to nurse. She feels real compassion for the mother who struggles bravely against the odds of illness or family disapproval to fulfill her own and her infant's need to breast feed, and she feels more and more bitter toward those doctors who continue to treat breast milk as if it were just another formula. These emotions, compassion and bitterness, make nursing mothers truly dedicated to helping other mothers to nurse.

La Leche League's First Ten Years

Six years after the idea for La Leche League came into being, there were forty-three groups, including two in Canada, one in Africa, and one in Mexico. By 1972, when La Leche League was about fifteen years old, there were over a thousand groups in all fifty states and fourteen foreign countries, and La Leche League became "LLLI," La Leche League International. Much of the work of this expansion fell on the shoulders of the original seven founding mothers, although as one of them, Edwina Froelich, pointed out, "We don't like to go overboard. One of the points we try to make is that husbands and families come first." Most of the founding mothers, who comprise LLLI's board of directors, have big families. President Marian Tompson has seven children, librarian-researcher Mary White has ten, vice-president Viola Lennon has ten, including breast-fed twins. So for years La Leche League work was sandwiched in and around housework and family life. Mothers stapled manuals together in the evenings instead of knitting, and answered correspondence instead of watching television. One mother had a thirteen-foot telephone cord so she could counsel a nervous nursing mother and load the washing machine or make corn muffins at the same time. Gradually, with the increasing scale of the work, enough money was raised through sales of the manual, donations, and other sources, to establish a full-time office with eighteen employees and an annual budget of over $250,000. A network of state and regional coordinators was established, to facilitate new group formation and to screen and train group leaders to insure that the basic emphasis on home and family, on good mothering through breast feeding, remains unchanged. La Leche Leaguers are constantly being asked to support and promote all kinds of related causes, from Zero Population Growth to boy dolls. They have steadfastly refused to take stands on any issues other than the teaching of breast feeding, and they especially avoid being committed on such touchy issues as abortion, even when individual members may have strong feelings pro or con. As one group leader put it, "La Leche League is an oasis of love for mothers, because here you can come just as a mother, regardless of other beliefs."

Many La Leche League mothers have become superb medical researchers, and the information sheets they put together on special medical topics are invaluable to mothers and medical personnel alike. League speakers travel worldwide, participating in medical conferences such as the 1970 White House Conference on Children. The League has distributed over half a million copies of a *Reader's Digest* article about its activities, and provides scientific exhibits for medical conventions and special packets for physicians, free of charge. Over 250,000 copies of *The Womanly Art of Breast Feeding* have been sold, and it is now available in French and Spanish also. League women speak in medical and nursing schools, high schools and colleges, on the art and advantages of breast feeding. Those who lecture to medical and nursing students always bring a nursing mother and baby to the lecture. It shocks the students at first and then tells them more than words ever could of the simplicity and importance of this natural function. La Leche League groups rally round and provide breast milk for highly allergic babies, and if possible help the mothers of such babies to relactate and establish their own milk supplies.

Fifteen years after founding, La Leche League International was participating in twenty medical research projects, ranging from studies of breast cancer to DDT to immunity factors. Public figures who are also nursing mothers have been very active in promoting breast feeding and the League. Especially conspicuous have been actresses Cloris Leachman, Dina Merrill, and Grace Kelly, who was the principal speaker at the League's 1971 convention.

A La Leche League convention has to be seen to be believed. At the 1971 convention in Chicago, the La Salle hotel was host to over 1500 mothers, 643 fathers, over 100 doctors, 209 older children, and 653 nursing babies. For three days, mothers, fathers, and doctors attended panel discussions on such subjects as nursing the premature baby, maternal emotions, fatherhood, and making contact with "inner city" mothers. The atmosphere was noisy, cheerful, and casual. Aisles were full of runabout toddlers, and it was not unusual to see a well-dressed woman speaking to two or three hundred people on late weaning or hospital rules or medical problems, with the microphone in one hand and her other arm around a baby at the breast. Although no one would have dreamed of disconcerting passersby by nursing in the hotel's public areas, nursing couples were a commonplace sight on the convention floors. At first bellboys' and elevator operators' eyes popped, but in a day or two the hotel staffers were pulling out pictures of their grandchildren and expounding on the beauties of motherhood, and often an overtaxed elevator girl would be coaxed into a smile as a baby reached for a gold uniform button or a mother put an arm around her and sympathized, "This must be hard on you."

There were very few crying babies. "Rock and rest" rooms were provided, and playrooms for the toddlers, and nursing babies don't cry much anyway, as long as Mother is nearby. Most of the parents backpacked their babies—no strollers were in evidence—and the speakers were accustomed to a gentle hubbub of children. President Marian Tompson, speaking to the banquet hall and an audience of fourteen hundred people, calmly requested, "Please hold your applause. Some of the babies have dropped off to sleep."

The hotel sold less liquor and twice as much food as at any other convention. Room service took to sending up double-size breakfasts, free of charge—a nursing mother with a husky baby may be producing one thousand calories a day in addition to her own needs; and the hotel iceboxes were jammed with fruit and milk provided free by the League for day-long snacks for mothers and older children. Twenty-four hours before the convention, the hotel's food manager called League President Marion Thompson in a panic: "Six hundred babies coming, and babies mean formula and formula means refrigeration, and you've got all my iceboxes filled with oranges and bananas!" It took her ten minutes to convince him that in this case six hundred babies would be guests with no bottles at all!

Experienced La Leche League mothers, though their educational and economic backgrounds vary widely, are remarkably at ease in public, poised and warm and calm. Among fifteen hundred women, in a crowded and demanding situation, in three days I never heard one cross word or saw two people in conflict. Leaguers speak easily on their feet. They really know their subject, they really believe in it, and the group meetings accustom them to taking the floor among strangers. And they're busy mothers, who don't believe in wasting time, so they speak to the point.

Many mothers whose own babies are weaned stay on in the League because they and their families take pleasure and pride in the simple but effective counseling that they do. Many, as their children grow up and move away, are finding part-time careers for which they are particularly suited, as lactation consultants in hospitals, as pediatric assistants, labor coaches, teachers on breast feeding, and writers and film makers in the area of family-centered maternity care.

Without degrees, without aggressiveness, without abrasive professionalism, in communities across the country these young mothers are infiltrating the medical establishment, subverting too-rigid hospital systems, unbending resistant doctors and neighbors and grandparents. They ease their way into the social services: a white, middle-class woman may be viewed with suspicion when she steps into a big-city hospital ward full of unmarried, black, newly delivered young mothers. But when she sits down on a bed and unbuttons her blouse and talks across her nursing baby's head the barriers start to fall. First individually, then in groups, and now, increasingly, across society, La Leche League mothers are spreading joy and comfort and love in a world which needs these things desperately.

8 · Attitudes Toward Breast Feeding

STATUS AND THE MODERN NURSING MOTHER

When safe artificial feeding of babies was first developed in the United States, it quickly became something of a status symbol. Doctors and mothers alike seemed to view the baby bottle as tangible evidence of woman's liberation from drudgery. In the 1920's, when the public was beginning to really appreciate the wonders of modern science, feeding a baby by clock and scale and measure seemed intrinsically superior to old-fashioned methods. The mothers who were quickest to take up bottle feeding were the well-educated and comparatively well-off young mothers, who could afford not only the milk and bottles, but the fees of that new specialist, the pediatrician, to tell them what to do; who enjoyed being modern and scientific with their babies; and who perhaps relished this additional way of pooh-poohing the turn-of-the-century customs of their own parents. Babies were not, on the whole, in fashion; but if one must have a baby, then the chic thing to do was to feed him by bottle.

136

As hospitalization for childbirth became customary throughout the nation the accompanying systematized care of the newborn made breast feeding physically less feasible. Soon bottle feeding not only had the status conferred on it by fashion and medical approval but seem'ed to be the only method possible for most women. The people who continued to breast feed were those who were too poor to buy milk and bottles, or recent immigrants who perhaps didn't know any better.

Today, bottle feeding has become universal. As status symbols do, it has spread from the privileged to the many. Routine bottle feeding, an innovation fifty years ago, has had ample time to reach every corner of the nation, and to be accepted without thought as normal by the majority of today's families. At present, those at the bottom of the economic scale, far from being the only people who breast feed, are the most adamant bottle feeders of all.

The mother who does breast feed today is not doing so from necessity or tradition. She is doing it by deliberate choice, and she is bucking the status quo to do so. Whether she succeeds or fails may depend upon the kind of help she gets. However, the fact that she decides to try at all, natural as the decision may seem to her, marks her as an unusual person in this bottle-feeding era. What kind of person is she? Statistics indicate what many doctors are observing in their own practices: Today's mother comes from what the staff of New York's Maternity Center refers to as "the top ten": She and her husband and family belong in the top 10 per cent of the nation, economically, socially, and above all educationally. She has the education that enables her to think for herself, in the matter of infant feeding as in other things. And she has the security and confidence to act on her own inclinations, without too much reference to what her friends or relatives are doing. Forty years ago she might have been the very one to depart from tradition, to take a job, bob her hair, bottle feed her baby. Today it is she and her husband who are educated enough to want more enlightened, family centered maternity care, and confident or dedicated enough to seek it. From that top 10 per cent come those parents who attend

childbirth education classes, who believe in natural childbirth, who campaign for rooming-in facilities, and who intend their babies to be breast-fed babies, or who drop out
of the system and manage the whole business themselves.

PREJUDICE AGAINST BREAST FEEDING

The mother who elects to breast feed often does not realize at first what a nonconformist she is. It's a shock the
first time she discovers herself being criticized, subtly or
openly, for nursing her baby. It's like getting criticized for
being a good cook, or attacked for loving her family. Yet
criticism does come, and usually from such unexpected
sources as hospital nurses or her best friends. Perhaps her
doctor, who she had assumed would heartily endorse her
intentions, is skeptical or even derogatory about her plans
to breast feed. Or a nurse, who has theoretically come to
help her at feeding time, tells her that her milk is no good
or her nipples are wrong or even that her personality is
unsuited to nursing. Or perhaps her own mother, though
gushing with praise, cannot quite conceal a feeling of dis-
gust at the act of nursing; or her best friend reveals that
she herself would not dream of breast feeding.

These attitudes are not based on rational objections.
They are pure prejudice. Like any prejudice, that against
breast feeding may be expressed in old wives' tales, subtle
threats, pointed jokes, or open hostility. Nobody ever gets
used to being a target for prejudice. Such an attitude can
undermine the confidence even of an experienced nursing
mother. When added to a new nursing mother's natural
doubts and fears about this unfamiliar art, prejudice in
those around her is almost certain to make her give up
breast feeding, through conscious decision, or unconsciously, through failure of the let-down reflex. The mother is especially vulnerable in the first days after birth,
when even one prejudiced remark can be enough to cause
lactation failure.

FEARS AND TABOOS

What are the reasons behind this unreasonable American prejudice? Like all prejudice, it is based on fear and ignorance. The fear of loss of status still affects some people. Today although truly poor people are most likely to bottle feed, some people still feel that breast feeding is a sign of poverty.

Simple ignorance about the nature of breast feeding is the basis for some of the prejudice against it, and can be cured by experience. Many mothers who declare they don't want to breast feed change their minds as soon as they learn more about it, or perhaps as soon as they experience a successful feeding or two. Both medical personnel and laymen tend to forget about some of their objections to breast feeding if they have a chance to observe nursing mothers and babies.

But the main cause for prejudice has to do with sex. We have come to regard the female breast as a sexual object, and an exclusively sexual object. Breasts used to be completely out of fashion; girls bound their breasts to make them unnoticeable—to such an extent that a woman doctor of the 1920s wrote, "Far too many young girls come to me nowadays with nipples at the level of their navels." Now breasts are very much in fashion; a recent editorial in *The Psychiatric Quarterly* states that one of the most obvious features of the American culture today is "the cult of the big breast."

Lest one think that the present admiration for breasts is merely fashion, started, say, by Jane Russell in the way that Jean Harlow set the style for platinum blondes, or Grable and Dietrich for legs, reflect for a moment on the unusual nature of the modern bosom up until the use of the braless look. The brassiered breast, whether covered by a bathing suit or an evening dress apparently had no nipple; it was a featureless geometric shape from which any trace of basic use had been eliminated, a firm cone, as immovable as the iron-armored bosom of a Valkyrie, with a combination of size and uplift which is almost never found

in nature (except, interestingly enough, in the lactating
breast, which is supported by the milk within). Psychiatrists describe this as a phallic breast; with its thrusting rigidity, it was really more of a male symbol than a female
one.

This curiously altered breast has nothing to do with babies. It is a sexual organ, and, by association, a genital
organ. Thus the idea of breast feeding can arouse feelings
of shame in two ways. First, we do not show our sexual organs to any but acceptable partners; therefore to show the
breast in nursing, or to allow the baby access to it, has implications of perversion which of course intensify as the
baby grows older. Second, exudations from the breast
seem like excrement; breast feeding becomes an unclean
act, to be performed in private like evacuation, and even
spots from leaking milk are offensive.

The rise of the braless look, and the custom in the
1970's, especially among the young, of allowing the breasts
and nipples to show very naturally through the clothing,
may represent a revolt against this artificial and essentially
hostile sexuality, rather than, as it is often considered to be,
a rejection of masculine and feminine roles or a glorifica-
tion of hedonism.

These taboos affect some people so seriously that they
can never develop a normal attitude towards breast feeding. A neurotic woman may find the very thought ab-
horrent, and cringe at the word "suck." A similarly neurotic man may feel jealous and dispossessed at the sight
of his baby at his wife's breast. Many people simply try
to settle the conflict by acting as if breast feeding doesn't
exist. Doctors give lectures and write books on infant
feeding in which breast feeding is not mentioned. An
article in *Child-Family Digest* describes a booklet on
sexual development and reproduction printed by the
New York State Department of Health for use in high
schools. The booklet describes and illustrates such details
as the growth of axillary and pubic hair, and the development of a human embryo, but never mentions the female
breast; as the article's author comments, it seems as if
even the New York Department of Health does not know

what breasts are for. The nursing mother often runs into this blind spot, this reluctance to think about breast feeding. Gone are the days when a nursing mother could turn her back to the room and count on being left politely alone. Some relatives, seeing her holding the baby closely, may repeatedly try to look at the baby's face, or even to take it from her arms, without seeming to realize he is nursing. One mother finally forced her family and in-laws to stop forgetting she was nursing by pinning a sign to her sweater reading "Lunchtime" when she fed the baby.

MILK EMOTIONALISM

Possibly as an offshoot of our breast taboos, we in the United States also have very unusual ideas about milk, and these too have repercussions on the nursing mother. While breast milk is devaluated, milk in general has an almost magic significance. Many other nations make some use of milk, especially in cooking or as a source of butter and cheese. For these purposes milk is taken from cows, goats, horses, donkeys, camels, yaks, and so on. But we are virtually alone in considering that animal milk is indispensable for growing children or that it is even suitable as a food for adults. (Certainly no other species of mammal includes milk in the adult diet. From a biological standpoint the idea is quite impractical.) In this country the dairy industry is a powerful force in the government itself. Milk and milk products are not only used by adults but form a substantial part of the adult diet, and the child who happens to dislike drinking milk is a great source of anxiety.

Only in this country do four-color ads proclaim, "You Never Outgrow Your need for Milk," while the milkman, judging from schoolbooks, is practically a folk hero. Dr. D. B. Jelliffe writes:

Milk (i.e. animal milk) plays such a dominant part in present-day infant feeding in Europe and North America that it is difficult for anyone brought up in these parts of the world to realize that it is not a necessary foodstuff for any age-group and that, in fact, children have been and are habitually reared in many . . . countries and on some Pacific islands without milk being used at all. This Western attitude has been termed "milk emotionalism."

This attitude towards milk handicaps the Western mother, who puts her baby to the breast for the primary and often sole purpose of getting milk into him. Since she can't see and measure the milk, it is hard to tell if he is getting too much, or not enough, or indeed any milk at all. She is prey to fears that there is no milk. What milk she does see, perhaps a few pale droplets at the beginning and end of meals, seems far less potent a source of nourishment than the milk she can prepare in the kitchen, which pours richly from the can, and fills bottle after bottle brimful.

Margaret Mead has stated that undue admiration for milk is one of the most harmful ideas that we Westerners give to other societies, not only because it encourages women in primitive environments to abandon breast feeding in favor of artificial feeding, but because it suggests that the only purpose of breast feeding is the giving of milk. The non-Western mother gives the breast without reservation. She doesn't worry about when the baby ate last, or whether the breast seems full or empty. She isn't nursing to get milk into the child, anyway; she's nursing to keep him comfortable and happy. If he cries, she offers the breast; if he gets hiccups, or bumps his head, or feels shy of a stranger, she offers the breast. In the process, the baby gets all the milk he needs, but the milk is incidental.

However, when the giving of milk becomes paramount, then the mother feels free to withhold the breast if she supposes that the baby has had enough, or is not hungry. From the baby's point of view, the comfort of the breast is lost. It becomes the mother, not the baby, who makes the decision as to whether the baby needs the breast, and when he gets it. This is a profound change from the normal pattern of most cultures; it makes a visible difference in the personality development of the babies, and hence eventually in the culture itself. (There are a few primitive cultures which, like our own, have rigid rules about the giving of the breast, and which thus deny the baby from early infancy the solace all human infants crave; and from all reports they are very unpleasant cultures in every other respect too.)

CULTURAL FEMININITY VS. BIOLOGICAL FEMININITY

All this cultural rejection of breast feeding is but a symptom of the basic attitude our culture has towards women. We glorify sexual attractiveness and debase motherhood. We admire the pliant, ineffectual, "feminine" woman, and regard as undesirable and unfeminine the qualities of aggressiveness, competence, and resourcefulness. These are qualities with which Mother Nature has endowed the female as well as the male, and for good reason, since in nature it is the female who must aggressively protect her young, and who, especially during pregnancy and lactation, must be supremely competent and resourceful in finding food and shelter. Niles Newton, in her book, *Maternal Emotions,* has defined this as the conflict between cultural femininity and biological femininity.

The woman who accepts the dictates of cultural femininity places primary emphasis on sexual attractiveness, and down-grades other biological functions. Perhaps the epitome of cultural femininity in our society is the fad in some communities for early dating, with mothers putting their ten- and twelve-year-old daughters into evening dresses and lipstick, with couples going steady at fourteen or fifteen, and with the marriage age often falling to eighteen and less. This is an irrational denial of biological reality. In our culture, or any other, ten- and twelve-year-olds are not ready for courtship, nor fifteen-year-olds for monogamy and the adult role. And this custom has nothing to do with, say, the Polynesian concept of sexual freedom in adolescence; the goal here is not sex but status.

Most of the women's magazines, with their emphasis on grooming and sexual attractiveness, on interior decoration, which is an extension of personal grooming, and on the happiness and rewards to be gained exclusively through sexual love, are directed at the culturally feminine woman. And in keeping with her needs they deal with other female biological functions in a highly negative way ("Must Childbirth Be a Lonely Ordeal?"; "Tell Me, Doctor . . ."; "Why Can't I Nurse My Baby?"). Under the guise of offering good advice, they actually present these functions as being full of pain, fear, and disappointment.

The culturally feminine woman quite naturally tries to avoid or minimize what to her are the unpleasant functional aspects of womanhood. She cannot understand why others might enjoy them. It is she who most vigorously wields the weapons of prejudice against breast feeding. This has been going on since civilization began. Medical authors from Hippocrates onwards have complained about the tendency of wealthy women to refuse to breast feed. And the culturally feminine woman, past or present, tries to discourage others from breast feeding. Observe this Mom at work in Rome in 600 A.D.:

When he had asked how long the labor had been, and how severe, and had learned that the young woman, overcome with fatigue, was sleeping, he . . . said, "I have no doubt she will suckle her son herself." But the young woman's mother said to him that she must spare her daughter and provide nurses for the child in order that to the other pains which she had suffered in childbirth might not be added the wearisome and difficult task of nursing.

The culturally feminine woman can become positively insulting in her condemnation of breast feeding. The strength of feeling she shows suggests that the woman who has herself rejected breast feeding is made guilty by the sight of a close friend or relative nursing a baby. Despite the fact that society has endorsed her own refusal to breast feed, she feels reproached. Possibly also she feels envious; she will never know the calm enjoyment and self-containment of the nursing couple; and these emotions of guilt and jealousy make her show hostility. Those men (doctors included) who admire cultural rather than biological femininity may also attack breast feeding with more emotion than the situation warrants, perhaps from similar motives of guilt.

THE ATALANTA SYNDROME

Rejection of biological femininity can be costly. The culturally feminine woman may show a pattern of physical symptoms which British psychiatrist Desmond O'Neill has called "the Atalanta syndrome," after the Arcadian nymph who raced with, outran, and spurned her suitors. Dr. O'Neill grouped together such symptoms of malfunction as painful or abnormal menstruation, frigidity, complications of pregnancy and labor, and lactation failure. He found that women who accept their biological role might show an occasional symptom; but women who disliked the biological demands of femaleness consistently showed four or more symptoms. Their emotional conflict was reflected in physical malfunction in almost every part of the reproductive cycle.

Acceptance of the biological role can reverse matters. Many young American mothers probably suffer from the Atalanta syndrome at first, but gradually improve after they have had a child or two, and have learned to value themselves as women and to enjoy motherhood. Menstrual cramps and irregularities no longer occur, subsequent pregnancies and deliveries are free from trouble, and sexual adjustment improves as the conflict within them fades.

A CHANGE IN THE WIND

The present generation of young parents seem to be discovering what many other cultures take for granted: that the biologically feminine role enhances a woman's charm, rather than detracting from it. Perhaps previous generations took the first steps, by establishing legal rights for women, and securing acceptance of women's right to enjoy sexual relationships. Now we are going the rest of the way, and we assume that without forfeiting freedom or sexuality, women also have the right to enjoy old-fashioned motherhood. Both men and women feel this way.

That "top ten per cent" young husband doesn't feel that his wife is less attractive, a less suitable wife, because she earns a master's degree, or writes TV plays, or runs an office; he prefers her to be capable and productive, at home or away from home. On the other hand, he doesn't think pregnancy is embarrassing or inconvenient; he likes his wife pregnant. He is interested in childbirth, and willing, when instructed, to do a spot of midwifing. He likes his wife to nurse their babies, and his enthusiasm for breast feeding may be the one thing that keeps her going in the face of difficulties. In short, he does not want a culturally feminine wife; he wants a real woman.

The concept of the true worth of biological femininity is beginning to spread into other fields. The "nurturing" professions, those which require a gift of warmth and concern for others, such as nursing, teaching, and social work, depend upon women to fill their ranks. And the ranks are infinitely better filled by women who are good wives and mothers than by women who are not. However, this means that, in these or any other professions, the hours in a day and years in a life-time that are devoted to the biologically feminine role must be left free. This is beginning to be done, for example by schools and hospitals that set up short shifts, so that mothers with young children can work part time; by businesses that make clerical and research work available to be done at home; by universities that offer postgraduate work for women whose families have grown.

One of the most conspicuous aspects of the counterculture movement is its emphasis on biological as opposed to cultural femininity. The casual garb and "unisex" appearance deplored by the older generations has its basis in freedom from feminine artifice, from makeup, elaborate hair styles, constricting clothes, unnatural shoes, and all the devices that emphasize a woman's role as subordinate and physically restricted, and which treat her body as bait. The Women's Liberation movement essentially takes the same tack; that women need neither act nor look like men's playthings, nor be dependent. Sometimes Women's Lib rejection of unhealthy cultural femininity goes overboard and rejects healthy biological femininity, too, but excess is perhaps inevitable in a revolution. The net effect is that more and more people—and not just young people —are trying to abandon the artificial values of our culture, including false images of what is feminine and what is womanly, and to substitute for them something a little more open; less structured, and closer to biological reality.

Part Two

9 · Before the Baby Comes

GETTING READY

The months when you are nursing your baby can be among the pleasantest of your whole life. However, it is up to you to make them so. Unfortunately, American civilization is not set up to accommodate the needs of the nursing mother. It takes a little advance planning if you are to avoid some of the circumstances, common in our society, which make delivery and breast feeding less pleasant and less successful than they should be. Experienced nursing mothers, who have successfully breast fed several babies, generally make the kind of arrangements that are suggested here, so that they themselves are free to relax and enjoy the new nursing baby without unnecessary obstacles to their physical well-being or their peace of mind.

CHOOSING A HOSPITAL

It is not hard to find competent medical care, even in a town where you are a stranger. You simply select an ac-

148

credited hospital, and go to the doctors on its staff; or you ask your family's doctor at home to recommend some one in good standing. But how can you find obstetrical and pedtiatric care that is not only medically competent but that will give you the kind of emotional support and practical help you want to have, both in delivering and in nursing your baby?

The best place to start is with the hospitals. Find out over the telephone if any of the hospitals in your area have rooming-in units. Breast feeding is much simpler if you have the baby near you all the time, and the existence of a rooming-in unit is a good indication that at least some of the hospital staff are oriented to "family-centered maternity care," that the doctors use some of the very valuable natural childbirth techniques, and that the nurses understand breast feeding, and are trained to encourage it. If no hospital in the area has rooming-in facilities, find out which one has the most nursing mothers, and which one leaves the babies "out" with the mothers the longest. The nursery or maternity ward nurse will tell you this, over the phone. Be prepared for an earful of the nurse's own opinions on breast-feeding, rooming-in, and natural childbirth, which may be highly negative if she does not have much experience with these techniques.

Some hospitals which do not have any rooming-in units will allow you to keep your baby with you if you take a private room. However in such hospitals, where rooming-in is rare, the nursing staff sometimes object to it as a disturbance of their routine, and either interfere too much or give you no help at all. A private room will cost you from two to fifteen dollars more per day; whether it is worth it is up to you. For more on the pros and cons of rooming-in, see Chapter 6. If you can get rooming-in, or wish to have the baby "boarding" with you in a private room, you may want to make the arrangements a few weeks before you go to the hospital, by visiting the hospital's business office. Then you won't have to be bothered with administrative details at the time the baby is born.

CHOOSING A DOCTOR

The Obstetrician: Your obstetrician's job is to keep you healthy during pregnancy and to deliver your baby, not to supervise your lactation. You will be asking the pediatrician most questions on breast feeding. However, you will still be in your obstetrician's care while you are in the hospital, and his attitude can make a great difference to you in the first days of breast feeding. If he understands breast feeding and is enthusiastic about it, he will see to it that your breasts are prepared during pregnancy for the job of nursing. He will make sure you do not receive any drugs to suppress lactation, and will prescribe mild pain relievers or anything else you may need to make you more relaxed and comfortable, so that your milk flows more easily. He will be capable of helping you if any problems arise such as engorgement or nipple soreness. The obstetrician who is not interested in breast feeding, and is not convinced of its importance, will not be able to give you this kind of help, and is much more skillful at suppressing lactation than at keeping it going. Although you can probably lactate with perfect success without any help from your obstetrician, it will be at least a convenience for you if he sees things your way, and it may save you a few arguments in those postpartum days when you will want to be peacefully getting to know your baby without having to argue about anything.

To find the kind of obstetrician you want, you may have to shop around a little. The most "brilliant" man, or the man all your friends go to, may not necessarily be the one for you. While both you and the doctor may shy away from the term "natural childbirth" as smacking of faddism, nowadays every doctor who has *real* understanding of and consideration for his maternity patients uses a great many of the natural childbirth techniques. Such a man is more likely to be helpful and experienced about breast feeding.

If you have been able to locate a hospital that encourages breast feeding, you can expect that at least some of the doctors on the staff will be the kind you are looking for. The maternity floor nurses may be able to tell you which doctors allow husbands in the labor rooms, which doctors hold prenatal classes for parents, which doctors have the most patients who breast feed; all of these practices are associated with modern, enlightened childbirth techniques.

When you have a list of possibilities, make an appointment with each one for a consultation. If you later decide that this is not the man, the consultation will only have cost you five dollars or so, whereas a full examination may cost fifteen dollars or more. Sometimes you can easily spot the obstetrician who is especially skilled with natural deliveries; his outstanding characteristics are apt to be gentleness and endless patience. He seems interested in you as a person, not just a pelvis; he listens to everything you ask, with no hint of impatience. He is not in a hurry, no matter how full the waiting-room is. He doesn't joke much. He is gentle, never brisk or rough. He explains everything he does, at great length. This care and patience may make the office visits longer; but it makes the delivery far easier.

An occasional physician will be very annoyed to find that you are "shopping" for medical care. This is not the man for you. The doctor who has had experience with spontaneous deliveries, and who has seen many happy nursing mothers, will understand very well why you are being careful to select a physician who appreciates these matters.

The Pediatrician: It is a good idea to pay at least one visit to your pediatrician before the baby comes. Once you have selected an obstetrician, he will be glad to recommend one or two pediatricians, and may be able to suggest someone who is especially interested in breast-fed babies. The hospital nurses may be able to tell you which pediatricians in town are the greatest champions of mother's milk for babies.

Pediatricians are more accustomed than obstetricians to mothers who are shopping for a doctor. They aren't apt to resent being questioned. However, don't start out by asking bluntly, "Are you in favor of breast feeding?" You put the pediatrician on the spot; he doesn't know if you want him to say yes or no. You can tell him that you plan to breast feed, and would like to have rooming-in (if it is available), and see what he says. If he tries to talk you out of both, you probably have the wrong man. You can ask him how many of his mothers breast feed, and for how long. If 25 per cent or 50 per cent do, and if he seems proud of them, you can be fairly sure he gives them help and encouragement. On the other hand, if *very* few of his mothers nurse their babies, no matter how convincing his explanations for that fact may be, you can be sure he does *not* give them help in trying to breast feed. Finally, you can ask him if he has children himself, and if they were breast fed. If they were not, he may regard the question as impertinent. If they were, he will enjoy telling you so, and you will know that he is personally acquainted with the normal course of lactation.

Suppose you already have a pediatrician you are satisfied with, but who does *not* encourage breast feeding? His lack of interest in the management of lactation has nothing to do with his skill at preventing complications of measles, or clearing up middle-ear infections. You need not feel obliged to change to some other doctor just because you and he don't see eye to eye on breast feeding. Don't let him shake your confidence. You can nurse your baby satisfactorily on your own.

"CONTRA-INDICATIONS"

It used to be thought that a mother with an Rh factor problem could not breast feed. This is not true. Rh antibodies may exist in the milk but they have no effect on the baby.

If a mother has t.b. or whooping cough she can have no contact with her baby at all, since these diseases are terribly dangerous for her newborn. Naturally in such a case she could not breast feed. She *can* nurse her baby if she has a cold or the flu or some other contagious disease. Breast-fed babies show remarkable immunity to such ailments, and often escape getting sick even when the whole family comes down with a "bug." Epileptic mothers sometimes have a medical conflict if they wish to breast feed; some drugs prescribed for epilepsy do adversely affect the nursing baby.

If the mother is desperately ill from some chronic disease her doctor may justifiably forbid her to breast feed, since she needs every bit of energy for herself. However, the mother who is temporarily incapacitated after a difficult or surgical delivery is better off breast feeding than not, although she may have to postpone initial feedings for two or three days. Lactation gives her an excuse to get more rest during convalescence, and saves her from the multiple chores of bottle feeding. Lactation can be of the same benefit to the mother with a heart condition.

THE DISADVANTAGED MOTHER

The mother who is physically handicapped deserves more than ever to breast feed her baby. A mother who must live in a wheelchair, or who is blind, will find breast feeding infinitely easier than trying to cope with bottles and formulae. It is no more difficult for her than for any other new mother to learn to nurse, and she gains a sense of joy in her self-sufficiency that goes far to combat any feelings she might have that she cannot give her child as much as other mothers do. Kathy Beaudette, a blind La Leche League group leader, says that breast feeding is "the only way to go" for a blind mother, that it fosters independence in both mother and child, and that it offered for her, even after weaning, "the miraculous closeness to my son that only touch could bring."

La Leche League International offers a variety of loan material about breast feeding and child care, including their manual and this book, on tape and in braille. *Nursing Your Baby* is or soon will be available on tape from the Library of Congress.

BRASSIERES

Wearing a well-fitted brassiere during pregnancy will help prevent loss of breast shape. Maternity bras should not have too much elastic in them; elastic does not survive washings very well. You will probably find you have to replace your bras about halfway through your pregnancy, as they all lose their fit after much laundering. You can wear nursing bras during pregnancy, but since they also wear out fairly quickly you will have to replace them anyway, so you might as well save them for afterward.

Before you go to the hospital, pack two or more nursing bras in your suitcase. These are the kind that have a flap that lowers, so you can feed the baby without losing support. Bras do get wet with milk, at first, so you will need at least one to wear and one to wash. If you don't bring any bras the nurses will probably insist on wrapping you up in breast binders, which are not nearly as comfortable. Nursing bras may be bought at lingerie shops, maternity shops, or any department store or mail order house such as Sears Roebuck. The plain cotton drop-cup type costs about two dollars. If you don't want such institutional-looking underwear, you can find very pretty nursing bras at some better stores, costing $4 or more. Or write to the maternity department of Saks Fifth Avenue, Fifth Avenue at 50th Street, or Bonwit Teller, Fifth Avenue at 56th Street, New York, New York, for their maternity booklets.

During late pregnancy and lactation you can expect to be about one full cup size larger than you used to be, with variations upward depending on the amount of milk present. If you started out as a skimpy A you will probably be no larger than an ample B, and will get adequate support from any well-fitted bra. If you started out as a B or C you will probably need the sturdy maternity bras. By six months after weaning your breasts will be back to their previous size and shape.

BREAST CARE

Because human nipples are overprotected by the clothing we wear, they tend to be supersensitive and easily damaged in the first days of nursing. It is wise to prevent this by proper care during pregnancy. Blondes and redheads, whose skin is naturally delicate, tend to benefit most from preventive breast care.

No breast care is necessary in the first six months of pregnancy. In the last three months, it is probably wise to stop using *any* soap on the breasts. The skin secretes protective oils which help to make nipple and areola strong and supple. By scrubbing with soap you remove this natural protection. The protective skin secretions are mildly antibacterial; it seems likely that nature is guarding your breasts and preparing them for the job of nursing better than you could.

To desensitize the overprotected nipples, doctors sometimes recommend scrubbing with a rough towel or (horrors!) a brush. A Connecticut clinic has found that it is simpler and less uncomfortable to trim a circle of materials from the tips of the cups of your brassieres so that the breast is supported but the nipple is exposed. Normal chafing against clothing will quickly desensitize the nipple. You may wish to stitch around the openings to prevent unravelling.

Some girls have nipples that are flat and retracted, or even inverted. The hormones of pregnancy will tend to improve the shape of the nipples, without any other help. The standard advice is to pull the nipple out daily with the fingers; however, research indicates that this does not improve the shape, and most girls dislike doing it. Wearing bras that are open at the tips will help, as the edges of the cut-away circles pull gently on the margins of the areolas, which helps to make the nipples more prominent. Once lactation begins, the nursing of the baby will soon draw the nipple out normally; however, the retraction will recur when the baby is weaned. Extensive tests in England show that the mother whose nipples are so inverted that she fears she will never be able to nurse can achieve normalcy with a device called the Woolwich breast shield, developed by Dr. Harold Waller. These lightweight plastic shields are worn inside the bra, and exert a gentle pressure on the margins of the areolas, and a mild suction on the nipples. Worn daily for several weeks they are said to overcome even a severe degree of inversion. (They can be ordered from La Leche League, 9616 Minneapolis Avenue, Franklin Park, Ill. 60131, $3.00 a pair.)

One experienced lactation consultant, a nurse working for a group of obstetricians, feels that retracted nipples are seldom seen in women whose love life involves a lot of breast play. Some couples tend to avoid this area of the woman's body, others make much of it. It is of course a matter of personal preference. However, it seems at least possible that the tender attentions of a man to this highly erogenous area are part of nature's way of preparing a young woman's body for the task of nursing a baby.

Recent research indicates that it is unwise to put alcohol, friar's balsam or other "hardening" agents on your nipples. These irritants, often recommended by nurses, are worse than useless if only because hard skin cracks more easily then soft, supple skin. Anointing the nipples with oils and creams is apparently harmless, if the preparations are water-soluble and rinse off easily. Hydrous lanolin is cheap and suitable. It may be bought from the druggist. Applying it at least has the merit of making you feel you are doing something constructive during the last tedious weeks of waiting for the baby.

It is possible that a mild shortage of vitamins A and D makes the skin sensitive. These vitamins are sometimes added to skin preparations. Taking a good vitamin supplement during pregnancy is worthwhile and may increase resistance to chafing and tenderness of the nipples as nursing starts.

SEDATIVES

We all know now of the drastic harm done to a developing human embryo by the sedative Thalidomide. This drug, like certain virus diseases such as German measles, can cause deformity, but only if it reaches the embryo during the crucial early stages of development in the first months of pregnancy.

Once the baby is fully formed, the danger of physical abnormality is past. However, drugs do continue to pass through the placenta, and can affect the baby's behavior. For example, it is thought that some sedatives such as phenobarbital, if taken in the last days of pregnancy or during labor, may suppress the baby's sucking reflex for as long as five days after birth.

Therefore, although it can be hard to sleep comfortably during the last two weeks of pregnancy, and you may feel you'd give anything for a good night's sleep, it is wise to avoid sedatives during this period, especially sedatives your doctor has not recently prescribed for you. This includes the kind you can buy without a prescription. Review the section on drugs and medication in chapter 3.

Household Help

If you want to enjoy the first weeks of nursing your baby, instead of struggling through them exhausted, don't go home to a house in which you must do the work alone. It is tempting to think that you can manage without any help. But you must protect your returning strength in these first weeks, or the baby's milk supply may suffer. And your husband, willing though he may be, may not be accustomed to housework. It may take him four times as long as it takes you to clean up the kitchen or put a few loads of laundry through the machine. All too soon you will find yourself helping out, and getting overtired, which is bad for your morale and your milk.

If you aren't sure that you will need or can afford some kind of steady, daily help while you are convalescing, read Dr. Spock on the subject; he is most convincing. Probably one of the nicest baby presents a grandmother can give is the money for a few weeks of paid household help. Communal living, if the community is emotionally stable, offers one solution for the new mother, as she can really rest, and let others do her tasks, as long as she needs to.

Sometimes a neighborhood in which there are a lot of young families can organize to make things easier for a new mother. For instance, a neighbor can take the toddler or older children for the afternoon, so that the new mother can nap. It is wise to institute this as a routine before the baby is born. One Chicago neighborhood has organized a housewives' round robin in which each woman takes a turn doing the morning housework and bringing in a cooked dinner in the household where there is a new baby. Since there are some twenty families in on the arrangement, the mother who comes home with a new baby receives twenty days of having her housework done and her husband's dinner fixed for her.

The one kind of help you don't need is a baby nurse. You may find yourself cleaning house and fixing meals for the nurse while she takes care of your baby. However, almost every city has a visiting nurse association, and you should certainly take advantage of this free service. Ask your doctor to arrange it. The visiting nurse can tell at a glance how the baby is doing, can help you with baths and other new tasks, and will also keep a weather eye on your own state of health. She is a good source of advice about diaper services and other methods of saving your energy.

Mothers in New Jersey should ask their doctor about arranging for a Visiting Homemaker from this state's wonderful low-cost service. In almost any large city you can look under "Babysitters" in the telephone book for trained, experienced mother's helpers.

SHORT CUTS

After you have arranged for help in the house for two weeks, and have set up a way for your older children to be away from home a couple of hours a day, try to set up as many other short cuts as you can to lighten your workload in the first month after you are home. Here are some suggestions:

1. Arrange for diaper services for the first few weeks

at least. This saves a tremendous amount of work. If you
live in the country and cannot get diaper service, get a few
dozen disposable diapers for the first few days at home.

2. If you can possibly afford it, now is the time to get
major appliances that you don't have. A washer and a
drier are more important than living room furniture. A
dishwasher will be worth more to you than wall-to-wall
rugs. There will be time for interior decorating again in
years to come, but while your children are very small the
most important purchases are those which reduce the
drudgery and give you more time and energy for being a
wife and mother.

3. A high school girl (or boy) can be a great help by
coming in for an hour or two after school to supervise
baths and supper for your small children.

4. Stock the cupboards with quick, nourishing foods,
with the emphasis on proteins. If you are alone with the
baby most of the day you may not feel like going to the
kitchen and cooking; yet especially at the start of lactation
you need plenty of nourishing food, or you will feel tired
and depressed. You're less likely to skimp, or fill up on
coffee and doughnuts, if something better is easily available. Suggestions: quick-cooking oatmeal; canned cheese
sauce, Welsh rarebit, or cheese spreads, for omelets, for
serving on toast, for heating with frozen vegetables;
canned tuna, chicken, Spam, sardines, and salmon; cheese
for snacks; canned spaghetti with meatballs, tuna and noodles, etc., or frozen casserole and pot-pie products, with
extra canned hamburgers, beef or other meat added for
extra nourishment; canned beans, canned brown bread,
and canned or frozen tamales.

5. If you have a freezer, or can borrow some space in
a friend's freezer, make and freeze as many dinners as you
can. Commercial TV dinners usually don't have enough
food in them to satisfy a nursing mother's appetite, but
you can buy trays and make your own more generous and
better tasting meals. Include your favorite meals and des-
serts; make your convalescence a time for treats. You can
make meals up for your other small children too. Then

your husband can fix dinner, or you can fix a hot lunch, simply by taking a meal from the freezer and heating it.

6. Husbands often don't like to market and sometimes don't have time. Even in these days of supermarkets you should be able to find a neighborhood store that will take an order over the phone and either deliver it or hold it until it is picked up. This is a great timesaver in the first weeks.

7. Address your birth announcements ahead of time.

8. Even if you have a washer and drier, you may wish to cut the laundry down to a minimum for a few weeks by sending your sheets and towels out to the laundry. Most laundries have delivery service. Furthermore, you might be able to get a linen service, which, just like a diaper service, will supply you with clean sheets and towels, pick them up weekly and substitute new ones. This means you could have clean sheets and towels every day, if you wished, without doing any laundry or buying any extra sheets. These services are listed in the telephone book under "Linen Supply Services." The cost is moderate: from about thirty cents for a double sheet to ten cents for a bath towel.

DIET AND REST

Now, in late pregnancy, is a good time to learn to nap. Any book on natural childbirth, such as *Understanding Natural Childbirth,* by Dr. Herbert Thoms, will tell you how to relax enough to fall asleep in the daytime. A nursing baby is usually less trouble at night than a bottle-fed baby. But he will be hungry, and only you can feed him, so you are bound to lose a little sleep. To keep your spirits up and your milk supply bountiful in the first weeks of lactation, it will help if you have practiced and learned the knack of napping, really sleeping, once or even two or three times a day.

Pregnancy is also a good time to improve your own eating habits. You may not feel like going to the trouble of changing your ways once you are preoccupied with the new baby. If you acquire the habit of eating well now, you will find that after delivery you have more energy and a better disposition, both of which are vital to the nursing mother. Few of us pay much attention to nutrition; the word brings to mind complicated pie-shaped charts and lists of food items which seem to have no bearing on our own meals. To figure out whether one's daily diet contains enough ounces of protein or the right-colored vegetables is about as much fun as balancing a checkbook. To me it seems easier to improve the family nutrition by cutting out what Spock calls the "cheat foods" rather than by trying to include some of everything on the various lists and charts. There are two very good books on how to do this: Niles Newton's *Family Book of Child Care*, which has an excellent section on marketing and meal planning that will save you both work and money; and Adelle Davis's *Let's Have Healthy Children*. The latter is a very unscientific book which is frowned on by home economists, but it is lively reading, and will give you a real appreciation of how much junk there is on the supermarket shelves. It includes a section on good food for the nursing mother.

FITNESS

During pregnancy, during childbirth, and during lactation you will have an easier time of it, enjoy yourself more, and be more of a help and pleasure to those around you, if you are fit. Staying fit, strong, and supple can be fun, rather than a duty, and it is never the wrong time to start; the smallest effort will bring some improvement.

Half an hour of fast walking outdoors, daily, will do a lot. *The Fitness Book,* by Bonnie Prudden, is a painless guide to toning yourself up; and don't think you don't need it. Few of us, unless we are professional dancers, athletes, or yoga teachers, are the healthy animals we could be.

It is easier to be consistent if you get a friend to limber up with you two or three times a week. What about your children for company? Bonnie Prudden has also published *Fitness from Six to Twelve.* Yoga exercises, most of which are peaceful stretches and balancings, are good for your breathing and your peace of mind as well as your body. Many of them can be accomplished without strain or fatigue even during pregnancy, and they fit right in to natural-childbirth and post-partum exercise programs. Several good books are available on yoga.

The benefits of looking after your body's well-being are many: you don't get so tired, you don't get winded, your plumbing problems disappear, you feel more cheerful; all especially valuable during pregnancy, but definite benefits at any time. It's nice to know, too, that the fitter you are, the brighter your eyes and the prettier you look.

Reading Up

You may want to order the La Leche League manual, *The Womanly Art of Breast Feeding,* or the LLL *News,* for further moral support after the baby comes. Other pertinent reading may be selected from the suggested reading lists at the end of the book.

By all means, pack a new and tempting book or two in your hospital suitcase. If you have something good to read you will enjoy your hospital stay more.

A Change of Pace

A mother often has the feeling, especially with a first baby, that after the pregnancy is over everything will get back to normal: The housework will get done again, she will wear her normal clothes again, and return to normal life. The trouble is this doesn't exactly happen. As Jean Kerr says, "The thing about having a baby is, from then on, you *have* it." If you already have several small children, one more doesn't make too much difference. But if this is the first baby, or if it has been a number of years since you had an infant in the house, the usual tendency is to try and fit the baby's care and feeding into your life and still do all the things you used to do, but didn't feel like doing in the last months of pregnancy, such as keeping the floor waxed and the glasses polished, going out a couple of nights a week, cooking fancy meals, and finding time for volunteer work, hobbies, and so on. This attempt to lead two conflicting lives at once, that of busy American wife and that of nursing mother, frequently makes breast feeding fail.

Perhaps one should postpone the return to "normal." Having taken a few months off to have a baby, you can plan to take a few months more to nurse him. In a way you can look at these months of nursing as your reward for the hard job of pregnancy and childbirth. This may be the only time in your life when you can legitimately sit down occasionally in the daytime, put your feet up, and watch television or read a mystery story, because you are feeding the baby. Especially in the first weeks he will want to nurse often and for long periods. Perhaps this is nature's way not only of insuring that the baby gets enough milk but that you get enough rest for an easy convalescence. The housework and the world's work will always be there; but the nursing relationship is soon over. It is worth taking time off to enjoy it.

10·In the Hospital

LABOR

When you get to the hospital, an intern or resident doctor will probably examine you. Tell him that you intend to nurse your baby, and that you want to make sure that no drugs are given to you to suppress lactation.

When your own doctor arrives, remind him too that you intend to breast feed; in the excitement of delivery it can happen that someone will follow the usual routine of administering drugs to "dry up the milk," without checking with you first. Reminding the doctors will prevent this. Your husband should remind them too, in case you forget. If you are given any such drugs by accident you will still be able to nurse, provided the baby is allowed to suck often.

DELIVERY

The ideal arrangement is to nurse the baby for half an hour or longer as soon as it is born. Few hospitals allow

164

this. However, talk it over with your doctor; he may be willing to make special arrangements for you. If he can't, don't be upset. One of the secrets of successful nursing is staying calm; and that means staying calm about hospital regulations, whatever they may be. You will feel very rewarded if you can just look at your baby, and perhaps touch and hold it, in the delivery room. There's plenty of time ahead for nursing.

What if you have twins?: Nursing twins is much less work than bottle feeding them. Go right ahead with your plans for breast feeding. Some of the tricks that help in nursing twins are described in the next chapter.

What if your baby is premature?: He will need your milk more than ever. Many, many mothers have been successful at pumping their milk out by hand or with a breast pump until their baby was big enough to bring home. Your milk can be saved and given to your baby while you are in the hospital and perhaps even after you go home.

What if you have a Caesarean section?: If you have a Caesarean section you may not feel well enough to do anything, even feed the baby, for a day or so. Thereafter things will proceed normally. Caesarean section mothers can manage rooming-in perfectly well by the third day. When you get home you will be glad of the extra rest you get, as you sit or lie down to nurse the baby, when you would otherwise be on your feet scrubbing and boiling bottles.

THE FIRST DAY

Your baby will probably be brought in to you for the first time between six and twenty-four hours after delivery, depending on how you are feeling. If he is sleepy there's no rush to feed him. Feel free to take time to get acquainted. Most new mothers have an urge to undress the baby and get a good look at him from head to toes. Follow that urge if you feel like it; don't worry if you can't get the baby wrapped up again as neatly as before.

Sometimes the nursery nurse will scold you for unwrapping the baby. They try to keep everything sterile in the nursery, and when you undo the wrappings you "contaminate" the baby's clothing. However, you have a right to look at your own baby at least once, even if it does mean more work for the nurses. If the nursery must maintain sterile conditions be sure to warn the nurse that you have undressed the baby.

HOSPITAL RULES

Maternity care is in a state of transition. It has only been in the last fifty years that having babies in hospitals has become commonplace. In the last twenty years some hospitals have been developing new systems of maternity care, more like the care a mother would ideally get in her own home. But many hospitals still run their maternity wards in the same way that the rest of the hospital is run. It is hard to train personnel to make exceptions to general rules, just in one part of the hospital. On the surgical wards the minor infraction of a rule can make the difference between life and death; it is no wonder nurses are sometimes unreasonably firm about minor rules on the maternity ward too. Likewise, with temperatures being taken, and medication and all other treatments being given exactly on schedule all over the hospital, it seems reasonable that babies should be fed right on schedule too. Without special training in family-centered maternity care, the nursing staff cannot always make allowances for the mother who breast feeds. Sometimes they tell a mother the wrong things. Sometimes, when the work load is heavy and the nurses are few, a new nursing mother is very much on her own.

So don't be distressed if things are not perfect; stay calm. The hospital stay is brief. You and your baby will soon be home, where things will be more normal for both of you.

THE PREMATURE BABY

If your baby is premature, there is no reason why you should not plan to nurse it. You must enlist the support of your doctor and the nursery staff. If the baby is too small to be brought to you to nurse, perhaps you can be allowed to nurse it in the nursery; premature babies need the touch of a mother's hand and the feel of her body against their skin as much as older babies, and the sight of the baby may be stimulating to your milk supply and let-down reflex and will be good for your morale and help you to persevere. You can also learn to draw your milk off with an electric pump; if the hospital is cooperative, your baby can be fed your milk until it is strong enough to nurse. Many, many mothers have kept a milk supply going until their premature baby came home, even if it took a month or more. It is an effort, but the little one who starts at a disadvantage needs and benefits from mother's milk more than ever. You might refer also to the section in chapter 11, "The Sick or Handicapped Baby." By all means contact your local La Leche League if there is one. They will know of other mothers who have had similar experiences and who can help and cheer you.

PUTTING THE BABY TO THE BREAST

Probably the nurse will help you get comfortable and get the first feeding started. If not, you can manage by yourself. You can nurse sitting up or lying down. If you are sitting, don't lean back. Lean forward a little, and rest the baby partly on your lap, like the mothers in the first four plates following p. 138. That way the nipple is easier for him to grasp, and your arm won't get tired from holding him. You can use your free hand to guide the nipple into his mouth. (See Fig. 1.)

If you are more comfortable lying down at this stage, ask the nurse to put the baby beside you, so that you are lying on your side and he is on his, facing you. You can raise or lower the nipple by the roll of your body, and steady the baby with your free hand. It is a little harder to make connections this way until you and the baby are more experienced; but you may not want to sit up much yet. You can nurse from both breasts while lying on one side (figs. 2 and 3) or you can change sides without get-

FIG. 1

ting up, by hugging the baby and turning over with him. (Fig. 4.)

When the baby nurses, he takes the nipple and all or much of the areola into his mouth. Touch his nearest cheek or the corner of his mouth with the nipple, and he will turn towards the touch. Don't touch the other cheek or he will turn away.

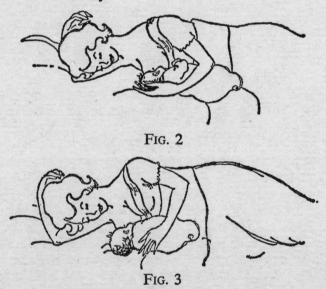

FIG. 2

FIG. 3

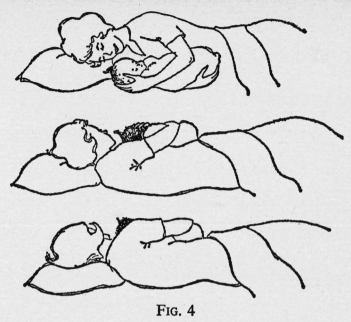

FIG. 4

For the first few feedings you may have to hold the breast away from the baby's nose so that he can breathe. (Fig. 5.)

Use both breasts at each feeding, and alternate the breast you start with. The nurses may give you other advice, but this really does seem to be the best system in the early weeks. You can pin a safety pin to your bra to remember which side you started with last time.

FIG. 5

PRIVACY

If you feel self-conscious because your roommates can watch and hear you, ask the nurse to put a screen around your bed while you are feeding the baby. This is not false modesty. Most of us need time to get used to breaking a life-long taboo against showing the breasts. Your baby will nurse better and get more to eat if you are not feeling embarrassed, and if this means you must have privacy, by all means ask for it.

GETTING THE BABY TO LET GO

A nursing baby can suck remarkably strongly. If you try to pull the nipple away he will just hang on harder. To get him off without hurting yourself, stick your finger in the corner of his mouth and break the suction. Then you can take him off without any trouble (Fig. 6.)

FIG. 6

BURPING AND SPITTING UP

Doctors usually advise "burping" babies after feedings, by patting them to bring up any air they may have swallowed. The nurse will show you how if you don't know. All babies spit up sometimes. Before your milk has come in, the baby may spit up a little of the yellowish colostrum. Occasionally a baby burps so heartily that he spits up a great gush of milk. This is nothing to be alarmed about.

BREAST CARE

Remember: soap, alcohol, and most other medicines and ointments are actually harmful to your tender skin. If you keep your clothes clean, nature will keep your breasts clean. A daily bath with plain warm water is plenty.

Unfortunately some hospitals still have rules about scrubbing or sterilizing the nipples before nursing. Just agree with the nurses who give you these orders, and then do as little as you can. The nurses will not have time to check up on you.

COLOSTRUM

Even a little colostrum is very beneficial to your newborn baby as mentioned earlier. While it may not seem to you that your breasts are producing anything in the first forty-eight hours, the baby who is interested in sucking (many are not, at this point) may swallow from one to several ounces of colostrum during early feedings. This is good for him and good for your future milk supply.

THE SECOND DAY

IN THE HOSPITAL NURSERY

Ask your doctor to leave orders in the nursery that your baby receive no formula or sugar water. Your baby is born with extra fluids in the body, which will see him through until your milk comes in, even if that takes several days. Naturally he will lose weight as he gradually loses these fluids. This loss need not be made up with formula or sugar water, which kill his appetite for your milk. Sucking on a rubber nipple can alter the baby's normal mouth movements and may make him a poorer sucker at the breast.

SCHEDULES

Rooming-in mothers usually nurse a baby eight or nine times during the day, and sleep with the baby at the breast at night. Each feeding may last half an hour or more. This prolonged, liberal nursing is the *best* way to avoid breast troubles such as soreness, engorgement, and infection, because it establishes an abundant, free-flowing milk supply from the beginning. This is nature's way to start breast feeding. If you must leave the baby in the nursery, ask to have him brought to you for an hour at each feeding. If this is impossible, ask for a three hour schedule. Don't let the nurses talk you into skipping the 2 A.M. feeding. If they forget to bring the baby out ring the buzzer and remind them. Your beasts need this feeding as much as the baby needs it.

SUCKING LIMITS

Every hospital has its own pet rules about how long the baby may suck. These rules are aimed at preventing nipple soreness. If your nipples are going to get sore at all, limiting sucking time to five minutes, or even one minute, will simply postpone the peak of soreness. When the milk comes in, a sucking limit will just keep the baby from getting as much milk as he needs. Let the baby make the decisions on how long he sucks; but if you are feeling sore, know that he will get most of the milk in the first ten minutes per side, and compromise with him after that.

SAFEGUARDING YOUR OWN COMFORT

If you feel sick, or uncomfortable from stitches, hemorrhoids, afterpains, or anything else, be sure to tell the doctor and the nurses. Any kind of discomfort makes it harder for you to relax while you are nursing the baby.

You are justified in asking for something to relieve discomfort, especially before feeding times. Even an aspirin helps. Some doctors prescribe a glass of beer or wine.

If you feel upset or depressed tell your doctor. Some people find that a mild sedative or tranquilizer is beneficial during these early days. They are, as psychiatrist Helene Deutsch points out, "happy but anxious days." You will feel better as the milk comes in and you and your baby settle down to being a happy nursing couple.

THE NURSES

A nurse who has breast fed her own babies can be a truly wonderful help to you and your baby. But many nurses are young and unmarried. They have never nursed a baby and they really don't understand the kind of help you need. Sometimes maternity care seems dull to them; they would rather be up in surgery. If you think a nurse is being particularly brisk and careless with you, it often helps to ask her for advice (not necessarily about breast feeding).

In many hospitals the nurses cannot afford the time to coach nursing mothers, even if they would like to. Mealtimes are rushed, and they must sometimes take the baby back to the nursery just when he is getting started. "Please," "Thank you," and a pretty smile can coax indulgences such as a longer feeding time from even the strictest supervisor. Be diplomatic with the nurses, and they'll forgive you for "upsetting the routine by taking the notion to breast feed."

In some hospitals, where everyone is in favor of breast feeding, each and every nurse may devote herself to helping you at each and every feeding. The nurses are apt to have gotten their training at different schools, in different decades; so each nurse may have rules for managing breast feeding which contradict what some previous nurse has told you. Also, different doctors may leave differing orders, so the poor nurses must tell one patient one set of rules and others another. Stay calm; don't let them bother you. Feel free to tell the nurse that you can manage alone, thank you. Don't get into arguments with the nurses—they have the upper hand! Luckily, nurses are busy, shifts change, and no one is going to have time to check up and see if you are following her particular brand of instructions. And sometimes you'll run into a wonderful nurse who really makes you feel at ease, and really knows how to help. Let her!

THE THIRD DAY

THE "LAZY" BABY

Lots of babies are not too interested in nursing, in the first few days. If the baby does not seem to want to nurse don't be discouraged. Don't try to force him into nursing, or keep him going once he's started, by such tricks as shaking or prodding him, tickling his feet or his cheek and so on. Efficiency may be on your mind or the attending nurse's but it's not on his, and this kind of treatment just upsets and scares him. It may make him retreat even further into sleepiness and lack of interest. The sleepy baby needs and appreciates your warmth and voice and nearness, even if he cannot yet nurse well. Let him doze on your chest or stomach, while you doze too. Babies seem to love this, and perhaps he draws strength from being so near, and will wake up to nurse later on. In these days before the milk comes in, the sleepy baby is a peaceful companion, warmer and more dear than any childhood teddy bear; if he spends most of his feeding periods just being held and cuddled that's doing him good too.

WHEN THE MILK COMES IN

When the colostrum changes to milk, the breasts start producing more abundantly; sometimes too abundantly. Long and frequent nursing, by a relaxed, experienced mother, can bring this change about within twelve to twenty-four hours after delivery. Nursing on a four-hour schedule postpones this, so that for most American mothers the milk comes in three to five days after delivery; it takes longest with the first baby.

The baby's appetite usually increases wonderfully when the milk comes in. But still he may not be able to keep up with the burgeoning supply. Your breasts, in addition to being full of milk, may be swollen as blood circulation increases: Nature is "marshaling her forces" for this big new job. All this fullness is an unusual feeling, and may make you uncomfortable; don't worry, it is only temporary.

Lumps, bumps, and swellings are to be expected as the glands fill up with Grade AA mother's milk. Some areas of the breast do not drain freely at first, and may feel lumpy even after a feeding.

RELIEF

Rooming-in mothers have a real advantage during an initial rushing flow of milk. They can pick the baby up whenever they feel too full, and in any case the baby usually wants to nurse so often that the breasts don't get too overloaded. If you find yourself getting too full for comfort, and you don't have your baby nearby, you can express milk manually by compressing the areola between your thumb and index finger, behind the nipple; or you can use your thumb and the edge of a glass or cup. (Fig. 7.) Try to get the hang of this when the breast is not too full, perhaps just after a feeding. What you are doing is forcing the milk forward out of the large ducts that lie beneath the nipple. Usually there are many little openings in the nipple. At first the milk will come in drops, and then in a dribble, and then in a fine spray. This a chore but it is worth doing if it relieves uncomfortable overfilling. By all means tell the nurses and your doctor if you are getting overfull. There are medications that can help. The nurse can help you express your milk, or show you how to use an electric breast pump, if one is available. (Manual expression is better than using the small glass and rubber bulb pump which produces painfully strong suction and is not very effective.)

FIG. 7

Sometimes it is hard for the baby to grasp the nipple when the breast is very full, because the areola is distended and tense. It can hurt like the dickens when he tries too. If this happens you can express some milk before the feeding, to make the areola more flexible or you can hold the breast so that the nipple protrudes better. (Fig. 1.) If you have bras which you have cut open at the tips, wear those. Nipple and areola will protrude, but the brassiere holds the full breast back and out of the baby's way a little.

LEAKING, DRIPPING, AND SPRAYING MILK

When this happens, it is wonderful news. It means that your let-down reflex is starting to work. The let-down reflex must work if the baby is to get the milk he needs. Any female can secrete milk. Successful breast-feeding mothers are the ones who establish a good let-down reflex: who not only *have* milk but can *give* milk.

At first, unless you have nursed babies before, you

probably won't feel the let-down reflex working. But you can recognize the signs of it: leaking or dripping of milk, especially during nursing from the other breast; afterpains or uterine cramps while nursing (these are caused by the same hormone that makes the milk let down); sore nipples just at the start of nursing, or a feeling that the baby is biting, which fades away as he nurses (the pain stops when the milk starts letting down). When the milk lets down you can sometimes hear the baby start to gulp, swallowing with every suck instead of after every four or five sucks. Later on you may be able to feel the let-down reflex, a sort of pins-and-needles sensation that brings with it a sense of relief and relaxation.

As your milk comes in, you may be warned again by nurses about sucking time limits. But it is bad for your let-down reflex to be fussing about how many minutes you nurse. The baby may need a few minutes to settle down, you may need a few more to let down your milk, and the feeding may not really start until many minutes have passed. Even if every other mother in the room is obediently taking her baby off the breast according to whatever system the hospital fancies, you put your watch away in a drawer and continue to let the baby decide how long to nurse.

How to Tell When the Baby Is Full

He signals satiety by relaxing his clenched fists; by a cute little grimace of a smile; sometimes by arching his back and growling, in a gesture of refusal; and, of course, by falling asleep. Don't try to prod him into nursing longer, or to force more into him. If your let-down reflex was working well, he may have gotten a huge meal in four or five minutes. In any case, he alone knows how hungry he was. Sometimes a baby will wake up and nurse again, when he is switched to the other breast. If not, take his word for it: He may be hungry again in an hour, but he's full now.

GETTING ACQUAINTED

You and the baby are learning to know each other. It is amazing how much personality tiny babies have; each one is an individual, responding to his mother in his own way. Dr. G. R. Barnes, Jr., writing the *Journal of the American Medical Association,* divided new babies into five types, depending on how they behaved at the breast. Which is closest to your baby?

BARRACUDAS: When put to the breast, these babies vigorously and promptly grasp the nipple and suck energetically for from fifteen to twenty minutes. There is no dallying. Occasionally this type of baby puts too much vigor into his nursing and hurts the nipple. (You can guess it was a mother who named that type! These babies are the easiest kind of all to breast feed. They don't *really* bite, they just nurse eagerly. They do all the work for you.)

PROCRASTINATORS: These babies often seem to put off until the fourth or fifth postpartum day what they could just as well have done from the start. They wait till the milk comes in. They show no particular interest or ability in sucking in the first few days. It is important not to prod or force these babies when they seem disinclined. They do well once they start.

GOURMETS OR MOUTHERS: These babies insist on mouthing the nipple, tasting a little milk and then smacking their lips, before starting to nurse. If the infant is hurried or prodded he will become furious and start to scream. Otherwise, after a few minutes of mouthing he settles down and nurses very well. (Mothers who have nursed these gourmet babies seem to think that this early dallying and playfulness at the breast often turns out to be a sign of a lifelong humorous turn of mind.)

RESTERS: These babies prefer to nurse a few minutes and then rest a few minutes. If left alone they often nurse well, although the entire procedure will take much longer. They cannot be hurried.

Dr. Barnes goes on to say that there are many babies who fall between these groups and others who fall into groups not described because they are less common. The above grouping serves merely to emphasize the fact that each baby nurses differently and the course of the nursing will depend on the combination of the baby's nursing characteristics, the mother's personality, and the quality of the help from the attending nurse.

A Restful Routine

While you are getting to know your baby, feedings will go ever more easily if you guard your own strength. Don't worry about finishing the birth announcements. Don't read, however interesting the book, when you feel like sleeping and have a chance to do so. Limit your visitors to a few minutes (except your husband, of course). Eat as much as you want—by this time you may have a ravenous appetite—but don't fill up on candy, which people are always giving to new mothers. Candy kills your appetite for the foods you do need. Drink lots of fruit juice and milk, all they offer you; they are good for your plumbing. But don't drink too much tea or coffee, which might make you restless, so that you can't nap. If you like beer maybe the nurses will let your husband bring you a cold bottle or two before dinner; it may be good for your milk supply, and it is certainly good for your morale.

THE FOURTH DAY

Sore Nipples

Sore nipples are a problem for some women, especially delicate-skinned blondes and redheads. Usually this soreness consists of a pain that makes you wince (or even brings tears to the eyes) as the baby first grasps the nipple, and which fades away as the milk lets down. *Soreness generally starts around the twentieth feeding, gets worse for twenty-four to forty-eight hours, and then rapidly disappears.* Thus rooming-in mothers are getting better already by the fourth day, while mothers on a four-hour hospital schedule will not be over their soreness until the sixth day or so. Limiting sucking or skipping feedings only postpones the peak of soreness.

Sometimes the nipple looks a little red and chafed. Sometimes it looks very sore, or cracks and even bleeds. The nipple will heal by itself in spite of sucking provided that no harmful substances, such as soap, alcohol, and vaseline, are applied. Lots of medicaments get the credit for miraculous cures that nature would have accomplished alone.

Keep a sore nipple dry and exposed to the air between feedings. This will help it to heal. Sun bathing or *very cautious* use of a sun lamp can help too. If lack of privacy means you cannot go around with the flaps of your bra down to let the air reach your nipples, have someone bring you a couple of little sieves from dime store tea strainers. You can put these in your bra over the nipples, and they will allow the air to circulate and keep you dry.

Don't chicken out now! It is normal to favor a cracked nipple somewhat; you can reduce nursing time on the sore side to eight or ten minutes, which is enough to insure that the baby gets the milk out. But too much skimping on nursing can make soreness worse or lead to other problems. To minimize discomfort and speed healing:

Start all feedings on the least sore side; once the milk has let down, you can switch.

If both sides are sore express milk manually until it lets down, then feed the baby.

Ask your doctor for a pain reliever to take just before feedings. Aspirin or wine will do the trick.

Try not to let the baby chew on the nipple itself, or hang on, sucking but not swallowing, for prolonged periods.

Keep up frequent, ample nursing.

Soothe the nipples between feedings with hydrous lanolin.

Nurse the baby in a different position each time: Lie down or sit up, or hold him under your arm at your side, or lie down and let him lie across your chest to nurse. This distributes the stress more evenly, rather than having pressure fall on the same part of the nipple at each feeding.

Nipple shields, which are very popular in some hospitals, are glass shields which fit over the breasts, with a rubber nipple on which the baby sucks. These protect your nipples entirely, but the baby must get milk by suction alone and usually gets very little. This is bad for your milk supply; it is better, in the long run, to grin and bear it. Above all, don't nurse for a brief period and then take the baby off before the milk lets down. It is the putting on and taking off that do the damage, especially if the milk has not let down.

If a nipple cracks and bleeds, you may see blood in the baby's mouth. This is an alarming sight but not too uncommon. Forget it. The nipple will heal by tomorrow or the next day.

THE FIFTH DAY

GOING HOME

Check over chapter 9, "Before the Baby Comes," to see if there are any ways you may have overlooked in which you can lighten your responsibilities at home. Before you go you may want to make a few phone calls to arrange for diaper service, afternoons away from home for an older child, or morning help for yourself.

Probably you will go home on the fifth or sixth day. The hospital may give you a bottle of formula to take with you. Don't take it! You might panic into using it. Some mothers find that the fatigue of going home causes a temporary drop in their milk supply, but that is no reason to stoke the baby with formula. Just let him nurse more often and the milk supply will return. Other mothers find that they have much more milk available for the baby when they get home than they did in the hospital, probably because their milk lets down better in familiar surroundings.

If lactation did not get well established in the hospital, your pediatrician may be suggesting that you give up the idea of nursing. Here is where your husband can really give you support. Tell the doctor together that you wish to continue learning to breast feed. You can give the baby a little formula if your own milk supply is still very low, but you will soon be able to build up your supply at home, where "rooming-in" and "demand feeding" are yours for the asking, as well as privacy, good food, and the tender, loving care of your husband and family.

THANKS TO THE STAFF

Do take time before you leave to thank any nurse who was especially helpful to you. If the nurse who helped you is off duty get her name and leave a note. Getting a mother and baby off to a good start can be almost as rewarding for the dedicated nurse as it has been for you. She won't expect to be thanked for her kindness and skill—and probably hasn't been in years. But she will feel pleased. Maybe it will encourage her when the next nursing mother comes along who needs her help.

11 · One to Six Weeks:
The Learning Period

HOMECOMING

Even if you enjoyed your hospital stay it is nice to be going home. Probably you feel fine, and were beginning to chafe at your idleness in the hospital. But it is surprising how tiring the trip home can be; you may be glad to lie down when you get there.

Before you get home, have your husband put the baby's bed near your own, so you will be able to feed him or reach over and pat him without getting up. If you have other small children arrange for them to be out of the house when you first get home. Then you and your new baby can be settled *in bed* before the welcoming tumult. You might want to make sure the day before you leave the hospital that there are enough groceries in the house to last a few days, so that you won't be obliged to plan meals and make lists right away.

A Few Good Rules

Thirty years ago, mothers spent about two weeks in the hospital and then went home and spent another two weeks or so in their bedrooms, with orders not to go up and down stairs. This effectively eliminated any chance that they would take over the housework too soon. Today mothers are sent home after five days in the hospital, which is not really a very restful place. In a world of apartments and one-story development houses, orders involving stairs wouldn't be of much use; and many physicians actually hesitate to make much of a to-do over getting more rest at home, lest a mother "take advantage" or "think she's sick."

But people recover from childbirth at widely varying and quite unpredictable speeds: The hothouse flower who catches every cold that goes around, and never does anything more strenuous than pick up a bridge hand, may feel perfectly fit in two weeks, while the former tennis champion is still feeling weak six months after giving birth. You may well find that you need a month or so of virtual idleness in order to convalesce completely from pregnancy and childbirth. The more work you do in that first month, the more months it will take you to feel strong again. Doing too much too soon is especially hard on the nursing mother, who is using her strength to make milk as well as to recuperate from pregnancy and delivery.

Dr. E. Robbins Kimball, who has helped hundreds of mothers to nurse their babies successfully, sends each patient home with a list of rules which all nursing mothers might do well to follow.

1. *Spend the first three days in bed*. This does not mean lying down whenever you get a chance; if means staying in bed, and getting up only to go to the bathroom. Keep the baby near you or in your bed. Let your husband get breakfast and dinner and bring it to you, and let whoever is helping you with your housework fix lunch. Don't even rinse out a diaper. If your household situation would require that you do the laundry, you can use disposable

diapers for a few days. Stock up on mystery stories or magazines or whatever you like to read, or move the TV into the bedroom. Remember, you don't have a baby every day, and when you do, you deserve to enjoy life for a little while. Naturally, when you come home from the hospital you can see all sorts of things that have been neglected in your absence. But don't even straighten a pillow; instead, make a list of what you ought to be doing, and plan on doing it after your three days in bed. Three days from now you may find that the things on the list don't seem quite as vital as they did at first.

If you have another small child, and there are hours in the day when there is no one to watch him but you, just shut the bedroom door and keep him in your room with you. Even an eighteen-month-old can amuse himself with books and crayons, and likes to be read to, and he will soon learn to take his nap on your bed.

Because you are in bed visitors will not overstay their welcome, or expect you to serve coffee or drinks. Feel free to tell people that the doctor instructed you to stay in bed, even if he didn't.

2. *Take three one-hour naps a day.* During your first three days in bed, pull the shades and sleep. For the rest of the month you should use your ingenuity to get into bed and sleep for each one of these naps. Sleep while the children sleep, sleep before dinner while your husband takes the baby for a walk in the fresh air, sleep after breakfast while a neighbor watches the toddler. Don't read; don't write notes; you can do those things while you nurse the baby. SLEEP. These three naps a day will do you more good, and do more to make breast feeding a pleasure and a quick success than anything else you do in the first weeks. (Fig. 8.)

3. Remember that *it takes two or three weeks to learn how to nurse and a couple of months to become an expert.* Don't regard every little event as a signal for panic. Sure, there will be days when you don't have enough milk. There will also be days when you have too much. There will be days when the baby "goes on a four hour schedule," or so it seems, and days when the baby wants to eat

FIG. 8

all the time, every two hours or oftener. These "frequency days" are nature's way of making your milk supply increase to keep up with your fast growing baby's needs. Researchers have found that the first two "frequency days" are apt to occur around the sixth and fourteenth days of life. The experienced mother hardly notices them, but the mother who is still clock-watching and counting each feed is very conscious of them. All the events of the early days of nursing your first baby loom very large, just like the events of your first pregnancy. Just remember that you (and your baby) are still learning. Breast feeding will be easier and easier as you go along.

MECHANICAL AIDS TO LACTATION

The simplest aid to lactation is a nasal spray containing oxytocin, the let-down hormone. This is especially helpful to the nervous nursing mother. See chapters 2 and 6 and discuss them with your doctor.

Donating milk to a milk bank is very stimulating to your own milk supply. If there is a milk bank in your area, discuss the idea with your doctor.

Tranquilizers help some nursing mothers, but for all

their vaunted safety, are potent drugs which should be used with care. See your doctor first.

CONDITIONING THE LET-DOWN REFLEX

Sometimes a new mother's let-down reflex doesn't work very reliably, even after two or three months of nursing. She may be losing a lot of milk through leaking, or she may never seem to have quite enough, so that her baby does not gain very fast, and sometimes cries at the breast. Such a mother needs to make a deliberate effort to induce her let-down reflex to function smoothly and reliably; nursing will be much more satisfactory when this is done. Here are some suggestions;

1. Cut out extraneous stresses, such as dinner guests (accept invitations, but don't give them), the Late Late Show, and so on.

2. Watch your own schedule: two or three one-hour naps, no skimping on meals or staying downtown shopping too long.

3. Put the baby on a schedule, starting with his first feeding at 4, 5, or 6 A.M., or whenever he wakes. Pick a reasonable time interval—two-and-a-half or three hours— and feed him regularly. This doesn't mean you have to let him cry. It just means don't let him sleep four or five hours, while your milk production slows, or your milk leaks and goes to waste. Train the baby and your breasts to a standard time interval.

4. If your milk suddenly lets down, pick up the baby and feed him, even off schedule; associate the let-down with the sucking. Then feed him again at the next scheduled time.

5. If you have a chance, take five minutes before feeding to sit down, put your feet up, close your eyes, and think about nothing.

6. Your body responds well to routine. Nurse in the same comfortable quiet spot at each meal; take a drink of water before your nurse. Your let-down reflex will associate itself with these habits.

7. Remove distracting influences. You can't let down

your milk well if a disapproving relative is glaring at you,
or if the phone is ringing, or if your three-year-old is getting into trouble in the kitchen. Later on, when you're an
old hand at nursing, these things won't bother you. Now,
while you're just beginning to get the hang of it, shut the
door on the relative, take the phone off the hook, and read
a nice story to your three-year-old.

8. Don't cheat yourself through altruism. A mother
tends to feel that it is more important to get the laundry
done, the house clean, the children well organized, the
yard presentable, the errands caught up with, and the
meals out on time than to get enough rest or a good breakfast for herself. But none of these things is as important to
your family— especially to your husband and to your
nursing baby—as a relaxed, cheerful mother. Learn to
look at taking care of yourself as your duty to your family,
rather than as self-indulgence.

9. Even though you need rest, don't let the baby skip
night feedings; get up at least once. At this point you may
have limited storage capacity; if your breasts get too full,
milk production slows down. Don't go so long between
feedings that you feel lumpy.

FOOD

Part of enjoying life in these first six weeks is eating
heartily and well. This is not the time to "diet"; lactation
is the best "diet" there is, anyway. A few months or a year
of giving milk can strip unnecessary weight from you without the slightest effort on your part. Some mothers think
that the most enjoyable thing about lactation is that for a
few happy months they can dive into meals with gusto,
eating cream on the cereal and two helpings of everything,
and never gain a pound.

This does not mean that you should fill up on "cheat
foods" such as cake and sweet rolls and coffee. These
things provide few of the elements needed in the milk you
are making. While the sugary, starchy foods are adding to
your body fat, the mammary glands go on raiding your
body for vitamins, minerals, and protein needed for milk

production. You don't lose weight, and you tend to feel tired and "used up." The answer is to eat plenty of high protein foods such as meat, cheese, eggs, and so on. The whole-grain cereals and breads provide protein as well as extra flavor. Fruit and fruit juices can give you as much "quick energy" from sugar as any soft drink can. Then you can satisfy your appetite, which just at first may be tremendous, by having a hearty "milk-making" snack whenever you feel hungry. Of course you will have plenty of breast milk no matter what you eat; milk is produced independently of diet. But you will feel better if you eat good food, and as much of it as you want, during the first few weeks. It's your "vacation." Enjoy it.

DRINK

If you are tired or preoccupied it is easy to forget about taking enough fluids. There is no need to force yourself to drink copious quantities of liquids, but you do not want to go thirsty. If you drink a glass of water or milk or juice every time you nurse the baby, that will be plenty; taking this much liquid will also help to prevent the constipation that plagues so many women after delivery. You may feel intensely thirsty at the moment the milk lets down; nature is reminding you to take that glass of water.

You do not need to make a special effort to drink milk. In most parts of the world nursing mothers drink no milk at all. Cheese, meats, and even salad greens provide you with plenty of calcium.

In this fast-paced modern life, alcohol has special virtues for the nursing mother. An old German baby nurse swears that all her maternity patients succeed in breast feeding because of her prescription: a big bowl of sugared and creamed oatmeal for breakfast, and a glass of port wine at 10 A.M. and 4 P.M. Dr. Kimball's succinct rule for nursing success is *Booze and snooze.* This does not mean you should drown yourself in double martinis, but a glass of wine or a bottle of beer before or with lunch and supper can make a nap more enticing, undone housework less worrisome, and the baby's tears less likely to provoke your own. This judicious tippling does not destine you for a drunkard's grave. By the time you are on your feet you will neither want nor enjoy a 10 A.M. glass of port. But this is one time in life when the therapeutic qualities of alcohol are a blessing.

Beer, which Dr. Kimball calls "the *sine qua non* for the nervous nursing mother," has special advantages. The imported brands particularly are rich in B complex vitamins which may contribute to your energy and good humor, and which may be of specific value during lactation.

YOUR HUSBAND

Nursing mothers owe a lot to their husbands. A husband's admiration for this new womanliness is one of the greatest rewards of nursing. It is your husband's pride and confidence in you that keeps you nursing, when you are a novice at the job. It is your husband who dispels your doubts, who reassures you and steadies you. He saves you from rushing for the bottle just because the baby has had an extra-hungry day and your supply hasn't caught up with the demand, or because your breasts seem empty and someone remarks, "You can't just let that child starve!" It is your husband who brightens the routine of your life by coming home every night with comments and anecdotes from the outside world; who reminds you that there are things worth thinking about besides housework and babies. It is your husband who takes over the essential work of the household when there is no one else to do it, and when you just can't manage; and who uses his authority to *make* you rest, when your tired conscience is urging you to overwork.

And it is your husband who appreciates the advantages of nursing, not only to you and the baby, but to himself: a happy baby to play with; a slim contented wife for his companion; and no heating up bottles at 2 A.M.! (Figs. 9, 10.)

FIG. 9

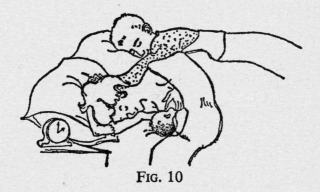

FIG. 10

YOUR CHILDREN

If you have several children, but this is the first one you've breast fed, you may feel strange at first about nursing in front of them. But children soon get accustomed to the sight and take it for granted. The child closest in age to the baby sometimes wants special attention while you are nursing. This is easy to deal with. Make the baby's meal-

time a special time for the older children, too, in which
you read to him and cuddle him. A nursing baby makes a
very good book rest, and you can quite easily hold two
children in your lap, or put your free arm around the older
child. (Fig. 11.) You can enjoy your peaceful private
meals alone with the baby now and then when the other
child is asleep or outside playing. Don't let yourself resent
the older baby's intrusion; if you seem to enjoy his
company when you are nursing, and perhaps give him a
special half-hour of play or attention at some other time,

FIG. 11

he won't think of nursing as disadvantageous to himself.
Of course you don't have to let the older child tease or
annoy you or the baby at feeding times. After all, you
have a right to breast feed, and your new baby has a right
to his mother's milk, regardless of how the older child
feels about it. Most toddlers and older children soon learn
to regard nursing as just what it is: a nice, friendly, and
very convenient way to feed a baby.

An older child who sees the baby at the breast may
want to try nursing too. The best way to discourage this

idea is to let the child try. He won't be very successful and he'll find that after all, it's just milk, and not the ambrosia the baby seems to think it is.

Your Mother

The emotionally mature grandmother is usually very pleased that her grandchild is being breast fed. Watching the new baby at the breast, she remembers her own days of new motherhood; and she feels fonder than ever of her daughter or daughter-in-law for being such a good mother to this new member of the family.

But it is not given to all of us, even grandmothers, to be mature all the time. Mingled with her pride is often a certain amount of jealousy. A grandmother may well be more skillful with the baby than is its inexperienced mother, and she may be secretly anxious to have her son or son-in-law see what a good mother *she* is; but there is one thing she cannot do for the baby (in our culture, at least) and that is, nurse it. So she is jealous because you are the only person who is really indispensable to the baby. At the same time, she is jealous of the baby, because it takes you away from her. Especially during nursing, the closed circle, the rapport between mother and baby may make a grandmother feel very excluded. She may break in with remarks that are more thoughtless or even cruel than she realizes, in her anxiety to regain your attention. The cure is simple; seek privacy during nursing, and at other times make a special effort so that she feels welcome and appreciated. Her feelings of jealousy will soon pass.

Nursing as an Antidote to Harassment

Perhaps the greatest advantage of nursing is that it brings peace. Sitting down to nurse the baby allows you to withdraw, momentarily, from all your other cares and duties. For a little while all problems can be answered with the words, "I'm feeding the baby, I'll be there in a few minutes." The plumber on the doorstep, your mother-in-law wanting to know where to put the laundry, the phone ringing, the four-year-old demanding a drink of water—all can wait. Behind the closed nursery door, curled in a rocking chair with the baby, you can restore yourself with the almost physical feeling of peace and tranquility that comes with nursing. These moments of solitude are a simple but rare blessing in the lives of most mothers.

If you are naturally the high-geared, hyperactive type, you especially will come to enjoy these brief excursions into tranquility. Later on, at the end of a strenuous day out, you'll absolutely crave to get home and sit down with the baby. If you are the nervous type, you can probably be an extremely successful nursing mother (dairymen say that the high-strung cows give the most milk) once you get into the swing of relaxing with the baby, instead of struggling with him. One new mother, who all her life had suffered from a severe rash during periods of emotional stress, described to La Leche League an especially ghastly day which ended with her husband's being painfully cut by the lawn mower. True to past experience, she broke out in the rash; then she sat down to nurse her twin babies, certain that she would have no milk. Instead, the milk let down quickly. As she nursed the babies, she began to feel relaxed for the first time all day; and by the time the meal was over her rash was gone.

These restorative moments of complete relief from stress are the reward that nature has always meant nursing to give to the mother. While her baby was at her breast, the cave woman could forget about cave bears and saber-toothed tigers, and the pioneer woman could stop thinking about hard work and Indians, and enjoy a brief retreat into leisure and peace. Among today's mothers, it is the woman who has six or eight children who *really* appreciates being able to breast feed; but the rewarding tranquillity that means so much to her can be just as pleasant, if not so sorely needed, to the mother of one.

Nursing a "Dividend" Baby

The mother who is most apt to have a hard time in sticking to her decision to breast feed is the mother who already has several children, and then, when the youngest is ten or twelve years old, has another baby.

Somehow a baby born out of season is always at a disadvantage, whether it be a fall colt or a Christmas lamb, or a child who arrives as a dividend to the family that already seemed complete. Even if the mother breast fed all her previous children with complete success, she may find that she doesn't seem to do well with this one. The baby nurses, but he just doesn't gain.

The problem is basically one of practicality. Once you get out of the habit of orienting your life around infants and toddlers, it is very difficult to get back into that habit. Life becomes so different for most women, once their children are all in school, that they cannot go back easily to a nursery world of long peaceful feedings, of two daily naps and neglected housework. It means giving up too many satisfactions such as abundant social life and useful community work. Besides, a family of older children entails a host of new responsibilities such as chauffeuring and chaperoning, laundering school clothes and fixing school lunches, that further intrude upon the mother's freedom to nurse the baby.

The result is that nursing time is curtailed so that the milk supply dwindles, or, sometimes, the let-down reflex is inhibited so that what milk the baby does get is simply rather low in calories. Although the conscientious mother *wants* to nurse, nature makes the decision for her; she can't.

If you are in this situation, nursing a little "dividend" some years after your last baby, and you do want to continue to nurse, stop and think ahead a little about how many changes this is going to make, temporarily, in your household. This baby does deserve his mother's milk, just as much as any of the rest did; but making this possible will take a special effort not only from you but from all the family. Let them get into the habit of doing some of their own work "for the duration," of expecting just as much from you in the way of love and kindness but perhaps a little less in the way of goods and services. Get into the habit, yourself, of resting more and doing less, so that you can enjoy this baby the way babies were meant to be enjoyed. All too soon this one, like the others, will be grown.

The mother who has her first baby rather late in life, after many years of marriage, paradoxically may have a very easy time breast feeding. Just having a baby in a childless household is such a big change that the changes necessitated by nursing can easily be accomplished simultaneously. The nursing relationship is a special blessing for an older mother, making this unexpected child doubly enjoyable and helping her to be casual and easygoing about motherhood.

THE SICK OR HANDICAPPED BABY

The baby who is born with a serious abnormality, such as Mongolism or a harelip, can still be fed his mother's milk. Nursing a disadvantaged baby may take immense patience and dedication. The retarded or brain-damaged infant may have little or no sucking reflex. A harelipped or cleft-palate child may have to be bottle or spoon-fed milk which the mother has expressed. However, the worried mother of such a child is often exceptionally willing to make the extra effort. It is one thing she can clearly do to help, and it brings profound emotional relief to her. One mother who nursed a normal baby and simultaneously expressed enough milk to maintain its harelipped twin put it this way:

"I believed Steve needed the nutritional advantage of the milk and thus I wanted very much to give it to him. The day I took him home from the hospital and began to express my milk for him, I experienced a great sense of relief and my anxiety over his condition seemed to dissipate. The act of providing breast milk for him in the unconventional way of a bottle provided me with great peace of mind and a feeling of usefulness. I felt I had climbed Mt. Everest when I succeeded."

The mother of a Mongoloid baby, healthy and nursing at eight months, said, "It is all I can do for her, to make her feel close and happy, and to give her the best start towards growing up that she can have. I often feel so thankful I can share this much, at least, with her."

It is always a shocking experience for both mother and child when a very small baby has to undergo major surgery. Here again the maintenance of a supply of breast milk is the most useful thing a mother can do for the child. Feeding of breast milk rapidly corrects the chemical chaos in the bodies of infants who have undergone stress. Many mothers have expressed milk and carried or sent it to the hospital daily. In one case where an infant with a heart anomaly was underoing major surgery in a military hospital, the mother's milk was picked up every day in an ice chest by an Air Force ambulance.

It is not always easy to maintain a full supply of milk exclusively by pumping or expressing, especially for a first-time mother who lacks nursing experience. But once a hospitalized baby is well enough to come home, and strong enough to nurse, a full milk supply can usually be developed in two or three days if the mother has maintained even a partial supply. Babies can tolerate surgery well; they are, as one doctor put it, designed to live. But the postoperative baby particularly needs not only the protection of breast milk, but the mother that goes with it—the body contact, the touching, the warmth. Perhaps especially in the case of an infant with neurological difficulties, being carried, sleeping with his mother, being bathed, and stroked, feeling her message of love and care through his skin and body as well as his mouth, can work wonders.

A mother with a seriously ill baby can always contact her local La Leche League, or, if there is none nearby, the main La Leche League offices in Franklin Park, Illinois, for guidance and support. She may have her hands full with her own emotions, and nothing helps so much as talking to someone who has been in the same boat. La Leche League can also guide her in ways to get along with the hospital staff and to enlist their support without harassing them. LLLI has several pamphlets on relactation, or reestablishing a milk supply. A useful reference for mothers and doctors concerned with breast feeding the sick or disadvantaged baby is *The Medical Value of Breast Feeding,* published by the International Childbirth Association, which contains an extensive bibliography.*

SCHEDULES

Niles Newton says, in an article on breast feeding which is written primarily for doctors, "The advice given by Southworth in Carr's *Practice of Pediatrics,* published in 1906, is still worth remembering, since at that time successful breast feeding was the rule rather than the exception." Southworth's schedule was:

First day: 4 nursings	
Second day: 6 nursings	
The rest of the first month:	10 nursings in 24 hrs.
Second and third months:	8 nursings in 24 hrs.
Fourth and fifth months:	7 nursings in 24 hrs.
Sixth through eleventh months:	6 nursings in 24 hrs.

He assumed the baby would have night feedings until six months old.

What a far cry this normal breast feeding schedule is from the four hour schedule that modern formula-fed babies are put on. Even the baby fed formula "on demand" is expected to fall into a roughly four hour schedule within a few weeks. But the nursing baby should not be expected to do so. Throughout the first four weeks many a nursing baby eats ten times in twenty-four hours; which means there is an average two and a half hours between feedings. Naturally, if he sometimes sleeps four or five hours at a stretch at night he may well double up in the daytime, and take some meals at even shorter intervals. If it seems to you that your baby is "always hungry," keep track for one day and see if he doesn't fall into the standard ten nursings a day pattern, and if his apparent insatiability isn't a result of your expecting him to go three or four hours between

---

* Available from the ICEA Supplies Center, 208 Ditty Building, Belluvue, Washington 98004.

every meal, as a baby fed on slow-digesting cow's milk does.

We sometimes make a concession to the small or weak formula-fed baby, and start him out on a three-hour schedule. But the breast-fed baby may not work up to a three hour schedule—one which averages out to eight meals a day—until the second or third month; and Dr. Southworth did not expect breast-fed babies to cut down to six meals a day, or a four hour schedule, until they were six months old! No wonder so many mothers in the previous generation could not nurse their babies, when a four hour schedule was flatly insisted on from birth, and when it was also customary to tell a mother to nurse from one breast only at each feeding. The woman who secreted so much milk that she could feed a baby adequately, despite the limited sucking stimulation given by offering only one breast every four hours, must have been rare indeed.

Suppose your new baby does not fit Southworth's description? The La Leche League manual says:

Occasionally, we see a baby who goes to extremes in one of two ways. One baby may seem to be exceptionally active, fussy and hungry all or most of the time. If we nurse him more often than every two hours which is what he seems to want, he only gets fussier and more restless, but will go right on nursing! This type of baby is often getting more milk than he really wants. What he wants is more sucking, without the milk; so use a pacifier between feedings, and keep him on a two-to-three hour schedule.

The other extreme is the too placid baby. He will sleep peacefully for four, five, or more hours between feedings, be fairly quiet, and nurse rather leisurely. As time goes on, he may seem to get even quieter, and you think, "Such a good baby. He certainly is doing well." Then comes the shock, when you take him to the doctor for his check-up and find out to your amazement that he has not gained an ounce, and in some instances has perhaps even lost weight.

Here again, remember that the breast-fed baby needs to be fed, as Dr. Carr advises, about every 2-3 hours, with perhaps one longer stretch a day. The exceptionally sleepy, placid baby must be awakened to be fed more often, and should be urged to take both sides at each feeding. The trouble in this case is not a lack of milk on your part nor a lack in its quality. It is the baby who needs to be regulated. By increasing the number of times he nurses, you will automatically increase your supply and soon the baby will be gaining as he should.

How to Tell if the Baby Is Getting Enough Milk

1. What goes in must come out. Does the baby have good bowel movements? The new nursing baby may have several bowel movements a day; some may be just a stain on the diapers. Later he will have one every two to four days, but it should be fairly big. The baby who is not getting enough to eat has scanty stools which may be greenish in color.

2. Does he have lots of wet diapers? If you are not giving him extra water, which he doesn't need anyway, those wet diapers are an indication that he is getting plenty of breast milk.

3. Is he content with eight to eleven feedings per day, the typical nursing schedule? If you are nursing him this often, and letting down your milk at feedings, he is undoubtedly getting enough.

4. Is he gaining? La Leche League says, "A good rule to follow, in a healthy baby, is that he should be gaining from four to seven ounces a week, but that less than this in a given week or two is not in itself cause for alarm." This does not mean you should rush off and buy a scale; home scales are usually quite inaccurate anyway. And weighing before and after feedings would be a great waste of time. Instead, if you feel dubious about your own production capacity, or if the baby seems too quiet and "good," weigh the baby once a week at the supermarket. Their scales are very accurate, by law, and the check-out girls usually don't mind if you hastily weigh the baby if you choose a quiet time of day to do it. Take along duplicates of what the baby is wearing, and weigh the closing after you weigh the baby. Subtract the weight of the clothes and you have a fair idea of how much the baby has gained. (Fig. 12.)

There is a tremendous amount of emphasis these days on how much weight a baby gains; formula-fed babies sometimes put on a lot of weight, and rate of gain has become the yardstick by which the baby's health is measured, by mothers and often by doctors too. Don't be rattled if someone insists your baby "isn't gaining fast enough," as long as he is happy and healthy and you nurse him long and often.

FIG. 12

CONFIDENCE BUILDERS

All of us have doubts sometimes about our nursing ability, even if we have nursed babies before. When the baby is fussy, or the doctor is noncommittal about whether the baby's doing well, or a friend criticizes, it is hard not to worry. You can't see the milk going into the baby; so there's no way to tell what he's getting. You start to concentrate so much on the fear that he's getting no milk that you get tense at feeding time, and lose the easygoing sense of teamwork and friendship with the baby. When these good feelings are there, the milk is there automatically;

you don't have to worry about it any more than your happy nursing baby does.

If you are still having doubts, try these suggestions:

1. Find another nursing mother, past or present. If you don't know anyone ask your neighbors and acquaintances. Now is the time to pack up your baby and visit someone else who has had more experience. See if there is a La Leche League in your part of the country. Or you might ask your doctor for the name of some other patient who is an old hand at breast feeding, explaining that you would like a few practical pointers and don't want to bother him about such trivial matters. One phone call with another, experienced, nursing mother can boost your morale for a week.

2. Even your pets can inspire your own confidence. One nursing mother wrote about her cat having kittens:

While the actual birth was a bit of a surprise to the cat (the first kitten was born on the back doorstep) by the time the others arrived she was already confident in her new role of mother. During the first week Domino was with her babies constantly. She didn't seem to mind their continuous nursing. No one suggested that the milk of Cindy Lou, the cocker spaniel next door, might be more nourishing for newborn kittens or at least would help them to sleep all night. And when she did leave them for a while, it took only the tiniest meeow to bring her leaping back into the box. Watching Domino raise her family is a continuing delight and inspiration . . .

3. If you can't believe the invisible milk is there, try expressing it manually for one feeding, and giving it to the baby in a bottle. Seeing a four-ounce bottle fill up with one's own milk will convince anyone that the milk is real. You may even find that you've expressed more than the baby can drink at one meal.

4. Remember that breast milk is tailored to the needs of your baby. You might say that two ounces of breast milk contains as much "goodness" as three or four ounces of cow's milk formula, even though the breast milk normally looks thin and blue. So your baby is getting plenty

of nourishment even when the amount of milk he takes seems scanty compared to the bottleful after bottleful that a formula-fed baby may take.

5. Don't judge how much milk you have by how full your breasts seem. Often we feel *very* full in the hospital; then, when we get home, the breasts are no longer burstingly full and it seems as if the milk has gone. But the fullness in the hospital is only partly caused by milk; some of it is due to increased circulation and some swelling in the tissues, which quickly dies down. And once the letdown reflex is working well, the milk stays back in the breasts until it is needed; there may be several ounces of milk available to the baby in a breast which feels hardly full at all.

6. If your baby cries often, try the pacifier between feedings, and give him lots of body contact. A rocking chair is the nursing mother's greatest tool for relaxing the mother as well as the baby, not just during feedings, but between and after feedings when a little snug cuddling is in order.

7. Take comfort from the thought that some babies just *are* more fussy than others. A pair of breast-fed twins supplied a good example, reported in the La Leche League *News*:

"Chatty Cathy," the smaller twin, is a little "fuss pot"—squirming and spitting, sleeping only in short hauls, and gaining rather slowly. Charlotte nurses peacefully, lives life in an easy-going way, and is gaining much faster than her sister.

The same mother, the same supply of milk—no supplement, no solids—and two very different babies.

8. Don't permit yourself to worry in the evening. When you are tired, little worries become big ones. You are especially likely to worry about the milk supply in the evening, or in the middle of the night. Force yourself to think of something else, to put the milk question out of your mind until morning. Let your husband walk the baby or rock him. Take a shower; have a drink. Remember that the best prescription for a fussy baby is *not* a bottle—bot-

tles bring problems of their own—but more rest for the mother.

And if you ever get to feeling nursing "isn't worth the bother" of learning, try rereading chapters 1 and 3.

Your Own Health

You must take care of your own health; nobody else will do it for you. Your pediatrician is primarily interested in your baby's health, and not in yours. Your obstetrician is primarily interested in your pelvic organs, and not the rest of you. All too often a new mother drags on for weeks with anemia or bronchitis or some other ailment which neither her obstetrician nor her pediatrician notice, though she may see both of them during that time, and which she herself tries to ignore, often simply because she feels too tired to bother going to another doctor.

If you catch a cold or run a fever or have continued cramps or vaginal bleeding or any other physical problem, by all means call a doctor and get something done about it. And if you feel really unwell don't drag yourself down to the doctor's office; find one who will come to you. Although house calls are a rarity these days, if anyone has a right to request a house call it is a sick mother just home with a new baby.

If you should happen to get sick you may find that your milk supply is lowered, particularly if you are running a fever. Don't worry; it will bounce right back up again in a day or two. You can continue to nurse your baby even through pneumonia; others have. The baby is already exposed to your germs anyway, and in fact is apt to be very resistant.

See chapter 3 for more about the medicines and drugs that can affect the baby through your milk.

Mastitis

Mastitis, or infection within the breast, is a not uncommon event during lactation. What happens is this: A duct gets plugged, or let-down is incomplete for a few feedings, or for some other reason the milk fails to flow from one section of a breast. Stasis sets in; the milk backs up, the area may become tender to the touch or slightly reddened, and infection begins to develop. Often the mother's first clue is that she feels sick and feverish; she may not at first associate this with the little sore place in one breast.

If the precipitating cause of "caked breast," as it used to be called, is stasis, then the obvious first thing to do is get that area flowing again. Hot compresses on the sore area (wet washclothes wrung out in hot water, not a heavy hot-water bottle) and frequent nursings on that side should be instituted at once. Let the baby nurse from the breast as often as you can get him to, twice as frequently as normal if possible, and try to relax so that your letdown will function well. R. M. Applebaum, M. D., a pediatrician whose patients are almost 100 per cent breast fed, is an authority on this ailment. In his advice to physicians ("The Modern Management of Successful Breast-Feeding," in *Pediatric Clinics of North America,* February 1970) he recommends the following:

An antibiotic should be taken immediately and for forty-eight to seventy-two hours. For this you should call your doctor. Under no circumstances should you wean the baby or stop nursing on the affected breast. There is nothing in the milk that will harm the baby, nor will the antibiotics or pain relievers you might take have any noticeable effect on the baby; and taking the baby off the breast immediately aggravates the backed-up milk problem and can make the whole situation much worse.

Anyone who has seen one of these small infections run rampant and turn into a breast abscess never wants to see another one. For this reason many doctors mistakenly advocate immediate weaning of the baby when a little breast infection develops. They are afraid of abscesses developing, and think of them as a result of nursing, when they are perhaps more truly a result of wrong advice!

One doctor who has made a study of mastitis believes that its occurrence can almost always be linked to what he calls a "lactation indiscretion." Something in the mother's day or week has caused a lapse in her normally free-flowing let-down. It might be too many late nights, a visit from tension-inducing relatives, a bad scare. Sometimes an area of the breast can get plugged up for purely mechanical reasons; a tight bra or the habit of sleeping on your stomach. If you are large-bosomed, arm exercises such as swimming or just stretching may be beneficial. In any case, the treatment is the same. If you develop a sore place in the breast, and especially if you feel as if you're getting the flu at the same time, get an antibiotic prescription from your doctor (Dr. Applebaum recommends Doxycycline, 100 mg. immediately and 50 mg. every six hours for two to four days). Put a hot compress on the affected area every hour for five or ten minutes, if you can, and step up the nursing on that side. The whole thing should be over in a day or possibly two.

LITTLE PROBLEMS

There are lots of little events in the early days of nursing that may seem like problems because they are new to you. Three months from now you won't even be able to remember them.

Leaking and clothes: If you leak primarily during feedings, you can open both bra cups and hold a clean diaper to the fountaining breast while the baby drinks from the other. Or use handkerchiefs, cut-up diapers, or the nursing pads you can buy at the drugstore, to wear inside your bra. Mild leaks can be controlled with the flannel and plastic liners that may sometimes be bought with nursing bras. Fixed feeding intervals can help if you leak continually. Sometimes you can stop the milk from leaking out by pressing down flat on the nipples with your hands or forearms, when you feel the milk let down.

Low milk supply at suppertime: The early evening meal does seem to be the scantiest. If you have nursed the baby a lot that day, naturally your breasts are empty at suppertime; and yet even newborns sometimes wake up and act hungry when they smell food cooking, so you can find yourself putting the baby to the breast *again* when you sit down to eat. Instead of feeding the baby, let your husband amuse him, or offer the pacifier. After a shower, a drink, and a good dinner, you may find you have a surprisingly ample dividend of milk that will send the baby off to a good sleep.

Too much milk: In the early days of nursing, supply and demand fluctuate. It takes a couple of months for you and the baby to get together, and even then there may be days when you have a little more or a little less milk than he wants. A day of overfilling is sometimes followed by a day of insufficiency. A day of skimpy milk and constant nursing may well be followed by a day of superabundant milk.

If your baby is sleeping six or eight or ten hours at night, so that you wake up every morning groaningly full of milk, you should waken him in the night and feed him. A new baby would probably feed off and on all night, if he slept in your bed. Sleeping separately, he sometimes sleeps through meals that both he and you need. Getting too full every morning tends to lower your total milk production. In another month or two both you and the baby will be able to go longer between feeds.

Night feeds: Just take the baby in bed with you, and doze while he drinks. There's no danger of rolling on him, really. We all do this, and mothers have slept with their babies since the beginning of humanity. You can put him back in his own bed, if and when you wake up.

Criticism: If a friend or relative criticizes you for nursing, reread Chapter 8, to understand why they do it; then turn a deaf ear.

Going out: Don't go out yet, unless you feel very lively and the four walls of your bedroom are really beginning to get you down. If you do go, take the baby—a nursing baby is so portable! Pleasant adult company is sometimes a real tonic, if you are careful not to overexert yourself in new surroundings. Sometimes just a drive in the car is a welcome change of scene, and of course you can nurse the baby in the car. How about a drive-in movie?

IF SORE NIPPLES PERSIST

The chance of nipple soreness diminishes after you have left the hospital and the early days of nursing are past. However, occasionally a nipple can get sore once you are home and should be treated as you would have treated it in the hospital. Sometimes an inexperienced nursing mother gets into trouble because she does not know how to treat a sore nipple, does not want to ask her doctor for fear that he will insist she wean the baby, and so goes on nursing on a nipple that gets worse and worse, until it is really injured. In such a case, where damage is severe, the only thing to do would be to put the baby on a bottle temporarily, removing milk by pump or, if that is too painful, taking dry-up pills and letting milk secretion subside; and then, in two or three weeks or more, when healing is complete, gradually to begin breast-feeding again. See the section in Chapter 12 on "Unweaning a Baby."

NURSING TWINS

It is much, much easier to breast feed twins than it is to fix sixteen sterile bottles of formula every day. It is also much better for the twins, who are often rather small at birth and need the extra boost of mother's milk. Lots of mothers have nursed twins. Dr. Spock, in a *Ladies' Home Journal* survey of mothers of twins, found that the mothers who breast fed twins were far better organized and felt better than the mothers who bottle fed them. La Leche League *News* often reports on League mothers who nurse twins. "From LLL in Denver comes exciting word that Kim Van Diesen had twin girls, Tracy and Kelly, in November. Kim's pediatrician had never known of anyone nursing twins, 'and said so.' The first month the girls each gained 2½ pounds. The following month showed another 2½-pound gain for each. And Kim is such a small person." In the same issue, a Chicago mother of three-month-old twins was reported as doing "just fine—no formula, no solids," despite having another twenty-two-month-old child to chase after.

Most mothers of twins nurse them simultaneously. This seems clumsy at first, but the fact that both breasts are emptied at once when the milk lets down may account for the superabundant milk that nursing mothers provide for their twin babies. In the old days, professional wet nurses probably increased their supplies, in order to feed two or even more babies, by this method of simultaneous feeding. For comfort, try tucking one twin under each arm, supported by pillows or the arms of a big chair. Or put one twin in your lap and use its stomach as a pillow for the other twin. You can expect to have plenty of milk for your twins, without adding cereals or anything else, at least until the combined weight of the twins is twenty or twenty-five pounds. This is usually where they are around five or six months old, when you would begin adding solids anyway.

It is customary to advise mothers of twins to rotate the babies, that is, to nurse each baby on each breast, and not always keep the same baby on the same side. The theory is that the stronger sucker will then be able to stimulate both breasts to higher production. However, in all animals that have multiple young, scientists have found that each baby has its own favorite nipple, and after some confusion in the early days soon learns to go to the same place for every meal. In this way each gland adjusts its secretion of milk to the demands of the particular baby that nurses on it. It may be that human twins can regulate their milk supplies individually and that keeping them always on the same breast would simplify matters. An extreme difference in demand may make you look a bit lop-sided; on the other hand production may differ without any difference in appearance. One mother pumping milk for a sick twin produced thirteen ounces regularly from one breast, and seven from the other, each morning, and yet both breasts were the same size.

The mother nursing twins may have to make a special effort to get enough calories. With supermarket shelves full of unnourishing products such as corn flakes and Jello, it is easy to eat a lot without actually getting much food. To nurse twins (or nurse one baby and give milk to a milk bank) without losing too much weight, a mother may need one or even two extra meals a day, with emphasis on meat and potatoes, and perhaps some hearty snacks as well. Like any nursing mother, if she finds herself losing weight or feeling tired or depressed, she may need additional B complex.

TRIPLETS

Yes, you can breast feed triplets. La Leche League International has more than a dozen mothers in its membership who have successfully nursed triplets. Some mothers feed two at once, some feed them all individually; some keep a schedule and others let all three babies demand-feed. Triplet mothers find themselves spending more time nursing than mothers of single babies, but not as much time as they would spend trying to make all those bottles! Most mothers of triplets feel that the individual love and attention each baby gets while nursing is much more than he would get if bottle fed, and just as important as the milk itself.

Triplet mothers agree that one should hunt before the birth for a cooperative pediatrician. Triplet babies gain just as well as twins and singles, on mother's milk, and do not need early solids or any other supplement, as a rule. Some mothers report that a few ounces of formula may have to be given to one baby on days that the mother is overtired, and that a mother nursing triplets runs a higher-than-normal risk of breast infection if she lets herself get worn out. Triplet mothers need to be very careful to get enough fresh air and exercise and rest, and to eat a nutritious diet themselves. Counseling from an experienced triplets mother is helpful, and can be obtained through La Leche League.

Changes around One Month

A great many babies get weaned to a bottle around the age of one month or six weeks, not because their mothers don't have enough milk, but because the mothers *think* they don't. They lose their confidence because the baby seems to be fussier than ever. Why? First, a one-month-old baby is often a rather crabby soul. He is far more aware of things than he was at two weeks, and that means he is more aware of cold, heat, wet diapers, loneliness, and his not-very-grown-up insides. So he cries. Second, around a month or six weeks after delivery you begin feeling pretty good. You do more. You no longer have household help; you do all the housework, and you are more and more tempted to take up your social life and outside interests again. So you get tired; and the immediate result of your fatigue is a fussy baby. Consider, again: The first treatment for a fussy baby is more rest for the mother. When the baby is not happy or is not getting enough milk, you need to slow down and spend more time peacefully nursing him.

Many of the mothers who quit around the one month mark do so simply because they are discouraged. They feel as if they are going to spend the rest of their lives with a baby at the breast, constantly nursing. There will never be time again for getting the house clean or taking an evening out; they will never sleep through the night again; the idea of breast feeding presents a picture of endless months of being tied to a constantly demanding baby, just as they've been tied in the past four or six weeks.

But this is no time to get discouraged. This is the turning point. From about six weeks onward, breast feeding becomes quite different. The baby rather abruptly drops about two meals a day, so that he is nursing eight times in twenty-four hours, instead of ten. You begin getting one six-hour stretch of sleep at night, and your ever improving let-down reflex works so well that some feedings are over in five or ten minutes, and you hardly notice that you had to lay down your iron or your broom and feed the baby.

Going out becomes easy; you can take the baby, or leave him with a bottle of breast milk. And you begin having the strength to come and go as you please, without detriment to your milk supply. The little problems such as leaking and overfilling will disappear in the weeks to come. These first six weeks have been trying, in some ways: you and your baby have been learning to breast feed; your baby has been adjusting to the strange and not always pleasant world he has been born into; you have been gradually recovering from the prolonged demands of pregnancy, and from the effort of childbirth; if this is the first baby, you have also been making the emotional change over from being a wife to being a wife and mother. These have been demanding tasks, but most of the work is behind you now. At the six week mark, you look forward to a change: the "reward period" of nursing your baby.

12·The Reward Period Begins

CHANGES AFTER TWO MONTHS

You and Your Baby

A new baby is fascinating, but a two-month-old baby is more fun. By two months, a baby is pink and pretty, instead of red and strange-looking. He can "talk" and smile his wonderful smile. He looks at people, and takes an interest in colors, and obviously enjoys the society of his father and any brothers or sisters he is lucky enough to have. He is a lot easier to care for than he was a few weeks previously; he is more content, and when he does want something, you can often "read" his cries and tell if he is hungry, or uncomfortable, or simply lonesome for you.

By the time two months have passed, you feel almost back to normal yourself. The problems associated with the learning days of nursing—leaking, milk fluctuations, nipple soreness—no longer exist. You are beginning to take the reins of the household in your own hands again, and to

213

get out of the house more, sometimes with your baby's company and sometimes without it.

You are beginning, too, to sense the nature of the nursing relationship, the warm spirit of mutual affection that unites the nursing couple. A brand-new baby is having such a time trying to get fed that he hardly has attention for anything more. But a baby of two months looks at you with his bright little eyes as he nurses; he knows you from all other people, and he loves you. He enjoys your company; he waits trustingly for you to feed him, and he wants to be sociable before, during, and after meals. He is no longer a perplexing bundle of contrariness, or a cute but frighteningly helpless doll, to be dressed and undressed and bathed and fussed over; he is your own little friend, and caring for him is second nature, like caring for yourself. Perhaps you used to feel a sense of relief whenever the baby went to sleep, and of apprehension when he stirred; now you find you enjoy having him around and don't worry about him, whether he's asleep or awake. In fact you may feel uncomfortable and anxious if you are away from him. You are becoming a happy, indeed an inseparable, nursing couple.

CONTINUING THE HOLIDAY

Now you can probably safely cut down from three naps a day to two; you can not only do some of the housework, but you can make short excursions, such as doing the marketing, or visiting a friend, or even going out to dinner, without getting too tired. But you are still convalescing, a fact which friends seem to forget. People who wouldn't dream of imposing on someone who is in late pregnancy, sometimes completely overlook a mother's need for rest after delivery. Once the six week mark is past, you may find yourself being considered available again for car pools, bridge games, cub scout leading, and so on and so on. Fortunately, nursing gives you a fine excuse to say no, for the time being. As the baby gets older, you will be able to do all these things, and eventually even hold down a job or go back to school without weaning the baby. Right now you are probably delighted to have such a good reason to avoid whatever jobs and invitations you really don't have the strength or inclination for. One excuse—"I'm so sorry, the doctor has told me not to accept any outside commitments while I'm still nursing the baby"—will take care of everything.

PICKING UP THE BABY

Sometimes babies cry because they are lonely and frightened. Don't think that just because the baby stops crying when you pick him up he's spoiled. That's a favorite remark of grandmothers, and it's very unfair. Of course he stops crying when you pick him up, if picking up was what he needed. He's not "testing" you at this age; he really needs comforting. Scientists are beginning to find that babies need lots of body contact and handling. Plenty of human contact is as important to their emotional growth as plenty of good food is to their physical growth. Isn't it convenient that breast feeding supplies both!

Grandmothers and husbands, and even, or perhaps especially, brothers and sisters, can carry and hold and rock a new baby when he needs comforting and you are busy; they don't have the pleasure of feeding him, so they like to share him in other ways. When you are all alone and your baby is fretful, and yet you are too busy to sit and rock him, you might try that time-honored device, the baby sling or backpack.

NIGHT FEEDINGS

You can expect a breast-fed baby to go on needing at least one night feeding, plus a late evening or very early morning feeding, for five or six months. Your milk supply may need this feeding too. The mother who at this point feels exhausted because she has to feed in the night isn't getting enough rest in the daytime.

CLOTHES

Depressing, isn't it. For months you looked forward to getting your waistline back so that you could wear your own clothes again; and now that your waistline is normal, you still can't get into any of your clothes because you are so bosomy. If there are one or two things in the closet that you can manage to get into, they probably button up the back or zip up the side and are very inconvenient for nursing. The girl who has been flat-chested all her life can enjoy this predicament; in fact, her clothes may fit and look better when she is lactating than when she is not. But even she may have the problem of finding something decent to wear that enables her to nurse the baby without getting completely undressed. This can be crucial when the baby suddenly decides in the middle of a morning of shopping that it is mealtime, and you then realize that you can't nurse him without taking your dress completely off. (Emergency solution: Find a dress shop and nurse him in the fitting room. Fig. 13.)

FIG. 13

The problem of finding clothes that can easily and dis-creetly give nursing access has always been with us. Paint-ings of Madonnas and other mothers from various periods and countries show all kinds of solutions. Some simply take advantage of a rather low-necked dress, perhaps using a shawl for modesty. Others have been portrayed in dresses that unbutton or untie in front, or that have slits concealed in drapery. The most exotic solution is perhaps that shown in a Flemish painting in which the Madonna wears an elaborate, high-necked gown with two rows of gold ornaments down the bodice, which on close inspection are found to be hooks and eyes holding closed an opening on each side.

Things are easier nowadays. All you need are a few things that pull up from the waist or button down the front: cardigans, skirts and shirts or overblouses, shirt-waist dresses. Since you'll be nursing for quite a while, you'll probably find it's worth buying a couple of unbut-toning drip-dry shirts or blouses to wear when you and the baby go out of the house. Pick material that won't show dark wet spots if you should happen to leak. To nurse dis-creetly, unbutton the *bottom* buttons rather than the top.

The most convenient and least revealing kind of tops are those which do *not* unbutton, but which can be lifted from the waist for nursing: overblouses, jerseys, sweaters, and so on. Some kind of pull-up-able top is invaluable if you want to nurse the baby while you have visitors, and hate to miss the conversation; or while traveling, or at a movie, or indeed anywhere away from home. The baby covers your slightly exposed midriff, your sweater or blouse conceals your breast, and you will find that no one can tell whether you are nursing the baby or whether you are just holding him.

Nursing bras were discussed briefly in Chapter 10. You do not have to wear a nursing bra, although they are con-venient. You can nurse in an ordinary bra by unhooking the back or by slipping a strap off your shoulder. In fact, you do not absolutely have to wear a bra at all, unless of course you are uncomfortable without one. A good bra can improve circulation by uplifting a drooping breast; it can keep you comfortable when you are very full; and it improves the line of your clothes. But a bra that hikes up in back and sags in front doesn't do any of these things, and the bra that is too tight may impede circulation and milk flow. How much a bra does to protect your figure is a matter of opinion, and perhaps of heredity. One woman who wears bras night and day, massages the skin of her breasts with lanolin during pregnancy, and forgoes nursing lest she damage her figure, may still wind up with striations and loss of shape; while another mother who can't stand bras and never wears them may bear and nurse three or four babies without losing the upstanding bosom she started with. So it's up to you. If you really want to be cautious, then wear a well-fitted bra twenty-four hours a day while you are nursing and for six months after weaning.

Slips sometimes present a problem in nursing access. Half-slips are the simplest answer, but if you don't care for them you can alter full-bodice slips by cutting the straps free of the bodice in front, and then sewing hooks onto the slip straps and eyes onto your bra straps. You can hook the straps together, and tuck the top edge of the slip into the top of your bra, or pin it to the drop cup so that it opens and closes with the bra. Sometimes department stores carry strapless slips to wear under summer dresses. These have shirred cotton backs and an elastic top, and are perfect for the nursing mother.

If you sew neatly you can sometimes alter a one-piece dress that has no front opening, by opening up the darts under the bust. If there is enough material the two sides of the dart can be overlapped and snaps sewn in; or you can filch a little material from the hem of the dress to face the dart edges with.

Fresh Air

You should try to spend at least half an hour walking outdoors every day, even if it's winter. Take the baby; it's good for him, too. Being indoors all day tends to make you concentrate too much on your indoor work and the imperfections of your surroundings. You actually need sunshine, in any case, for vitamin D. A short walk in the late afternoon improves your appetite for dinner, and lifts your spirits too. And maybe it helps your milk supply. Dairymen have demonstrated that cows give more milk at the evening milking if they are turned out of the barn for an hour or so in the afternoon.

Nursing Away from Home

Many nursing mothers really dislike leaving their small babies behind, no matter how competent the baby sitter; often the happy nursing couple hates to be separated, even briefly, during these early months. So take the baby along. It is just as easy to take a nursing baby with you as it is to leave him at home and then miss him all evening. All you need is a blanket and a couple of extra diapers; the bottle-feeding mother may have to portage half a drugstore. Nursing babies are usually cheery and quiet, if they are near their mothers; you can take a small nursing baby on a camping trip, to a dinner party or a restaurant, a football game or a formal dance, with complete aplomb. Feed him in the car on the way there. If he is hungry again before it is time to leave, take him to some quiet corner such as your hostess' bedroom, and feed him again; and that will usually hold him until the drive home.

To take the baby shopping with you, or to the park, feed him just before you leave the house (plan on taking time to do it; don't hustle him, you might hurt his feelings). Or you can feed him in the car, after you get where you're going. This will give you a reasonable amount of time before he is hungry again.

If you must feed the baby before you get back to the car probably the most comfortable place to do so is a ladies' lounge. Usually there is a chair or couch where you can sit. Buy a magazine to read, if you don't want people to talk to you. Don't feel self-conscious about other women noticing you; you'll find that most will go by without noticing, except for an occasional older woman who will be delighted to see a young mother nursing, and an occasion-

al mother who will look at you longingly and then tell you
how she tried and failed to nurse.

In emergencies you will probably find that you can
nurse quite unnoticed even in public places such as a park
bench or a restaurant booth. You will *feel* conspicuous but
you won't be nearly as conspicuous as you would be with
a screaming, hungry baby in your arms. Or you can do as
one city-dwelling mother does, and take a bottle of your
own expressed milk with you to give the baby if he gets
hungry when circumstances prohibit nursing.

MANUAL EXPRESSION

Expressing your milk manually is a skill that is easier
for some than for others. It's a handy knack to acquire if
you must go out in the evening and would like to leave
some milk for the baby, or if you need to relieve your own
overfullness while you and the baby are apart. It's a necessary skill if you must leave the baby often or long.

To get started, massage the breast from its perimeter towards the center for a minute or so, then compress the
areola, behind the nipple, between your thumb and the
knuckle of your first finger, squeezing the milk within the
sinuses out the nipple. If your milk does not let-down, try
for no more than five minutes a side, and try again in an
hour or so. Or stand under a warm shower and try expressing; this usually works like a charm. A warm bath is
relaxing, too, and you can catch the milk in a cup and save
it. Like any other skill, manual expression gets easier with
practice. To save the milk, pour it into sterilized bottles
and freeze it. It freezes in layers, which looks funny, but it
will mix again when thawed.

RELIEF BOTTLE

If you express all the milk left in each breast after each
feeding, in twenty-four hours you will probably have at
least four ounces. Express it into a boiled, sterile, wide-
mouthed baby bottle and keep it in the refrigerator or the
freezer. You can use this if you want to take the baby to

church or some other place where nursing would be inconvenient, or if you want to leave the baby behind with a sitter.

Some nursing babies do not like the taste of formula, but will take a bottle if it contains breast milk. Some will refuse a bottle in any case, and would rather wait until you get home. You'll find that the older your baby gets the more obliging he is; if you come home from an evening out, absolutely bursting with milk, the baby will gladly nurse and ease your discomfort, even if he *has* had a bottle.

SEX AND NURSING

The closeness of a mother and her nursing baby, while it brings joy to the father, sometimes partially eclipses the mother's need for other close relationships, including sex. This may in part be due to temporary abeyance of the menstrual cycle, with its mood swings and peaks of desire. The nursing mother may feel compliant about sexual relations without actually being eager. Perhaps also nursing a baby provides some of the fringe benefits of sex; closeness to another person, a feeling of being admired and cherished, and the reassurance that one is needed and wanted; and so a mother may turn less often to her husband for the balm of touching and physical closeness. Husbands need the balm and reassurance of physical closeness too, of course, and a mother who notices a reduced need for sex in herself during lactation should take thought to be generous and affectionate to her man.

Some women on the other hand find that the experience of lactation intensifies their physical affection for their husband. The hormonal patterns of sex and of lactation are very closely allied. One mother, having nursed her first child, found that from then on, when her husband kissed and fondled her breasts, she was swept by a palpable wave of deep affection, almost adoration, such as she had once felt for her infant. The play of hormones can be downright startling. Oxytocin, the hormone responsible for the letdown reflex, is also released during orgasm. Many a couple has been astonished to discover that, as the wife reaches climax, her milk may let down so sharply that it sprays into the air six inches or more in twin tiny-streamed fountains, likely as not catching her unwary mate full in the face. This phenomenon, like accidental let-down in other circumstances, generally abates as lactation becomes more fully established and the let-down reflex more controlled.

An occasional baby, even a tiny baby, seems invariably to wake up and fuss and want attention precisely when its parents are making love: an aggravating situation, especially for fathers! Perhaps such an infant should sleep in another room, with the door closed, at least some of the time.

Some men, due to their own upbringing, feel conflict about whether a nursing mother's breasts belong to the husband or to the baby. Some doctors, no doubt with conflicts of their own, warn against the dangers of infection if a husband touches the wife's breasts or kisses them, during lactation. In fact there is nothing in mutually agreeable love play that should be avoided during lactation; a couple can be as free with each other's bodies then as at any other time; and if a little milk comes into the picture one way or another, it's harmless, and the baby won't miss it. There's always more where that came from.

In our culture some parents and more than a few grandparents feel a little uneasy about a boy baby nursing at his mother's breasts for more than a few months. Nursing is such an intense physical pleasure for a baby that it is not uncommon for boy babies to have erections as they nurse —they often do so before urinating, too—and the thought of a male child still nursing when he is "old enough to know what he is doing," (whatever age that might be!) seems to have disquieting sexual overtones. While it is a rather difficult thing to demonstrate scientifically, the practical experience of many families suggests that male and female nursing babies alike take their mothers' bodies for granted in a healthy, accepting way, no matter how long they are nursed. One might speculate that the fetishistic attitude of many American men towards the female breast is at least partly due to having been deprived during infancy of the experience of long nursing, and a natural awareness and acceptance of the female body.

EARLY FEEDING OF SOLID FOODS

Breast-fed babies do not need any "solid" foods until they are five or six months old. Bottle-fed babies *do* need these early supplements, because cow's milk does not contain all the nourishment they should have. (Chapter 3.) Some doctors do not take this into account and prescribe early solids anyway. Your breast-fed baby does not need solid foods to be "satisfied," no matter how big and husky he is. A pacifier will do just as well, or an extra nursing on a fussy day. Every mouthful of cereal or fruit you put into him simply substitutes for the most nutritious breast milk.

Young breast-fed babies often act as if they knew this. They cry and struggle when getting their solid foods, or they take only a mouthful or two. It is a sad sight to see a mother trying desperately to do as her doctor ordered (do doctors know how seriously we take their instructions, when we're inexperienced?) and get two tablespoons of apple sauce down a frantic, crying baby. One such mother wrote about this problem to a nationally syndicated medical columnist. Her doctor had ordered her to feed her small baby solids, "as much as she wants," the baby fought every mouthful, and mealtimes had them both in tears. The columnist doctor responded with three hundred words on how to get a little cereal into a reluctant baby, and then scolded the mother for "taking the job of mothering too seriously." No one suggested that it was not the job of mothering, nor the baby's important feelings, but the doctor's important-sounding rules that were being taken too seriously.

So forget about solid foods right now, despite the brochures and free samples from baby food companies that are arriving in the mailbox. (Of course those companies are interested in seeing you start solids early.) Sometime between four and six months your baby will begin showing eager interest in what the rest of the family is eating. You can safely wait until then.

VITAMINS

Breast milk is a much better source of the vitamins babies need than is cow's milk. Your nursing baby does not really need vitamin drops, especially if you take the vitamins yourself. Most nursing babies hate the strong taste of vitamins; why make them suffer?

The one exception is vitamin D, which comes from sunlight. You and your baby should both get half an hour or so of sunlight every day, if you possibly can. If you cannot get any sunlight because of the climate you at least should take a vitamin D supplement.

ALWAYS: FLUCTUATIONS

Babies grow and mothers recuperate somewhat in the style of the algebra problem involving the frog in the well that jumped up two feet and fell back one. Sometimes a three-month-old baby goes on a four hour schedule for a day, like a much older baby; sometimes he falls back to eating like a much younger baby for a while. You too may find you gain strength in spurts, as it were, and occasionally fall back to needing that extra nap or rest period you had been doing without.

Your milk supply will fluctuate somewhat, in relation to sucking stimulus. If your baby is a steady, hearty eater, who wants the same big meals day after day, you may experience very little fluctuation; with the Gourmet type of baby who may want a banquet today and only hors d'oeuvres tomorrow, your milk supply may often be in a state of change. Also you can continue to expect occasional frequency days, when your baby nurses extra hungrily, thus emptying the breasts and stimulating milk production to rise, over a period of the next day or two, until supply again equals demand.

At three months your baby will probably get his first immunization shot, the DPT shot which protects him against diphtheria, tetanus, and whooping cough. This will make him fussy and feverish, and he may want to nurse off and on all day, purely for the comfort of it. The mother who has raised both bottle-fed and breast-fed babies can really appreciate what a blessing it is to have such a sure-fire way of comforting a fretful baby.

CHANGES AT THREE AND FOUR MONTHS

While the growing baby can now get a full meal in five or ten minutes, he sometimes likes to nurse on and on until he falls asleep at the breast, now dozing, now and then sucking, until you finally lay him down, still dreaming of sweet milk, and sucking in his dreams. To get the baby to bed without wakening, take him off the breast, and hold him until he subsides again. Then take him to his crib and lay him down, but keep your hand on his back, if he stirs, until he sleeps once more. It is sudden desertion that makes him roar.

Around four months, the baby develops a new trick. He interrupts himself. Suddenly he is very interested in noises, the human voice especially. If someone else in the room starts talking, or if you speak suddenly while nursing, the baby may drop the nipple and jerk his head around to locate the voice. He may jerk his head around without letting go too! The TV distracts him, and you may find you can't even read a magazine, because he gets interrupted by the rustle of the turning pages. An exceptionally aware baby may be unable to start nursing again when interrupted by noises, or may cry at such interruptions.

Fortunately, in about two weeks the baby will have learned to nurse and listen at the same time. Meanwhile, keep your own voice down while nursing; put your hand over the baby's ear, to keep sounds out; and sit so that the baby can see the source of any disturbance. If he does break away from the breast, you can usually coax him back with soothing words and a gentle pat.

Once the baby has learned to look, listen, and drink at the same time, he takes a genuine interest in his surroundings, watching the faces of others as he nurses. By five

Fig. 14

months, if you cover his ear, he will reach up and pull your hand away; he wants to hear everything. He may also play at the breast, waving his free hand about and watching it, playing with your clothes, patting your face. A five-month-old baby is apt to get hold of a button on your blouse and try and put it in his mouth, while he is nursing. He loves to watch your mouth as you talk to him while he eats, and his biggest problem is trying to smile at you and nurse at the same time. (Fig. 14.)

Another feature of the four- or five-month-old baby's awareness of the world is that he may refuse to take a bottle. Although you may have left him with a sitter before, and he may have taken bottles occasionally in the past, he suddenly refuses them. Now, apparently, he would rather wait for his own warm, good-smelling mother, and her sweet milk, than drink heaven-knows-what from a cold glass and rubber contraption in the arms of a baby sitter. Luckily, by his age he can wait three or four hours in the daytime, which is long enough for you to get errands done without him. And in the evenings almost every baby is willing to eat at five or six, and then sleep through until one or two in the morning. This gives you enough span for an occasional night out. You may be able to get around his persnicketiness by leaving a bottle of breast milk or by having the sitter offer milk in a cup or spoon. In a month or two the baby will accept the bottle again.

THE BABY SLING

The oldest labor-saving device in the world is probably the baby sling. Every human society seems to have some version of it, some way to carry a baby comfortably and safely on your body instead of in your arms.

Many families nowadays "backpack" the baby instead of using a stroller, out in public. But have you ever thought of doing it at home, when you have a thousand things to do, and the baby is fussy and fretful with a stomachache or a tooth coming in, or plain lonesomeness? Mothers who have tried this are astonished at the tranquility it produces. There is something extremely soothing to a baby about being closely, snugly, wrapped on his mother's warm, loving back, looking over her shoulder at the interesting things she is doing, or being lulled to sleep simply by the rhythm of her breathing and moving. A half-hour of being carried on someone's back may tranquilize a baby all day. One mother says that when she has company coming for dinner she always carries the baby for an hour or so while she is cleaning up and getting the meal started; then the baby is quite happy to be alone in playpen or crib while she cooks and talks with her guests.

Carrying your baby properly, on your back (or on your chest, if it is a tiny baby), is far less tiring than carrying him in your arms. You can carry quite a heavy baby for hours and never notice it. Did you ever see pictures of children in India or China, with heavy baby brothers or sisters on their backs, and wonder how they did it? The answer is that the weight is properly located. Your legs are doing most of the work, rather than your easily fatigued back and arm muscles. Carrying the baby in a sling can actually make you feel better, because it improves your posture; the extra weight keeps you from slumping and slouching. Meanwhile, you have both hands free to peel potatoes and dust and iron. And you can get more work done because you aren't being interrupted to soothe a fussy baby. Some psychologists feel that the warm, impersonal body contact provided by a sling is more soothing and beneficial to the baby than lots of cooing and fussing and playing with him would be.

There are two excellent baby carriers available on the market. The "Happy Baby Carrier" is a cloth sling-seat which can be worn either on your back or your chest. It comes in a range of prices, according to fabric, from $8.95 to $11.95, and can be ordered from La Leche League International or from Happy Baby Carrier, 932 Calle Miramar, Redondo Beach, California 90277. They also sell a doll-size Happy Baby Carrier and a doll to go with it for little girls who want to be like their mothers.

Another excellent product is the Gerry Carrier. This is an aluminum-framed baby backpack which will hold a baby from five months to two and one-half years. I have also seen it used for six-month-old twins, facing sideways, back to back. This is a well-engineered piece of equipment, a favorite with fathers, and a godsend for the hundred-pound mother with a twenty-five pound year-old baby. Prices run from $10 to $16 in baby stores and department stores, or the carrier may be ordered from Gerry Designs, Inc., P. O. Box 998, Boulder, Colorado 80302. At the La Leche League Convention in 1971, among fifteen hundred mothers I saw one stroller, but hundreds of babies in Gerry Carriers or Happy Baby Carriers.

Psychologists point out that the backpacked baby, in addition to feeling loved and secure from body contact, meets the world at eye level and facing forward, which is better for his confidence and morale than seeing everything from knee-level in a stroller.

Gerry Designs, Inc. also provide an excellent strap system for keeping a baby or toddler safe in an automobile, while allowing him more freedom and comfort than a car seat gives.

TRAVELING

Traveling is much, much easier with a nursing baby than with a bottle-fed baby. In the first place, your baby doesn't care where he is as long as he's with you. Nursing is such a comfort and reassurance to him that your lap and your arms make even the strangest places quite acceptable. He doesn't cry for his familiar crib, or get thrown off schedule because he happens to be on an airplane or in a car; you, not cribs and schedules, are the center of his world, so he is completely nonchalant about travel. You can accompany your husband on a six weeks' business trip, or a fishing trip in the wilderness, and take your baby along, and all three of you will enjoy yourselves.

FIG. 15

Nursing is infinitely more practical than bottle feeding while you are on the move. The logistics of supplying a baby with sterile formula during, say, a car trip from New York to California are formidable. Pity the poor bottle-feeding mother, with her insulated bag of formula (How long will it stay cold? How long will it be safe to use?)

heating a bottle under hot water in the motel sink, while the baby screams; or, several days from home, mixing dry milk powder with tap water in a far from sterile bottle and hoping the baby "won't mind." The breast-fed baby is the *only* baby who can be safely taken traveling in the Near East, Africa, rural Latin America, or other spots where sanitation is poor. If your husband is likely to be stationed abroad, or if you have a chance to travel for some other reason, this is a real point in favor of making breast feeding a success.

FIG. 16

If you plan to fly with your nursing baby, you may want to choose a night flight. Darkness, and fewer passengers moving up and down the aisles, mean more privacy for you. Get to the airport early and select the first seat in a given row. For the person in this seat a bassinette or baby bed can usually be affixed to the bulkhead or partition, so you won't have to hold the baby all the time. Some foreign airlines, such as TEAL in the Pacific, have a "nursing corner" on the plane, a curtained alcove that will provide you with privacy for nursing. But you really don't need this. With a two piece suit that can be lifted from the waist, even the stewardess won't be able to tell that you are nursing, and may be very perplexed because you don't ask her to warm a bottle for the baby.

While you are traveling, let your husband do the work. Your baby depends on you not to get exhausted; and if you get overtired your baby will respond by being fussy, and spoiling the trip. You can keep rested if you stay cool, don't rush, and let your husband do all the driving and cope with tickets and baggage. If you must travel alone, plan your schedule reasonably, so that you will have time for some relaxation. It's not impossible; one professional woman recently took her five-month-old nursing baby on a lecture tour, with complete success.

IF YOU EVER FEEL LIKE QUITTING

Sometimes, when you are feeling tired, or your milk seems skimpy, or some relative is pressuring you to do things her way and put your baby on the bottle, it seems easy to say, "Well, I've nursed this baby three months—or four, or five—I'll put him on a bottle now, and perhaps I'll have better luck and be able to nurse the next one longer."

Don't kid yourself. First, you'll never again have as much time or leisure as you have with the first baby, in which to learn the womanly art of breast feeding. Secondly, it is a common fallacy to assume that breast feeding becomes less and less valuable as the baby grows older. From the nutritional standpoint this may be so. But breast feeding continues to provide protection against illness, for as long as it is continued; this can be extremely valuable for a baby of eight months or even eighteen months, just as it is for one of a few weeks. Nursing continues to be practical, too, saving time, smoothing out stresses, and keeping the baby happy, healthy, and close, for as long as it continues. Unless you have really decided that this biological femininity bit is for the birds, keep nursing; you'll be glad you did.

How to Unwean a Baby

Suppose somewhere in the last few weeks you lost your confidence, or your doctor came out strongly for bottle feeding, or you suffered some misadventure such as mastitis, and you are now giving your baby supplementary formula. There is no reason why you cannot gradually build up your supply again until your baby is entirely breast fed. If you don't make the effort to eliminate bottle feeding entirely, your milk supply will continue to dwindle until the baby is entirely bottle-fed.

If your baby is receiving a total of four to six ounces of formula a day, whether in one feeding or in small portions after several feedings, pick a day when you can count on peace and quiet, and omit the formula altogether. Nurse the baby several extra times during the day for as long as he will nurse. That is what will bring your supply back. It will probably take forty-eight hours—two days and two nights—of long and frequent feedings before you notice results. (Extra feedings at night should be compensated for by an extra nap in the daytime.) On the third day your supply will have increased more than enough to make up for the amount of supplement the baby was getting.

If your baby is getting *more* than the equivalent of one bottle, remove the bottles one at a time. Of course he will be hungry. You want him to be. When you have cut out, say, the morning bottle, for three or four days, and your milk is making up the difference, cut out one more bottle. Again he will be hungry; again your supply will rise. Over a period of three weeks or so, you should be able to feed him all by yourself again, and he will be gaining well and thriving.

Sometimes a baby who has gotten used to a bottle can be very unpleasant about being asked to nurse on a nearly empty breast. He sucks for a moment and then screams and wrenches away. Try the midwife's trick of putting honey on the nipples; once he is nursing, you can soothe him so that he stays on the breast, by rocking, patting him, and talking or singing to him. You can also try luring him on by using an eyedropper to trickle a little milk into the corner of his mouth as he nurses; this will encourage him to redouble his efforts.

If your baby is far along the road to being weaned to the bottle, and you are now nevertheless anxious to bring him back to the breast, you might find helpful a device called "Lact-aid," designed to speed up the process of "relactation," or re-establishment of a milk supply. See page 258, "Relactation."

It is always worth making the effort of unweaning a young baby, if only for the pleasures and convenience of being able to nurse him for as many months as he needs you to do so; but it is especially worthwhile if you have a family history of allergy, or if your baby is the type who is allergic or who catches colds easily, and who needs the extra protection only mothers' milk can give.

THE WORKING MOTHER

Some mothers have no choice but to go back to work while their babies are still small. If you must work and still wish to breast feed, it's quite possible; many others have done it. First, consider whether you could work at home; if you are a teacher, perhaps you could tutor at home instead of working at a school, for example. Or you might consider a night job, which would free you to nurse in the daytime. Or you might do what working mothers do in Jamaica, and teach the baby to nurse at night and sleep during the day. Try not to go back to work until you are physically strong. If you're not ready you can get sick or worn out and it will cost you more in recuperating time in the long run.

It's easier to work and nurse if you don't start until the baby is four or five months old. How does it work? You nurse the baby in bed before breakfast—such a peaceful way to start the day. Some mothers express a bottle of milk before the first morning feeding, and leave it for the baby's lunch. Then you go to work. You may find you have to express your milk at the lunch hour to keep from overfilling; if you have access to a refrigerator, this milk can be saved. Then you nurse the baby once again when you get home, once before bedtime, and perhaps once in the night.

One mother, a school teacher, went to work when her baby was three weeks old and still nursed for five months. She drank a milk shake and pumped her breasts first thing in the morning. Then she nursed the baby and took the morning's milk in a bottle to the sitter's. On her half-hour lunch break she went to the school nurse's room and expressed her milk, which took twenty minutes to do, and ate her sandwich in the remaining ten minutes. The milk went into the home-ec teacher's freezer. After work she took the frozen milk to the baby sitter's and left it in her freezer for the next day.

Working mothers agree that you must have an understanding husband who will help you as much as possible at home and with the baby. A cooperative baby-sitter is important, too. One working mother took her sitter to the La Leche League meetings so she could share the mother's enthusiasm for breast feeding.

Rest is also vitally important if you are working and nursing. Lie down in a dark room with the bare baby against bare you and rest and nurse when you first get home; the skin contact is calming for both of you. Lie down on the couch to nurse or to play with your older children. Extra B complex vitamins will help remarkably to reduce your fatigue; you are really carrying a stressful load and you need them. Brewer's yeast is the best all-around source. Watch your nutrition, make sure you get enough calories and protein. Take care of yourself.

Paradoxically, when the baby is nine or ten months old or older, it is almost easier to work or finish school if the baby is nursing than if he is not. The closeness of the nursing relationship, the reassurance of the breast when you come home each day, makes your absences easier for the baby to tolerate, and makes him a cheerier, less demanding baby when you are home.

No matter what the baby's age, the mother who works and nurses should really be proud of herself. She is working extra hard and doing the best she can do for her child.

CHANGES AROUND FIVE MONTHS

A five-month-old baby has probably settled down to two naps a day. He may sleep ten hours at night, especially if his mother is well rested so that daytime nursings are ample. He has learned to anticipate, and whimpers or calls for meals rather than crying. He is well aware of the difference between you dressed and you undressed, and will lie quietly in your arms while you uncover the breast. However, he will roar in righteous indignation if you answer his whimper by picking him up, and then put him down again before you feed him!

This is probably the peak of the nursing cycle. Soon your baby will be taking more and more nourishment from other sources. Now he is still growing fast, and has reached nearly twice his birth weight, and may be taking one and a half pints or even a quart of milk from you every day. You find this reflected in your own larger appetite and greater thirst. You may find, too, that some of your physical energy is definitely being given to milk making. Even though you feel strong and are getting plenty of rest, unusual physical exercise such as pushing a lawn mower or scrubbing a ceiling may leave you breathless and drenched with perspiration. If so, put off all the heavy jobs for a few more weeks; you will find that you can tackle them with greater efficiency when your nursing baby is seven or eight months old.

A baby of five or six months has a characteristic gesture in coming to the breast. The arms are raised, fists clenched; when he nurses, the baby hugs his mother, one arm on each side of the breast; he may or may not hold on to her clothes. This gesture enables him to home in on the breast almost without help from her, and is especially useful at night; it also helps to keep him in the nursing position even when his mother, carrying him on one arm, gets up to answer the phone or turn down the stove. You can see this gesture in a bottle-feeding baby of the same age, who raises his clenched fists up on either side of his head while he drinks; but of course in his case the utility of this apparently instinctive gesture is lost.

Around five months a baby may suddenly become extremely efficient at the breast. He hardly gets started before he's all through, and wants to get down and play, and you can't believe he got any milk in that brief time. Actually the baby nurses so strongly and the milk lets down so well that he may easily empty both breasts and get a full meal in five minutes or less. Don't interpret this speed as a sign that he is losing interest in the breast. It is still an important part of his life.

Solid Foods

You can tell that a baby who is nearing the six month mark is ready for solid foods. His first teeth are coming in, and with them an urge to put everything he gets hold of into his mouth. This may soothe his gums and it also serves to teach him the difference between food and nonfood. He can put finger and thumb together and pick up a crust of bread. He can creep about. If the adults of the family sat on the ground and ate with their hands, as our cave men ancestors must have done, this baby would be ready to join right in and help himself.

Doctors usually recommend that you start the baby on mashed bananas and cereal, which are both digestible and tasty. Since your baby is not used to spoons, he may bite down or try to spit the spoon out. Lay him in your lap and sort of drop the food into his mouth. He'll catch on quickly, and will soon be sitting up and leaning forward, with his mouth open like a baby bird. When he is taking puréed fruits and cereals, you can add other foods, according to your doctor's instructions. Because of the current fashion of starting solid foods very early, your doctor may have been loading you up with free samples. But since until now your baby has been thriving on nature's menu alone, you have probably put all the little cans and jars on the shelf. Canned puréed baby foods are very convenient, especially for the bottle-fed baby who must have food supplements very early in life, and cannot handle anything that is not virtually a liquid. But you may find that your baby regards these preparations as being pretty insipid, and is much more interested in sitting at the family board and helping himself with his fingers to everything that looks good. He can manage anything he can mash up with his tongue and gums, and will enjoy scrambled eggs, cottage cheese, avocado, bologna, cooked carrot or sweet potato, pieces of soft pear or melon, bread, rice and so on. He also likes something fairly firm to hold in his hand and chew on: A beef hot dog is excellent since it doesn't make crumbs or leave juice. A cube of cheese will be relished, as well as a hard old heel of bread for trying those teeth on. Don't bother with the packaged teething biscuits; they make a sticky mess and contain a lot of sugar, to start your baby on the road to the dentist.

The most useful of the prepared baby foods are the meats which provide the protein and iron your baby is beginning to need. Prepared "dinners" seem to be mostly starch; they are handy for traveling or other emergencies if your baby likes them but are not as valuable as the good fresh food from your own table.

The principles to follow in choosing your baby's foods are the same principles of good nutrition that you follow in feeding the rest of the family. His meals should be high in meats, vegetables, fruits, and whole-grain bread or cereals, and low on sugar, fats, and calories-only foods such as puddings and noodles. If you have other small children he can probably eat just about what they eat, either from a high chair or a less tippy low feeding table. Both he and your other children will enjoy being together at mealtime.

THE CUP

A baby of five or six months may enjoy drinking water and juice from a cup, or he may refuse it. You can also offer regular cow's milk in a cup (if your doctor agrees), but chances are your baby won't take it. The breast-fed baby's usual reaction to his first cup of milk is to taste it, and then laugh and push it away, as if that were the most ludicrous place to find milk. By nine or ten months, when he can manage a cup more or less by himself, he will take more pleasure in drinking from it.

BITING

About this time your nursing baby may try out his teeth on you. Usually he will do this at the end of a meal; so if he shows an inclination to bite don't let him dawdle, but take him off the breast as soon as he seems to be through. If he does bite you can tell him firmly that he may *not,* and take him right off the breast. After one or two tries, he'll get the idea. Occasionally a baby of six or eight months may bite deliberately, if you try to feed him—perhaps because you are planning to go out—when he isn't hungry.

REFUSING A BREAST

Occasionally a baby will develop a predilection for nursing from one breast but not the other. A smart baby will sometimes reject one breast temporarily because you have tried to slip him vitamin drops or medicine while he was nursing on that breast. You can fool the baby into taking the "wrong" breast by holding him under your arm instead of across your lap, so that the breast he has been rejecting is on the same side of his face as the one he likes would normally be.

Of course you could nurse him on one breast only, if you had to.

Sometimes the baby is taking so much solid food as well as milk in a cup that he is actually weaning himself, without your knowing it. One can, without noticing it, favor one breast for convenience, so that the baby nurses longer and more often on that side. Then the other breast will produce less and involute more rapidly. As the milk supply wanes, it reverts somewhat to colostrum in both taste and appearance, and the baby may come to reject the breast because the milk in it really does taste different to him.

FATIGUE

Around five or six months is another "danger" period, similar to that around one month or six weeks, when a great many mothers wean their babies. The reasons are the same: the baby is bigger, the mother is going out more, and doing more, and getting too tired. The baby responds by being fussy and wanting to nurse more often, and it seems as if the milk is going. Or the baby is doing well but the mother feels tired all the time, and the convenience and pleasure of nursing no longer seem worthwhile.

Fatigue starts a vicious circle. It is only when you are tired that dust under the bed or dirty windows or a clutter of toys seem unbearable, so that you drive yourself to do more and more work just when you most need the rest. Poor nutrition also contributes to a feeling of fatigue, and again the fatigue kills your appetite, so that your nutritional situation becomes worse and you lose weight, and *that* makes you feel tired.

At this point many mothers find that a B complex supplement such as brewer's yeast makes all the difference. Synthesized B complex vitamin pills may also help but don't seem to be as effective over a long period of time as is brewer's yeast.

SPACE-AGE HOUSEKEEPING

No woman ever got all her work done. One prominent psychiatrist says, "Show me a woman with a perfectly kept house and I'll show you a woman with deep psychological problems." Take a tip from newspaper columnist Heloise Cruse: It's not the dirt and dust that gets us down, it's the mess and clutter and disorganization in the house. What we need are a few quick ways of getting the effect of neatness; then we feel like good housekeepers, and there is more time and strength left for enjoying husbands and babies, and for other housekeeping tasks that take effort but don't really show.

As Heloise suggests: When your husband leaves for work, quickly make the bed; then at least *something's* done. Put the breakfast dishes (all right, and last night's dinner dishes too) in the sink, and cover them with hot soapy water. That gets them out of sight, and meanwhile the grease and food is soaking loose. Then take a very big paper bag, and walk around the living room and bedrooms, putting everything into the bag that needs to be disposed of: crumbs, ashes, newspapers, magazines, opened envelopes, bits of toys, and all the other clutter a room acquires in a day. You can put pillows back and gather up toys as you go. Don't put everything away separately; never walk down a hall or up the stairs with just one or two things in your hands. Put things that belong in other rooms in a pile at the door, then take them along when you're going there anyway.

Then take a pad of toilet tissue, wet it with alcohol, and quickly wipe the bathroom fixtures. Alcohol is cheap, disinfectant, leaves no odor, and makes chrome shine. Then with a broom or carpet sweeper, quickly clean up the middle of the living room and kitchen.

Now, sit down and relax. You've worked about fifteen minutes, and your house is clean and neat looking. If someone drops in, you won't be embarrassed. If you never get a chance to do another thing all day, you're still ahead, because the depressing, overwhelming mess is gone.

Later on, you can rinse off those dishes—that's about all they need, after all that soaking—and start the laundry. Then plan what you're going to have for dinner. That way there will be no last minute scramble in the cupboards at five o'clock, only to find out that you don't have some ingredients you need, or that the dinner you do have available should have been started an hour ago.

In the late afternoon, take a walk in the sunshine. Then, just before your husband comes home, go around the living room quickly, and set the table. He will see that everything is nice and neat, and if the table is set, he'll feel optimistic about the chances of getting dinner pretty soon— even if it won't be ready for an hour, or even if *he* is going to cook it. Then you have time to sit down with him over a drink, or a cup of soup, nurse the baby, hear the day's news, and relax.

This kind of quick "top cleaning" is more important than all the other jobs, such as vacuuming under beds and washing windows, because this is what soothes your nerves, and takes away that feeling of pressure and futility. To make it even easier:

1. Go through every room in the house and throw or give away everything that you haven't used in a year. (Heloise Cruse suggests that you do this when you are mad; you'll be more ruthless.) That dress you were planning to make over but never will, that waffle iron that always burns the waffles, all the old clothes that no one is wearing, that fill up your closet and drawers and crowd and wrinkle the clothes that you do wear, that ugly chafing dish you don't use, and all that stuff in the kitchen drawer that you might want sometime. Have you wanted it in the past year? No! Then throw it out! Give it to the Salvation Army; they will be glad to have it. It's much easier to keep half-empty closets and shelves clean and orderly. Do you really use those hand towels? Will you ever mend that old sheet? The fewer linens and clothes and possessions you can get along with, the fewer things you will have to wash and clean and sweep around.

2. Before you acquire something in the way of furniture or interior decorations stop and think: Will this make my life easier, or harder? Will it have to be cleaned, or guarded from scratches? As La Leche League suggests, before buying something for the house, ask yourself: Wouldn't I rather have that nice empty corner or bare tabletop?

3. Confine the children's toys to one room. Concentrate on toys that are discarded after use, such as paper dolls, or on activity toys that are sturdy and can be used by several children, instead of clutter toys with a hundred parts for you to pick up. Big baskets or even cardboard boxes are good for keeping toys—and boots and sporting equipment —in one spot and out of sight. Convenience is more important than style.

4. To quote the La Leche League manual, order before

prettiness, convenience before style, and above all, people before things. Sure, it would be great to have the floors waxed all the time, like those on the TV commercials, and to have interiors with that un-lived-in look, like the cover of a magazine. But it is far more vital that you get a nap, and a walk in the sunshine, and time to nurse your baby. It is far more vital to do just a little jiffy top cleaning and save your strength and good humor for smiling at your family and listening to what they have to say. Your husband wants a certain amount of neatness, but most of all, he wants your good company. Your children need clean clothes and hot food, but most of all they need a cheerful, loving mother. People—including yourself—before things.

For a wonderful collection of back-saving, time-saving, morale-saving suggestions from a Navy wife who really sympathizes with housewives because she is one, read *Heloise's Housekeeping Hints* by Heloise Cruse, published by Prentice-Hall.

THE CREATIVE URGE

A creative woman, one for example who ordinarily is a productive artist or scientist, may find that her work flourishes during lactation, or she may be inclined to give up creative work entirely during the months that she is breast feeding. While loss of interest in one's work can be exasperating, it is only temporary. Psychiatrist Helene Deutsch suggests that breast feeding can bring its greatest benefits to the woman who is usually immersed in serious creative work. Nine months or more of a happy nursing relationship can provide a rare interlude of peace and satisfaction in a demanding lifetime. In her classic *Psychology of Women* she describes women who have set their creative work aside to nurse their babies, and then returned reinspired to their callings. Dr. Deutsch observed that these women were sometimes rather strict or abstracted with their children, but that the children nevertheless seemed to retain their affectionate early relationship with the mother, and grew to be happy, stable people.

EMERGENCY SEPARATIONS

What can you do if you must be suddenly separated from your nursing baby for a few days? What if one of you has to go to the hospital, or you must make a sudden trip to a dying relative, or some other emergency arises?

First, do what you can to prevent the separation. You can take your nursing baby with you, even to a distant funeral, and that will be less trouble to you than trying to dry up your milk, and worrying about your baby while you're away. When a nursing mother or baby must be hospitalized, it is very often possible to let them go together, and share a private room. The mother can continue to nurse, if she is the patient, and if the baby is the patient, he really needs his mother's milk. This is especially important if the baby is at the stage where he likes *only* mother's milk from the breast and will not take a bottle. (Some babies may do better if the bottle is fitted with a Nuk-Sanger nipple, which imitates the function of the human nipple.)

If the baby will take a bottle when hungry, and most babies will, you can express your milk either manually or by renting an electric breast pump from a druggists' supply house, and send it to the baby. If you are too far from the baby to do that, you can pump your milk and discard it, just to keep the supply going until you can get together again, while the baby is fed by cup, spoon, or bottle.

La Leche Leaguers, in emergencies when a mother had to go away, have solved this problem by leaving the baby with another nursing mother. They have found that babies, of course, can tell the difference; a baby may object to nursing at the breast of a stranger, but can sometimes be induced to nurse if his face is covered with a handkerchief so he cannot see the unfamiliar mother's face.

CHANGES AFTER SIX MONTHS

Your baby may drop night feedings by six months of age. Chances are he will still want one very early morning

feeding, around dawn. Some nursing babies never give up
this feeding voluntarily until they are weaned.

.During the day the baby of six or eight months will
probably eat three meals of solid food with the rest of the
family or just before them. But he may still want four or
five nursings in each twenty-four hours, and these feedings
still provide a useful excuse for you to get off your feet for
a while. Sometimes he'll be through with the breast in five
or ten minutes. Sometimes he'll want to linger. When you
can give him the time (perhaps after lunch, when both you
and he are planning on a nap) you can get a good deal of
vicarious enjoyment out of letting him nurse half an hour
or more until he nurses himself to sleep. Falling asleep at
the breast would certainly appear to be one of life's most
satisfying luxuries; just watching your baby as he blissfully
relaxes is enough to make you fall asleep yourself.

MENSTRUATION AND PREGNANCY

Because you are a successful nursing mother, you probably are finding that your menses continue to be suppressed. You probably will not menstruate until the baby
is from eight to eighteen months old. Until you have had
at least one period, and probably two or three, you are unlikely to conceive again.

Don't count on it, though! People have conceived before that first period; one doctor feels that this can often be
traced to a few busy days, or perhaps an illness of mother or baby, which led the mother to nurse less frequently
so that lactation was reduced or suspended "long enough
to let an egg slip through." If you do not wish to get pregnant, there are several good methods of contraception
presently available, although not in every state. See your
doctor or a family-planning clinic; cross the state line to
get good advice if you have to. Don't rely on luck, timing,
douching with 7-Up, or anything else but good medical
advice.

Some doctors will not prescribe birth-control pills or install an intrauterine device until after you have had your
first period. When your periods do start up, this will in no

way affect your milk supply. Someone might tell you that you "can't" nurse on the days when you are menstruating or that the baby will be fussy on those days, or the milk will diminish or taste different. All false. Sometimes, however, you yourself are irritable during or before your period, and this will be reflected in your baby's behavior; he may be cranky too, or want to nurse more, for reassurance.

Suppose you became pregnant while you are still nursing? While it might be a strain on you to nurse all the way through pregnancy, there is no need to come straight home from the obstetrician's office and wean the baby. You can plan on weaning him very gradually over a period of many weeks, as described in chapter 13.

Some mothers never bother to wean their baby when they become pregnant again, and thus find themselves, at the end of nine months, with two nursing babies! This event is common enough nowadays to have a name, "tandem nursing." Some mothers find that their milk supply dwindles to nothing during pregnancy and that the baby weans himself. An occasional mother complains of pain in the breast while nursing during late pregnancy, which is presumably an indication from Mother Nature that nursing should stop, and that the present baby should receive his love and attention in ways other than at the breast.

The Persistent Night Feeder

By the time a baby is seven or eight months old, he doesn't need a night feeding as a rule although many are loath to give up the pre-dawn snack. Since your storage capacity is ample, and your milk production in any case is somewhat less than it was, now that the baby is getting some solid foods, you can lactate steadily without the stimulation of night feeds. If you feel you would like to give up feeding the baby at night there are three methods to try. You can let him cry it out, which may be ghastly for everyone; for some babies your abrupt desertion is very frightening but for others this works like a charm. You can try rocking or singing to him, without feeding him; sometimes company and reassurance is what he really wants, and forty minutes of singing the first night becomes twenty minutes the second, five minutes the third, a called-out reassurance the fourth night, and peace and quiet from then on. Or you can let father take over. Amazingly enough, some babies (girls, especially) will go right back to sleep because their fathers have told them to.

Don't think that you can have uninterrupted nights by weaning to a bottle. Your baby may give up his midnight snack if it no longer consists of breast milk, and then again he may not. There are plenty of bottle-fed babies who go on demanding a bottle in the night well into their second year. A survey published in the *Journal of Pediatrics* in 1969 indicates that sleep patterns in infants are individual and utterly unrelated to whether they are breast fed or bottle fed. This does not mean that you must tolerate the behavior of a fifteen-month-old baby who wakes you up for company once an hour all night; you have some rights too. But some babies just can't bear to give up that last night feeding. If you can't break the habit, resign yourself. Something so terribly important to him isn't worth fighting over. Take a nap in the daytime, for your own sake, and try again in a month or two.

Changes at Eight Months

By now the reassuring nature of breast feeding as a sign of love is almost more important to your baby than the fact that it satisfies his hunger. He may want to nurse for comfort, if he bumps his head, or has been frightened. A baby of this age can be very bossy about feedings; when one breast is emptied he may fling himself across your lap and indicate that you should make the other available, and pronto. If you are carrying him, and he decides to eat, he may pull at your clothes, wriggle and wrench down to breast level, and all but help himself. His purposefulness is hilarious but it can create problems; he is no respecter of persons, and may all too obviously decide to have a snack when you are standing at the supermarket check-out counter, or talking to your minister's wife or your husband's boss. Fortunately people who are not used to breast-fed babies sometimes don't realize what he is doing.

Now that your baby can sit up, and perhaps creep and stand, he likes to nurse sitting up too, straddling your lap, and regarding the world as he eats. He is quite dogmatic about this; you may wonder what's wrong as you try to make him lie down on your arm and nurse, and he wriggles and complains, until you discover he has a change in mind. He may also like to hold onto the breast that he is not drinking from, as if it might go away before he gets to it.

CHANGES IN THE LET-DOWN REFLEX

After the baby passes the six month mark, and is beginning to get nourishment from sources other than you, you may find that the let-down reflex no longer operates promptly when he is put to the breast. He may have to suck for fifteen seconds or more before the milk lets down. Gradually the interval will become longer and longer, as your baby grows older and begins to wean himself. This delay in milk flow is reason in itself for some babies to lose interest in the breast, at or around the age of nine months.

CHANGES AT NINE MONTHS

In *A Baby's First Year* Dr. Spock writes of the formula-fed baby:

Around nine months of age babies begin to divide into two groups as far as feelings towards the good old bottle are concerned. Of one the mother says: "He's getting bored with it. After a couple of ounces he stops to fool with the nipple and grin at me. He likes milk from the cup." Such a baby seems ready for gradual weaning.

But the mother of a baby like Dana [the subject of Dr. Spock's book] will say: "She loves her bottle more than ever ... she usually drains it to the last drop, stroking it and murmuring to it. She's gotten suspicious of the cup lately." Such a baby seems to be saying, "I'm nowhere near ready to give it up."

Exactly the same thing is true of the breast-fed baby. Some babies will wean themselves rather abruptly, at or around the age of nine months. You start by giving the baby a cup of milk at breakfast, or perhaps dinner, because you are busy and the baby is too restless to nurse, and it just seems easier. By and by the baby expects a cup at every meal, and your own milk supply diminishes correspondingly. Without really noticing it, you find he is weaned. He may cling to one favorite feeding, early morning or a bedtime snack, for a few more weeks—and then all by himself, he is through with nursing and ready to go on to more grown-up things.

Other babies, at the age of nine months don't give up the breast at all. They become even fonder of being cuddled and nursed, and while they may only nurse three or four times in twenty-four hours, those feedings are terribly important to them. With such a baby, you can plan to continue nursing as long as is convenient for you, and as long as you both enjoy being a happy nursing couple.

13·Nursing Your Older Baby

The older baby really enjoys nursing. You can see that it means more to him than being just a way of filling his stomach, and that you mean more to him because of this. He wants to nurse for comfort and reassurance, as much as for food. If you leave him with a sitter he welcomes you home by scrambling into your lap for a swig of milk. If he hurts himself, or is frightened, nursing consoles him. When he is tired and ready for bed, nursing is his soothing nightcap.

Often he continues to like to nurse sitting upright, unless he is sleepy, when he goes back to lying in your arms like a little baby. For some reason the older baby likes to play by putting a finger in your mouth while he nurses.

Many babies do not have a visual association with the breast until they are twelve months old or so. To such a baby, the things that mean "Mother's going to nurse me" are being held in the nursing position, having her undress, and feeling the breast against his cheek. Perhaps because

249

he does not look at the breast as he nurses, the sight of the breast has in itself no meaning for a surprisingly long time. Some babies of course do make visual association earlier, and may dance up and down in their cribs, demanding to be fed, whenever they catch a glimpse of mamma dressing or undressing.

FIG. 17

TALKING

Naturally as the baby learns to talk he can tell you when he wants to nurse, in whatever terms your family uses. This can be disconcerting, as when a toddler climbs into your mother-in-law's lap, plucks at her blouse, and asks, politely, "Mi'k?" Some babies even make jokes with their minuscule vocabularies, like the sixteen-month-old baby who started to nurse, then pulled away from the breast in mock haste and said, "Hot!" and burst into laughter.

The ability to converse can also be handy. The baby who at eight months imperiously insisted upon being nursed right now in the middle of the Sears Roebuck house-wares department, can at twelve or fourteen months be dissuaded by verbal explanations: "Pretty soon," "When we get to the car," and so on.

How Long to Nurse

When you are down to one or two or three feedings in twenty-four hours, your baby is not exactly "breast fed" because he is getting most of his nourishment from other sources. But he is still a nursing baby, and those one or two feedings may be very warm and dear moments for both of you. There's no need in the world to cut off abruptly just because someone says the baby is "too old" to nurse, or no longer "needs" to nurse. Suppose he hangs on to a pre-bed snack, or likes to welcome you home by nursing, until he's two? Why shouldn't he? How many children of two—yes, and three and four—have you seen in the supermarket sucking on a bottle for dear life? Cherish these moments of closeness with your older baby; all too soon he will be a baby no longer. The time to stop nursing altogether is when either partner is really ready to quit.

Weaning Customs

In this country, the rigid child care systems of the 1920s and subsequent decades included abrupt weaning. Here and in Europe, when a doctor decides that it is time a patient ceased breast feeding, he may instruct the mother to give no more access to the breast whatsoever; the mother must take "drying-up" pills, bind her breasts, restrict fluid intake and cease producing milk as promptly as can be arranged, while the baby is expected to complete the transition to being fully bottle or cup fed, with equal speed.

This system is workable only when lactation has been mismanaged to such an extent that milk production is already very inadequate, so that the baby gladly abandons the unsatisfying breast for the bottle which fills his stomach. Engorgement and distension are not too much of a problem when feedings are suddenly halted, if the mother has not been secreting much milk anyway.

But such sudden weaning is rough on both parties if it is undertaken when the baby is still nursing happily, and the mother is producing well. Then the mother has to be a stoic indeed to obey orders to cease nursing completely.

The doctor may forbid all nursing on the grounds that sucking stimulates milk secretion, which is what he is trying to stop. But letting the baby drink off enough milk, once or twice, to ease the mother's discomfort, probably provides an insignificant amount of stimulation. There is hardly a mother in existence who, in this predicament, hasn't resorted to the forbidden relief, and, however guiltily, allowed the baby to nurse for one last time.

Fortunately, Dr. Spock and other advocates of more relaxed handling of infants have introduced the concept of more natural weaning, gradually, and with the consent of both parties. This system, which is common throughout the world, is beginning to be customary in this country, for weaning babies both from the breast and from the bottle.

Weaning the natural way takes place extremely slowly. The baby who abruptly loses interest at nine months provides the exception: he may go from five meals a day to none in the space of three weeks. But the baby who goes on to nurse for many months more loses interest in the breast very gradually. Sometimes you are too busy to feed him; sometimes he is not interested in nursing. Gradually you forget about one meal and then another, until he is nursing regularly only at one time in the day, his favorite feeding, which is apt to be either the early morning or the bedtime feeding.

Of course there are days when he is tired, or teething, and "backslides" to taking two or three feedings again for a while. But the general trend continues. Slowly the favorite meal too is abandoned. He sleeps through his early morning feeding or sometimes gives up his evening meal because you are out for the evening, and then begins going without it even when you are home. A day goes by when you don't nurse him at all; then, a week later, two days go by. Now your milk is really almost nonexistent. Still, occasionally your baby likes to lie at the breast and recall his infant comfort. Then one day you realize he hasn't nursed in a week. Perhaps he remembers, and tries again, but the empty breast is really not very interesting. He may nurse a moment, and then give up, perhaps with a comment, like one twenty-monther who suddenly asked for the breast after three weeks of not nursing. He tried it briefly, and gave up, remarking matter-of-factly to his nearby father, "Nope, Mamma's mi'k aw gone."

With this kind of weaning there is no crying, heartbroken child who cannot understand why the dearest person in the world is denying him the thing he wants most; there are no discomforts, no problems. It is so gradual that often a mother cannot remember just exactly when nursing stopped. Neither can the baby.

Sometimes we can't help wishing that the baby would get things over with and give up the breast, much as we love to nurse him. Perhaps mothers too are subject to inner taboos against long nursing. La Leche Leaguers note that it is often the first baby who "spontaneously" weans himself at nine months, whereas subsequent babies tend to be nursed indefinitely. You can see, probably, how to encourage your baby to wean himself, without making things hard for either of you. Give him lots of other kinds of attention. Anticipate his needs for food and drink. You can sometimes tell him to wait if you are busy, or even promise to nurse him some other time, at bedtime perhaps. Don't begrudge him the breast if he really longs for it, and don't be too sudden. Let him linger on with his favorite meal for a few days or weeks. When he wants to nurse only once a day, it is hardly a great inconvenience for you, and you can satisfy prying relatives who ask, "When are you going to wean that baby?" by saying, "I *am* weaning him." One meal a day soon dwindles to an occasional meal, and then to none. What a pleasant, peaceful way to bring to a close the pleasant, peaceful experience of nursing your baby.

The Nursing Toddler

The more experienced you are as a mother, the longer you are likely to keep the baby on the breast. La Leche Leaguers report more and more League members with a baby that is still "snacking," or nursing at bedtime or occasionally for comfort, at two years old, or three, or even older. The more familiar one becomes with breast feeding, the less susceptible one is to fad or fashion or criticism; so the baby is not weaned according to the customs of others. Also the very essence of the nursing relationship is to set no rules, to just let it happen; the more a mother becomes attuned to this receptivity, the less likely she is to be arbitrary about weaning; and so breast feeding, for comfort and affection rather than nutrition, lingers on.

The nursing toddler is a perfectly normal phenomenon in many cultures. Psychologically and biologically there is no reason why a two- or three-year-old should not still nurse. Nursing is terribly important to some toddlers; they obviously draw immense reassurance and security, as they begin to explore their world, from being able to return from time to time to the breast.

The mother with the nursing toddler must expect some criticism; "What are you going to tell his kindergarten teacher?" is the commonest wisecrack. She can also expect some friction with the baby. Two-year-olds can be both negative and bossy, and one sometimes sees a nursing toddler who has learned to wield his demand for the breast as a weapon over his mother. Perhaps the mother is intellectually convinced that she must not "reject" her baby by refusing the breast. Therefore she gives in and nurses, even when she doesn't really want to: when it means leaving her company, or interrupting a shopping trip. She feels resentful, secretly, and she is right to feel resentful! The mother of a two-year-old doesn't have to be, and shouldn't be, the omnipresent, all-giving mother that the same baby needed at two months. Nature decrees that both mother and baby should be feeling moments of independence. However, the mother who feels she has no right to refuse to nurse, since the baby's needs come first, sometimes prolongs a nursing relationship which is really a running battle. The mother resents nursing, at least some of the time; the baby feels the resentment and becomes even more demanding and aggressive about nursing, wanting reassurance more than ever, but also expressing the anger which his mother's repressed anger arouses.

Sometimes a toddler demands the breast just for lack of anything better to do. What do mothers do when they're bored? Go to the icebox for a Coke, right? So the baby asks to nurse when he would be just as happy with a sandwich or a glass of juice, or some company or amusement. It's the mother's job to sense this, and adjust as the baby grows; she is not doing the baby any favors if she allows him to substitute suckling for a romp on the lawn or being read to, at an age when he needs to be exploring and experiencing more and more.

Sometimes a mother clings to the comforting nursing relationship when her baby is ready to outgrow it. A woman who has an unhappy marriage might tend to postpone weaning her child. The youngest child in a big family is sometimes encouraged, and not just by the mother, to cling to his infant ways, including nursing. And late weaning, like early weaning, can become fashionable. In nonnursing circles, the announcement that you nursed the baby two years has a certain shock value which can be gratifying, but among groups of nursing mothers one sometimes gets the feeling that long nursing has become competitive, with the mother who nursed thirty-two months enjoying more status than the mother who nursed twenty-two months. Finally, some mothers use the nursing relationship aggressively. This kind of mother will snatch up her toddler and put him to the breast almost forcibly, because he is making too much noise or straying too far, and she wants to shut him up; paradoxically, she is nursing the baby so she can take her attention *off* him. Also, it's not just the mother who can use breast feeding unfairly. In one family older brothers and sisters habitually carried the toddler to Mom and told him to nurse, just to keep him out of their hair and their toys.

When the nursing relationship has deteriorated to the point where either partner uses the nursing to manipulate the other partner unfairly, then it ought to be stopped. That is not a happy nursing couple anymore; relations between mother and child need to be rebuilt on a more grown-up basis.

Tandem Nursing

Suppose that a mother is nursing a toddler completely agreeably, and another baby comes along? Some mothers nurse through pregnancy and continue to let the older baby nurse, at least occasionally, after the new baby has arrived. "It's so important to him," is the usual feeling. This so-called tandem nursing can be reassuring all around. The danger is that the mother begins to feel it is an obligation rather than a pleasure. She needs to listen to her own body and her own heart. If nursing during pregnancy becomes uncomfortable, or wearing, she should politely stop. If she feels resentment, feels that the older baby is taking the newcomer's milk or stealing her attention from the newborn, she should stop. Being resented is much harder on a child than being weaned.

In this case the resentment is not an emotion over which one should feel guilty; it is a biologically natural phenomenon. Animal mothers disassociate themselves from their young ones as the young ones mature and before the next babies arrive. In wild horse herds a mare may be followed by her yearling and even her two-year-old, and she will graze with them and keep company with them, but she will kick and nip them if they try to nurse.

Viola Lennon, a La Leche League founding mother, who had a large family quite close together, was asked how it happened that she never found herself tandem nursing? "Because Mother Vi didn't let it happen," was her sensible response. Weaning a toddler, when you have had enough of breast feeding, is common sense too. How long to nurse is a matter to be decided between you and your baby, and at this point you both have equal rights.

Weaning is part of the baby's growing up, but it is sometimes part of the mother's growing up, too.

TODDLER WEANING PROBLEMS

What if the toddler has been freely indulged in nursing, and now at the age of two or three is nursing many times a day, often at night, and has temper tantrums if nursing is denied or postponed even for a few minutes? Weaning such a child by just refusing the breast may be pretty traumatic for the baby, the mother, the rest of the household, and even the neighbors. Tact and perhaps a little duplicity is called for. In rural Mexico, mothers put a little chili pepper on their breasts. (Angostura bitters, a flavoring sold in liquor stores, might be gentler and safer.) When the child reacts to the bad taste, the mother feigns surprise, offers sympathy, and agrees that it's too bad the milk has turned so funny tasting. A few tries over a few days is usually enough to discourage future nursing, and meanwhile the mother can be sure to spend extra time going for walks, playing, and giving the youngster other attention. In some parts of the Pacific women wean late-nursing children by painting their breasts or nipples an odd color with a harmless dye; the changed appearance is sufficiently alarming to discourage the child. Food coloring would be safe to use if a fed-up mother wanted to try this dodge.

A practice that is common in Europe is for the mother to take a four or five day vacation from home, perhaps visiting relatives, while the father and other members of the household take care of the youngster. The mother who has let herself slip into a longer and more demanding nursing situation than she enjoys has really earned a little vacation. Usually in her absence the toddler will grow fully accustomed to being happy without nursing. Though he may ask to nurse when she first returns, the firm statement that the milk is all gone now, coupled with lots of affection but refusal to let him try nursing, should soon put an end to the problem, and without the child having had to endure the active rejection by the mother that he might have experienced had she been physically present during the first days of weaning.

AFTER WEANING

If a baby is weaned abruptly, the mother's breasts first fill with milk, and then gradually become empty and slack, over a period of several days. Slowly, as the breasts change to the nonproductive state, they return to their former, smaller size. A complete return to normal takes about six months.

If a baby abandons breast feeding very gradually, over a period of many months, the breasts return to normal during that period. By the time the baby is nursing once every few days, there is almost no milk in the breasts, and their appearance is pretty much as it was before pregnancy.

Long after the baby has ceased nursing altogether, it remains possible to express manually a few drops of milk from the breasts. Gradually, the drops that can be expressed change in appearance to the clear, yellowish look of colostrum. Finally, perhaps a year after weaning, even this disappears. However, even then it would be possible, by putting a baby to the breasts often enough, to start up milk secretion all over again through the stimulus of the baby's sucking.

RELACTATION: NURSING ADOPTED BABIES

Many women are finding that they can successfully nurse an adopted baby, months or even years after their own last pregnancies. The advantages are obvious; the adopted baby gets the health and protection and perfect nutrition of breast milk, and both mother and baby enjoy the closeness of the nursing relationship. A mother who cannot have a second child, or who chooses not to have more than one biological child, can nevertheless convey the full benefits of biological mothering to subsequent adopted infants. The techniques for relactating have been well worked out by a number of adoptive mothers who are now researching and counseling in this area. In general, every effort is made to initiate lactation before the adopted baby arrives, by manual expression, pumping, perhaps borrowing a nursing baby. The new baby is then started out on formula, but encouraged to nurse before, during, and after feedings, to stimulate milk secretion.

It is often infuriating to a baby to suck on an empty breast, especially if he is very hungry; techniques for keeping him interested range from putting honey on the breast to trickling milk into the corner of his mouth with an eyedropper. Perhaps the most successful aid is the nursing supplementer called Lact-aid, developed by the father of an adopted baby. This device consists of a sac which holds the formula, and which can be pinned inside the mother's bra, and a tiny tube which can be laid alongside the mother's nipple so that the baby draws milk from it as he nurses. An adopted baby may be thus fed all his supplement while actually at the breast. Amounts of supplement are then gradually decreased or diluted as the mother's milk supply develops, and the baby nurses strongly and well, without frustration. Some startling results have been obtained with this device; a full milk supply, with no supplements or solids, has been developed in one to two weeks in mothers who weaned their previous babies up to six years previously. A mother who lactated after miscarrying at four months maintained some milk flow by manual expression for another four months, and then established lactation using the Lact-aid with her new adopted baby in three short days. A number of adoptive mothers who have never been pregnant have been able to establish a partial milk supply with this device. Adoptive mothers who have never been pregnant and who may never develop more than a modest flow of milk find joy in using the Lact-aid to feed their baby *at* the breast, if not *by* the breast, and thus to establish a happy nursing relationship. The Lact-aid, in a handsome and well-designed kit, and much information on relactation and nursing adoptive babies, may be obtained from J. J. Avery, Inc., P. O. Box 6459, Denver, Colorado 80206. Several booklets on relactation are available from La Leche League International.

It is important, in considering nursing an adopted baby, to have the help of an enthusiastic doctor. Many doctors have never heard of such a thing, but will usually become supportive if presented with some of the La Leche League medical literature on the subject. Some adoptive mothers find that the case workers are suspicious of a mother's interest in nursing an adopted baby. Tact and discretion are called for in pressing the idea; one couple were refused as adoptive parents when the agency discovered the mother planned to try nursing the baby. Also it is generally impossible to interest a baby in nursing if the baby is over four months old when it comes home. The smaller the baby, the more likely it is to nurse strongly and persistently and thus bring in the milk supply.

Some mothers have used relactation techniques to establish breast milk for foster babies placed with them temporarily by state agencies. Again, social workers are often horrified at first. One agency forbade a foster mother to breast feed because the milk wasn't pasteurized! However, a foster mother who is willing to breast feed her charges even if only for a few weeks can virtually save the life of a sickly or malnourished infant, and the rapid change in such an infant is usually enough to convince even the most prejudiced case worker. In nursing foster children the babies need to be kept familiar with the bottle, so they can switch over when other homes are found for them, and the social worker needs to learn to give the mother a few days notice when the baby is to be moved, so that she can taper off comfortably.

EXTENDING MOTHERING SKILLS

Breast feeding is not an end in itself, though it may seem so in the weeks and months in which you are learning about it and enjoying it. The end goal, of course, is a happy and healthy baby and a fulfilled mother. Breast feeding does so much to ensure this. The benefits of the nursing relationship linger long beyond weaning. Your baby will be healthier for months, perhaps years. And don't you have the feeling that he is a happier person than he might otherwise have been? Happy nursing babies are all kinds. of people—introverts, extroverts, thinkers or doers—but they tend to share certain basic traits: a generous, affectionate nature, coupled, after weaning, with an almost comic self-sufficiency. Probably your youngster, too, has these qualities which are typical of the little child who has spent most of his first year of life, or longer, as a happy nursing baby.

And for you, the benefits of being half a nursing couple continue, too. Looking back over the months of nursing, you remember the pleasures, not the little problems. Do you sense how much you may have learned? Dr. Robert Applebaum says that to him the one word which describes true femininity is "receptivity." Think of the difference between "passive" and "receptive." There is a partnership implicit in being receptive, a partnership which is the very nature of the nursing relationship. But the warmth and receptivity one sometimes first develops in becoming a nursing mother doesn't vanish with the milk. It can extend into the rest of your life, for the rest of your life. It can become the heart of your relationship toward your husband, toward your family, toward the rest of the world. Our society values achieving; it does not much value perceiving. The nursing mother, however restricted and unfeeling her own upbringing might have been, learns as she nurses her baby more and more about perceiving, about awareness of others, about reaching goals by means of receptiveness, instead of aggressiveness.

We have long lives now, and many women have small families. Women have more education than in the past. There are many years ahead, and many opportunities, to put the lessons of the nursing relationship to work in other ways. If there's one thing every part of society could use right now—from the crowded cities to the medical establishment, from the arts to big business—it's the womanly art of gentle living, the receptive way of achieving together —and with Mother Nature—instead of at odds with nature and against each other. The nursing relationship is a glimpse of how things can be. Some of this enlightenment can carry over into the rest of your life. To quote nursing mother Grace Kelly, "Motherhood begins at the breast; it doesn't end there." Perhaps in the return of breast feeding we are witnessing a small but infectious sample of revolution, a humanizing revolution of our own culture.

Selected References

The references which follow are listed in general under the first chapter to which they pertain. These references constitute the principal published source material for this book; they are by no means a complete or even fully representative listing of the literature on human lactation and related subjects. The literature on rooming-in alone is now very extensive. The serious reader is referred to the bibliographies in the works listed here.

To the science-oriented reader I would especially like to recommend R. J. Williams' thought-provoking book, *Biochemical Individuality*. Also, every reader who is intrigued by the problems of instinct will thoroughly enjoy Konrad Lorenz's delightful and illuminating book about animals, *King Solomon's Ring*.

A certain amount of the material in *Nursing Your Baby* comes, of course, not from the literature but from experience, my own and that of others, and from interviews and letters. I would be glad to hear from readers with additional or contrasting information, experiences, or opinions on the subjects considered here.

CHAPTER 1. THE NURSING COUPLE

ALDRITCH, C. A., M.D. "The Advisability of Breast Feeding." *J. Am. Med. Assoc.*, 135:915, 1947.

BAKWIN, H., M.D. "Psychological Implications of Early Child Care." *Am. J. Nursing*, 51:7, 1951.

BARTEMEIER, L., M.D. "The Contribution of the Father to the Mental Health of the Family." *Am. J. Psychiatry*, 110:4; reprinted, *Child-Family Digest*, Nov. 1953.

BEVAN-BROWN, M., M.D. *The Sources of Love and Fear*. Dunedin, New Zealand; Coulls, Somerville, Wilkie, Ltd., 1950.

BOWLBY, JOHN, M.D. *Child Care and the Growth of Love*. Baltimore, Md.: Penguin Books, Inc., 1953.

BRODY, SYLVIA. *Patterns of Mothering*. New York: International Universities Press, Inc., 1956.

DEUTSCH, HELENE, M.D. *The Psychology of Women*, 2 vols. New York: Grune & Stratton, Inc., 1945.

DICK-READ, GRANTLY, M.D. *Childbirth Without Fear*. New York: Harper & Row, 1944.

ESCALONA, SIBYLLE. "Interaction of Mother and Child." From *Problems of Infancy and Childhood*, Transactions of the Sixth Conference, Josiah Macy Jr. Foundation, New York, 1952.

GESELL, A., M.D., F. L. ILG, M.D. *Feeding Behavior of Infants*. Philadelphia: J. B. Lippincott Co., 1937.

GOLAPAN, C. "Effect of Protein Supplementation and Some So-Called Galactagogues on Lactation in Poor Indian Women." *Ind. J. Med. Research*, 46:317, 1958.

HEARDMAN, HELEN. *A Way to Natural Childbirth*. Edinburgh and London: S. Livingstone, Ltd., 1948.

HYTTEN, F. E., M.D. "Clinical and Chemical Studies in Human Lactation." *Brit. Med. J.*, i:175; i:249; i:912; ii:844; ii:1447, 1954.

ILLINGWORTH, R. S., M.D. *The Normal Child*. Boston: Little, Brown & Co., 1957.

KING, A. G., M.D. "Suppression of Lactation and Its Relation to Cancer of the Breast." *J. Med. Assoc. of Georgia*, July 1958; reprinted, *CFD*, Sept.-Oct. 1958.

La Leche League. *The Womanly Art of Breast Feeding*. La Leche League of Franklin Park, Inc. 3332 Rose St., Franklin Park, Ill., 1958.

LINDBERGH, ANNE MORROW. *Gift from the Sea*. New York: Pantheon Books, Inc., 1955.

MIDDLEMORE, M. P., M.D. *The Nursing Couple*. London: Cassell & Co., Ltd., 1941.

MOLONEY, JAMES CLARK, M.D. "The Cornelian Corner." *Psychiatric Quart.*, Oct. 1946; reprinted in *CFD* Dec. 1949.

MONTAGU, ASHLEY. "Neonatal and Infant Immaturity in Man." *J. Am. Med. Assoc.*, Oct. 1961. Excerpted in *Briefs*, 26:6.

NEWTON, NILES. "The Relationship Between Infant Feeding Experiences and Later Behavior." *J. Ped.*, 38:28, 1951.

————. "The Influence of the Let-Down Reflex in Breast Feeding on the Mother-Child Relationship." *Marriage and Family Living*, 22:18, 1958.

ROBINSON, MARIE N., M.D. *The Power of Sexual Surrender*. New York: Doubleday & Company, Inc., 1959.

SMITH, H. *Letters to Married Ladies*. London, 1765. Quoted in G. F. STILL, M.D. *The History of Paediatrics*. London: Oxford University Press, 1931.

SPOCK, BENJAMIN, M.D. and JOHN REINHART. *A Baby's First Year*. New York: Duell, Sloan & Pearce, Inc., 1955.

THIRKELL, ANGELA. *Love at All Ages*. New York: Alfred A. Knopf, Inc., 1959.

WINNICOTT, D. W., M.D. *Mother and Child*. New York: Basic Books, Inc., 1957.

CHAPTER 2. HOW THE BREASTS FUNCTION

BHAVANI BELEVADY, SWARAN PASRICHA, and K. SHANKAR. "Studies on Lactation and Dietary Habits of the Nilgiri Hill Tribes," *Indian J. Med. Research*, 47:221, 1959.

CRONIN, T. J. "Influence of Lactation Upon Ovulation." *Lancet*, 2:422, 1968.

DAVIES, V., and J. P. PRATT. "The Stimulation and Maintenance of Lactation." *Am. J. Nursing*, 46:242, 1946.

DODEK, S. M., M.D., *et al.* "Intrapartum Initiation of Lactation Control." *J. Am. Med. Assoc.*, 154:309, 1954.

EGLI, G. E., *et al.* "The Influence of the Number of Breast Feedings on Milk Production." *Ped.*, 27:314, 1961.

FOLLEY, S. J. *The Psysiology and Biochemistry of Lactation*. London: Oliver and Boyd, 1956.

LEWISON, E. F., M.D., and L. W. ALLEN, M.D. "Antecedent Factors in Cancer of the Breast." *Am. Surg.*, 138:39, 1953.

MEITES, J., *et al.* "The Central Nervous System and the Secretion and Release of Prolactin." From *Advances in Neuroendocrinology*. Edited by A. NALBANDOV. Chicago: Univ. of Illinois Press, 1963.

NAISH, CHARLOTTE, M.D. *Breast Feeding*. London: Lloyd-Luke, 1956.

NEWTON, MICHAEL, M.D. "The Management of Breast Feeding Disorders." *Southern Med. J.*, 49:514, 1956.

————and G. E. EGLI. "The Effect of Intranasal Administration of Oxytocin on the Let-Down of Milk in Lactating Women." *Am. J. of Ob. and Gyn.*, 1958, 76:103.

NEWTON, MICHAEL, M.D. and NILES NEWTON. "The Let-Down Reflex in Human Lactation." *J. Ped.*, 33:698, 1948.

————. "Breast Abscess, a Result of Lactation Failure." *Surg., Gyn., and Ob.*, 91:651, 1950.

———. "The Normal Course and Management of Lactation." *Clin. Ob. and Gyn.*, 5:44, 1962.

NEWTON, NILES. "The Sexual Implications of Breast Feeding." *CFD*, Nov. 1952.

———and MICHAEL NEWTON, M.D. "Relation of the Let-Down Reflex to Ability to Breast Feed." *Ped.*, 5:726, 1950.

NICOLSON, W., M.D. "Does Breast Feeding Help *Prevent* Cancer of the Breast?" *CFD*, June, 1954.

Physiology of Lactation. World Health Organization Technical Report, Series No. 305. Geneva, Switzerland: WHO, 1965.

RICHARDSON, FRANK H., M.D. *The Nursing Mother.* New York: David McKay Co., Inc., 1953.

Rocky Mountain Metal Products Co. *Progress Report*: R. M. Nuk Sauger Preventative Orthodontic Program. Rocky Mountain Metal Products Co., P.O. Box 1887, Denver 1, Colo., 1962.

SALBER, E., *et al.* "The Duration of Postpartum Amenorrhea." *Am. J. Epidemiology*, 82:347, 1966.

SCHAEFER, O. "Cancer of the Breast and Lactation." *Canad. Med. Assoc. J.*, 100:625, 1969.

WALLER, HAROLD, M.D. *Clinical Studies in Lactation.* London: H. K. Lewis and Co., Ltd., 1939.

———. *The Breasts and Breast Feeding.* London: William Heinemann, Ltd., 1957.

WEAVER, H. "Why Nurse Your Baby?" *CFD*. Nov. 1949.

WEISCHHOFF, H., M.D. "Artificial Stimulation of Lactation in Primitive Cultures." *Bull. Hist. Med.*, 8:1403, 1940.

ZAKS, N. G. *The Motor Apparatus of the Mammary Gland.* Springfield, Ill.: Charles C. Thomas, Pub., 1958.

CHAPTER 3. MILK

ACHESON, E., and S. TRUELOVE. "Early Weaning in the Aetiology of Ulcerative Colitis." *Brit. Med. J.* pp. 929-933, Oct. 1961.

ANTHREYA, B., *et al.* "Poliomyelitis Antibodies in Human Colostrum and Milk." *J. Ped.* 64:7982, 1964.

ARIAS, I. M. "Prolonged Neonatal Unconjugated Hyperbilirubinemia Associated with Breast Feeding." *J. Clinic. Invest.* 43:2037, 1964.

BLAXTER, K. L. "Lactation and the Growth of the Young." From *Milk: The Mammary Gland and Its Secretion*, Vol. II. Edited by S. K. KON and A. T. COWIE. New York: Academic Press, Inc., 1961.

DAVIDSON, M. "Breast Feeding." *Pediatrics*, 14th edition. Edited by H. BARNETT. New York: Appleton-Century-Crofts, 1968.

DRAKE, T. G. H., M.D. "Infant Feeding in England and in France from 1750 to 1800." *Am. J. Dis. Child.*, 39:1049, 1930.

GLASER, J. "The Dietary Prophylaxis of Allergic Diseases in Infancy." *J. Asthma Res.* 3:199-208, 1966.

GOPALAN, C., and B. BELEVADY. "Nutrition and Lactation." *Fed. Proc.* 20, Suppl., 7:1777, 1961.

GRAVER, T. "Muscles, Malformation, and Malocclusion." *Am. J. of Orthod.*, 49:429-431, 1963.

GRYBOSKI, J. "Gastrointestinal Milk Allergy in Infants." *Ped.* 40:354-360, 1967.

GYORGY, P., M.D. "The Late Effects of Early Nutrition." *Am. J. Clin. Nutr.*, 8:344-345, 1960.

———, S. DHANAMITTA, and E. STEERS. "Protective Effects of Human Milk in Experimental Staphylococcus Infection." *Science*, 137:338, 1962.

HAIKE, D. "The Medical Value of Breast Feeding." Bellevue, Washington: International Childbirth Education Association, Pub., 1971.

HARFOUCHE, J. "The Importance of Breast Feeding," *J. Trop. Ped.*, 135-175, 1970. 200 references on protective aspects of breast feeding.

HODES, H. "Colostrum: A Valuable Source of Antibodies." *Ob-Gyn Observer*, 3:7, 1964.

HOLZEL, A. "The Prevention and Treatment of Gastroenteritis in Infancy." *The Practitioner*, 204:46-54, 1970.

HYMANSON, H., M.D. "A Short Review of the History of Infant Feeding." *Arch. Ped.*, 51:1, 1934.

HYTTEN, F. E., M.D. and A. M. THOMSON. "Nutrition of the Lactating Woman." From *Milk: The Mammary Gland and Its Secretion*, Vol. II. Edited by S. K. KON and A. T. COWIE. New York: Academic Press, Inc., 1961.

JELLIFFE, D. B., M.D. *Infant Nutrition in the Subtropics and Tropics.* Geneva, Switzerland: World Health Organization, 1955.

JELLIFFE, D. B., and E. F. P. JELLIFFE, ed. "Symposium: The Uniqueness of Human Milk." *Am. J. Clin. Nutr.*, 24:968-1024, Aug. 1971.

KASDAN, SARA. *Love and Knishes.* New York: Vanguard Press, 1956.

KNOWLES, J. "Excretions of Drugs in Milk." *J. Ped.*, 66:1068-1081, 1965.

KON, S. K., and A. T. COWIE, ed. *Milk: The Mammary Gland and Its Secretion*, 2 vols. New York: Academic Press, Inc., 1961.

KRON, R. "Newborn Sucking Behavior Affected by Obstetrical Sedation." *Ped.*, 37:1012-1016, 1966.

La Leche League, Inc. "On Early Introduction of Solid Foods," *LLL News*, reprinted, *CFD*, July-Aug. 1959.

LOWE, L., and F. CORMIA. "Atopic Exema." *Current Therapy*, Philadelphia: B. W. Saunders Co., 1967.

MACIE, I. C., M.D. and E. F. DONELSON. "Human Milk Studies." *J. Nutr.*, 7:231, 1934.

———and H. J. KELLY. "Human Milk and Cow's Milk in Infant Nutrition." From *Milk: The Mammary Gland and Its Secretion*, Vol. II. Edited by S. K. KON and A. T. COWIE. New York: Academic Press, Inc., 1961.

MELLANDER, O., *et al.* "Breast Feeding and Artificial Feeding: the Norbotten Study." *Acta Paediatrica*, 48: Suppl. 116, 1959.

MEYER, HERMAN F., M.D. *Infant Foods and Feeding Practice.* Springfield, Ill.: Charles C. Thomas, Pub., 1960.

MICHAELS, R. "Studies of Antiviral Factors in Human Milk and Serum." *J. of Immun.*, 94:262-263, 1965.

MILLER, G. H. "Does the Pill Impair Nursing?" *Med. World News,* May, 1969.

MONTAGU, ASHLEY. "Natural Selection and the Origin and Evolution of Weeping in Man." *Science,* Dec. 1959; reprinted, *CFD,* Jan.-Feb. 1960.

MORGAN, AGNES FAY, M.D. *Nutritional Status, U.S.A.* Berkeley: Univ. of California Press, 1959.

MURILLO, G. J. and A. S. GOLDMAN. "The Cells of Human Colostrum, II." *Pediat. Res.,* 4:71, 1970.

NEWTON, MICHAEL, M.D. "A Test for Lactation Success." *Am. J. Ob. and Gyn.,* 64:397, 1952.

SMITH, C. W., and A. S. GOLDMAN. "The Cells of Human Colostrum, I." *Pediat. Res.,* 2:103, 1968.

SMITHELLS, R., and D. MORGAN. "Transmission of Drugs by the Placenta and the Breasts." *The Practitioner,* 204:14-19, 1970.

STEIHM, E. R., and J. RYAN. "Breast Milk Jaundice." *Am. Dis. Child.,* 109:212-216. 1965.

STILL, G. F., M.D. *The History of Paediatrics.* London: Oxford University Press, 1931.

TANK, G. "Relation of Diet to Variation of Dental Caries," *J. Am. Dental Assoc.,* 70:394-403, 1965.

WIDDOWSON, E., J. SLATER, B. HARRISON, and A. SUTTON. "Absorption, Excretion and Retention of Strontium by Breast-Fed and Bottle-Fed Babies." *Lancet,* 2:941-944, 1960.

WILLIAMS, ROGER J. *Biochemical Individuality.* New York: John Wiley & Sons, Inc., 1956.

CHAPTER 4. WHAT HAPPENED TO MOTHER INSTINCT?

BLAUVELT, HELEN. "Dynamics of the Mother-Newborn Relationship in Goats." From *Group Processes,* Transactions of the First Conference, Josiah Macy Jr. Foundation, New York, 1955.

————. "Neonate-Mother Relationships in Goats and Man." From *Group Processes,* Transactions of the Second Conference, Josiah Macy Jr. Foundation, New York, 1956.

————. "Further Studies on Maternal-Neonate Interrelationships." From *Group Processes,* Transactions of the Third Conference, Josiah Macy Jr. Foundation, New York, 1957.

BRAZELTON, T. B. "Effect of Prenatal Drugs on the Behavior of the Neonate. *Amer. J. of Psychiatry,* 126:95-100, 1970.

CRAIG, W. "Male Doves Reared in Isolation." *J. Anim. Behavior,* 4:121, 1914. Quoted in W. H. THORPE. *Learning and Instinct in Animals.* Cambridge: Harvard University Press, 1956.

GRAY, P. H. "Theory and Evidence of Imprinting in the Human Infant." *J. Psych.,* 46:155, 1958.

GUNTHER, MAVIS, M.D. "Instinct and the Nursing Couple." *Lancet,* 1: 575, 1955.

HINDE, R. A. "The Establishment of the Parent-Offspring Relation in Birds, with Some Mammalian Analogies." From *Current Problems in Animal Behavior*. Edited by W. H. THORPE and O. L. ZANGWILL. Cambridge: Harvard University Press, 1961.

LEHRMAN, D. S. "On the Organization of Maternal Behavior and the Problem of Instinct." From *L'Instinct dans le Comportement des Animaux et de l'Homme*. Paris: Masson et Cie, 1956.

LEVY, DAVID M., M.D. *Behavioral Analysis*. Springfield, Ill. Charles C. Thomas, Publisher, 1958.

LORENZ, KONRAD Z. *King Solomon's Ring*. New York: Thomas Y. Crowell Company, 1952.

MOLONEY, JAMES CLARK, M.D. "Post-Partum Depression." *CFD*, Feb. 1952.

MONTAGU, ASHLEY. *Touching: The Human Significance of the Skin*. New York: Columbia Univ. Press, 1971.

NEWTON, NILES, and MICHAEL NEWTON, M.D. "Mothers' Reactions to Their Newborn Babies," *J. Am. Med. Assoc.*, 181:206, 1962.

SALK, L., M.D. "Effects of Normal Heartbeat Sound on Behavior of Newborn Infant: Implications for Mental Health." *World Mental Health*, 12:4, 1960.

SCHNEIRLA, T. C. "Family Life and Adjustment in Animals." From *Problems of Infancy and Childhood*, Transactions of Fourth Conference, Josiah Macy Jr. Foundation, New York, 1959.

SPITZ, RENÉ A., M.D. *No and Yes on the Genesis of Human Communication*. New York: International Universities Press, Inc., 1957.

THORPE, W. H. *Learning and Instinct in Animals*. Cambridge: Harvard University Press, 1956.

———. "Sensitive Periods in the Learning of Animals and Men." From *Current Problems in Animal Behavior*, Part III, Chap. VIII. Edited by W. H. THORPE and O. L. ZANGWILL. Cambridge: Harvard University Press, 1961.

YERKES, R. M., and M. I. TOMLIN. "Mother-Infant Relations in the Chimpanzees." *J. Comp. Psych.*, 20:321, 1935.

CHAPTER 5. DOCTORS WHO DON'T HELP

ALDRITCH, C. A., M.D. "Ancient Processes in a Scientific Age." *Am. J. Dis. Child.*, 64:714, 1942.

BARTEMEIER, L. H., M.D. "Concerning the Cornelian Corner." *Am. J. Orthopsychiatry*, 17:4, 1949; reprinted, *CFD*, Nov. 1949.

BEAL, V. A. "The Acceptance of Solid Foods and Other Food Patterns of Infants and Children." *Ped.*, 20:448, 1957. Quoted in *LLL Newsletter* and *CFD*, July-Aug. 1959.

BLUM, L. H., M.D. "The Pediatrician in the Role of Psychologist and Educator." *Am. J. Dis. Child.*, 80:238, 1950.

CARITHERS, H. "Mother-Pediatrician Relationship in the Neonatal Period." *J. Ped.*, 38:654, 1951.

CORBIN, HAZEL. "Emotional Aspects of Maternity Care." *Am. J. Nursing,* 48:20, 1948.

DANIELSON, E. "A Study of Breast Technic." *Am. J. Nursing,* 33:462, 1933.

HILL, L. F., M.D., *et al.* Report of the Committee on Nutrition: "On the Feeding of Solid Food to Infants." American Academy of Pediatrics. *Ped.,* 2:685, 1958.

ILLINGWORTH, R. S., M.D. "Common Difficulties in Infant Feeding." *Brit. Med. J.,* 2:1077, 1949.

JELLIFFE, D. B., M.D. "Breast Milk and the World Protein Gap." *Clin. Ped.,* 7:2, 96, 1968.

MCBRIDE, A., M.D., and W. DAVISON. "Rooming-In," *North Carolina Med. J.,* 16:159; reprinted, *CFD,* Oct. 1955.

MORSE, J. L., M.D. "Recollections and Reflections on Forty-Five Years of Artificial Infant Feeding." *J. Ped.,* 1935.

NEWTON, NILES, and MICHAEL NEWTON, M.D. "Recent Trends in Breast Feeding: a Review." *Am. J. Med. Science,* 221:691, 1951.

POWERS, G. "Infant Feeding, Historical Background and Modern Practice." *J. Am. Med. Assoc.,* 105:753, 1935.

RICHARDSON, FRANK H., M.D. "On Too-Early Feeding of Solids." *CFD,* 18:4, 81, 1959.

SALBER, M. B., *et al.* "Patterns of Breast Feeding." *New Eng. J. Med.,* 259:707, 1958.

WALLER, HAROLD, M.D. "Early Failure of Breast Feeding." *Nursing Mirror,* 1949; reprinted, *CFD,* June-July, 1950.

WEINFELD, G., and BENJAMIN SPOCK, M.D. "Pediatrics and Child Psychiatry." *Am. J. Orthopsychiatry* 11:423, 1941.

WELBOURN, H. F., M.D. "Bottle Feeding: A Problem of Modern Civilization." *J. Trop. Ped.,* March, 1958. Excerpted in *CFD,* Sept.-Oct. 1958.

WOLFENSTEIN, M. "Trends in Infant Care." *Am. J. Orthopsychiatry,* 23:120, 1953.

CHAPTER 6. DOCTORS WHO UNDERSTAND

American Academy of Pediatrics, Committee on Nutrition: "On the Feeding of Solid Foods to Infants." *Ped.,* 21:685-692, 1958.

APPLEBAUM, R. M., M.D. "The Modern Management of Successful Breast-Feeding." *Ped. Clin. N. Am.,* 17:203-225, 1970.

CARNEY, OTIS. "They Deliver Your Baby at Home—Safely." *Collier's,* Nov. 22, 1952; reprinted, *CFD,* May 1953.

CORBIN, HAZEL. "Changing Maternity Service in a Changing World." *Pub. Health Nursing,* 42:427, 1950.

GUTHRIE, H., and G. GUTHRIE. "The Resurgence of Natural Feeding." *Clin. Ped.,* 5:481-484, 1966.

GYORGY, PAUL, M.D. "Orientation In Infant Feeding." *Fed. Proc.* 20, Suppl. 7:169, 1961.

HAIRE, D. "The Nurse's Contribution to Successful Breast Feeding." *ICEA* publication, ICEA Supply Center, Bellevue, Washington, 1971.

HARRIS, A. "A Public Health Nurse in Rooming-In." *Pub. Health Nursing*, Oct. 1952; reprinted, *CFD*, Jan. 1953.

HAYDEN, F. "Maternal Mortality in History and Today." *Md. J. Australia*, pp. 100-109, Jan. 1970.

HOLDAWAY, GARTH, M.D. "A Year's Experience of Rooming-In in a Maternity Home." *New Zealand Med. J.* 58:163; reprinted, *CFD*, Nov.-Dec. 1959.

JACKSON, E. B., M.D. and G. TRAINHAM. "Family-Centered Maternity and Infant Care." Suppl. I to *Problems of Infancy and Childhood*, Transactions of the Fourth Conference, Josiah Macy Jr. Foundation, New York, 1950.

JORDHEIM, A. F. "Having a Baby in Norway." *Am. J. Nursing*, 52:1; reprinted, *CFD*, April 1952.

KIMBALL, E. R. "How I Get Mothers to Breastfeed." *Physician's Mgement.*, June 1968.

KING, F. TRUBY, M.D. *Natural Feeding of Infants.* New Zealand, London: Whitcombe and Tombs, Ltd., 1918.

KOOPMAN, A., *et al.* "Stress Without Distress." *R. N.*, Sept. 1953; reprinted in *CFD*, Dec. 1953.

KRUSE, M. "The Relief Housewife in Denmark." *Am. J. Nursing*, 51:105; reprinted, *CFD*, July 1951.

LADAS, A. K. "How to Help Mothers Breastfeed." *Clin. Ped.*, 9:12 p. 702, 1970.

LAKE, E. "Breast Fed Is Best Fed." *Reader's Digest*, June 1950.

McBRYDE, A., M.D. "Compulsory Rooming-In in the Ward and Private Newborn Service at Duke Hospital." *J. Am. Med. Assoc.*, 145:9; reprinted, *CFD*, June 1951.

McCLURE, MURIEL, H. "When She Chooses Breast Feeding." *Am. J. Nursing*, 56:1002, 1956.

MEYER, H. "Breast-Feeding in the United States." *Clin: Ped.* 7:708-715, 1968.

MILLS, A. C. "Babies Born at Home in Great Britain." *Canadian Nurse*, Nov. 1959. Excerpted in *CFD*, Mar. 1960.

MOLONEY, JAMES CLARK, M.D., *et al.* "Newborn, His Family and the Modern Hospital." *The Mod. Hosp.;* reprinted, *CFD*, Oct. 1949.

MONTAGU, ASHLEY. "Babies Should Be Born at Home!" *Ladies' Home Journal*, Aug. 1955; reprinted, *CFD*, March, 1956.

NEWTON, MICHAEL, M.D. "Nine Questions Mothers May Ask About Breast Feeding." *Consultants*, pp. 27-30, Feb. 1967.

————and NILES NEWTON. "Psychologic Aspects of Lactation." *New Eng. J. Med.*, 277:1179-1188, 1967.

NEWTON, NILES. "Breast Feeding—Psychological Aspects." *Phila. Med.*, 46:49, 1951; reprinted, *CFD*, Jan. 1952.

————. "Childbirth Under Unusually Fortunate Circumstances." *CFD*, Sept. 1953.

————. "The Medical Case for Routine Rooming-In." Unpublished. Available from ICEA, Bellevue, Washington, 1962.

ODELL, G. " 'Physiologic' Hypobilirubinemia in the Neonatal Period." *Med. Intell.* 277:193-195, 1967.

RICHARDSON, FRANK H., M.D. "Progress of Breast Feeding in New York State." Read at the seventy-eighth annual session of the *Am. Med. Assoc.*, Washington, D. C., May 20, 1927.

――――. "Breast Feeding Comes of Age." *J. Am. Med. Assoc.*, 142:863, 1950.

――――. "Breast Feeding: Going or Coming? And Why?" *N. Carolina Med. J.* 21:102, 1960.

ROSS, H. "Ante-Natal Preparation for Breast Feeding." *CFD*, Nov. 1958.

SALBER, E. and M. FEINLEIB. "Breast-Feeding in Boston." *Ped.* 37:299-303, 1966.

THOMS, H., M.D. and R. H. WYATT, M.D. "One Thousand Consecutive Deliveries Under a Training for Childbirth Program." *Am. J. Ob. and Gyn.*, 61:205, 1951.

CHAPTER 7. WOMEN WHO SHARE

FRISBIE, R. P. "The Womanly Art of Breast Feeding." *Everywoman's Family Circle*, May 1960.

GYORGY, PAUL, M.D. "Are Human Milk Banks Still Necessary?" *J. of the Maine Med. Assoc.*, Jan. 1962.

Medical Review, 1960. The Evanston Hospital Association, 2650 Ridge Ave., Evanston, Ill.

NEWTON, NILES. "New Help for Nursing Mothers." *CFD*, Sept.-Oct. 1960.

SHORT, FLORENCE. "Breast Feeding Saves Baby's Life." *Ladies' Home Journal*, Aug. 1958.

SMITH, BEVERLY BUSH. "Begins Nursing to Save Baby at Eleven Weeks." *Chicago Sunday Tribune*, Aug. 14, 1960. Reprinted, with comments by F. L. Richardson, M.D., *CFD*, July-Aug. 1960.

CHAPTER 8. ATTITUDES TOWARD BREAST FEEDING

ADAMS, W. "Is Your Wife Too Civilized?" *Better Homes and Gardens;* reprinted in *CFD*, Jan. 1960.

Breast Feeding. Children's Bureau Folder No. 8, Revised, 1947. U.S. Dept. of Health, Education and Welfare, Washington, D. C.

BRECHER, R. and E. BRECHER. "What They've Been Learning About Breast Feeding." *Ladies' Home Journal*, Dec. 1955; reprinted in *CFD*, April, 1958.

COUNTRYMAN, BETTY ANN. *Breast Feeding.* New York and Indianapolis: The Bobbs-Merrill Company, Inc., 1960.

FOOTE, J., M.D., "An Infant Hygiene Campaign of the Second Century." *Arch. Ped.*, 37:173, 1920.

JELIFFE, D. B., M.D. Letter re.: "Gunther: Instinct and the Nursing Couple." *Lancet,* 268:1024, 1955.

KINSEY, A. C., M.D. *et al. Sexual Behavior of the Human Female.* Philadelphia: W. B. Saunders Co., 1955.

LYON, A. B. "The Sexual Aspects of Breast Feeding." *CFD,* Dec. 1955.

MOLONEY, JAMES CLARK, M.D. "Maternocentric Child Rearing." *Merrill-Palmer Quart.,* Winter 1956; reprinted, *CFD,* Nov.-Dec. 1956.

MOSHER, CLELIA, M.D. *Woman's Physical Freedom.* The Woman's Press, 1923.

MURDOCK, G. P., and J. W. WHITING. "Cultural Determination of Parental Attitudes." from *Problems of Infancy and Childhood,* Transactions of the Fourth Conference, Josiah Macy Jr. Foundation, New York, 1950.

NEWTON, NILES. *Maternal Emotions.* New York: Paul Hoeber, Inc. (Harper & Row), 1955.

O'NEILL, DESMOND, M.D. "Incidence of the Atalanta Symptoms." *Postgrad. Med. J.* London, reprinted, *CFD,* Dec. 1954.

The Psychiatric Quarterly. Editorial: . . . "It Broke the Baby's Teeth." *Psych. Quart.,* 30:131; reprinted, *CFD,* 14:3, 1956.

ROLFE, J. C., trans. AULUS GELLIUS: *The Attic Nights.* Loeb Classical Library, 2:353, New York: G. P. Putnam's Sons, 1927.

SPOCK, BENJAMIN, M.D. *The Common Sense Book of Baby and Child Care.* New York: Duell, Sloan & Pearce, Inc., 1945.

STENDLER, C. G. "Sixty Years of Child Training Practices." *J. Ped.,* 36:122, 1950.

CHAPTER 9. BEFORE THE BABY COMES

DAVIS, ADELLE. *Let's Have Healthy Children.* New York: Harcourt, Brace & World, Inc., 1951.

GOODRICH, F. W., M.D. *Natural Childbirth.* Englewood Cliffs, N. J.: Prentice-Hall, Inc., 1950.

HOFFMAN, J. B., M.D. "A Suggested Treatment for Inverted Nipples." *Am. J. Ob. and Gyn.,* 47:346, 1953.

THOMS, H., M.D., and L. G. ROTH, M.D. *Understanding Natural Childbirth.* New York: McGraw-Hill Book Co., 1950.

CHAPTER 10. IN THE HOSPITAL

BARNES, G., M.D. *et al.* "Management of Breast Feeding." *J. Amer. Med. Assoc.,* 17:192, 1953.

Easy Breastfeeding. Pub. of the Natural Childbirth Trust of Great Britain, 26 Seymour St., London, W. 1.

GUNTHER, MAVIS, M.D. "Sore Nipples: Causes and Prevention." *Lancet,* 249:590, 1945.

MONTGOMERY, T. "Immediate Care of the Newborn." *Clin. Ob. and Gyn.*, 5:30, 1962.

NAISH, CHARLOTTE, M.D. "Common Complaints in Breast Feeding and Their Treatment." *Childhood*, Mar.-Apr. 1949; reprinted in *CFD*, March 1951.

NEWTON, NILES. "Nipple Pain and Nipple Damage." *J. Ped.*, 41:411, 1952.

NORVAL, M. A. "Sucking Responses of Newly Born Babies at Breast." *Am. J. Dis. Child.*, 71:41, 1946.

SVEDRES, M. F. "Rooming-In Is Not Enough for Me!" *CFD*, Nov.-Dec. 1957.

TRAINHAM, G. and J. MONTGOMERY. "Seif-Demand Feeding for Babies." *Am. J. Nursing*, 46:766, 1946.

WEIDENBACH, E. *Family-Centered Maternity Nursing.* New York: G. P. Putnam's Sons, 1958.

CHAPTERS 11, 12, 13. ONE TO SIX WEEKS: THE LEARNING PERIOD; THE REWARD PERIOD BEGINS; NURSING YOUR OLDER BABY

"Baby Sling Helps Mother." Anonymous letter, *CFD*, Aug. 1950.

CRUSE, HELOISE. *Housekeeping Hints.* Englewood Cliffs, N. J.: Prentice-Hall, Inc., 1962.

FROEHLICH, EDWINA. "When and How Shall I Wean My Baby?" *LLL News*, 1:5; reprinted, *CFD*, Mar.-April 1959.

MOLNER, J. G., M.D. "Your Health: Don't Battle Baby Over New Foods." *The Sunday Advertiser*, Nov. 27, 1960, Honolulu, Hawaii, 1960.

MCCANE, R. *"The Maintenance of Stability in the Newborn." Arch. Dis. Child.* 34:361-370, 1959.

NEWTON, NILES. "Why I Weaned My Second Baby Late." *CFD*, Nov. 1950.

OLMSTED, R. W., M.D., and E. B. JACKSON, M.D. "Self-Demand Feeding in the First Weeks of Life." *Ped.*, 6:396, 1950.

RICHARDSON, FRANK H., M.D. "Can a Working Mother Nurse Her Baby?" *Today's Health*, Feb. 1951; reprinted in *CFD*, April 1951.

SMALLPIECE, V., and P. DAVIES. "Immediate Feeding of Premature Babies with Undiluted Breast Milk." *Lancet*, pp. 1349-1352, 1964.

SMITH, BEVERLY BUSH. "Weaning Your Breast-Fed Baby." *Today's Health*, July 1962.

TRAINHAM, G., *et al.* "A Case History of Twins Breast-Fed on a Self-Demand Schedule." *J. Ped.*, 27:97, 1954.

RECOMMENDED FILMS

"A Better Beginning." 16 mm. sound film about the Evantson Premature Babies' Milk Bank. Available on free loan to interested groups. Film Library, Speech Annex, Northwestern University, Evanston, Ill.

"Breast Feeding—A Family Affair." 16 mm. sound, color film. Association for Childbirth Education, Mrs. William H. McCafferty, distribution chairman, 2763 N.W. 70th, Seattle 7, Washington. Fee, $5 per showing.

"The Okinawan" and other films on family life, infant care, and mental health in other cultures. Dr. James Clark Moloney, 240 Daines St., Birmingham, Michigan.

"Hospital Maternity Care—Family Centered." An excellent film. Soon to be available with sound track in French and Spanish also. Write Exhibit Manager, Mead Johnson Laboratories, Evansville 21, Indiana. No charge.

"Talking About Breastfeeding." 16 mm. sound film, *cinema verité* style. A touching, warm glimpse of what it is like to be a nursing mother; good teaching aid or introduction. Polymorph Films, Inc., 331 Newbury St., Boston, Mass. 02115. Rent or purchase.

MAGAZINES, PAMPHLETS, AND PRODUCTS

Abreast of the Times. R. M. Applebaum, M.D. A guide for mothers by one of the nation's leading medical experts on breast feeding. La Leche League International, 9616 Minneapolis Avenue, Franklin Park, Ill. 60131. $2.50 plus .25 postage.

Best-Fed Babies. Forty pages of questions and answers about breast feeding. Association for Childbirth Education, 2763 N.W. 70 St., Seattle, Washington 98167. $1.00.

Breast Feeding and Natural Child Spacing. Sheila K. Kippley. K. Publishers, 845 E. Minneapolis, Salina, Kansas 67401. Also available from LLLI. $2.95 plus .25 postage.

Briefs. A digest of current articles on maternity care and related subjects, published six times yearly by the Maternity Center Association, 48 E. 92 St., New York, N.Y. 10028, $2.00 per year.

Child and Family. Box 508, Oak Park, Ill. 60303. $4.00 per year.

ICEA News. Bulletin of the International Childbirth Education Association. Annual Membership $10.00. Subscription, $1.00 from Mrs. Donald Gollnick, 1310 N. 26 St., Milwaukee, Wisconsin 53205.

Instructions for Nursing Your Baby. Hospital pamphlet approved by the American Academy of Pediatrics and the American College of Obstetricians and Gynecologists. $2.25 per 100 from ICEA Supplies Center, 208 Ditty Building, Bellevue, Wash. 98004.

Mamasan Nursing Dresses. Instructions on converting dress patterns for nursing. $.50 plus self-addressed, stamped envelope. Mrs. Martin Klein, 570 Grand Boulevard, Brentwood, N.Y. 11717.

The Normal Course and Management of Lactation, by Michael Newton, M.D., and Niles Newton, Phd.; and *Modern Management of Successful Breast-Feeding,* by R. M. Applebaum, M.D., available as a single reprint from *Child and Family."* Box 508, Oak Park, Ill. 60603. $.50 ea., discounts on quantity.

Nuk-Sauger Nipples and Pacifiers: Nuk-Sauger Preventative Orthodontic Program. P. O. Box 1887, Denver, Colorado 80206.

The Nurse's Contribution of Successful Breast-Feeding. and *The Medical Value of Breast Feeding* by Doris and John Haire. Convincing medical information and extensive bibliography. ICEA Supplies Center, 208 Ditty Building, Bellevue, Washington 98004.

Lact-aid Nursing Supplementer. J. J. Avery, Inc., P. O. Box 6459, Denver, Colorado 80206.

Please Breast-feed Your Baby. Alic Gerard. Signet Books, The New American Library, Inc. 1301 Avenue of the Americas, New York, N.Y. 10019. $.75 per copy.

Relactation: A Guide to Breast Feeding the Adopted Baby. Elizabeth Hormann, LLLI, $1.00 plus $.30 postage.

"Symposium: The Uniqueness of Human Milk." Excellent articles by the Jelliffes, the Newtons, Dr. Paul Gyorgy, Marian Tompson of La Leche League, and others. $1.75 from the *American Journal of Clinical Nutrition,* 9650 Rockville Pike, Bethesda, Maryland 20014.

Woolwich Breast Shields for retracted nipples. LLLI, $2.75 a pair plus $.50 postage.

For lists of pamphlets and reprints on a wide variety of subjects related to breast feeding, ranging from history and folklore to specific medical problems, write to:

Child and Family, Box 508, Oak Park, Ill. 60303

La Leche League International, 9616 Minneapolis Avenue, Franklin Park, Ill. 60131

International Childbirth Education Association Supplies Center, 208 Ditty Building, Bellevue, Washington 98004.

MILK BANKS

(Milk available only by doctor's prescription.
Donors must live within driving distance of milk banks.)

Breast Milk Bank, Clifford Lanter, Asst. Director, Southwest Blood Bank of Arizona, 4 South 12th Ave., Phoenix, Arizona.

The Directory for Mother's Milk, Inc., Miss Cornelia MacPherson, General Director, 221 Longwood Ave., Boston 15, Massachusetts.

Evanston Premature Babies' Milk Bank, c/o Chairman, Evanston Hospital, Evanston, Illinois.

Mothers' Milk Bank, Inc., Mrs. R. D. Jessee, President, 2032 Webster St., San Francisco 15, California.

Mothers' Milk Bank of Wilmington, Mrs. Allen T. Hill, Director, Delaware Hospital, Wilmington, Delaware.

LA LECHE LEAGUE

For a current list of La Leche League groups and similar nursing mothers' circles, write to La Leche League International, Inc., 9616 Minneapolis Avenue, Franklin Park, Ill. 60131.

Breastfeeding help at any time: (312) 455-7730 (Illinois).

LLLI Pamphlets:

How the Nurse Can Help the Breastfeeding Mother. $.20.

When You Breastfeed Your Baby. $.10.

Index

Milk tension, 34-35
Miscarriage, 20
Moloney, Dr. James Clark, 83, 84, 113
Montagu, Ashley, 8
Mother, nursing, 4-5, 7-8, 11-13, 23-26, 66
"baby blues," 76
clothes, 216-18
diet, 58-60, 160-61, 179, 188-89, 209-10, 235
disadvantaged, 153
and doctors, 88-90, 95-98
donor, 122-23, 124
fatigue, 36, 239
and groups, 130-31
heartbeat, 72-73
malnourished, 59
and mastitis, 97, 103, 106, 204-06, 232
nursing couple, 2, 4-8, 14-15, 213-14
rest, 160-61, 184-85, 188, 194, 203, 211, 215, 234
self-care, 187-88
triplets, 210
twins, 208-10
vitamins, 49-52, 224
weaning, 6-8, 251-53, 254, 257-58
working, 146, 233-34
see also Mothers
Mothering
and animals, 68-70
and humans, 67-68, 76-80
skills, 260-62
Mothers,
after delivery, 74-75
fitness, 161-62
primitive, 98-100
see also Mother, nursing
Mothers' helpers, 157-58
Mothers' Milk Bank of San Francisco, 117-18

Naps, 160, 185, 214
see also Rest
Nasal spray, 32, 112, 186
Natural childbirth, 105
Newborns
and body contact, 83
and colostrum, 75-76
New Jersey, Visiting Homemakers of, 112-13, 158
Newton, Dr. Michael, 84, 92, 103
Newton, Niles, 84, 92, 103, 114, 143, 161, 198
Night feeding, 188, 207, 215, 245-46
Nipples
care of, 170, 171
desensitizing, 155-56
"hardening" agents, 156
human vs. bottle, 73-74
and let-down reflex, 30-31, 32, 34
Nuk-Sauger, 42
retracted, 89-90, 155-57
shields for, 180
sore, 31, 32, 92, 172, 179-81, 205, 208
Noises and baby, 225-26
Nuk-Sauger nipple, 42
Nurse, baby, 158
Nursery, hospital, 106-09, 171-72
Nurses
and breast care, 156
and breast feeding, 72, 87, 90, 138, 173-74
helpful, 4, 182
labor, 115
lactation, 110-11, 114
nursery, 165
and rooming-in, 106, 108-09
visiting, 157, 158
wet, 34, 37, 118-20, 209

The Practice of
Policy Analysis

Forty Years of Art & Technology

The Practice of Policy Analysis
Forty Years of Art & Technology

by Peter W. House and Roger D. Shull

Foreword by Aaron Wildavsky

THE COMPASS PRESS
WASHINGTON, D.C.

DISCLAIMER

This book is an account of work sponsored by the United States government. Neither the United States nor the National Science Foundation (an agency of the U.S. government) nor any of their employees makes any warranty, express or implied, or assumes any legal liability or responsibility for the accuracy, completeness, or usefulness of any information, apparatus, product, or process disclosed, or represents that its use would not infringe privately owned rights. Reference herein to any specific commercial product, process, or service by trade name, mark, manufacturer, or otherwise does not constitute or imply its endorsement, recommendation, or favoring by the United States government or any agency thereof. The views and opinions of the authors expressed herein do not necessarily state or reflect those of the United States government or any agency thereof.

Edited by Michael Cannizzaro
Book and Cover designed by Anne Meagher-Cook
Printed (alk paper) and bound in the U.S. by Edwards Brothers, Ann Arbor, Michigan

Library of Congress Cataloguing-in-Publication Data

House, Peter William, 1937–
    The practice of policy analysis: forty years of art and
technology / by Peter W. House, Roger D. Shull; foreword by
Aaron Wildavsky.
    p. cm.
Includes bibliographical references.
    1. Policy sciences—Case studies. 2. Energy policy—United
States—Case studies. 3. Environmental policy—United States—Case
studies. I. Shull, Roger D. (Roger Don) II. Title
H97.H67   1991   320'.6—dc20 91-24363
ISBN 0-929590-03-1 (cloth)
ISBN 0-929590-04-X (paper)

The Compass Press is an imprint of Howells House
Box 9546, Washington, DC 20016

Contents

Illustrations

Figures

Foreword

Peter House and Roger Shull are known for their critical acumen in describing government and personal experience with the effort to use large-scale mathematical models. They have demonstrated, to anyone who is amenable to argument, that these large-scale models, even if run on mainframe computers, were of limited value which decreased with the political complexity of the problem. They reflect substantial political sophistication: they have been around too long not to know, for instance, that imposing massive requirements for analysis of new regulations or of environmental impacts has the purpose of delaying things some people don't like as well as just possibly contributing to enlightenment. Nor do they suppose that the advent of desktop computers is going to change fundamental political facts of life, although it does enhance the prospects for more widespread use of simpler models.

Somewhat to their surprise, they have concluded that growing data bases and the computer power to manage them have, rather than introducing a new era of large-model systems analysis, revalidated the more modest, step-by-step cost-benefit analyses and feedback approach known as "incrementalism" in an earlier era. A technocratic decision process managed by mathematical experts would not be for them even if it were feasible, which it is not; instead, their book is about making incrementalism work better.

Throughout this book, which gives the reader the best of academic knowledge and of practical experience, we see how far the field of policy analysis and the authors have come. Analytical methods have been simplified and their accuracy increased, and all sorts of difficulties in applying analysis have been recognized so that earlier pretensions are gone. The authors have cut mere analytical expertise down to size, illuminating many areas for which existing knowledge and know-how is inadequate—including the limitations of cost-benefit analysis; they not only acknowledge the important role played by conflicting values but build it in to the discussion of what analysis can and cannot do. In short, everything connected with analysis has become more modest as the field has gained the experience of practice in the real world. As it should.

Just as the analytic community's awareness has grown, however, there have been challenges that would reject all analysis as it has been practiced up until now—the better along with the worse. For readers to take to heart the subtle and discerning discussion of strengths and weaknesses of analysis that House and Shull provide, they must be persuaded that the analysis itself is worthwhile, or at least not join those who wish to dissolve all facts into their values.

A quarter of a century ago, when I first became aware of those new-fangled modes of analysis (systems analysis, cost-benefit analysis, and program budgeting), I thought they did not take political factors sufficiently into account. I included as "political" not only people with different values competing over rival visions of public policy, but also the need of government for public support. The economists with whom I differed in those days felt that my strictures would create anarchy in their pristine models. It took me some time to realize that we all agreed on the general idea of weighing the pluses and minuses of a particular array of alternatives and expressing (when relevant, feasible, and accurate) comparisons roughly in quantitative terms. It is this even more general model of cost-benefit analysis, however, that is now under attack.

Returning for a moment to the bad old days, even then there was a radical rejection of cost-benefit analysis. Since, the argument went, the political economy was immoral and unproductive, and markets perpetuated and exacerbated inequalities, models that assumed the validity of these institutional structures were unacceptable. If one dislikes democratic capitalism because one believes democracy is a sham and capitalism is coercion, then one certainly does not want to accept cost-benefit or any other type of analysis based on analogies to these systems.

The logic was then and remains impeccable. The empirical question was whether these allegations were true, especially in comparison to any other known alternative. For if the allegations were true but alternatives were worse, one might have to hold one's nose and accept the lesser evil. One could even claim that there was a greater good to be found and diligently seek it, but, until it was found, the lesser evil would represent a more moral course. In light of the utter failure and popular rejection in Eastern Europe and the Soviet Union of communist command economies, the principal alternative to democratic capitalism, these old assertions appear rather shopworn. If the political economy you prefer produces results you condemn, you have a moral as well as logical conflict.

The present challenge to cost-benefit analysis comes not from those who doubt democracy or capitalism but from those who believe such analysis is dangerous to the survival of the earth and humanity. The new challenge to cost-benefit analysis does not extend to counting costs: There is great interest in estimating the damage that industry and technology do— indeed, one objection to current cost-benefit analysis is that it does not value highly enough environmental damage. The central objection, however, is not to the measurement of costs but to counting benefits—and, in particular, to offsetting the benefits to some against the costs to others. Rather, if any new substance harms anyone, it should be prohibited. I say that this is a rejection of cost-benefit analysis because without the criterion of *net* benefit there is no point in analysis at all.

Why is it deemed not only inappropriate but immoral to offset "harms" by "goods"? One notion is that there is so much harm around already that adding to it is criminal. This policy of minimizing regret implies that losses are much more important than gains and therefore no losses are acceptable whatsoever. One might argue that if modern technology produced only unmitigated damage, most of us wouldn't be around to argue the point, but this argument is invalidated by a second and more compelling notion—namely, the idea of impending catastrophe.

In this sort of "final straw" scenario, as applied to the environment, the implicit hypothesis is that, at some point, a single increment of pollution or global warming could create irreversible environmental damage. This form of incrementalism—in which a single molecule of harm is enough to kill— stands in stark contrast to traditional incrementalism, the piecemeal engineering in which feedback from small moves is used to calibrate future actions so that some good might be done while avoiding great harm. If one increment can kill, we cannot have increments at all.

The acceptance of these notions would make cost-benefit analysis irrelevant: either the cost side would be so high as to dwarf any benefit, or the benefit side would be ruled out altogether. Thus the authors' hope in this book to encourage incrementalism as a strategy for improving public policy is challenged on two fronts—on the one hand, by the rejection of the concept of *net* benefit, and, on the other, by the rejection of even incremental changes bearing potential dangers.

Yet, the reading of this book will be equally edifying for those looking for signs of policy analysis in its death throes as for those seeking to improve it. Everyone knows that not everything is subject to analysis, any more than people are market commodities. Many, if not most, things are decided by agreement, not calculation. For House and Shull, this fact is fundamental to their positioning of public policy analysis in the general scheme of things. And, they note, even when there is agreement, there is not always a policy by which to achieve the agreed objectives.

The authors also join several of the most perceptive and outstanding scholars in the field (Graham, Raiffa, and Vaupel) in the observation that some policy problems are simply beyond our understanding—an extension of the widely recognized notion of cognitive limits on rationality. Further, in an extension of Michael Polyani's concept of "tacit knowledge," they suggest that managers, private as well as public, would often do better to conduct their own informal analyses because it is the manager, not the analyst, who can draw on a fund of practical experience and deal with the realities of a particular organization. Thus, the authors predict, policy analysis in the future is likely to place a greater premium on expertise in the substantive discipline at issue than on analytical expertise per se.

As for the values which frame and structure policy analysis, House and Shull complete the picture by noting that democratic government recognizes the people as sovereign and that no one but they, through their elected representatives, can decide what values should prevail. As the authors have maintained in earlier writings, this means that policy analysis in the public sector must be recognized as a limited and discreet, albeit important, function of the responsibilities of political leaders to frame the questions at the beginning and to select an alternative, regardless of the analytical results, at the end. But above all, it means that the selection of values must be part of the public political process. I agree.

Lately, although I still share this view, I am less certain that it will always work for good. Some issues—child welfare, for example—may be removed from the realm of calculation and determined in the realm of values. This is understandable. But when more and more advocates find it advantageous and are able to politically exempt their issues from the scrutiny of analysis, more and more facts become subordinated to values and, reminiscent of Hume's warning against the will becoming servant of the passions, the polity grows contentious and consensus on values dissipates.

Moreover, an unwillingness to face facts creates grave risks of its own: An organism can die from internal exhaustion by using up its resources to combat false alarms just as well as it can perish from failing to recognize a real threat. But the subtler points to be made, and they are implicit in this book, are that a society's values can be no more perfect than the political system that defines them, and that not only do those values need to inform analysis, but analysis must also inform them.

A society that bases all its decisions on cost-benefit analysis using market analogies would lack important degrees of compassion and creativity; a society that essentially abandons cost-benefit analysis would make its people not only poorer but sicker, duller, and more cruel—we have the experience of communist societies to vouch for that. There should be exceptions to cost-benefit analysis, as House and Shull remind us, but when the exceptions become the rule, decency declines along with the economy.

It is fitting and not surprising, therefore, that at this point in the history of the art of policy analysis, the most basic techniques humans have applied to decision-making ever since they have been human—incrementalism and cost-benefit analysis—should be revalidated. Like democracy and the market economy, their strengths and imperfections are not only recognized but also understood better than systems subjected to less trial and error, and thus remain the best game in town.

Aaron Wildavsky

Preface

Professional government policy analysts provide facts, figures, and forecasts to help political executives and legislators develop, implement, and monitor the results of policy agendas. The practice of policy analysis now involves extensive quantitative manipulation of data but, over the years and among different types of issues, the relative level of contribution of quantitative analysis has vacillated.

The choice of a public policy from a set of alternatives is based on political objectives, observed facts, value judgments, and perceptions of the potential results of various policies. Quantitative analyses can contribute to all of these decision factors, but are most suited to clarifying the facts involved in the issue. In the early days of mainframe computers, many new mathematical tools were developed for all phases of policy analysis. Unseasoned developers pushed them as cure-alls, touting the ability of the computer and mathematical algorithms to make final decisions with little or no effort on the part of the politician. The modeling philosophy of the time was "comprehensiveness"; i.e., the model attempted to simulate all conceivable factors impinging upon the issue at hand, rendering the politician omniscient regarding all likely outcomes of a policy choice, given any assumed set of influential factors. This philosophy was offered to replace older, more limited techniques, pejoratively dubbed "incremental analysis."

Incrementalism is the name for a specific approach to public administration defined by Yale political economist Charles Lindblom in the late 1950s. It is based on the idea that one can never comprehend adequately the totality of a government system and, thus, public administrators should apply only incremental policy changes to most important problems until the desired solution is achieved. If the incremental actions cause unwanted secondary effects, then policies can be altered. If the desired effect is achieved with no undesirable secondary effects, no additional actions are necessary. This approach has many positive points, but many theorists, especially those with physical science, engineering, or business backgrounds, where things are designed from scratch and systems are totally controlled, consider incrementalism merely "a band-aid approach" or "crisis management."

The Art of Public Policy Analysis and *The Rush to Policy,* two of our earlier works, offered extensive first-hand documentation of the successes and failures of attempted application of large mathematical simulation and decision models to federal policy issues. This work continues to draw on that experience, including the development, implementation, and laying to rest of the Strategic Environmental Assessment System (SEAS) at the Environmental Protection Agency, described in Chapter 2.

Although noble in intent and mathematically logical in structure, the big comprehensive models that ran on mainframe computers were of limited utility. Complex as they were, they were still unrealistically simple representations of the real world. Their predictions were most accurate when the real world changed slowly and steadily, but the simple, inexpensive "back-of-the-envelope" extrapolation models also worked well then. Whenever the real world experienced shock changes of a nature not previously experienced, the comprehensive models failed as miserably as the simple models. Furthermore, the big models had been developed at the cost of several million dollars each, and required dozens of technical experts to operate.

By the 1980s, proponents of detailed quantitative methods had gained enough credibility with politicians that such methods were incorporated into laws and executive orders.

The most famous of these is Executive Order 12291, signed by President Reagan in his first month in office, which required detailed cost-benefit analyses for all new federal regulations. Ostensibly, this rule was imposed to assure that federal regulatory agencies thoroughly study the impact of proposed regulations on all concerned parties before promulgation. A second motive may have been simply to slow down the production of new regulations, one of Reagan's campaign promises. *Rush to Policy* highlighted the problems caused by Executive Order 12291 and similar rules, and suggested the appropriate place of quantitative analyses in public-sector decisions.

Although based on two different periods and on different types of analytical models, both of our earlier books conclude that the contributions of mathematical policy analyses to real policy decisions are indeed limited. In the short period since we wrote *Rush to Policy* in 1985, the large, centralized, mainframe computer has now been almost completely replaced by the desktop microcomputer (personal computer, or "PC"). This represents a substantial technological advance which has had profound effects on the use of quantitative methods in policy analyses. Microcomputers offer numerous new capabilities, and traditional analyses can now be performed and replicated with almost incredible speed.

This book, like the earlier two, addresses how to and when not to use quantitative methods in policy analyses. However, with the new PC technology, the endorsements and cautions are very different. Our more recent applications undertaken at the National Science Foundation (NSF), such as benefits assessments and risk analysis, described in Chapter 3, and a user-friendly, PC-based central data base, described in Chapter 4, have pushed us towards supporting a "new incrementalism." Based on our experience at NSF, where we have been at the frontiers of the new technology, we hope to demonstrate how the effectiveness and efficiency of policy analysis can be vastly improved; at the same time we describe those areas of policy analysis where the personal computer is of no help at all.

Methodologies have tremendous inertia and are only replaced by a better approach by strong managers. Federal policy analysts who have developed, nurtured, and lived with their large models are reluctant to let them go. Some large-scale models have survived, and are still in use, such as the Department of Energy's national energy supply and demand models, although they produce only background information rather than policy analysis. The more academic the question and the audience, the greater the interest in comprehensive models, because they are more conceptually interesting and educational. Thus, even if policy analysts never use comprehensive models, they should be aware of their abilities and limitations so as to avoid false expectations.

Executive Order 12291 is still on the books. Policy analysts in regulatory agencies across the government are doing their best to estimate benefits, costs, and risks of various proposed regulations, and public interest groups are continually challenging implementation of the executive order by the Office of Management and Budget. Whether or not regulatory analysts support the executive order, they will find that the new powers of the PC as described herein will prove enormously useful in their work.

While in the 1980s the computational capabilities of desktop computers approached those of 1970s vintage mainframes (and far surpassed their user-friendliness), mainframe computer technology has itself advanced significantly, fostering more reliable simulation of physical science phenomena such as meteorology and oceanography. In certain cases, however, such as global warming, the processes are still so complex that computers cannot credibly predict future conditions. A model for understanding global warming must a priori be comprehensive, accounting for the many sources and sinks of global gases and energy. But such models are useful only for scoping the physical aspects of the problem. Analysis of national or world policies to control global warming involves complex international economic and political issues. Comprehensive computer policy analysis models had already exceeded available data and understanding of political phenomena in the 1970s; therefore extension of computing capabilities has contributed virtually nothing to this vein of policy analysis. The ultimate use of the mainframe computer may be as a tool for the policy researcher to access extremely large data sets and perform extensive calculations to inform and complement the capabilities of PC-based analytical methods and systems.

Rather than revive the potential for comprehensive models, the new microcomputing technology has provided for more robust and defensible analyses at the primary effects level. The new technology allows quicker and more precise definitions and explanations of the current conditions of an issue, the time trends, and the outside factors most affecting the situation, thus yielding prompt short-term projections. The controlling variables in the simulation can be varied over all feasible ranges, offering an understanding of possible future situations. The policy information produced by these models is essentially as valuable as that developed on the large comprehensive models. And the simulations can be conducted with incredible speed in the PC environment, with a level of sophistication commensurate with the quality of available data. After years of building, justifying, and promoting comprehensive computer models for policy analysis, we end up in this book arguing that, with the new tools, the old (pre-systems analysis) methods are more effective. We are, in essence, promoting a revalidation of incrementalism.

This conclusion may disappoint those hoping to design more powerful or elegant analytical methods, but we foresee no hope that tough social and political problems can be "solved" by quantitative analysis. New ways of thinking about social problems and of making decisions will always be of value to political executives, but what counts in the real world is the knowledge of the science involved and, in a democracy, of the politics involved. In this regard, our views have not changed over the past decade, and the experience of our peers in Washington and recent writings of our academic colleagues support them.

1.

Introduction

The inclination to rely on numbers has been a prevailing fact of life in the legislative and executive branches of the federal government for decades. This book is not about numbers, per se, but about how policy analysts have used, are using, and will be using numbers—concocted with highly sophisticated computer systems and analytic techniques—in studies for federal, state, and local governments. Whatever their titles or organizations, government policy analysts are supposed to bring empirical know-how into the political arena. Over the years, methods have changed and the amount of information and analytical capabilities available to policy analysts have grown, but the political elements remain, in a democratic society, decisive in the choice of policy.

Policy analysis is simply the comparison of the effects of an existing or proposed set of operating rules to the impact of some other option. Staffs in regulatory agencies prepare policy analyses called "regulatory impact analyses" every time a new or revised standard is proposed (e.g., raising highway speed limits to 65 miles per hour). Such analyses address who would be helped, who would be hurt, and how much the policy would cost or save. Policy analyses range from five-minute, "back-of-the-envelope" calculations to $100 million, decade-long research studies such as the federal acid rain research effort. The issues always involve politics, and the process usually requires some quantitative analysis, but what is often not fully appreciated by the public is the extent of interaction between the political process and the informational and quantitative analyses.

Policy analysis is as old as civilized government. Indeed, Grier, reviewing ancient history, claims that the first risk analysis consulting firm was established about 3200 B.C. in the Tigris-Euphrates Valley.[1] The use of scientific advice by government executives in the early days of the United States was rare, but not completely absent. In 1830, the Secretary of the Treasury, guided by a congressional resolution, contracted with the Franklin Institute of Philadelphia to develop the specifications to meet appropriate safety standards for steam boilers, explosions of which had claimed many lives in the previous decade.[2] The National Academy of Sciences was created by public law in 1863 to coordinate the provision of scientific advice to the government during the Civil War, but organizational problems rendered the Academy ineffective until World War I.[3] In 1922, the Bureau of Agricultural Economics was created within the U.S. Department of Agriculture (USDA) to study the relationships between agriculture and the rest of the economy and to develop policies to avoid economic depressions.[4] In the depths of the Great Depression, President Hoover appointed a committee on social trends, whose work included analysis of the growth of governmental functions. The committee suggested that its analysis ". . . might supply a basis for the formulation of large national policies looking to the next phase of the nation's development."[5] President Roosevelt was aided by a group of new-age economists (dubbed the "Brain Trust" by the press) who favored government-business cooperation and helped him design and implement the New Deal.[6] The Office of Scientific Research and Development was established in 1941 to coordinate scientific activities during War World II.[7] In creating the Council of Economic Advisors by the Employment Act of 1946, Congress formally recognized that the executive branch should make use of expert knowledge in guiding the country's policies. Passage of this particular law might be considered the birth of the era of formal policy analysis in the federal government.

Analysis of national policies is not a proprietary domain of the policy analyst, however; at least theoretically, everyone in America analyzes federal policies in one way or another. As policy analysts working on computer models at the National Science Foundation, the authors have had contact with a large number of the professional players in the analysis pool. Figure 1-1 portrays only the more prominent identifiable persons and institutions involved in the continuing federal policy review process. Those in the oval labeled "agency policy analysts" are relatively small fish in a huge sea of participants, each with individual analyses, judgments, opinions, and desiderata. Information and misinformation related to government policies and programs may come from any point of the compass, and from all types of organizations. In addition to providing their own independent assessments of the status quo and possible future events, policy analysts are also responsible for reviewing and evaluating all other sources of information and propositions and for advising their executives on the veracity of challenging claims and rhetoric.

We make a distinction, as do many other authors,[8] between policy analysis and policy research. Policy analysis refers to the process of computation and arranging of data to help political executives respond to the many demands of assorted interests in a specific political context over a relatively short period of time. Policy research refers to the process of generating new detailed information and perspective on relevant policy issues over the longer term, in a more general political context.

Some agencies have a staff of researchers who gather and analyze new data and explore policy options and future scenarios. Other agencies subcontract policy research to think tanks, academic institutions, and nonprofit institutes. Policy researchers conduct detailed, rigorous studies of all facets of policy issues. In environmental, health, and safety regulatory

Figure 1-1
Participants in the Policy Process

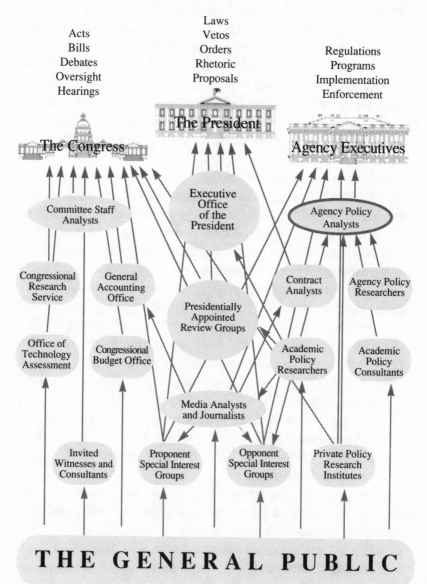

agencies, for example, policy research includes detailed basic research projects on cause and effect, measurements of safety levels, surveys of affected parties, economic evaluation of control strategies, and quantification of hazard risks of different populations.

To avoid potential conflicts of interest and influences on policy by those not duly authorized to play such a role, contract analysts and researchers are officially precluded from undertaking certain functions and making certain judgments. Office of Management and Budget (OMB) Circular A-76 prevents executive branch agencies from contracting ". . . a function which is so intimately related to the public interest as to mandate performance by government employees," including ". . . either the exercise of discretion in applying government authority or the use of value judgment in making decisions for the government." Interpretation of this rule, however, is left up to individual agency procurement officers, and several of the large agencies operating with limited personnel but large budgets for external research have pushed an increasing number of technical analyses onto private sector firms. Many critics argue that Circular A-76 has been clearly violated by these agencies, creating a "shadow government" run by unaccountable private contractors.[9] In Chapter 4, we will show how the expanded analytical capabilities of the personal computer have greatly reduced the need for contract technical assistance in policy analysis at the National Science Foundation, and how these capabilities can help other agencies regain control of their designated policy responsibilities.

Academic policy researchers may work directly for a sponsoring agency, either as consultants on demand to the policy analysts, or as principal investigators on longer-term research projects. They may also be sponsored by private foundations, interest groups, or their own institution. The research may be subject to strict guidelines of the sponsor, as in toxicology studies, or may be under very little sponsor control, as is the case with grants from the National Science

Foundation and private foundations. If not restricted, researchers under government contract can become active players in the policy debate by publishing their findings at a time or in a manner designed for political impact.

On particularly hot issues, such as AIDS, the space shuttle accident, or asbestos health hazards, the government often deflects issues to specially appointed objective or "multiperspective" committees. If the crux of the issue appears to be a scientific question, the special committee of experts is often hosted and managed by one of the national academies (e.g., the National Academy of Sciences, the National Academy of Engineering, or the National Institute of Medicine). These special committees rarely develop new fundamental information. Typically, they review several competing analyses and render pronouncements on their scientific validity. Although often advertised as "seeking the advice of the best minds in the country," this ritual is also recognized as a good way to deflect political pressures and to delay the need for action.

The Natural Tension

Policy researchers are essentially scientists, deriving their professional rewards and respect from their peers across many different institutions, including universities, professional societies, special interest organizations, industry, and government. They are schooled in the scientific method, drawing conclusions only after discovering unquestionable evidence. Detailed documentation, well tested theories, structured reasoning, precise calculations, and statistical reliability are all important attributes for the profession. Their products must adhere sufficiently to these attributes to elicit favorable review by peers. If the structured analytical process is not complete, when asked a question as to the results of the analysis, the appropriate response of the policy researcher is, "I don't know yet."

Policy analysts are sometimes described as translators,

carrying and interpreting messages back and forth between scientists and administrators.[10] The perspectives of managers and executives are different, sometimes radically so, from those of the scientist. Administrators work principally with people and situations, and decisions are made under pressure, based on experience, philosophies, objectives, and general management theories. The policy analyst must comprehend the technical principles and vocabulary of the issue well enough to be able to ask the right questions of the researchers and subsequently distill and clarify the researchers' responses so that they are comprehensible to the administrator. When the administrator asks the policy analyst for information on an issue, "I don't know" is not a helpful response.

A natural tension exists between policy analysts and policy researchers when they meet at the professional level. The same policy analysis that might have been commended for being prompt, clear, and crucial in guiding a policy decision may be faulted by policy researchers as being premature, misleading, and statistically unreliable. Conversely, a policy research journal article which received high marks during scientific peer review may be faulted by the policy analysis community as "too little, too late," naive, irrelevant, misdirected, or confusing.

Policy analysts and policy researchers often have similar academic backgrounds, but each has grown up in a different world, serving different masters. As a group, policy analysts yearn to produce more technically defensible products, just as policy researchers like their work to be relevant and helpful. But while the analyst must respond to the executive in simple terms within the specified time frame, the researcher must respond to the standards set by his peers. The resulting compromises lead to a mismatch of objectives and products. Recognition of this mismatch can help executives understand some of the criticisms of policy analysis, especially over very controversial issues.

Contemporary policy research usually requires complex

scientific and technical calculations, and the basic findings may be so technically sophisticated that their policy implications require interpretation. It is here that the question of values enters the picture, the role of the scientific expert ends, and the political debate begins. Since the implications from the scientific perspective may differ from those from the political perspective, a scholar commissioned by the government to conduct policy research may be disappointed by decisions apparently unsupported by the research findings. This contrast between experts' opinions and democratic principles has been debated since the time of Aristotle and Plato.[11]

While the experts may understand the scientific aspects of an issue, they are not elected representatives of the people, and thus cannot speak for them. Often, experts have difficulty separating their professional analyses and judgments from their personal values. In 1927, educator-philosopher John Dewey stated it this way:

> No government by experts in which the masses do not
> have the chance to inform the experts as to their needs
> can be anything but an oligarchy managed in the interests
> of the few.[12]

Various branches of government have shared this view during the creation of the different expert advisory boards. In 1947, after the American scientific community had played a major role in winning World War II, Congress approved the establishment of a federally funded National Science Foundation directed by an independent board of appointed scientific experts. President Truman vetoed the bill with the following message:

> It would, in effect, vest the determination of vital na-
> tional policies, the expenditure of large public funds, and
> the administration of important governmental functions
> in a group of individuals who would be essentially pri-
> vate citizens. The proposed National Science Foundation

would be divorced from control by the people to an extent that implies a distinct lack of faith in democratic processes.[13]

When an amended bill addressing this accountability problem was passed, Truman signed it into law, satisfied that the Foundation would be in the domain of the White House.

Scientists whose official role is to provide advice to executives on scientific issues often air their opinions about other political matters not related to science. President Nixon became so upset with the opposition to the Vietnam War publicly voiced by his science advisor and members of the President's Science Advisory Committee that he abolished the post of White House Science Advisor.[14] Congress re-established the position in 1976, but the conflict illustrates the likelihood that some advisors may find it difficult to restrict their advice to issues in their academic expertise.

For the most part, policy analysis is a discretionary commodity. Some political executives see a great need for analytical input, while others, particularly those in a newly elected administration who consider it their mission to make the changes promised in the campaign, see no need at all. Even a newly appointed or elected official who does seek analytical advice may view the career civil service staff as proponents of the policies of the previous administration. Survival for policy analysts, in these cases, depends on how well they can demonstrate that they and their skills are politically neutral and objective, and can be as useful to the new administration as they were to the old. Policy analysts, even career civil servants, who appear to have become politically tainted by the partisan use of analysis will be expected to depart along with their political patrons.

The most difficult aspect of the interaction between the analyst and the executive is in finding a precise definition of the question to be addressed. Analysts must understand why the executive is involved in the issue, what his or her perspectives are on that issue, and what the favored outcomes are and why. The policy question as seen by the administration often must be sorted from other issues introduced into the debate by outside participants. Analysts and executives must develop a vocabulary that enables them to communicate effectively. Once this understanding is achieved, policy analysts are able to monitor relevant events and provide an early warning capability for important emerging issues.

The criteria for evaluating policy alternatives must be worked out with the executive. Quantitative evaluations of policy alternatives typically emphasize costs, risks, or benefits, dealing with actual dollar costs of one alternative as compared to another. Public policies, however, affect economic sectors and political jurisdictions in different ways and cause political repercussions. Consequently, an analysis should measure the distributional effects of an action, in addition to net benefits (i.e., who wins and who loses what, and which of the official's constituencies will be affected).

The most valuable product of the policy analysis process is not a formal options paper, but the increased understanding of and confidence in decisions gained by the officials. The absolute truth behind any issue considered by the policy analyst may never be known, or noted only after it can make any difference. Therefore, much of the value of the analysis may be derived from the face-to-face, verbal interaction between analyst and executive without any formal documentation.

This interactive process, a major factor in public sector decisions for decades, is but one of many which guide managers to policy decisions. Consider a sub-cabinet-level, appointed government executive at the level of bureau chief, such as the Deputy Administrator for Federal Aviation under the Secretary of Transportation, or the Assistant Secretary for Land and Minerals Management under the Secretary of the Interior. On any given issue, he may take any or all of the following considerations into account in making a policy decision:

- the President's campaign platform (either specific statements about the issue or general views);
- the Secretary's public statements;
- informal guidance from the White House, Office of Management and Budget, and the department secretary;
- the executive's own political or career objectives;
- the positions of members and committees of Congress;
- the positions of influential private groups, including industry, the media, and campaign supporters;
- the views of advisors;
- quantitative data on the issue provided by outsiders as well as by his staff;
- the respective results of alternative decisions as hypothesized by outsiders as well as his staff.

The political context tends to determine the extent to which factual and quantitative analyses are used. For example, decisions regarding the abortion issues in the late 1980s were made almost entirely on the basis of principles, ideology, and, for some elected officials, political considerations. Numerical analyses were limited to simple points, such as how many previous abortions had been undertaken because of rape or incest. On the other hand, executives concerned with environmental issues such as acid rain and global warming were inundated by data, computer simulations, economic analyses, and forecasts.

The Constitution requires data collection and retention—specifically, Treasury receipts and disbursements and enumeration of citizens to apportion the House of Representatives. Other government functions, such as regulation of commerce, also require recordkeeping to demonstrate compliance with laws. Each executive agency has developed its own stable of recordkeepers, generating long tables and books of numbers to show Congress and the public that it is doing its job. Thus, the federal government seems not a government of men and laws, but of numbers. The evolution of recordkeeping in the mid-1960s tracks the aggressive movement of digital computer technology out of research laboratories, military laboratories, and the Census Bureau[a] into mainstream government data processing operations.

The Eras of Analysis

Although the application of computers to quantitative civilian public policy analysis has been an evolutionary process, there are four discernible eras:

* the Systems Analysis Era;
* the Comprehensive Model Era;
* the Decision Model Era; and
* the Personal Computer Era.

This book deals primarily with examples from the last three eras, as the first era has been exhaustively documented by such authors as Quade, Hoos, de Neufville, and Dorfman et al. (see Annotated Bibliography).

The discipline of systems analysis has its roots in military strategy analysis, a centuries-old concept which became a formal and highly successful occupation during World War II.[15] At that time, it was known as "operations analysis." During the 1940s, it appeared in several other incarnations, including "operations research," "management science," "optimization," "systems engineering," "cost-effectiveness analysis," and, finally, as coined by the RAND Corporation, "systems analysis."

The principle of systems analysis is to examine all parts of the system simultaneously, with the hope of finding better "answers" than if each part were considered alone. But the term "system" is ambiguous unless defined for a particular

---

[a]The Bureau of the Census was the pioneer federal user of computers, applying automated counting and sorting devices as early as 1900, and employing the UNIVAC computer as early as 1950.

problem. For example, in the Air Force, a "system" might be a landing gear, an aircraft, an aircraft weapons crew, or an entire air fleet, including support infrastructure. An aircraft carrier with all its planes and support ships might be considered a system. Deciding where to draw the "box" around the system was more often than not a political, judgmental, or intuitive task.

The tools of systems analysis are mathematical simulation and economics. Systems analysts try to construct a mathematical equation or algorithm which describes the behavior of all system components and an economic equation which describes the cost of each component as a function of its capability and reliability. Given a budget constraint, they can then calculate the best possible design. Conversely, given a design specification, they can calculate the configuration yielding the lowest possible cost.

Within the federal government, systems analysis remained a tool of the military through the early 1950s. By then, businesses had begun to explore its utility,[16] traffic engineers were beginning to use the techniques for determining the optimal size of new highways,[17] and civil engineers were beginning to use systems analysis in designing large river basin management systems.

Management of water resources was one of the first nonmilitary public policy problems subjected to systems analysis. The Harvard Water Program was initiated in 1955 in the university's Graduate School of Public Administration, now the John F. Kennedy School of Government. As in most succeeding programs, the analytical methods involved so many different academic disciplines that they required the inputs of a team of senior professionals from engineering, economics, mathematics, and political science. The early history of the program is extensively reported by its mentors, Maas, Hufschmidt, Dorfman, Thomas, Marglin, and Fair in *Design of Water Resource Systems*,[18] which became a bible to young water resource engineers and public-sector economists. The book espouses such economic erudition as efficiency objectives, income re-distribution, production functions, social benefit estimation, optimality, resource constraints, linear programming, stochastic modeling, queuing theory, Markov analysis, digital computers, and response surface analyses. It also includes a chapter describing how governmental factors conflict with ideal physical simulation, economic, and management theories. The following excerpts provide a quaint perspective of those early years:

> Analysis of a river-basin system is but one example of the diverse and complex problems that can be solved efficiently through simulation by modern computers. Other examples are simulations of vehicular traffic networks, combinations of warehousing and marketing, and constructs of the U.S. domestic economy.[b] Because it is the essence of simulation to reproduce, in some cognate way, the behavior of a system in every important detail, simulation problems typically are large-scale and complex. . . .
>
> Until digital computers of the magnitude of the Model No. 650 of the International Business Machines Corporation or the Univac I of the Remington Rand Corporation were constructed, the solution of large-scale simulation problems was not feasible. Even the storage capacity of these computers was not commodious enough to handle efficiently an analysis of the size and complexity of our simplified river-basin system. That had to await elaboration of the very large computers of the IBM 700 class,

---

[b]An indirect reference to the input-output modeling work of Nobel laureate Wassily Leontief across campus in the economics department, which would later become the source of the comprehensive model era.

with an internal magnetic-core storage capacity of up to 32,768 words.[c19]

The 1960s brought economic and social changes which fostered a "Golden Age" for systems analysis, policy analysis, data processing, simulation, optimization, and many other disciplines associated with scientific analysis and computer calculations. After the launching of the Soviet space satellite, Sputnik, the government formed the National Aeronautics and Space Administration (NASA) and set a goal of beating the Russians to the moon. At the same time, a more dispersed and mundane problem recognized in a growing number of metropolitan areas throughout the nation was the rapid, often haphazard, unplanned growth of industry and urban areas. Still basking in the afterglow of the technological victory of World War II, the nation looked to the federal government to develop technological solutions to these problems as well.

All federal transportation functions were consolidated and expanded under a new Department of Transportation, including an Urban Mass Transit Administration. Human resource functions were consolidated and expanded under the new Department of Health, Education and Welfare, with large increases in medical and air and water pollution research, and a new Department of Housing and Urban Development was created, with massive grant programs to rebuild America's cities. Federal resources were ample for these expanding programs, and the systems analysis community garnered its fair share. Both authors witnessed this rapid change while in graduate school; computations for master's theses were done with adding machines and slide rules, but doctoral research

---

[c]For comparison, a 1990 "notebook" computer ($8^{1}/_{2}'' \times 11'' \times 2''$, 4 lb.) had a magnetic core (now RAM) storage of 2 million words (bytes) plus rapidly accessible backup storage (hard disk with 30-millisecond response) of 40 million words. This represents roughly 1,000 times greater capacity in about 1/1,000 of the physical volume.

calculations a few years later were done on mainframe computers.

"Planning" became a buzz word in government at all levels. Just as mechanical failures in physical systems were blamed on poor design, the systems analysts attributed social and economic problems on poor planning. If government agencies would simply gather data, define and investigate the social "system" involved, project the social costs and benefits of alternative strategies, and implement the optimal strategy, social problems could be "solved." And systems analysts had all the tools necessary for such planning and design. Planning offices at all levels of government and in all fields of public service were created or, if extant, pushed to center stage. They were supported with growing budgets to hire systems analysts as consultants. All federal environmental legislation of the 1960s contained provisions and funding for long-range planning to ensure that environmental quality would be preserved once it had been recovered.

In the systems analysis era, emphasis was on methodology rather than subject matter. Thus, professional papers and conferences focused on procedures such as linear programming, Markov analysis, dynamic programming, game theory, stochastic modeling, Bayesian analysis, quasi-linearization, invariant embedding, general system theory, and feedback. Papers at these conferences frequently involved the application of systems analysis to a specific problem, but the problem was used merely as a set of data for testing and demonstrating an algorithm. Almost every application was custom-programmed, using basic algorithms copied from manuscripts.

The "transferability" argument, used by systems analysis promoters to justify federal funds, was that once developed, a new algorithm could be applied to all other similar social problems at very little cost. But successive applications were not simple "off-the-shelf" tasks that could be handled by government staff or even the average local government consultant. To make a complex computer model operate correctly, experienced personnel had to guide the collection, interpretation, and loading of data into the computer. The proprietors of successful models marketed these services to the government at substantial profit.

Systems analysts during this period should have been constrained by the lack of sufficient data to define component relationships in a statistically significant manner. Millions of dollars were spent gathering environmental, economic, and sociological data, but analysts had no idea whether or not many of the important functions programmed into the models actually simulated reality.

Most analysts addressed this shortcoming with their best guesses for technical coefficients for the models, reasoning that once the model was operating in a rudimentary sense ("first draft"), they could determine the relative importance of the poorly defined components and then gather improved data. This approach to the problem of data enabled the discipline to advance rapidly in the early days and actually carried over into the comprehensive model era. However, in the end, the data problem proved to be an Achilles' heel for both systems analysis and for comprehensive models.

Secretary of Defense Robert McNamara applied systems analysis throughout his department's budgeting process with the Program Planning and Budgeting System—or PPBS, an acronym long remembered (usually with no particular fondness) by federal bureaucrats. President Johnson called the system revolutionary, and directed that it be used in all federal agencies.[20] By the end of the decade, federal, state, and local governments had paid tens of millions of dollars to academic consultants and "Beltway bandits" (consulting firms which sprouted in the Washington suburbs along the Capital Beltway) to simulate plans and operations in such areas as the environment, energy, education, law enforcement, transportation, urban development, water resources, health services, and even national economic policy.

With all these components of social infrastructure now

subject to systemic analysis, the next step, as mainframe computer capabilities continued to advance, was to integrate each component as a "subsystem" in one grand, coordinated model of the region, state, or nation. This was the dawn of the era of comprehensive analysis.

By 1970, most federal agencies and the governments of the most populous cities and states had installed mainframe computers for financial management. Government researchers and their supporting contractors were learning the advantages of mainframe computers and a few agencies were beginning to use them for data storage and retrieval. But it took an act of faith, and a good deal of time and specialized assistance, to entrust a job to a computer instead of the traditional tools of analysis. Even after a clear specification of the algorithm was given to a computer programmer, the program keyed into the computer, and the job "submitted," time- and resource-devouring pitfalls remained. New programs never ran correctly the first time, so many cycles of programming and submission were required to produce results. Only then could one begin parametric studies with the program to determine its capabilities and utility for the purpose at hand; but even at this stage, computer results were simply long columns of numbers in stacks of fan-fold paper, so any graphic analysis required the services of a draftsman.

Yet computers played a major role in NASA's successful delivery of men to the moon and back. This accomplishment generated a chorus of what Ida Hoos called "doleful dichotomies"[21] in which the success of the lunar landing was compared to the failures of current social programs: neatness and order versus social disorder, holistic perspectives versus fragmentation, efficient management versus bumbling bureaucracy. Everyone, from the President on down, wanted to know why we couldn't use the technology that got us to the moon to solve social problems. This optimism, combined with sharp cutbacks in NASA's funding of support contractors as the Apollo program wound down, produced a large cadre of aerospace computer experts looking for new applications and a like body of government officials only too eager to engage them. Civilian federal agencies entered into large new contracts to develop computer simulations to solve problems in environmental quality management, urban planning, transportation planning, law enforcement, educational planning, health service delivery, energy policy, and economic policy. Hundreds of millions of dollars were spent programming the models, collecting and organizing data bases, and producing policy options from the computer output.

Unlike earlier efforts, which relied on incremental, partial, or unit analysis, most of the new models were "comprehensive." Using systems analysis techniques from military and aerospace applications, they linked empirical physical relationships, cost functions, damage functions, human behavior models, and other quantifiable related phenomena to produce simulations of the social system under different control, management, or assistance policies. But these computer models did little to solve the nation's social crises. In retrospect, the comprehensive models fell from favor for three principal reasons:

- they focused on the physical aspects of the problem, giving too little attention to social, psychological, institutional, and political factors;
- in many cases, there was insufficient empirical data on the simulated physical phenomena to support credible simulation models; and
- the models performed best when forecasting and describing evolutionary changes, which could be done just as well with older, simpler, cheaper methods; but they did not perform well in predicting or simulating abrupt or major changes, where they would have been most useful to executives.

The comprehensive model era persisted into the late 1970s, culminating in the Department of Energy's National Energy Plans of 1977 and 1979. Quantitative information in those documents was developed by linking national-scale models for the U.S. economy, the U.S. energy supply system, and environmental pollutant generation and control.

However, the intervening technological advances in computational powers did not banish the systemic problems of earlier modelling approaches, and many policy analysts had already become disenchanted with comprehensive models. They scaled back the size of the problems attacked and expanded the scope of simulated policy choices to make their computations more realistic as to choices among policy alternatives. Thus was born the era of decision analysis, a reaction to the overextension of the comprehensive era.

Considered as more compact and discrete packages, problems could be solved in less time on smaller mainframe computers—the minicomputers. More effort was now spent defining the full range of policy options and outcomes and specifying criteria for the best outcome to guide the executive. The key visual aid for this strategy was the decision tree, a series of diverging lines, theoretically representing all possible outcomes from a decision, labeled with the estimated probability of each outcome. To help guide policy decisions through this forest of possible outcomes, older evaluation theories were revived and new concepts were developed: cost-effectiveness analysis, cost-benefit analysis, risk analysis, decision theory, social choice theory, and multi-attribute utility analysis. These seemed to be more effective methods for informing public sector decisions, and some politicians were persuaded that the techniques should be codified and made a formal part of the decision process.

Now cost analysis is routinely used in government policy choice, but, while benefits analysis is attempted in many regulatory analyses, it is of limited use when the issue involves human life, pain, and suffering, or other values that cannot be measured in economic terms. Moreover, formal decision models were conceptually complex. As these limitations made themselves apparent, most proponents of decision analysis returned to military or private financial analysis. Few traces of their contributions remain intact in public policy analysis.

The retreat of decision analysis was hastened by the technological leaps in personal computing in the 1980s. The personal computer era, another step back from the comprehensive model, can be characterized as the extensive application of traditional techniques to specific policy issues.

The advancement of personal computer technology in one decade is nothing short of amazing. Although magnetic recording typewriters were in use at the Environmental Protection Agency (EPA) starting in 1970, and a mainframe word processor[d] was introduced in 1975, the first personal computers were not readily available until 1977[22] and IBM's PC did not arrive until the 1980s. Early PCs were used primarily for word processing and data base management, for which they were excellent, as long as the documents or data bases weren't large. Although assembly language and high-level programming languages (such as BASIC) were available on PCs, they saw very limited application in government policy analyses because such programming was not much easier on PCs than on mainframes. Thus, in the early 1980s, most quantitative federal policy analyses were performed on mainframe computers.

With the introduction of "user-friendly" software (allowing the user to perform complex procedures on the computer with little or no knowledge of programming), PCs were almost instantly adopted by quantitative analysts throughout business and government. Rapidly rising sales and profits drove PC developers to new, astounding achievements, increasing memory, data storage, and processing speeds by several orders of magnitude over five years. The most powerful

---

[d]IBM "Mag-tape" and "Mag-card" devices hooked to an IBM Selectric typewriter, and the WYLBUR word processor on a time-shared IBM 360.

new tool available to the policy analyst through the microcomputer was spreadsheet software,[e] which allows the computer user to conduct simple and complex mathematical operations on numbers appearing in a matrix on a screen that looks like an accountant's ledger sheet. Advanced spreadsheet software includes built-in automatic calculation procedures such as statistical, trigonometric, and common mathematical functions. Analyses can be converted to graphic displays on the screen in a matter of seconds, and high-quality paper copies of graphs or spreadsheets can be produced in about a minute.

Data base software, combined with large desktop data storage devices such as hard disks, Bernoulli cartridges, optical (compact disc) storage, and high-speed tape cartridges, permits virtually instant retrieval of specific data from a very large data base, requiring only a few dozen keystrokes selected from clearly defined menus. In addition, networking capabilities now enable an entire policy analysis staff to access the same software and data bases from separate locations, leading to several efficiencies as well as increased effectiveness through staff teamwork and sharing of data and knowledge.

By the end of the 1980s, nearly all of the federal policy analysis offices had personal computer facilities, often approaching one machine per analyst. The power of the hardware and the capabilities and simplicity of use of the software have combined to make the process of policy analysis significantly faster and cheaper, in addition to improving the quality of the result. These trends have important implications for the profession, introducing a host of technology-driven improvements:

- Better continuity and control: As the range and ease of application of contemporary software have eliminated

---

[e]VisiCalc, Multiplan, Lotus 1-2-3, Microsoft EXCEL, Quattro, and many others.

the need for most outside contracts with systems or mathematics specialists, most analysis can now be done by a relatively small in-house staff improving continuity and control of the policy analysis process.

- Better responsiveness: The significantly increased speed of computer-based analysis often enables the policy executive to interact directly with the analytical process, rendering the analysis more responsive to political or deadline requirements.
- Better analysis: The graphics capabilities of today's software greatly enhance the clarity and comprehensibility of the analysis to the user; more importantly, the speed and low cost of computation enables policy analysts to repeat procedures many times to determine the sensitivity of the outcome to different assumptions regarding critical criteria such as causal relationships, data accuracy, additional policy alternatives, or even more marginal policy alterations.
- Better analysts: The range of tasks and speed at which they can be accomplished by an individual not only makes analysis more cost effective by reducing analytical staff requirements, but can also broaden each analyst's perspective and experience through exposure to larger sets of issues.

In view of these advantages, it may be said that policy analysis is better now, and more valuable to the executive. However, the value of information is determined by the needs of the user; the influence of analysis on a particular policy decision compared to other considerations can never be ascertained.

The personal computer era nevertheless has made the policy analysis discipline healthier, more respected, and more useful to executives in carrying out their responsibilities. The balance of this book attempts to present to the reader the logic leading to this conclusion.

The widespread use of personal computers at all levels

of government is now a reality, and the presence of computer technology is fundamentally changing the way policy analysts operate. Detailed quantitative policy analyses that took months to perform in the 1960s can now be executed in a matter of hours, but this enhanced capability does not necessarily mean that more complex or larger mathematical models will become any more useful than they were in the previous era, nor will models that lack the requisite information for analysis (such as benefit or risk models) be any more relevant. However, the availability of powerful software and hardware to everyone in the policy community does mean that more effort can be spent on improving data collection and on matching data sets with other sources measuring the same phenomena. It is also easier for the analysts of opposing groups to check the claims of others to assure, for example, that an adversary's position is indeed supported by the facts or assumptions claimed.

But the effectiveness of numerical analyses can be limited by political considerations. During the energy crisis, environmental protection remained a strong popular cause, so when the White House hoped to return to coal-burning, an environmentally acceptable strategy to do so was sought. Millions of dollars were spent on developing data and analytical methods to support both sides of the environment versus coal debate but, regardless of the amount of information mustered, neither side would accept the findings of the other. Consequently, a large number of issues required a presidential decision.

Another example of the limits of sophisticated analysis emerged at the National Science Foundation several years ago during a public meeting of the National Science Board. The issue was the need for government assistance in the construction and renovation of research university laboratories. The NSF policy analysis group undertook a sophisticated survey of NSF grantees and their administrators to find out whether or not improved facilities were actually needed. Results showed that only a few projects were constrained by inadequate facilities, and that many were housed in newly renovated space. When this finding was presented to the Board, it was not well received, because the sentiment among many members was that financial aid for facilities was necessary. One member stated, "I don't care what the numbers say; we know there is a problem." As in the coal production debate, closely held political convictions and differing perspectives led to conflicting interpretations and obscured the factual data.

When introduced to a new policy issue, an analyst will try to determine whether technical analysis is mandatory, potentially helpful, or irrelevant to a choice of policy. In many regulatory issues, detailed economic and social impact assessments are required by law, but in some cases, like federal health-based air quality standards, economic factors are statutorily excluded from consideration. Another class of issues is so dominated by moral perspectives that, even though relevant numerical data are available, analysis would be irrelevant (e.g., school prayer, capital punishment, care for the terminally ill, and abortion). The number of issues exempt from quantitative analysis facing the Bush administration as it prepared to take office prompted one prominent Washington journalist to write an article entitled "The End of Economics?"[23]

Analytical procedures are best suited for technical issues. Complex issues affecting many jurisdictions and interest groups and involving many different technical factors (such as acid rain or global warming) might also be viewed as ideal candidates for detailed technical analyses because of the multitude of variables involved. However, the weighing and interaction of the variables in these complex issues are unlikely to be agreed upon clearly enough by the involved parties to be analyzed credibly. At the other extreme, single-variable issues (for example, whether to tighten or loosen a long-standing safety standard) have the greatest potential for being clearly specified. They often permit detailed calculations and allow resources to be focused, rather than dispersed across several aspects of the issue. In these cases, sophisticated techniques can be applied with reasonable expectation of useful results.

The availability of information also poses a dilemma for the analyst. On the one hand, the more information available, the greater the likelihood of producing a useful analysis; however, when executives think they fully understand an issue, they tend to have little patience with quantitative analysis even if there is extensive information. If the issue is new or highly technical, the analyst must find surrogates for the missing data or design studies to gather necessary information. In either case, as the results of an analysis become more condensed for executive consumption, the quantity and quality of available information becomes a hidden factor. Usually, the higher the level of the executive, the less time an analyst has to present analysis, and the greater the possibility that his results will be more descriptive than analytical.

The results are generally presented at the policy level in essence only, distilled to precise and stark contrasts. The top official expects all insignificant factors to have been purged from the issue and wants to see a simplified political judgment. In preparing these highly condensed briefing documents, analysts must use extreme caution lest they omit a conciliation that appears marginal at the time but which could create political repercussions under other circumstances.

In this book, policy analysis is presented as an art that is only broadly definable. The analyst provides only the facts and interpretation necessary to constitute the "substantial evidence" required by law that policy decisions are not "arbitrary and capricious." Policy analysis can quickly deteriorate, because the process provides the opportunity to shape the information to support a particular policy option. The professional policy analyst must recognize that his role is to provide the broadest range of perspectives he can usefully create, leaving it to the political executive to choose among them.

The promotion of sophisticated analytical techniques implies that somehow they are better or more appropriate than the current public policy decision process and, therefore, can inform the latter. In this work one should remember that a number of factors exogenous to the issue at hand make the analysis of a policy even more complex:

- Analytical approaches are said to improve the decision process by organizing thoughts, but that statement implies that somehow the present methods are flawed, that all people and professions think the same way as analysts, and that the analytical paradigms fit public policy problems sufficiently to replace existing processes.
- Decision-aiding techniques are often easier to talk about than they are to operate; missing data, misapplied theory, and experimental information have resulted in numerous fatal flaws in the paradigms.
- If a study suggests that the techniques available to the policy analysts are not ready to operate as hoped, analysts face a dilemma when directives require their use.
- If the use of sophisticated analytical techniques is judged to be a legitimate way to guide major public policies, improvements in informing and accomplishing policy goals can be expected; however, the goals themselves may be too ambitious, misdirected, or otherwise specious.

This book is designed neither to teach executives how to make decisions, nor to propose national goals, nor to promote one profession or analytical technique at the expense of another. It is constructed, rather, as an exploration of the future of professional policy analysis, primarily in the public sector, in light of past experience and the promise of new data and technology now available.

References

1. Grier, B., "The Early History of the Theory and Management of Risk," paper presented at the Judgment and Decision Making Group Meeting, Philadelphia, 1981, and "One Thousand Years of Mathematical Psychology," paper presented at the Society for Mathematical Psychology Convention, Madison, WI, 1980.

2. Franklin Institute, "Report," March 1, 1836, House Document 162, Series 289.

3. Dupree, A. Hunter, *Science in the Federal Government,* Harvard University Press, Cambridge, 1957, Chapter VI.

4. Gaus, J.M., and L.O. Wolcott, *Public Administration and the United States Department of Agriculture,* Chicago, 1940, p. 47–57.

5. Dupree, op.cit., p. 336.

6. Leuchtenburg, William E., *Franklin D. Roosevelt and the New Deal,* Harper Torchbooks, Harper and Row, New York, 1963, p. 33 ff.

7. Dupree, op.cit., p. 371.

8. Hanushek, Eric A., "The Policy Research Markets," *Journal of Policy Analysis and Management,* 9:2. p. 146, 1990.

9. Goldstein, Mark L., "The Shadow Government," *Government Executive,* May 1990, p. 30.

10. House, Peter W. and Roger D. Shull, *Managing Research on Demand,* University Press of America, Lanham, MD, 1985, p. 7.

11. Levine, Charles H., and Peter M. Benda, *Expertise and Democratic Decisionmaking: A Reader,* Report to the Task Force on Science Policy, U.S. House of Representatives, Congressional Research Service, Washington, December 1986, p. 3.

12. Dewey, John, *The Public and Its Problems: An Essay on Political Inquiry,* 1927, reprinted by Gateway Books, Chicago, 1946, p. 208.

13. England, J. Merton, *A Patron for Pure Science: The National Science Foundation's Formative Years, 1945–57,* National Science Foundation, Washington, 1982, p. 82.

14. Wells, William G., Jr., "Science Advice and the Presidency: An Overview from Roosevelt to Ford," *Technology in Society,* 2:1,2, 1980.

15. Quade, E.S., and W.I. Boucher, *Systems Analysis and Policy Planning,* American Elsevier Publishing Co., Inc., New York, 1968, p. 2.

16. Hanssmann, F., "Optimal Inventory Location and Control in Production and Distribution," *Operations Research,* 7:4, 1959, p. 483.

17. Carroll, J.D., and H.W. Bevis, "Predicting Local Travel in Urban Regions," *Proceedings of Regional Science Society,* Vol. 3, 1957, p. 194.

18. Maas, Arthur, Maynard M. Hufschmidt, Robert Dorfman, Harold A. Thomas, Jr., Stephen A. Marglin, and Gordon Maskew Fair, *Design of Water-Resource Systems,* Harvard University Press, Cambridge, 1962.

19. Morrice, H.A.W., and W.N. Allan, "Planning for the Ultimate Development of the Nile Valley," *Proceedings of the Institute of Civil Engineers,* 14:101, London, 1959.

20. Johnson, Lyndon B., "News Conference on Foreign and Domestic Matters," August 26, 1965.

21. Hoos, Ida R., *Systems Analysis in Public Policy: A Critique,* University of California Press, Berkeley, 1972, p. 89.

22. Levy, Steven, *Hackers: Heroes of the Computer Revolution,* Dell, New York, 1984, p. 269.

23. Samuelson, Robert, "The End of Economics?" *Newsweek,* July 24, 1989.

2.

The Comprehensive Era: The Pursuit of Omniscience

The comprehensive mathematical models developed during the 1970s were intended to be just that—comprehensive. Any design, however, was limited by money, time, personnel, and knowledge. The dilemma remains today: No matter how many interacting factors are included in a computer model by an analyst, it is always possible to find the ones left out.

The ability to build comprehensive models for public policy emerged from the interaction among mathematical specialists from several different professions, brought together as common users of mainframe computers. Macro-economists provided the integrated philosophy with their detailed "input-output" matrices of the U.S. economy, such as that done by Leontief at Harvard concurrent with the Harvard Water Project. At the same time, engineering professionals provided mathematical simulation of different physical and socio-economic activities and processes, while professionals in the interdisciplinary field of "systems analysis" actually integrated the many different areas of specialized knowledge into a functioning algorithm.

The demand for comprehensive analysis arose from the environmental awareness movement of the late 1960s and early 1970s, which highlighted the negative secondary effects of various public and private policies and projects. Thus, we could no longer build a new highway to speed the flow of traffic and improve highway safety without estimating also the social costs of the resulting property owner dislocation, the increased property development incentives, and the increased noise, air, water, and solid waste pollution. The National

Environmental Policy Act of 1970 (NEPA) required preparation of an "environmental impact statement" for every new major federal action. "Action" in this case was interpreted to be anything that involved federal funds or regulatory authority. Thus, any highway, housing, water, power, or airport project supported or authorized by the federal government required lengthy technical analysis of anticipated environmental harm which might be caused by the project. Soon, nearly all state legislatures had passed some type of environmental impact law, and new rules were devised to guide analyses of inflation impacts, regulatory impacts, urban impacts, arms control impacts, and paperwork burden impacts. Indeed, it is fortunate that Congress did not conduct an analysis of the impact of NEPA on the nation's forest resources, otherwise, the comprehensive public policy modelling era might never have materialized.

Traditionally, environmental scientists and engineers, particularly those skilled in pollution control processes, have tended to specialize in a particular environmental medium, i.e., air, water, or land. But if, for example, a new air pollution control process was proposed as a requirement by EPA, with the requirement to analyze secondary impacts, the agency would have to calculate how much water pollution or solid waste would be created by the residue of a new measure to control air pollution and propose methods for dealing with these secondary environmental effects. Next, it would be suggested that EPA determine the increase in volume of business in environmental pollution control industries that would result from implementing the new standard. It is easy to see that the search for such sequential problems could be pushed ad infinitum, and well beyond singular fields of expert analysis.

The comprehensive models were just what the doctor ordered. Input-output economists had successfully represented the relationships among all the nation's industrial sectors in matrix form. Pollution control engineers had begun to catalog the types and quantities of environmental pollutants produced by the different industrial sectors and could express costs and effectiveness of pollution control technologies mathematically. Systems analysts and computer programmers had the ability to solve very large sets of simultaneous equations using the power of the nation's fastest mainframe computers. Given these capabilities and the frustration of interwoven secondary effects of many different federal programs, it was natural that sooner or later someone would suggest that a single comprehensive model be developed that would simulate the growth of the U.S. economy and, in the process, calculate quantities of environmental pollutants captured and released, and the amount of money spent by each industry for pollution control.

The Strategic Environmental Assessment System

Such a system was indeed built at EPA beginning in 1974, when the authors designed and implemented the Strategic Environmental Assessment System (SEAS). More than $1 million was allocated annually to SEAS out of EPA's growing budget, and nearly two dozen analysts, including staff and outside contracts, were assigned to the project. SEAS was a large computer program used to assess the impact of environmental policies on the economy and the environment, in terms of both dollar changes in gross national product (GNP) and of pollutants released to the biosphere.

SEAS produced year-by-year forecasts up to 25 years in the future. These forecasts were regional as well as national, and took into account the interactions among various parts of the economy. SEAS also produced reports on 13 special interest areas corresponding to the 13 modules comprising the SEAS program as a whole. The interest areas are shown in Figure 2-1. The system accounted for the economic activities of materials extraction, goods production, transportation, consumption, and disposal. The specific core of the algorithms used was a detailed model of activities of the national

Figure 2-1
The Strategic Environmental Assessment System

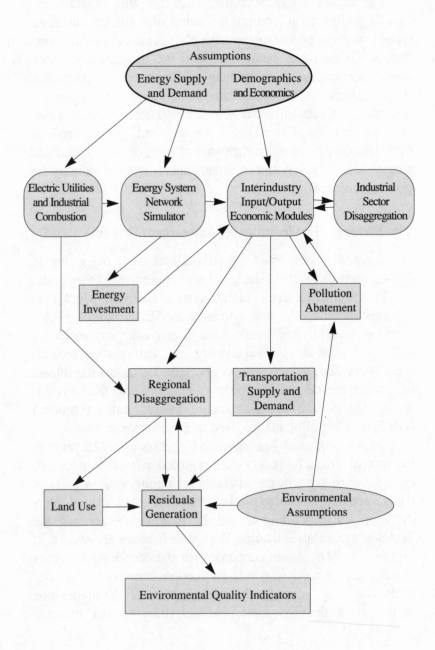

economy, developed at the University of Maryland, but modified to include considerations of materials flows, pollution abatement costs, and specialized consumption demands.

This system first produced predictions of a detailed national economic pattern and level for each year, forecasts which were used to generate other forecasts—such as energy use, pollution residual levels, and transportation demands. For example, the levels of activity of some 350 economic production subsectors were associated with the level of residuals (waste materials) and with the use of a given amount of raw materials. The system kept track of these waste and raw materials and produced estimates of their annual amounts.

Depending on further assumptions, the gross pollution residuals were converted to net residuals to simulate the effects of a set of pollution abatement strategies and processes. The system calculated the cost of each abatement process plus the national economic impacts of these costs. Assumptions transforming gross residuals to net residuals also included a certain amount of recycling of scrap and collected residuals. The recycled material (or a portion of it) was then added to the amount of raw materials available. Residuals released to air, land, and water were calculated, and transportation and land use were separately forecast, based on general economic parameters and the pollutant and stock usage totals.

The final portion of the national forecast used the estimates produced for one year to forecast detailed positive and negative feedbacks to calculate the subsequent year. For example, a heavy drain on a raw material in relatively short supply could cause a shift in its relative price, plus an increase in the level of capital investment. This would require a recalculation of the relative price table, making this raw material more expensive and drawing resources away from other uses. Further, in later forecast years, the increased capital investment could cause a shift toward lower import rates.

After the national projections were completed, SEAS assigned parts of the economic and residual national forecasts to different regional areas such as federal regions, states, standard metropolitan statistical areas (SMSAs), air quality control regions (AQCRs), and river basins. A set of general spatial models of land use, transportation, river drainage and flows, air diffusions, and storm runoff were used to calculate environmental quality impacts for regions of the country.

The SEAS system was modular, so that any program could be executed independently of the others, provided that all necessary input files had been previously created. Therefore, it was not necessary to run the entire SEAS system every time a forecast was desired, but merely to concentrate on those components of the system that were germane to the issue. Further, each program produced a detailed printed output report and an output file for processing by other programs. In addition, general-purpose report generators were available for the production of system summary reports.

All programs were autonomous so that they could incorporate but did not require user-supplied information. A "default scenario" reflected forecasts based on the best data available at any point in time. These data were overridden by any external input information desired by the user. SEAS had 13 functional modules: four national economic modules, five materials flow modules, and four regional modules, as listed in Table 2-1.[1]

SEAS was the most comprehensive simulation of America's energy, economic, and environmental systems ever attempted. It responded to the needs of strategic planners and thinkers in many fields. Moreover, SEAS required strategic analysts to share the same assumptions, whereas in the past analysts had to make their own assumptions about influential factors outside their particular field of interest or expertise.

The economic portion of SEAS simulated the outputs of 185 separate industrial sectors. Those sectors which included alternative production processes with different unit environmental emissions were disaggregated into separate components (stretching the 185 into 400 sectors), each with its own

Table 2-1
The Multipurpose Modules of SEAS

National Economic Modules

1. **SEAS/INFORUM**: An expanded version of the University of Maryland's INFORUM inter-industry input/output model, which could be driven by various national macroeconomic forecasts.
2. **Sector Disaggregation**: Disaggregation of INFORUM economic sectors to represent subsector growth and technological change in the greater detail required for policy purposes.
3. **Abatement Costs**: Capital costs and operating and maintenance costs associated with pollution control for each economic sector, subsector, and process.
4. **Price/Wage Impacts**: Adjusted industrial forecasts to account for the impacts on relative prices due to changes in the assumptions which produced the original table, i.e., pollution control activity or stock shortage.

Materials Flow Modules

5. **Stocks**: Accounts on domestic and worldwide reserves of critical resources and materials as determined by relative production price, investment requirements, and net import levels.
6. **Solid Waste**: Annual tonnage, disposal methods, and costs for nonindustrial and solid waste sources, and estimated levels of recycling.
7. **National Residuals**: Nationwide estimates of annual tonnage of air, water, and land pollution from stationary sources.
8. **Transportation**: Transportation demands, modal splits, and mobile source air pollution emissions at the national and regional levels.
9. **Energy**: Summary of energy use by fuel type and user category, consistent with national economic forecasts.

Regional Modules

10. **Regionalization**: Regionalization of national economic, pollutant, and abatement cost data.
11. **Land Use**: Forecasts of urban, rural, and agricultural land use and associated nonpoint residuals.
12. **Ambient Quality**: Surrogate measures of ambient air and water quality from air emissions and water effluent discharge levels.
13. **Benefits**: Value of the annual reduction in damages to the environment due to pollution abatement.

environmental coefficients. Because energy production was a major concern during the 1970s and is a major source of environmental emissions, when SEAS was used by the Department of Energy (DOE), the energy industry was broken down into the finest details. Whereas the INFORUM input-output model contained an aggregate sector called "Electric Utilities," SEAS considered electricity produced by coal, oil, gas, hydro, nuclear, and new sources such as solar, wind, and geothermal. Because different regulations applied, coal-fired utilities were further disaggregated into old and new categories. The "energy" module of SEAS accounted for 32 energy demand categories, 60 different energy conversion activities, and 22 different energy supply sources.

Base economic growth scenarios as defined by forecasts of GNP, were taken from official federal sources (e.g., the President's Council of Economic Advisors). National population forecasts came from the Bureau of the Census, and employment baselines came from Department of Labor data. Future energy demands and supply sources and technologies were provided by official DOE sources. Environmental emissions were programmed industry by industry and year by year according to EPA regulations and compliance schedules. Thus, projections of the future were consistent with all official perceptions of the future. If one of these perceptions were changed, the model could simply rerun the analysis with a different set of assumptions. SEAS seemed to be the dream tool of strategic planners and comprehensive analysts.

Although the concept of SEAS still sounds sensible and achievable today, it was an operational nightmare. Viewed in the context of the extremely user-friendly personal computer of the 1990s, which can solve many complicated problems in a matter of seconds and a few keystrokes, execution of the SEAS computer system sounds like a voyage back to the dark ages.

In its later stages, SEAS comprised about 50 separate "programs" totalling nearly 70,000 lines of FORTRAN code.

It accessed about 200 input files and produced 75 output files, required 3,000 computer disk tracks and the mounting of 25 separate tapes, and a full run required about a half-hour of IBM 360 mainframe CPU time and several hours of system analyst time for manually calibrating the various modules. Each run for a new future energy supply scenario required examination of about 3,000 pieces of data and the conversion of that data, by professional judgment, into more than 1,000 SEAS input variables. The computational process essentially monopolized the time-shared mainframe computer, so runs had to be executed at night when other users' demands were low. Data input errors were not discovered until the following morning's delivery of several 20-pound boxes of SEAS "output" (endless tables on 11" x 17" fan-fold computer paper).

If the policy question necessitated running three or four scenarios, it was not unusual for the entire process to take a full work week. Converting the tabular output into simple graphics or prose for presentation to policy officials or for publication as a report required many more man-weeks of effort. Answering detailed questions about these outputs required a team of highly trained senior analysts who could speak with credible knowledge on hundreds of different science, engineering, and financial topics. Maintaining the professional staff necessary to operate SEAS and stay aware of the system's idiosyncrasies continued to cost about $1 million a year in 1990 terms. SEAS was an expensive operation.

Other than providing spectacular entertainment for computer hackers, big thinkers, policy researchers, statisticians, environmental managers, planners, and other numerophiles, what were the benefits of SEAS? In 1979, Paul Cowan, a graduate student at the University of Pennsylvania, conducted an evaluation of the use of SEAS by the government[2]. He interviewed all senior administrators in agencies who had used the model for various purposes. None of the interviewees could identify any major policy decisions that were based on SEAS results. In fact, as described below, SEAS results muted environmentalists' concerns over the first and second national energy plans, obviating the need for modified policies. Thus SEAS played an important if unintended role not fully appreciated by the energy policy makers.

Does this mean the entire effort was worthless? For many reasons, the answer is no. First, at the agency level, even major policy decisions (major in the sense of importance to executives) are usually incremental or tactical, not strategic. SEAS projected the cost of implementing all phases of national air and water pollution control legislation—information useful for EPA's strategic planning, but of limited use for the politically sensitive task of establishing specific pollution control regulations for each industry. SEAS estimated capital and operating costs for air and water pollution controls for 10 years into the future for all significant industrial sectors. It also calculated costs for municipal sewage treatment and automotive emission controls.

The estimates were all based on the same economic assumptions, and included a readjustment of industrial output based on the growing pollution control equipment industry. Even viewed from long past the final forecast year, most of the projections were reasonably accurate, as indicated in Figures 2-2 and 2-3.[3] However, as reported in Cowan's study, information from SEAS never formed the basis for any memorable policy decision.

The SEAS output provided good news in general: for the next decade, pollution control costs would be less than 2 percent of the GNP, and growing pollution control activities would stimulate employment in construction and manufacturing. It provided bad news for specific cases: The pulp and paper, chemicals, electric utilities, iron and steel, leather tanning, and electroplating industries would be severely affected, spending more than 3 percent of their gross output on air and water pollution control.

But the policy battles were not fought at the strategic level. The main business of EPA was not strategy but

Figure 2-2
Comparison of 1975 SEAS National Air Pollution
Forecasts and Energy Use Assumptions

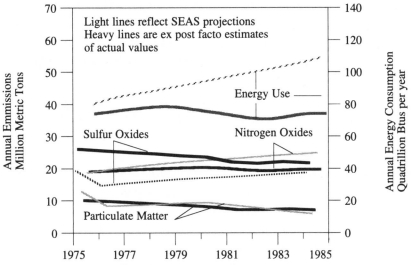

Sources: EPA 1975 Draft Report, EPA and USEIA 1988 Annual Reports

Figure 2-3
Comparison of 1975 SEAS Industrial Air Pollution
Control Costs With 1988 Ex Post Facto Estimates

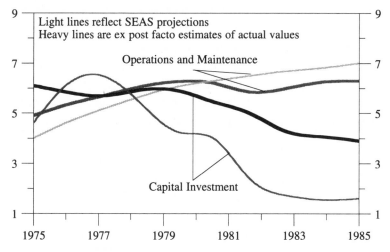

Sources: EPA 1975 Draft Report; Survey of Current Business,
U.S. Bureau of Economic Analysis, 1988

tactics—promulgating and enforcing emissions standards on individual industries sources. Although in 1970 the President consolidated in the new EPA the federal environmental authorities previously scattered around the executive branch, Congress did not consolidate the many environmental laws. Thus, EPA was simply an umbrella agency supervising loosely connected bureaucratic units which were implementing and enforcing the provisions of the Clean Air Act, the Clean Water Act, the Resource Recovery and Conservation Act, the Toxic Substances Control Act, the Safe Drinking Water Act, and the Federal Insecticide, Fungicide, and Rodenticide Act, among others.

Thus, even though it satisfied two particular statutory requirements (the cost estimates required by the Clean Air Act and Clean Water Act), SEAS provided little positive (and, in many cases, substantial negative) value to the regulators and enforcers on the front line. In fact, there was no high-level request to combine the formerly independent periodic cost assessments. That idea was conceived by EPA's Office of Research and Development (ORD), which volunteered to take over from the policy office the job of preparing the cost estimates. The authors were senior managers of the policy research group (then called the Washington Environmental Research Center, or WERC), which took on the tasks.

The WERC staff, composed of a dozen or so young Ph.D. economists, engineers, systems analysts, operations researchers, and planners, decided on its own that a giant comprehensive model was the only right way to do the job. The theory was that once the model framework was assembled, each year's new regulatory cost analysis report could be produced by simply changing a few numbers and rerunning the model.

But despite a heady attitude and vigorous effort by the WERC staff, the project was doomed from the start. Despite repeated revisions of report drafts, the document was never sent to Congress, but was finally published four years later as a research report.[4]

A post mortem analysis of the failure of the SEAS team to produce an acceptable analysis and report reveals one unanticipated pitfall of the concept: an organization's perception of a comprehensive computer model as a threat to existing bureaucratic power structures. A large system claiming to be able to simulate and integrate all the major functions of an agency can only be successful if endorsed and encouraged by the top agency executives, and housed in an organizational unit reporting directly to the "front office." Even then, there are likely to be considerable tensions between the "comprehensive" office and the individual line managers who are technical experts on the details of their assigned missions. As organizational support evaporated, SEAS succumbed to its own bureaucratic meltdown.

Although WERC held biweekly progress meetings through the first year of the project, EPA staff from other areas were rarely present. Greater success in effecting participation within the agency would probably have alleviated many subsequent problems, since lack of communication contributed to almost all of them. Any time major changes are made in a routine procedure, misunderstandings result.

The original draft report openly expressed the limitations of data and the fact that each time new industry information was obtained, a new cost estimate was inevitable. When regulations changed during the course of report preparation (a frequent event in that era of galloping regulatory revision), program offices demanded that analyses be redone to incorporate the latest information. The insertion of the new information into the draft was even more time consuming than revising the model and reporting the results. Hence, the report was always partly obsolete.

Agency program officials, not having a stake in the report, had no particular incentive to be responsive or cooperative when it came to reviewing the draft report, over 1,000 pages long. Furthermore, when the review was conducted, minor errors or recent changes in regulations weakened the credibility of the document. On top of everything, three other major units in the agency were involved in similar or related studies, but the existence of several of these studies was not discovered until late in the project period, when potential incorporation of their results had become difficult or impossible within the available time.

The program offices conducting these parallel investigations did not share the views of WERC regarding review of related cost analysis reports prior to public release. The related reports were not congressionally mandated, and did not require agency-wide concurrence for release, so they were reviewed within a single unit of the agency and then released to the public. Thus, the results in the reports rapidly earned the status of "accepted" values without the benefit of ORD review or concurrence. This immediately led to a confrontation, since modification of the comprehensive report values to conform to a particular independently conducted, detailed study was obligatory if the agency was not to be accused of giving two answers to the same question. Although the detailed studies had better information on particular industrial parameters, such as plant inventories, production technologies, and pollution control cost functions, they were conducted without regard to interactions with other industries or official national GNP forecasts, thereby tending to compromise the prime objectives of the WERC-initiated report. Hence, the obligated revisions were not well received by ORD or the supporting contractors.

The final blow came with the organizational dissolution of the WERC just prior to delivery of the first draft report, and the reduction of staff support for the project from six people to one part-time employee. The lone staffer lost his stature as an "expert" and was relegated to the position of recording secretary, required to respond to all changes requested by the other offices. These bureaucratic machinations made significant contributions to the protracted review period.

SEAS Redux: A National Energy Plan

Even as SEAS was being buried at EPA, a new lease on its life was being drafted in the form of the First National Energy Plan. A major priority of the new Carter administration was to do something to prevent the kind of energy crisis that had hit the previous administration. Under the guidance of White House energy policy staff, the Federal Energy Administration (FEA) and the Energy Research and Development Administration (ERDA) (predecessors of DOE) were developing a national plan for energy supplies that would render the country less vulnerable to embargoes on imported oil, which disrupted the economy during the 1973–74 winter. The plan was comprehensive and theoretical, calling for vastly increased domestic coal production and utilization, increased domestic oil production, plus stringent energy conservation measures and bold solar energy initiatives. Because the environmental community was a prominent component of Carter's supporters, he needed to assure that group that implementing his national energy plan wouldn't further degrade the environment.

What better tool to prove to the environmentalists that the new energy plan was acceptable than a national Strategic Environmental Assessment System? The plight of SEAS at EPA hadn't gone unnoticed by environmental policy professionals at ERDA and the White House energy policy staff. The staff were already using a large comprehensive computer model to simulate the nation's energy supply and demand networks. Thus, they were intrigued with adapting a similar concept from the environmental field to produce the environmental impact analysis quickly for their forthcoming plan. SEAS was forthwith taken under the wing of ERDA's Assistant

Administrator for Environment and Safety, and a staff of former EPA SEAS contractors and a couple of former EPA employees set to work to beef up the energy aspects of the model and adapt it to operate with results of the energy market models.

The mission was accomplished, and, for a brief moment in bureaucratic history, SEAS had an avid customer for comprehensive assessments. SEAS projected air pollutants, water pollutants, solid waste, radioactive waste, and land use to the end of the century, incorporating the policy initiatives proposed in the National Energy Plan, and contrasted those impacts with a future in which energy supplies and environmental controls continued as they had in the past. The assessment showed that if existing environmental regulations were strictly enforced on all industries, and if solar energy and conservation initiatives were successful, the nation's future air quality would, in general, be cleaner than it was in 1975.

Because the results were good news, (i.e., that the President's proposed energy plan was environmentally sound), the SEAS results were widely publicized, with special briefings for the press, members of Congress, and the White House energy staff. To give a further impression of environmental awareness, the results were presented as the first *Annual Environmental Assessment Report* (AEAR),[5] which would be repeated each year as the nation pursued its goal of decreased dependence on foreign energy sources. With the formation of the new Department of Energy on October 1, 1977, the SEAS project was transferred to the new Assistant Secretary for Environment, Ruth C. Clusen, a prominent environmentalist, and for a while became the Department's official environmental assessment protocol.

To help build support in the environmental community, Clusen directed preparation of a sequel to the first AEAR and chose a new title for the report, *National Environmental Impact Projection No. 1* (NEIP 1).[6] NEIP 1 was necessitated by the release of new national energy supply and demand forecasts by the Energy Information Administration (EIA), the quasi-independent statistical analysis unit housed in DOE. NEIP 1 received little response, positive or negative, from outside the Assistant Secretary's office for several reasons. First, it was meant to be a baseline against which to compare impacts arising from policies in the Second National Energy Plan, currently under development. Second, the energy supply demand scenarios represented continuation of energy policies in effect before passage of the National Energy Act of 1978. Third, EIA was, by definition, precluded from a policy-making role in DOE, so reports from that group could be used or ignored by anyone, including the top executives in the Department. Thus, no one opposed the report or its methodology. The SEAS team was in fat city.

Their period of glory was brief. In the autumn of 1978, when the DOE Office of Policy, Planning, and Management began developing the second national energy plan, officially called "National Energy Plan II" (NEPII), the inevitable conflicts between technology and environmental protection arose. Every energy production or conservation technology has some negative environmental impacts (even solar energy systems), and the SEAS team and related units were diligently discovering and documenting each and every effect and converting those effects into coefficients to load into SEAS. The SEAS team was also busy gathering energy performance data on various new energy production concepts and trying to ascertain the relative shares of each technology to be proposed in NEPII.

As might be expected, the publicizing of environmental effects of energy technologies was not appreciated by the technology offices in DOE, each pushing for more rapid adoption of its favorite energy technology, nor by the policy office, which was trying to put together a bold yet credible plan which would be favored by the President, the Congress, and the general public. Yet an environmental assessment was a statutory requirement of the same DOE Act that mandated the biennial national energy plans, so NEPII did have an environmental assessment, the computational part of which was produced by SEAS. But the assessment was published as a separate document,[7] and whereas thousands of copies of NEPII[8] were printed and widely circulated, the NEPII Appendix was printed in hundreds of copies, and distributed by request only. As far as DOE was concerned, SEAS and its environmental assessment were necessary evils.

SEAS' most valuable service was to help placate the environmental community by demonstrating that a sophisticated comprehensive environmental analysis had been done, thereby eliminating one of the government's vulnerabilities to environmentalists' objections. But the unwieldiness of SEAS as a quick response tool became evident once more, as it had in the EPA cost analysis.

With the success of SEAS in the first National Energy Plan, new staff at EPA's Office of Research and Development found faith in comprehensive modelling for technology assessment of various regional energy development scenarios and for guiding future research and development programs. Thus, EPA became a partner in maintaining and operating the system. But even with two agencies supporting the system with staff and funds for contractors, the question of whether the burden of maintaining SEAS was worth the utility of its output began to creep into the minds of analysts and managers alike.

Energy and industrial technology were rapidly changing and, to maintain its credibility, SEAS mathematical coefficients had to represent the industrial economy accurately. Energy supply and demand assumptions were changing even faster. Even after all the enhancements of the model supported by the EPA efforts and the DOE energy plan efforts, there was a long list of significant updates needed.[9]

To make matters worse, over the several years that SEAS had been used, it was becoming clear that SEAS results were simply uninteresting. Scenario values for pollutant emissions in the future were close to what an informed expert would guess, given the scenario assumptions. And when the model was rerun with different economic scenarios, such as high and low world oil prices, the projections of important variables were almost always within 4 to 5 percent of each other, well within the expected source of error. Thus, along with the rest of the nation near the end of the Carter administration, the SEAS team set about to retrench and re-assess its mission. The use of comprehensive national economic models for assessment of government programs began to fade and was virtually eclipsed by political events over the next few years.

No major federal policies were changed or chosen on the basis of SEAS analyses. But during the 1970s, when comprehensive analyses were de rigueur, SEAS was used by many bureaus to meet prescribed requirements for comprehensive studies on human and natural resource issues. Simply because of its centralization, SEAS became widely known around government, academe, and the consulting industry as a useful data base for energy and environmental analyses. SEAS computations or SEAS data were used for the following projects:

- Calculating the total costs of legislated air and water pollution controls (EPA);
- Assessing the effectiveness of water quality regulations (National Commission on Water Quality);
- Determining the environmental impacts of National Energy Plans (DOE and Council on Environmental Quality);
- Determining regional environmental impacts in concentrated energy supply areas (EPA);
- Determining secondary environmental effects of accelerated development of solar energy (Solar Energy Research Institute);
- Assessing natural resource impacts of population growth (National Institutes of Health); and
- Research and development planning (EPA and DOE).

But rarely did SEAS answer a specific policy question, nor was it asked to. It provided general information about broad policies, and quantitative results were generally good news, or no worse than expected. It provided quantitative answers to questions about secondary impacts, which typically were not of major consequence. It provided convenient sets of numbers and reports for general use by the agencies in responding to questions about the future. The most significant contribution was probably its demonstration that comprehensive models were expensive and rarely produced results any more enlightening than simpler, single-issue models.

References

1. House, Peter W., *Trading Off Environment, Economics, and Energy*, Lexington Books, Lexington, MA, 1977, p. 54.

2. Cowan, Paul J., "The Role of Models in the Department of Energy and the Environmental Protection Agency: A Case Study of the Strategic Environmental Assessment System," Master's Thesis, The University of Pennsylvania, 1979.

3. Shull, R.D., and House, P.W. (eds.), "Cost of Air and Water Pollution Control 1976–1985" (draft), U.S. Environmental Protection Agency, Washington, August 1975.

4. Shull, R.D., Project Officer, *Resources and Pollution Control: Demonstration of a Comprehensive Assessment*, EPA 600/5-79-010, U.S. Environmental Protection Agency, Washington, 1979.

5. Mitre Corporation, CONSAD Research Corporation, Control Data Corporation, International Research and Technology, Inc., *Annual Environmental Analysis Report*, prepared for Assistant Administrator for Environment and Safety, U.S. Energy Research and Development Administration, Washington, September 1977.

6. Mitre Corporation, *National Environmental Impact Projection No. 1,* prepared for Assistant Secretary for Environment, U.S. Department of Energy, Washington, February 1979.

7. Assistant Secretary for Environment, *National Energy Plan II,* appended by *Environmental Trends and Impacts,* U.S. Department of Energy, submitted to the Congress on May 7, 1979.

8. The Secretary of Energy, *National Energy Plan II,* submitted to the Congress on May 7, 1979.

9. CONSAD Research Corp. and Control Data Corp., "SEAS Briefing," prepared for U.S. Department of Energy, Office of Environmental Assessment, January 6, 1982.

of government is now a reality, and the presence of computer technology is fundamentally changing the way policy analysts operate. Detailed, quantitative policy analyses that took months to perform in the 1960s can now be executed in a matter of hours. But this enhanced capability does not necessarily mean that more complex or larger multidimensional models will become any more useful than they were in the previous era, nor will models that lack the requisite information for analysis (such as benefit or risk models). The difficulty is even greater. However, the availability of powerful software and hardware to everyone in the policy community does mean that more effort can be spent on improving data collection and on matching data sets with other sources, enhancing the comprehensiveness. It is also easier for the analysts of opposing groups to check the claims of others to assure, for example, that an adversary position is indeed supported by the facts or assumptions claimed.

But the effectiveness of numerical analyses can be diminished by political considerations. During the energy crisis, environmental protection remained a strong popular cause, so when the White House hoped to return to coal-burning, an environmentally acceptable strategy to do so was sought. Millions of dollars were spent on developing data and analytical methods to support both sides of the environment versus coal debate but, regardless of the amount of information mustered, neither side would accept the findings of the other. Consequently, a large number of issues required a presidential decision.

Another example of the limits of sophisticated analysis emerged at the National Science Foundation several years ago during a public meeting of the National Science Board. The issue was the need for government assistance in the construction and renovation of research university laboratories. The NSF policy analysis group undertook a sophisticated survey of NSF grantees and their administrators to find out whether or not improved facilities were actually needed. Results

3.

The Reagan Revolution and The Decision Model Era

The inauguration of President Ronald Reagan and the flurry of political housecleaning which began in January of 1981 sealed the end of the era of comprehensive models and helped to open the way for a simpler, more directed kind of modelling which is presented here under the rubric of the decision model.

Decision models include those which are designed to produce a correct answer, the right decision, or the best decision when applied to public policy issues, e.g., cost-benefit, risk, optimization, and decision analyses. Comprehensive models were never intended to produce a decision. Rather, they were intended to simulate the behavior of the comprehensive system (e.g., the U.S. economy) and, by producing different scenarios of the future under alternate decisions, make the best choice self-evident to executives.

Decision model theory, of course, was developed well before the decision model era described here. Cost-benefit analysis was used in the mid-19th century by the French engineer Jules Dupuit[1] to evaluate the merits of competing road and bridge projects. It has been a required assessment procedure for federal water resources projects since the 1950s,[2] and for all new federal regulations since 1981.[3] As with comprehensive models, statistical uncertainties are rarely considered explicitly in cost-benefit analyses (a notable exception being stochastic variability of river flows in water resources planning).

Risk analysis (determining the frequency of occurrence of specified events) was used in the 19th century by the statistician Bortkiewicz to analyze the risk of Prussian soldiers being killed by horse kicks,[4] and has been the analytic foundation of insurance companies since the 18th century, according to the *International Encyclopedia of Statistics*.[5] Some historians show evidence of the use of risk analysis in determining interest rates on loans as far back to 3000 B.C. in Mesopotamia.[6] It is now a principal analytic tool of federal regulatory agencies. Just as cost-benefit analysis does not a priori consider risk, risk analysis, per se, does not address costs and benefits.

Decision analysis attempts integrate the foregoing techniques to determine the most acceptable policy decision, considering uncertainties in knowledge about many different facets of the issue at hand. For example, decision analysis could help regulators to decide whether to ban an apple pesticide that is a suspected carcinogen even when they are not precisely sure of the human ingestion rate which precipitates cancer, the number of people who will eat apples, average yearly consumption, levels of carcinogens in alternative pesticides, cost to the apple industry of reduction in purchases, or the general public's willingness to trade cancer risk for aesthetically attractive apples. Decision modelers pointed to the fact that every number used in comprehensive models was an average or an estimate, often with significant uncertainty, and that the mathematical interaction of the thousands of uncertain variables in models like SEAS produced results in which the error bands for all scenarios would overlap each other as well as the base case. Leinweber and Squitieri of the RAND Corporation led the assault against energy/environment comprehensive models, in a paper published just after Ronald Reagan's election:

> All policy modelers acknowledge the uncertainties inherent in their trade. Data available for such efforts are often of poor quality, and current understanding of political and socioeconomic processes is sufficiently incomplete

to assure that policy analysis models in these domains are also incomplete and uncertain. . . .

Explicit consideration of the consequences of the propagation and compounding of errors in data passing through uncertain models is still rare.

Analysis should illuminate, not obscure, issues in the policy debate. Models have often been used to justify both sides of an issue. When there is a large range of uncertainty it is easy to drive the results of analysis to one side or the other. For almost any major issue one can find careful computerized studies that reach opposite conclusions. A model incorporating measures of uncertainty can show how both are "right" in the sense of being possible, but wrong in the sense of having selectively drawn appealing point estimates from a result that has a very broad underlying statistical distribution.[7]

In May of 1982, President Reagan sent proposed legislation to Congress which would abolish the Department of Energy.[8] Congress never took the proposal seriously, and throughout the administration's eight years, continued to appropriate more funds for DOE than requested by the administration. However, this didn't stop a general scaling back of the department in several areas, particularly those related to information and analysis. The number of policy analysts and supporting staff and extramural resources at DOE was reduced by about 90 percent during the first two years of the administration. Thus, there were no resources to maintain comprehensive models like SEAS, even without the attacks from the "simple model" community. The surviving policy analysts, when asked for quantitative information, had to rely on simple calculations which could be done manually or with short runs of the mainframe computer. Whereas the Second National Energy Plan described in the previous chapter comprised some 500 pages, including the environmental appendix, the Third National Energy Plan (NEPIII)[9], submitted to Congress in response to the same statute as NEPII, was a mere 26 pages, one-twentieth of the information in the earlier report.

Executive Order 12291

Ideally, governmental regulations should result in a net benefit to the nation. But often in the heat of the legislative process, a debate becomes so emotional that the cost of achieving a desired benefit is ignored or not weighed against the benefit. Similarly, according to conventional wisdom, the conversion of the benefits of the legislation into monetary terms weakens its chance of passage. Thus, many laws on health, safety, and the environment passed during the 1970s required zero discharge of pollutants and zero health risks. Of 32 frequently applied environmental, health, and safety regulations surveyed by the authors in an earlier work,[10] only seven required a cost analysis, and only four required benefits analysis. This syndrome eventually gave rise to what was seen as a regulatory overload on American businesses, which ultimately lead to the landmark Executive Order 12291.

Easing the regulatory burden on America's industries to enhance their international competitiveness became a significant issue in the 1980 presidential campaign. The Heritage Foundation, the conservative public policy research institution which provided much of the intellectual input for the Reagan campaign, strongly recommended a required cost-benefit analysis for all existing and new regulations,[11] and further recommended that it should be promulgated immediately after inauguration via Executive Order.[12] Executive Order 12291 was signed by President Reagan 28 days after inauguration, specifying:

- Administrative decisions shall be based on adequate information concerning the need for and consequences of proposed government action;

- Regulatory action shall not be undertaken unless the potential benefits to society from the regulation outweigh the potential costs to society;
- Regulatory objectives shall be chosen to maximize the net benefits to society;
- Among alternative approaches to any given regulatory objective, the alternative involving the least net cost to society shall be chosen; and
- Agencies shall set regulatory priorities with the aim of maximizing the aggregate net benefits to society, taking into account the condition of the particular industries affected by the regulations, the condition of the national economy, and other regulatory actions contemplated for the future.[13]

In support of Executive Order 12291, the Division of Policy Research and Analysis of NSF was asked to conduct an objective assessment of the current capabilities of benefits analysis relevant to regulatory analyses. The product of more than 100 national experts, scholars, and federal regulators, and completed in December 1984, the assessment offered a cautious endorsement:

There are a number of inherent difficulties in efforts to carry out benefits assessments in areas relating to health, safety, and the environment. For instance, many benefits that are intuitively felt to be most important are also among the most difficult to measure. It can be difficult to identify the full range of both benefits and costs. The choice of an appropriate discount rate for comparing benefits and costs over time is problematic. Even when benefits are quantifiable in principle and agreement can be reached on their valuation, required data may not be available. Thus, considerable uncertainty is built into most benefit estimates, even when they are based on the best available data.

[T]he concept provides a useful framework for thinking
about a proposed action or comparing alternatives even
when this cannot be done in a wholly quantified way.
However, without better resolution of the methodological problems, proponents of an action may tend to assign
unduly high values to those benefits which are important
but hard to measure, while opponents may tend to over-
emphasize the fact that the benefits which are easiest to
quantify and value are relatively small.

[T]he requirements imposed on [benefits analysis] can
exceed our current understanding of existing practices
and may well require substantial professional judgments
in areas of analysis where there may be no professional
consensus on the appropriate method for dealing with a
specific task.[14]

In democratic societies, citizens willingly sacrifice some
measure of personal liberty in exchange for collective benefits
such as security and stability. Therefore, theoretically each
new governmental restriction should produce benefits to the
citizens that outweigh the loss of the rights sacrificed. In many
cases, the costs of a proposed government action and the
economic benefits likely to accrue can be estimated, providing
the possibility for a cost-benefit analysis.

Generally, the cost-benefit criterion is that the cumulative net social benefit over the relevant time period must be
positive, taking into account the time value of money. Cost-
benefit analysis can be expressed mathematically as

$$S = \int_{t=0}^{n} \frac{B(t) - C(t)}{(1 + r)^t} \, dt$$

where S = the net social benefit accumulated over a period
of n years, $B(t)$ and $C(t)$ are the benefits and costs occurring
in year t, and r is the discount rate applied to devalue future

costs and benefits.[a] Because S is the sum of all the future net benefits discounted from the present time, it is often called the present value of the proposed action. An alternative way of presenting the same information is the cost-benefit ratio, or the ratio of the summation of benefits to the summation of costs. In this case, a ratio greater than 1.0 indicates a desirable action.

Time discounting is an important but problematic factor. For many capital projects, costs are incurred early in the period, so they are minimally discounted, whereas benefits may not start to accrue until late in the time period where they are subject to maximum discounting. Thus, a project which may intuitively seem beneficial may not have a net social benefit in the long term. What constitutes an appropriate discount rate is a matter of continuing debate. In 1990 Kolb and Scheraga[15] proposed a two-step procedure where investment costs are amortized using the marginal rate of return on private capital and then both benefits and costs are discounted using the social rate of time preference. The first rate is the cost of capital for the business sector, in the range of 5–10 percent. The second rate is the average investment earnings of private citizens, in the range of 1–5 percent. Conventional discounting procedures would apply the first rate to all time discounting. Kolb and Scheraga maintain that the social rate is more appropriate for discounting the time stream of benefits since business investment costs are ultimately passed on to consumers. They suggest analyzing an action with a range of discount rates and other assumptions, and approving only those projects which are clearly beneficial under all assumptions. The expanded calculation capabilities of personal computers make a substantive contribution to this process, since many more assumptions can be tested, and detailed sensitivity analyses can be performed for all important variables in the analysis.

---

[a]Guidance issued with Executive Order 12291 specified a discount rate of 10 percent.

However, the apparent benefit of many government actions will still depend strongly on the choice of discount rate, which will thus continue to be controversial. Decisions on such actions require political or judicial debate and decision. Kopp and Smith[16] report on a suit brought under the Superfund Act[b], for environmental damages due to release of hazardous materials by a mining operation into a recreational stream and underlying groundwater aquifer. The value of damages estimated by the plaintiff and defendant varied by two orders of magnitude (less than $500,000 versus more than $100 million). Kopp and Smith write that the differences were due to assumptions on the nature and duration of damages, the economic harm caused to individual recreators, and methods used for evaluating damages. Since all assumptions and methods fell within the realm of reasonableness, it was left to the court to resolve the issue, based on testimony by attorneys and expert witnesses.

A rational, but complicating, concept formally introduced in the federal environmental impact statement procedure[17] is the "zero option," or "do nothing," alternative. In other words, the present value of alternative proposals must be computed relative to present value of no new action. No matter what the subject of the proposed actions, the need for dual forecasts of the future with and without the proposed options immediately introduces significant uncertainty into the analysis.

Governmental actions most similar to private-sector activities are most amenable to cost-benefit analysis (e.g., increased shipping revenues resulting from a new or improved port or waterway). Cost-benefit analyses have been used to evaluate such projects for decades. In the last two decades, government policy analysts and scientists have struggled to

---

[b]Officially the Comprehensive Environmental Response, Compensation, and Liability Act of 1980 and the Superfund Reauthorization Act and Amendments of 1986.

apply the concept to less concrete phenomena such as human health, safety, and environmental, recreational, and esthetic values. The problem is that the value of many benefits in these areas is subjective, and can be weighed only by estimating society's willingness to accept the costs of changes.

Two approaches are used to estimate willingness to pay: revealed preferences and expressed preferences. The former is derived from observing what people do; the latter by asking them what they would do. Both methods can produce misleading results. For example, expressed preference methods may be inaccurate if questions are too general or too complicated, and individuals may intentionally or unintentionally misrepresent their true positions. Similarly, revealed preference evaluations may lose their validity when there are restrictions on consumer behavior in the market, when consumer information is limited, or when the goods or services in question are not available in the market.

Expressed preference advocates often present survey respondents with complicated questionnaires, requesting that the respondent choose among numerous options or rank the options. For this procedure to work requires selecting a sample of individuals sufficiently large and well constructed to represent adequately all conflicting interests and provide stable and reliable estimates of individual preferences. The revealed preference method appears more reliable on the surface, because it deals with actual data, but it is reliable only if all relevant aspects of individual preferences can be captured by or deduced from market data, which is often impossible. The following case study on air quality regulations provides some examples of problems policy analysts have met when applying benefit analysis to real-world issues.

The regulation of particulate matter is part of the National Primary and Secondary Ambient Air Quality Standards (NAAQS) under Section 109 of the 1970 Clean Air Act. Primary standards are set at levels that, "allowing an adequate margin of safety, are requisite to protect the public health."

Secondary standards are set to "protect the public welfare from any known or anticipated adverse effects." Initial standards were set for total mass of particles, irrespective of size:

Primary standards
- 75 micrograms per cubic meter (annual geometric mean); and
- 260 micrograms per cubic meter (maximum 24-hour concentration not to be exceeded more than once per year).

Secondary standards
- 60 micrograms per cubic meter (annual geometric mean, as a guide to be used in assessing implementation plans to achieve the 24-hour standard); and
- 150 micrograms per cubic meter (maximum 24-hour concentration not to be exceeded more than once per year).

There is technical evidence to show that coarse particles are less harmful to health than fine particles and thus to suggest that a size-specific standard should be considered. Since the passage of the 1970 Clean Air Act, two separate Supreme Court decisions (*Portland Cement vs. Ruckelshaus,* 1973, and *Weyerhauser vs. Costle,* 1978) held that benefits evaluations could not be considered in setting primary standards. Nevertheless, in December 1981, an economic analysis was performed for the Office of Air Quality Planning and Standards (OAQPS) of the EPA on the benefits of alternative standards for particulate matter. The legal irrelevance of the product notwithstanding, it was a diligent analysis and thus is reviewed here as an example of the state of the art.

In 1969, the National Air Pollution Control Administration, the predecessor of EPA's OAQPS,[18] published a document which identified and evaluated the effects of airborne particulate matter on health, climate, visibility, materials, vegetation, and public concern. Epidemiological studies cited in the document indicated an association between short-term exposures to certain concentrations of particulate matter and increased mortality and morbidity from damage to the respiratory system. The association between long-term community exposure to particulate matter and respiratory disease was "probable"; the association between long-term residence in a polluted area and chronic disease and death was described in the document as "conjectural."

These findings led to the development of air quality standards in 1971; these same standards prevailed until the new size-specific standard was promulgated in 1987. The benefits analyses described below, despite their legal inadmissibility, fostered a public discussion and assessment of the state of knowledge of particulate matter air pollutant effects and controls which indirectly played a role in promulgation of the new standard. However, as described below, knowledge gained from this process was officially ignored in promulgating the final rule. While students of environmental management would endorse cost-benefit analysis to select the standard from several alternatives, the wording of Section 109 invalidates such an analysis unless it applies to choosing the adequacy of the margin of safety.

The benefits analysis examined three primary standards, each of which would have been implemented in 1989. It did not examine any secondary standards. The three primary standards were expressed in technical terms, where micro means one-millionth and PM10 means that quantity of particles with a diameter less than or equal to 10 micrometers. Each alternative was represented as an average maximum and a once-a-year 24-hour maximum:

	In Microgram of PM 10	
	Maximum Mean	**Maximum 24**
Option 1	55	150
Option 2	85	225
Option 3	110	300

Once a new standard is established, control strategies (or "implementation plans") for emissions sources are developed state by state. State plans must demonstrate that particulate levels will not exceed the established standard.

Benefits were estimated by separately considering health effects, residential property values, hedonic wage rates, and reduced soiling. The benefits associated with each of these factors are not mutually exclusive and would have involved double-counting if they were simply added together. If the spirit of the law had been followed, health effects benefits would have been the same in all cases, since all three options would have been set low enough to "protect the public health." However, the analysis proceeded in textbook fashion, unconstrained by laws.

In using both epidemiological studies and economic studies, the analysis was able to exploit different types of information in estimating health effects. Epidemiological studies have an advantage over economic studies because they take into account several factors in addition to particles that influence the incidence of respiratory disease, including age, sex, race, occupation, and smoking. The report stated that such information makes "it possible to assess directly the level of risk to the individual, rather than inferring it from a 'population risk.'" On the other hand, the report indicated that because economic studies do not take into account as many health-related factors, they can use data sources that also do not take all these factors into account. Thus, economic studies have more data sources at their disposal. In addition, economic studies allow economic models to be revised and updated more easily.

Using both economic and epidemiological studies, the analysis developed dose-response functions that related levels of particulate matter for each regulatory alternative to the incidence of illness for each health effect category (e.g., acute exposure, acute morbidity, chronic exposure, and chronic morbidity). From these dose-response functions and several data sources, health benefits were estimated in monetary terms, based on the following assumptions:

- The base year is 1989;
- The time horizon is 15 years;
- The value of reduced morbidity is a function of both direct medical expenditures and lost workdays; and
- The value of a life ranges from $380,000 to $2,800,000 with a point estimate of $1,590,000 (1980 dollars).

The specific methodology used to estimate these benefits is too complex to summarize adequately here. Fourteen different studies were used to estimate the incidence of mortality and the benefits of reduced morbidity, and another six studies were examined to estimate the value of a life.

One of the most important of the studies considered was by Mazumdar et al.,[19] relating the level of smoke in London to mortality rates. A linear dose-response equation derived from this study was used to estimate mortality rates. However, the applicability of Mazumdar's findings was subject to question because the levels of "British smoke" in the study covaried substantially with levels of SO_2 molecules (which are distinct from particulate matter). Statistical techniques were employed in the benefits analysis to deal with this difficulty.

Property values were analyzed under the assumption that a household would pay more to live in a less polluted area, everything else being equal. This additional value placed on property was regarded as a reflection of a household's perceived benefits from living in a less polluted area. Hence, the difference in property values was viewed in the analysis as the monetary value that a household places on "perceived health, physical property, aesthetic, or psychic benefits."[20]

Using the data of previous studies, a hedonic price technique was employed to develop a cost relationship between property values and levels of particulate matter. The technique involved a regression of housing values onto a set of housing characteristics that included air quality. This then allowed for estimates to be made of the benefits of the regulatory alternatives. The report noted, however, that there are probably some benefits of reduced particulates that are not perceived by the household in its valuation of property. Thus, the analysis did not regard the estimated differences in property values as total measures of benefits.

Wage rates were evaluated in a hedonic manner similar to that used for residential property values. The general notion was that, all else being equal, individuals require more compensation to be willing to work in more polluted areas. Therefore, wage differentials associated with air pollution levels were regarded as equivalent to values placed on clean air. A hedonic price technique was used again in which wage differentials were related to the characteristics of individuals, jobs, and areas. This technique was complex; it involved an econometric model that contained functions for worker utility, production by the firm, profit maximization, and an "offer function." The offer function calculated (1) wages paid to the optimal number of workers and (2) alternative pollution levels, where both of these in combination would yield a constant profit level.

Several studies on soiling were reviewed, and four were used to estimate the benefits of reduced soiling in terms of decreased cleaning costs. The analysis did not involve the repair or replacement of any materials that might conceivably be damaged by particulate matter. Two models were developed, one to estimate benefits to households and the other to estimate benefits to the manufacturing sector. By using the relations provided in the studies, the analysis was able to derive cleanup costs from levels of particulate matter. The benefits of lower cleanup costs were estimated county by county for all U.S. counties expected to undergo a reduction in particulate matter. For each regulation option, benefits to counties were aggregated across Census regions and the United States, rendering total benefits.

Three types of benefits were considered: health effects, soiling and materials damage, and visibility and aesthetics. These were estimated by analyzing four factors: health effects, residential property values, wage rates, and reduced soiling. The analysis of health effects resulted in benefit estimates strictly pertaining to the reduced incidence of disease; similarly, the analysis of soiling resulted in estimates strictly pertaining to reduced cleanup costs. However, the analyses of residential property values and wage rates each yielded estimates of people's perceived total benefits of living or working in areas with different pollution levels. Therefore, the benefits estimated from comparisons of residential property values and the benefits estimated from comparisons of wage rates each represent the total of society's perceived health benefits, perceived cleanup benefits, and perceived visibility and aesthetics benefits.

The estimated perceived benefits derived from property values were subdivided by health, cleanup, and visibility and aesthetics benefits. This was done by adopting the general findings of a study by Brookshire et al.[21] The same was done for the benefits derived from hedonic wage rates. Health benefits were considered in two categories: perceived health benefits (the reduction in acute exposure mortality and acute exposure acute morbidity) and unperceived health benefits (the reduction in chronic exposure mortality, chronic exposure morbidity, and acute exposure chronic morbidity). Finally, assuming that households perceive the benefits of reduced soiling while manufacturing firms do not, soiling benefits were divided into perceived (household) benefits and unperceived (manufacturing firms) benefits. Non-manufacturing firms were not included.

In the analysis of Option 1 (55, 150), all benefits were estimated assuming a 15-year time horizon and a 10 percent discount rate. For health benefits and soiling benefits, the best estimate for each type of benefit was chosen from among the different results of different factors considered in the analysis. The analysis considered visibility and aesthetic benefits away from the residence, but did not estimate them, and examined and considered studies that were done on visibility and aesthetic benefits. Such benefits were not estimated (except by way of property values and wage rates) because there was no available information on the extent to which airborne particles below 10 micrometers in diameter hinder visibility.

There is close to a 20-fold difference between the minimum and maximum estimates of benefits, clearly indicating that there is considerable uncertainty in the analysis. Furthermore, because the analysis examines a wide variety of issues concerning particulate matter, there are many different sources of uncertainty. However, as indicated by the estimates of total benefits for Option 1, health benefits constitute the vast majority of the total benefits. This suggests that, of all sources of uncertainty, those pertaining to health effects are the most important. The analysis did not include distributional effects, and because only benefits were examined and not costs, the analysis could not address the issues of the variable impact of regulatory alternatives on different institutions. However, there are distributional effects associated with benefits as well, which the analysis could have addressed but did not.

The estimation of the value of life was also a major source of uncertainty. Any discussion of the value of life as a source of uncertainty, however, involves the implicit assumption that there exists some objective monetary value of life and that the "uncertainty" is uncertainty with regard to finding this value. This assumption requires two other implicit assumptions: (1) the value of life is strictly an economic consideration; and (2) if people have different valuations of life, then the "objective" value of a life is some average of these individual values. In essence, this philosophy assumes that the value of life can somehow be reduced to dollars, even if the estimates are highly uncertain. In contrast, other schools of thought raise moral and ethical objections to the concept of attempting to reduce life to dollars.[22]

The analysis ignored the benefits of reduced pain and suffering that result from the reduced incidence of illness. Although reduced pain and suffering may be difficult to valuate, one would expect that it is conceptually no more difficult than a valuation of visibility and aesthetics and of life itself, which the analysis did perform. Moreover, because reduced illness was by far the main contributor to total estimated benefits, reduced pain and suffering (of both those that are ill and their family and friends) would also likely be substantial. Although this issue applies in general to many federal policy decisions, Congress attempted to avoid the issue by careful wording of Section 109. Thus, there should have been no pain, suffering, or death associated with any legal alternative.

As illustrated earlier in this section, the results of the analysis indicate that benefits increase substantially with increases in the stringency of the standard, a result which was not expected by the agency.[23] The administration's principal reason for introducing benefits analysis into the regulatory process was to prove the reasonability of less stringent standards.

After another year of gathering data and refining the cost and benefit calculations in response to cognizant critics, the agency proposed the *least stringent* option (150 micrograms per cubic meter once-a-year 2-hour maximum and 50 micrograms per cubic meter annual average) for particles equal to or less than 10 micrometers in diameter.[24] After more than three years of additional public comment and additional research and analysis, EPA promulgated the 50–150 rule for fine particle ambient air quality as initially proposed. The revised cost and benefits analyses were included in the docket in response to Executive Order 12291 but, in deference to the previously cited court decisions, EPA claimed to have ignored the analyses in promulgating the standard. The following quote from the EPA's rationale presented in the regulation provides a snapshot of the utility of cost-benefit analyses for environmental standards as of 1987:

> In announcing the availability of the draft RIA [Regulatory Impact Analysis responding to Executive Order 12291], the Agency stated that neither the RIA nor the contractors' reports were considered in developing the proposed revisions. Subsequent to the release of the draft RIA, the public and other governmental agencies raised a number of questions regarding the underlying data bases and analyses discussed in the draft RIA. In response to these questions, the Agency modified the cost model used and made other, more limited, changes to the benefits analyses. The number and extent of the changes were constrained, however, by the underlying model structure and the available data. The Agency has carefully evaluated the revised analysis and has concluded that despite the significant improvement made, fundamental questions remain with regard to certain aspects of the methodology used, particularly with respect to the emission reduction/air quality improvement relationship which affects the subsequent cost and benefit calculations. Consistent with its past practice, the Agency has not considered the final Regulatory Impact Analysis of National Ambient Air Quality Standards for Particulate Matter in reaching decisions on the final standards.[25]

This statement was prepared by the EPA staff attorneys and policy analysts. The lack of guidance provided by quantitative analyses was also cited by the Clean Air Scientific Advisory Committee, an independent panel of scientists appointed to review the analyses of the EPA staff scientists:

> During the past decade, the link between visibility and fine particle mass concentrations has been convincingly documented. . . . The public cares about visibility and is willing to pay something for clean air. However, the

quantitative basis for establishing a psychological, economic, transportation or any other welfare cost associated with visibility impairment has not been established.[26]

And so, despite the extensive effort of dozens of experienced environmental scientists and economists, the new (in 1987) fine particle ambient air quality standard was chosen by political judgment.

Risk Analysis

Given the problems of quantifying effects into dollars, the "risk analysis" procedure was explored during the same era in an attempt to provide a rational set of physical (as opposed to economic) projections upon which to base the necessary political judgments. Unfortunately, risk analysis ran into many of the same problems as the cost-benefit procedures.

One of the principal responsibilities of government is to protect its citizens against threats which they cannot dispel themselves. Armies, police, firemen, public health officials, weather forecasts, flood control projects, and vehicular traffic controls are traditional examples of government intervention which attempts to lessen society's risk of injury, illness, or financial loss. Risk analysis is the process of evaluating the mathematical probability of a certain type of harm to an individual during some time period. Risk management is the deliberate act of trying to lessen the probability of harm.

People are continually subjected to risks. Cardiovascular disease and cancer are the greatest risks of death for the average American, as reported in the U.S. Statistical Abstracts[27] (Figure 3-1). But, of course, none of us is average. When the causes of death are compiled by geographic area, age, sex, socio-economic status, and type of employment, the patterns are much different. Cancer death rates vary from 831 per

Figure 3-1
Causes of Deaths for Americans in 1986

Accidental or Disease Deaths per Million Total Population

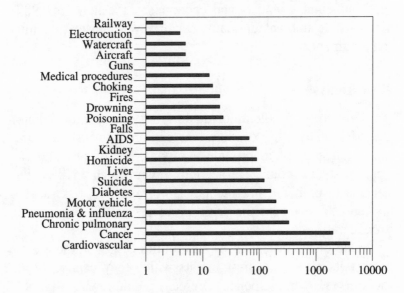

Source: *Statistical Abstract of the U.S. 1990*

million in Alaska to 2,666 per million in the District of Columbia (Figure 3-2). For young people, accidental death rates
are about double that for heart disease.

Even though the federal government has been regulating
threats to its citizens' health for more than a century, our
former colleagues Covello and Mumpower[28] list the following
changes over the past decade or so which have brought the
discipline of risk analysis to the front of the public agenda:

Figure 3-2
1988 Frequency of Cancer Deaths by State

Cancer Deaths Per Million State Population

Source: *Statistical Abstract of the U.S. 1990*

- A significant shift in the nature of the risks to which human beings are subject;
- A significant increase in average life expectancies;
- An increase in new risks fundamentally different in both character and magnitude from those encountered in the past;
- A significant increase in the ability of scientists to identify and measure risks;
- A significant increase in the number of scientists and analysts whose work is specifically focused on health, safety, and environmental risks;
- An increase in the number of formal quantitative risk analyses that are produced and used;
- An increase in the role of the federal government in assessing and managing risks; and
- An increase in the participation of special interest groups in the societal risk management process.

Just as with the comprehensive model, the fundamental theories and concepts behind the application of risk analysis to health, safety, and environmental regulations are flawless. However, gathering adequate data, marshalling the analytic skills, defining the regulatory objective, and distilling the analytic results into a form meaningful to executives entail so many difficulties that the techniques are of limited value as a decision aid. As an example of the complexity and many sources of uncertainty in using risk analysis to set an ambient water quality standard, consider the following mathematical expression, adapted from Lipton,[29] of the probability of a human developing cancer from consumption of seafood contaminated by carcinogens in wastes discharged into a waterway:

$$R_{jT} = \int_{t=0}^{T} \int_{m=1}^{M} \int_{i=1}^{S} , \frac{C_{im}(t)Q_m B_{im} F_{imt} I_{ij} * (1 - L_{ijm})}{W_j} \, di \, dm \, dt$$

The left hand side of this equation, R_jT, is the probability that a person in population subgroup j exposed to contaminated seafood from a specific waterway for a period of T years will contract cancer from this cause. The right-hand side of the equation consists entirely of measured or estimated variables, each of which has its own source of significant statistical errors. C_im is the concentration of carcinogen m in the environment of seafood species i. Individuals may consume several different types of seafood which have lived in an aquatic environment contaminated by several different carcinogens. Q_m is the human carcinogenic potency factor for carcinogen m, estimated as the upper 95 percent confidence limit of the slope of a linear dose-response curve. This parameter is usually derived from laboratory studies of nonhuman organisms exposed to elevated doses of the carcinogen. This procedure, as well as the linear extrapolation theory, is subject to continual debate among scientists and regulators. B_imt is the maximum bioconcentration factor for carcinogen m in species i, usually determined in laboratory studies, at the time t that it was caught. Aquatic animals may concentrate certain chemicals in their body tissues several times higher than the ambient environmental concentration. F_imt is the fraction of bioconcentration of carcinogen m attained by species i at the time t that it was caught. Bioconcentration is a function of time; younger organisms and migratory organisms may have low values of F_imt. I_ij is the mean daily ingestion of seafood species i by people in subgroup j. Of course, the variability of seafood consumption even among a small subgroup of the population is extreme, and this number must be estimated from surveys or observation of seafood catches or sales. L_ijm is the fraction of carcinogen m lost during the food preparation of species i prior to consumption by people in subgroup j. Bioconcentration generally occurs in certain organs of the seafood. If carcinogen m happened to concentrate in discarded viscera, L_ijm would be very high. If the concentration occurred in the edible flesh, L_ijm would be very low.

Finally, W_j is the average human body weight of people in subgroup j, again available only by survey or access to community medical records.

The integral signs mean that, to be comprehensive, the calculated risks should be accumulated for all kinds of carcinogens (m = 1 through M) present in all kinds of seafood (i = 1 through S) consumed by the subgroup. Also, since most of the variables are functions of time, the calculation of risk should be performed for each year and summed over the assumed exposure period (t = 1 through T). The integration across all types of carcinogens assumes that their carcinogenic mechanisms are independent and additive, an assertion that could be too stringent or too lenient depending on your perspective.

If an acceptable level of cancer risk were specified, for example one in 1 million, in principle, one can back-calculate an allowable concentration of contaminant $(C_i n)$, which would then become the ambient water quality standard. The specification of a population subgroup allows regulators to target their concern toward more susceptible or more highly exposed persons in the population. But such a selection is not easy. Should the calculation be for a 100-pound person who eats seafood from the same source three meals a day, every day of his or her life? This sounds extreme, but often, regulatory agency scientists, either because of legal specifications, lack of data for mathematical parameters, or a desire to err on the safe side, perform this calculation for the "maximally exposed individual."

Federal health, safety, and environmental protection laws have rarely specified exact numerical levels of acceptable risk, except for a few cases of "zero" risk. Usually they provide qualitative prescriptions of stringency which must be interpreted by the enforcing agency. Table 3-1 provides some common examples of the language that agency scientists and policy analysts must accommodate. The noted "Delaney Clause" of the Food, Drug, and Cosmetic Act is the clearest

Table 3-1
Risk Avoidance Language in Selected Federal Statutes

Law and Section	Risk Target	Risk Avoidance Language
Food, Drug and Cosmetic Acts, 21USC§348(C)(3)(A) "Delaney Clause"	Food Additives	"found...to induce cancer in man or animal"
Occupational Safety and Health Act, 29USC§655(b)(5), 1970	Toxic materials and harmful physical agents in workplaces	"will suffer material impairment of health or functional capacity"
Clean Air Act, 42 USC§7408, 7409, 1977	Common air pollutants	"cause, or contribute to, air pollution which may reasonably be anticipated to endanger public health or welfare"
Clean Air Act, 42 USC§742, 1977	Hazardous air pollutants	"cause, or contribute to, air pollution which may reasonably be anticipated to result in an increase in mortality or an irreversible, or incapacitating reversible, illness"
Clean Air Act, 42 USC§7521, 1977	Motor vehicle emissions	"cause, or contribute to, air pollution which may reasonably be anticipated to endanger public health or welfare"
Toxic Substances Control Act, 15USC§2603(f), 1976	Existing chemical substances or mixtures	"may be reasonable basis to conclude...will present a significant risk of serious or widespread harm to human beings from cancer, gene mutations, or birth defects"
Toxic Substances Control Act, 15USC§2604(f), 1976	New chemical substances, mixtures, or uses	"is a reasonable basis to conclude...will present unreasonable risk of injury to environment"

(requiring no risk at all to "man or animal"), but it is also the most frustrating to the food and drug industry and many professional risk managers. It applies to all food additives, not just suspected chemicals, and has been interpreted to mean that if any animal contracts cancer in a lab test, the material must be prohibited. There is no provision to balance the health or economic benefits of the additive. Furthermore, there is no latitude for comparison with other risks, such as the carcinogenic properties of many natural foods.

The sugar substitute cyclamate was banned because of the Delaney Clause. Saccharin would have been similarly banned, but since no alternative artificial sweetener was available at the time, Congress voted a special exemption. Many legislators recognize the infeasibility or extremely high costs of pursuing zero risk, but at the same time many don't want to be on record as voting in favor of "a little cancer" or "a few deaths." Consequently, the Delaney Clause will be on the books for years to come.

In the other cases in Table 3-1, where some interpretation is possible, regulators (particularly in the EPA) have attempted to set a benchmark of acceptable risk to rationalize their many different regulatory programs. But each new standard is a separate political battle, drawing out special interest groups from both sides. Former EPA Administrator Ruckelshaus often joked that, "If we get about the same number of protests from both sides I figure we must have picked the right value."

As a companion to the cost-benefit assessment discussed above, the NSF also assessed the capabilities of risk analysis procedures applied to regulatory impact analysis. This project also benefited from the opinion of more than 100 national experts in risk analysis.[30] The summary comments were far less optimistic than they might have been a few years before.

- Even the best risk assessment cannot provide exact answers. Due to gaps in underlying scientific data, and to a lesser extent to limitations of available methods, the results of risk assessments are, at best, useful approximations. Risk assessment is difficult to do and even more difficult to do well. Regulatory executives may feel uncomfortable with the fact that a good risk assessment will make the uncertainty and subjectivity underlying a decision explicit. Furthermore, the quantitative nature of risk estimates presents a potential problem in that they may be interpreted to convey a false sense of precision where none may be warranted. Like most other human endeavors, risk assessment is as much art or philosophy as science. It has weaknesses and limitations and can contribute positive value only if used with great care and understanding.

- It is unsound to conduct a risk assessment of regulatory options on the basis of risk estimates biased by conservative assumptions and models to degrees that are not obvious or specified. Such methods do not adequately differentiate best scientific judgment from societal value judgment. The issue is not whether conservatism is desirable in health matters, but rather how and by whom the conservative judgments should be made.

- The theory and conceptual underpinnings for risk assessment are well developed. The difficulty in practicing risk assessment comes from ignorance or lack of data in the particular application. Inevitably, many approximations and important judgments are required.

- Risk assessment cannot now, and perhaps never will, be reducible to a step-by-step, cookbook procedure. Instead, the methods selected and the way they are implemented must depend on the situation under study.

- Although the goal of risk assessment should be to reflect scientific information and uncertainty while introducing a minimum of value judgments, it must be accepted that many of the approximations and assumptions used, the outputs produced, and the ways they are presented have policy implications. It is, therefore, unrealistic to expect that guidelines for conducting risk assessment can effectively safeguard against the possibility of risk assessment being biased toward specific viewpoints or interests.

Aside from difficulties in finding common measures of risk in order to allow the rationalization of government risk protection programs, the variable perceptions and preferences for different types of risks by different individuals or groups preclude any type of standardized, scientific procedure for specifying acceptable risk levels. Risk analysis professionals have been studying this issue for over a decade and have managed to identify and catalogue several psychological issues. Camerer and Kunreuther[31] provide a good overview on this subject, with special reference to low-probability/high-consequence events, such as nuclear power plant accidents and plane crashes. They cite several different psychological behavioral theories which explain why, on the average, people are not fully aware of all their risks, and do not cope in any comprehensive economically rational way with risks of which they are aware. Yet, in deciding whether to adopt a regulation and at what level, risk analysis is often a formal part of the decision-making framework, despite the various incarnations of uncertainty in such an approach.

An analysis by Herbert Inhaber sponsored by the Atomic Energy Control Board (AECB) of Canada provides an excellent example of comparing risks from a large number of different activities. The document was widely debated by U.S. analysts, and thoroughly examined and critiqued by DOE. Inhaber was attempting to determine which type of energy technology was the safest from a comprehensive viewpoint. In fact, the AECB hoped the study would show that atomic power was safer than many of the other technologies currently in development. The project considered 11 technological methods for generating electricity-equivalent energy from coal, oil, natural gas, nuclear power, hydropower, solar thermal heating, methanol, wind, solar photovoltaic, solar space heating, and ocean thermal power.[32] These technologies were chosen not because they represent an exhaustive set of energy technologies but because the data necessary for analysis were available. Three major types of statistical data sources were used: health effects due to pollutants, industrial damage and disease, and materials and labor used for energy systems.

Inhaber analyzed two types of risk: catastrophic and non-catastrophic. The latter consisted primarily of risks to human health from industrial and occupational sources or from pollution effects. These risks were quantified for each fuel cycle, from extraction to energy end-use, based on a variety of sources and assumptions about the current state of technological development. Six sources of risk, corresponding to the six stages of each fuel cycle, were considered: material and fuel production, component fabrication, plant construction, operation and maintenance, transportation, and waste disposition and deactivation.

Inhaber included public health risk as a result of the other six sources of risk rather than an additional source of risk. Most of the risk calculations concentrated on three of the risk sources: material and fuel production, component fabrication, and plant construction. Material requirements and necessary man-hours to produce the materials, or construction man-hour requirements, were determined. Values for risk by source were obtained from statistics on injury, death, and disease rates for workers. The proportion of risk by source was then calculated for each technology. For coal and oil, most of the risk is due to air pollution resulting from electricity production or operation and maintenance; for natural gas and ocean thermal, the risk is due to fuel gathering and handling; for nuclear power, the risk is from materials acquisitions and waste disposal; and for wind, solar thermal heating, and solar photovoltaic, the risk results primarily from the backup systems required (assumed to be coal).

The total man-days lost per megawatt-year net energy output over the lifetime of each energy system were determined, with a death assumed equivalent to 6,000 man-days lost. Inhaber concluded that unconventional energy systems can create substantial risk for human health. Natural gas and nuclear power had the lowest values, and most of the unconventional technologies had values similar to coal and oil. The large volume of construction materials required and the risks associated with backup energy and energy systems storage resulted in high values for unconventional energy sources.

The Inhaber report met with mixed reactions. On one hand, a comparison of the risks of various technologies was a significant contribution to risk analysis literature. The idea of giving risk calculations a common base for all technologies studied (e.g., man-days lost per megawatt-year) was commendable, as was that of adopting a cradle-to-grave approach often missing from common perceptions of risk. Solar technologies, for instance, tend to appear exceptionally clean and without hazard, while nuclear power evokes fear and distrust. Inhaber's conclusions that nuclear was one of the two lowest risk technologies and that risk from wind, methanol, and solar was similar to that from coal and oil and much greater than that from nuclear, were surprising news, eagerly accepted by some, particularly proponents of nuclear power. Others were not so eager to accept the Inhaber report, which became the focus of in-depth critiques, numerous publications, and protracted accusations and denials. The major published response to the Inhaber report, a critique by Holdren et al., was, at 232 pages, longer than the document it criticized.[33] A review of this critique highlights the difficulties of risk analysis.

Holdren et al. organized their criticisms under categories of inconsistencies, conceptual confusions, inappropriate selection of systems and data, misreadings and misrepresentations of literature, improper calculating procedures, untenable assumptions and contentions, as well as typographical errors, internal discrepancies, and arithmetic mistakes. A major contention was that Holdren's own work, cited numerous times by Inhaber, had been misrepresented and misused.

In discussing inconsistencies, Holdren pointed out that the Inhaber report stated clearly that risks from conventional and unconventional systems were calculated in the same way, that the basis of methodology was the same for all systems, and that all systems were treated in the same way. Yet Holdren showed that only materials and labor requirements on site were included for conventional systems, whereas materials acquisition, component manufacture, and plant construction were also considered for unconventional systems.

Once this error had been committed, it tended to generate more error, as in the calculation of man-hours of labor needed from which man-days lost (Inhaber's expression of occupational risk) was ultimately derived. Although in this case Inhaber subsequently showed that the omissions and errors cited by Holdren made negligible numerical differences in the conclusions when the correct values were substituted, the damage to the credibility of the risk assessment had been done.

One of several conceptual confusions in the Inhaber report cited by Holdren was the addition of occupational and public risks to produce a value for total risk. Whereas, superficially, this would seem simple and appropriate, Holdren pointed out that the two risks are not comparable and therefore not additive. Risks to the public can be considered a net cost to society. Occupational risk is a gross cost, the net dependent on what the workers would otherwise have been doing (and the risk they would otherwise have incurred). To compare occupational risks of technologies, one would have to compare them on the basis of the net change in risk brought about by each technology. Another conceptual confusion against which Holdren warned was the aggregation of deaths from different causes, as if any death is equivalent to any other death. While conceptually this makes sense, in reality some deaths are more feared than others, and some illnesses shorten life more than others. Qualitatively, then, they are different.

Another apparent error was the choice of anthracite as the coal used in steel production. Anthracite makes up a small percentage of the coal mined (not enough for the amount of steel-making called for in Inhaber's calculations), is more dangerous to mine than soft coal, and requires more worker-hours per ton produced. The occupational risk estimated for coal acquisition for making steel may have been high by a factor of three, affecting considerably the hazard associated with the energy systems requiring the most steel, primarily solar space heating and methanol.

Perhaps one of the most likely pitfalls in any analysis is that which falls in the category of misreadings and misrepresentations. In one instance, Inhaber, according to Holdren, took information from the wrong column of figures in a reference document, resulting in greater materials requirement by a factor of 50 for windmills, and therefore greater risk. Often it is difficult to interpret reference material correctly, because it may not be written clearly or all of the data necessary for the correct interpretation are not present, and misinterpretation can raise the question of misrepresentation.

A more recent attempt to compare the risks of two technologies highlights the point that average statistics do not mean much to someone who is not the average person. Many participants in the policy process divide deaths by some very aggregate, easily obtained, value (as we did in Figure 3-1). In the case of Figure 3-1, the divisions are by one year and by the total U.S. population. Taking the total deaths in commercial aircraft accidents and dividing it by the number of passenger miles flown provides one measure of the risk of traveling by commercial airline. A similar figure can be calculated for travel by private automobile. Hence the oft-quoted statistic that our chances of dying in an aircraft are about one-twentieth that of dying in a car.

However, this is true only for the grand average, including all drunk drivers, young people, unsafe vehicles, and unsafe roads. Concerned that automobiles were unfairly judged by these gross averages, General Motors statisticians did some disaggregating and found interesting results.[34] Because commercial airline accidents happen primarily during landing and takeoff, longer trips do not have proportionately higher risks, whereas the fatality risk for auto accidents is approximately proportional to trip length.

The GM analysts calculated that the break-even point of equal risk is about 600 miles: for trips longer than 600 miles, planes are safer, but for shorter trips, autos are safer. And this is true for only the automobile front seat: for back-seat passengers, who suffer fewer fatalities, trips below 800 miles are safer by car. Furthermore, an experienced, sober, seat-belted driver on interstate highways is subject to a much lower fatality risk than the average driver, making auto travel for this sector of the population even safer. The important lesson here is that for any risk analysis, the risk varies considerably throughout the population exposed, and analyses and reports need to make clear which risk is being targeted and managed.

Decision Analysis

Decision analysis is a separate technical discipline, but with aspects similar to the other analytical approaches. Decision analysis techniques provide an analytical framework for structuring the choices of solutions to problems characterized by complex and interrelated issues and uncertainties over the nature and timing of outcomes, the dynamics of the problem, and value preferences.

The theoretical foundation of decision analysis is simply the proposition that the desirability of alternative courses of action should depend on the probability of the possible outcomes for each alternative and the preferences for those outcomes. Probability is estimated statistically, and desirability is measured by utility functions. Probabilities and utilities can be combined to calculate the desirability of each alternative.

Decision analysis is essentially statutorily mandated for the nation's energy security. This is a continuing function of DOE, although different administrations have different concepts about the "decision space," i.e., the range of available options. Conservative administrations tend to favor market solutions for most of our energy availability problems.[35]

Decision analysis concepts were used repeatedly to deflect congressional attempts throughout the 1980s to pass acid rain control legislation. Any type of control program proposed indicated large increases in electric utility rates for the central and eastern sections of the country. Acid rain, a result of the transport over hundreds of miles of SO_2 emissions from coal-fired power plants, requires large, complex meteorologic and air chemistry computer simulations to determine the effect of emission controls on exposed environments. As with all large models of this type, there is so much uncertainty in input parameters and output results that there is no certainty that a given control program will produce benefits at least equal to its costs. As each new bill to control acid rain was introduced in Congress, administration experts testified about the uncertainties involved; given the other economic issues facing the nation during the 1980s, this was enough to kill the bill.

To find an example of true quantitative decision analysis actually used in the civilian side of the government, we had to reach back to the Nixon administration. This example, taken from Howard et al.,[36] began as a study for the Environmental Science Service Administration, predecessor of the National Oceanic and Atmospheric Administration, to see if decision analysis could be useful for planning and analysis of National Weather Service operations. The question of whether to try to change the path and intensity of a hurricane by cloud seeding provides a classic example of the complex issues for which decision analysis was designed.

Seeding is a process of inducing rainfall from clouds by dispersing fine particles from aircraft. Based on theory and limited empirical data, there was some probability that seeding might lower the intensity of hurricanes or change their paths. To determine whether or not the current limited knowledge justified seeding storms actually threatening the mainland, this decision analysis focused on estimating property damages that would result from seeding or not seeding a hurricane. Possible injuries and deaths were not explicitly considered in the analysis.

There is considerable uncertainty in wind changes for both seeded and unseeded hurricanes, therefore probabilities on wind speed had to be determined. Property damages were assumed to be a function of the wind speed. Wind speed probabilities and the damage function together determined a probability function for property damages. Probabilities of wind speed changes in the 12-hour period prior to landfall for both seeded and unseeded hurricanes were determined after discussion with knowledgable meteorologists. Probability functions were computed, based on experience with previous storms, for changes in wind speed, given that seeding may have a beneficial effect, no effect, or a detrimental effect.

Given that seeding has no effect (i.e., is equivalent to not seeding), the latest scientific knowledge indicated that the change in wind speed over a 12-hour period was given by a normal distribution with a mean of zero and a standard deviation of 15.6 percent. Given that seeding was beneficial, the distribution on the change in wind speed was represented by a normal distribution with a mean of –15 percent and a standard deviation of 7 percent. Conditioned on seeding being detrimental, the distribution for wind speed change was taken to be normal with a mean of 10 percent and standard deviation of 7 percent.

The path and behavior of hurricanes are highly variable, and empirical evidence was limited to two seedings of the same hurricane while it was far from shore. Thus, even though maximum wind speed dropped following each of the two seedings, there was a significant probability that this drop was not caused by the seeding. Atmospheric scientists at the time judged the probabilities as follows: 9 percent that it was beneficial, 9 percent that it had no effect, and two percent that it was detrimental. Since the average political executive has limited knowledge of complex statistics, these probabilities were the fatal flaw in this particular application of decision analysis. The scientists were hardly more certain about the effects of seeding than they would have been about the results of a coin toss.

The damage function, a power function of the maximum sustained wind speed in miles per hour, was determined using data from the American Red Cross. A linear least-squares fit of the logarithms was used to calculate the empirical constants, and probability distributions for property damage were then developed for a "nominal" hurricane, both seeded and unseeded. The statistics for expected damages are shown as a continuous function in Figure 3-3, and for discrete values in the two bars in Figure 3-4. Discrete probabilities were assigned to specific changes in maximum wind speed using the appropriate conditional normal distributions and the probabilities of the conditioning events (i.e., beneficial, neutral, detrimental). The figures show that seeding a nominal hurricane (one whose maximum wind speed at landfall is the same as that 12 hours earlier and causes property damage of $100 million) reduces the expected property damage by about $20 million (1971 dollars). Extensive sensitivity analysis of the conditioning probabilities and the parameters in the damage function indicated that property damages are reduced about 10 to 30 percent by seeding. A risk-averse utility function for property damage increases the value of seeding even more. The decision analysts claimed that despite the uncertainties, the decision should always favor seeding because the expected damage was always lower for the seeding option.

The executives, however, were averse to the risk of being blamed by the media for causing more damage than would have occurred if they hadn't authorized "fooling around" with such a powerful act of nature. The decision analysts calculated a liability cost to the government based on the 2 percent probability of exacerbating the storm, and still concluded that seeding was the proper statistical decision.

**Figure 3-3
Expected Decreased Damage
After Hurricane Seeding**

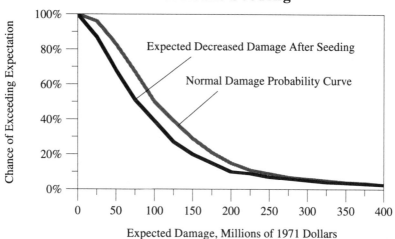

Source: Howard et al., 1972

**Figure 3-4
Hurricane Seeding Decision Analysis**

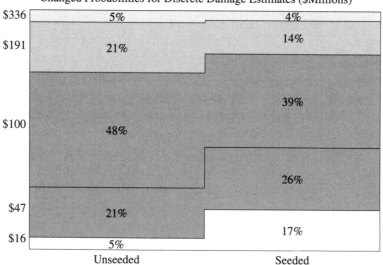

Source: Howard et al., 1972

These calculations, however, did not convince the executives. Seeding was not chosen that hurricane season, and has not been seriously considered since. Additional numerical analyses since that time have concluded that the maximum possible effect that could be caused by the seeding process is minimal compared to the scale of potential natural changes in the storm.[37]

One lesson to be learned here is the futility of complex statistics for analyzing one-time events. Even though the chance of strengthening rather than diminishing the storm was only 2 percent, statistics provide no insight as to whether one of the 2 percent cases will be the next one or not. All the scientists were saying was, "Out of 100 storms, we would guess that two might actually be enlarged by the seeding process." The executives focused on the frightening consequences of the 2 percent case, even though a rational person with a long time perspective should have chosen the seeding option based on available information. Faced with anything as uncertain as a coin toss, most executives would rather go with their instincts.

The foregoing quantitative models provided simpler, more focused and transparent procedures for using experiential knowledge and data to aid in making decisions on complex public policy issues. Despite extensive research, testing, and trial applications over the past several years, none of these methods holds promise for significantly improving the federal decision-making process in the near future, except to the extent that they provide a rhetorical framework for discussion. Many of these methods have demonstrated their effectiveness in smaller-scale, more limited decisions in the private, military, and aerospace sectors, and in small municipal governments. In each of these cases, however, objectives are clearer, the number of decision participants limited and they share more common interests, decision options are more precisely articulated, and input information is apt to be more quantitative than in federal regulatory decisions. When applied to the problem of choosing the appropriate stringency of federal regulations, however, all the methods pale before the challenge. The methods are patently unusable in many different aspects.

Classic cost-benefit analysis seeks to monetize all new costs and new benefits (often avoiding current or projected damages) that would occur under various proposed regulatory alternatives. We now know most of the categories of costs and benefits associated with a broad-scale federal environmental regulation (e.g., the banning of DDT), such as mortality, morbidity, production costs, loss of market, loss of employment, relocation costs, option preservation, changes in property value, esthetic costs and benefits, psychic costs, and ecological damages. But it is extremely difficult and expensive to estimate a defensible monetary value for even one of these cost or benefit categories even in one area, let alone aggregating them nationwide. In most previous attempts to apply this method to federal regulation, there have been too many uncertainties and unknowns to produce a credible estimate of net social benefit or cost.

Risk analysis provides a framework for systematically collecting and analyzing risk data but there is little scientific data on risk. In many instances, the estimate of a risk to human health is based on extrapolation of data from animal experiments (e.g., under the Delaney Clause). The validity of the data and of subsequent decisions, however, depend on a number of assumptions. For example, decisions concerning whether a drug or food additive is safe for human use are based on data from animal experiments and, in turn, on assumptions regarding the similarity of dose-response relationships of animals and humans. Any revisions of these technical assumptions could result in completely different conclusions and, hence, policy decisions. Another significant problem of risk analysis is that there is no universally acceptable level of risk; with no benchmark to determine whether or not an incurred risk should be considered acceptable, decisions must be subjective.

Moreover, there is no way to assess or compare aggregated decisions, as most policy decisions are made independently of one another. In questions of health and safety, there
is a tendency to drive the desired risk to zero. Why accept any
risk at all in any one instance? Another problem concerns
balancing short-term and long-term risks. How should auto
accident risk be compared with possible cancer after 30 years'
exposure to a substance? There is no paradigm for this sort
of trade-off other than a long-term economic benefits analysis,
the shortcomings of which have already been discussed. Finally, the aggregation of risk itself is a problem. The simplifying assumption that magnitude and probability can be multiplied to estimate risk has no empirical basis. The approach
may have some value for comparing hazards of the same order
of magnitude, especially those in the moderate to high range
of probability. There are definite problems, however, when
comparing hazards that are dissimilar.

Decision analysis, however, deals with uncertainty in the
most systematic manner of all the methods discussed. The
alternative actions open to executives and the important consequences of those actions are identified and predicted. Probabilities for uncertain events or behavior are estimated, even
if the probabilities are subjective. In addition, the sequence
of possible decisions, uncertain events, and eventual outcomes is explicitly structured, usually in the form of a decision tree.

A distinguishing feature of decision analysis is the use
of utility functions as a means for ranking results. Utility is a
measure of preferences including the executive's preference
for certainty as well as personal values for certain outcomes.
A government official may not approve a project that has only
a one-in-a-million chance of killing a million people nearly
as readily as another project that has an expected accidental
death rate of 10 persons, even though the damage expected
of the first project is smaller. Although the considerations
here are complex, the important point is that preferences for

risks and rewards are not linear functions of the level of risk or size of reward, nor are they proportional to the expected value. Utility takes such factors into account in assessing preferences for outcomes. Decision analysis, however, involves individual preferences and has difficulties similar to those of social choice theory in dealing with group preferences.

The idea of decision analysis is that executives should maximize their expected utility. Given this rule and the decision tree structure, complete with probability assignments, the tree can be "solved" to indicate which choice is preferred at each decision node in the tree. Working backward from the final outcomes, each path can be assigned values, and a value for the first decision (which is the only one that matters at the moment) can be derived.

The most important advantage of decision analysis is its treatment of risk and uncertainty. The possible outcomes of actions have policy significance, even though some outcomes are only remotely possible. Some actions may have risks of irreversible damage. The main information problem with decision analysis is akin to those in cost-benefit and risk analyses: national regulatory issues usually contain far more unknowns than knowns. Although the procedure permits substitution of unknowns with numerical opinions of experts, when subjective data begin to dominate the analysis, the executive may ask the very valid question, "Why is the mathematical manipulation of several hunches any better than my own intuitive decision?" The more serious problems with decision analysis relate to its relevance to and compatibility with the practical principles of our government.

Another way of assessing the problems with currently proposed quantitative decision aids is to consider their relevance to the principal policy questions. Nearly all environmental, health, and safety laws have been reactions to growing, obvious national problems or isolated catastrophic incidents of national significance. Consequently, the stakes are high in the political debate, and the Congress is rarely inclined to depend on the executive branch to determine, through objective research and analysis, the appropriate level of protection. Instead, laws are written specifically to ensure that the levels of protection are adequate, as judged in political terms, and are promptly promulgated and enforced. In many cases, a specific numerical value or a specific piece of equipment is written into the law (e.g., the allowable automotive emissions in grams per mile in the Clean Air Act, or seat belts in the National Traffic and Vehicle Safety Act).

In the majority of these cases, there is not sufficient information to justify such numeric specifications, and the Congress determines requirements without reference to costs. In some cases, compromises have allowed economic rationalization to temper restrictions—such as "best conventional technology" in the Clean Water Act, the fuel additive regulations in the Clean Air Act, and vehicle safety standards other than occupant restraint systems—but these instances are the exception rather than the rule.

The early versions of environmental, health, and safety laws, for the most part, instructed the executive branch to specify standards or criteria for acceptable environmental quality (i.e., tolerable contaminant concentrations, usually called "ambient standards"). Where enforcement of these standards proved to be difficult, however, or where there was insufficient information to derive ambient standards, legislative amendments began to specify particular procedures, equipment, or equipment performance requirements for sources of pollutants or other hazards. These standards, usually initiated to simplify and accelerate the enforcement process, are commonly known as "technology standards."

There are considerable variations in the specificity of the standards-setting sections of the various environmental, health, and safety laws. Some prescribe a precise numeric value for the standard (e.g., auto emissions), in which case the executive branch has almost no discretion. The regulation simply mimics the law, and the cost, benefit, risk, and effectiveness, rather than analyzed, are implicitly sanctioned by Congress. Only slightly less restrictive are the laws that mandate a particular action, procedure, or piece of equipment. For example, the Resource Conservation and Recovery Act requires the closing of all open dumps; the Surface Mining Control and Reclamation Act specifies mining procedures at a level of detail found in an operating engineer's handbook. Again, studies of the costs, benefits, and effectiveness of proposed regulations are not considered in the rule-making process.

Most ambient standard laws specify levels of risk in qualitative terms, such as "protect the public health," "no significant risk," and "protect public welfare." In these cases, the executive branch is charged with determining the numerical ambient concentration limit that will achieve these qualitative objectives. There is no discretion to determine the social benefits of alternative objectives through cost-benefit analysis. Technology standards also use this method when not enough information is known to specify a number, or when the number is so complex that many different values are appropriate for the many different types of sources. Qualitative technology standards commonly contain language such as "best practicable," "best available," "lowest achievable."

While many of the "qualitative" standards are uncompromising, some allow or encourage broad-based, reasoned judgment in rule-making. Some allow a cost reasonableness test (e.g., "best available treatment technology economically achievable"). Other laws, like the Clean Air Act New Source Performance Standards, expand this area of discretion, but stop short of requiring an actual cost-benefit analysis: "best system . . . (taking into consideration the cost of achieving such emission reduction, and any other health and environmental impact and energy requirements)." In such cases, monetized national benefits estimated to result from alternative proposed standards may sometimes be considered admissible evidence in rule-making. Out of the scores of individual sections of the many federal environmental, health, and safety laws requiring standards-setting, only a few specifically refer to the term benefit. The Clean Water Act's best conventional technology and water quality standards exemptions are the best examples. This is the only type of law where the full application of Executive Order 12291 is relevant in development of regulations.

Application of quantitative decision aids is relevant to the regulatory development process in only a small minority of the environmental, health, and safety laws. Thus, devoting a large effort to calculating benefits of alternative standards in these cases may be a waste of resources, since the results may never be used. In contrast, quantitative risk, cost, and effectiveness analyses are used in a larger area of regulations.

If federal policy analysts bear allegiance to the Constitution, as they undertake to do in their oath of office, it seems that, in the most extreme interpretation of the oath, they should not use or suggest methods or make decisions that are contrary to the general principles of legislative debate, judicial review, or separation of powers clearly stated therein. This is only relevant to the extent that such methods are proffered as a replacement for the adversarial process. Merkhofer assembled an extensive series of comments by scholars on the incompatibility of quantitative methods with Constitutional principles, social norms, ethics, and other factors.[38] His findings are augmented by the authors' experiences and discussed below.

Perhaps the biggest problem with cost-benefit analysis in federal regulatory policy decisions is its inability to deal with distributional equity among social classes, interest groups, states, or regions. Analysts are prone to aggregate total national benefits and costs for a regulation. Indeed, Executive Order 12291 seeks a net benefit for national society. But every regulation causes a shift in the economic status quo. A cleaner environment in one region may mean loss of jobs in another. Safer working conditions in an industry may mean higher costs to consumers or increased foreign competition in that industry. Solving the acid rain problems in the Northeast could impose greater costs on the Midwest than the economic benefits obtained.

There is no obvious answer to these problems and the net national benefit is of interest primarily to the academic or theorist. Individuals and groups generally tend to pursue their own net benefit. The resulting conflicts can be solved only through the political process. The most that cost and benefit calculations can do is to provide ammunition for political debates. Many benefit evaluations involve placing a value on human life, suffering, willingness to pay for certain conditions, and the value of traditions, beliefs, and principles.

The political perils of valuing human life are obvious and yet federal regulators are forced implicitly to value lives every day. Willingness-to-pay surveys are frequently used, but do not help when people in low income brackets want clean air but may not be able to pay for it. On the other hand, benefit analysis can deal with the preservation of the species, scenic vistas, and religiously or anthropologically significant sites only if they can impute a value through willingness-to-pay surveys for preservation. Thus, national decisions based solely on cost-benefit analysis of the net national interest would be appropriate only in a pragmatic, uncultured, technocratic monarchy.

Risk management laws and regulations find many conflicts with individual liberty; for example, many motorcyclists are seriously offended by helmet regulations designed for their own safety. Many factory employees do not appreciate air pollution regulations that force their employer to curtail operations to benefit the health of their own community.

If all citizens were exposed to the same mix of risks and had the same physical dexterity and genetic background, mathematical formulae could tell us where to spend our scarce resources and which human activities to constrain to maximize the average life expectancy of society. Of course, every citizen is exposed to a different mix of risks, is affected differently by them, perceives their probability of occurrence differently, and has a different mix of risk preferences. Among the many choices among risks that cannot be easily or consistently made by individuals, even if precisely quantified, are the following:

- Is a high-probability, low-consequence risk preferable to a low-probability, high-consequence risk (e.g., fossil-fueled utility air pollution versus a nuclear-powered utility accident)?
- Should the government force auto manufacturers to add expensive airbags to all cars to provide protection in addition to that already offered by underused shoulder belts?
- Should the government spend more resources on building safer highways, cleaning up hazardous wastes, reducing air pollution, controlling pesticides, or researching cures for cancer?
- Wouldn't banning smoking save more lives nationally than banning ethylene dibromide (EDB) as a pest control on grains and fruits?
- How safe should industrial working conditions be? Is it worth a few cents more per loaf of bread to the nation's consumers to require dust controls at grain elevators to prevent one or two explosions per year?
- How much money should the nation spend on air traffic safety?

These are all difficult questions of social choice, involving fundamental Constitutional issues of governmental responsibilities and powers, individual liberties, and the transfer of wealth. Quantitative risk analyses cannot answer these questions—only the political, institutional, and legislative processes can. In fact, the presence of quantitative risk information might actually complicate and prolong the political decision process on such matters by muting some of the emotional and rhetorical positions involved. In addition, where logical trade-offs or alternatives might actually be admissible to the political debate, precise quantitative information may be available for one risk factor, while the risk of new alternatives is uncertain (e.g., aspirin versus acetaminophen).

As with cost-benefit analysis, the lack of clear, pragmatic, achievable objectives in the risk management statutes render risk analysis a dubious decision aid for trading off risks at the federal level. This is not to say that research on the severity of hazards should be discontinued—only that the resulting data should not be oversold as a magic solution to complicated social issues. Thus, while quantitative risk analysis may be useful in placing proposed regulatory actions in perspective against the many risks to society, it can make only a limited contribution to public sector decisions because of the highly variable and often unpredictable perceptions and preferences of risk of the public.

Decision analysis comes closest to an actual decision aid—it incorporates all available quantitative risk and economic data, provides methods for incorporating subjective probability (expert guesses), and allows consideration of the executive's preferences. It can even help lead to consensus decisions among multiple adversaries who have some goals in common. It has been used successfully in business decisions for several years, where objective functions and players are clearly defined.

In public-sector decisions, however, it may be incompatible with Constitutional principles or of limited utility in resolving extremely adversarial issues. It is most appropriate within an individual agency for selecting the best proposal for a single regulation where the agency head is statutorily provided with discretionary powers, for example, determination of "adequate margin of safety" in the Clean Air Act. In these cases, the administrator and staff can consider several alternative standards for a given pollutant, evaluate the probable reactions of the prominent interest groups, and choose the option that would "maximize utility" for the nation.

The proponents of quantitative decision models argue that, at minimum, these methods introduce order and rigor into the decision-making process, helping the executive to make a "better" decision. However, since the analysis is, in many instances, short of information, irrelevant to, or incompatible with the real decisions and issues, quantifying the issue will not a priori lead to better decisions. The development and marketing of these techniques by the academic community seem to be based on the assumption that the current decision process could be improved and made more rational or even honest with formal, analytical processes. This may or may not be true.

If an issue rises to the policy level, the chances are it is complex and probably emotionally charged. People do not often agree on either the scope of the issue, its desired outcome, its implementation strategy, or all of the above. Groups and factions align on all sides of issues, and "solutions" to issues lie in the realm of politics, and the appropriate player is the political professional, the specialist in the art of politics. Issues that are amenable to analytic or routine solution do not require executive decision. This is not to say that the more politically problematic issues could not benefit from some analytic input. The choice of the significant variable, from a political perspective, is, however, just as likely to depend on considerations normally not measurable, such as the concerns of political figures about some secondary impacts of a policy on their constituencies.

That the cost and benefit variables are chosen by a political process does not necessarily mean that analysis would not result in the same policy recommendation but cost and effectiveness measurements are in fact politically significant only in illustrating who bears the cost and who benefits from the effects. The use of data from this perspective results in a judgment of "political heat," where the cost is assessed in terms of whether it would be bearable to those affected, regardless of the absolute costs and benefits. The recipients of the benefits are also characteristically chosen on the basis of returns to the politician, not in societal or absolute terms.[c]

In the decision model era, government policy analysts were introduced to many new problems. Simultaneously, many new sources of data were generated, and many new analytical techniques were designed and tested to simplify and streamline the massive regulatory agenda. Risk analysis and cost-benefit analysis are permanent fixtures in the regulatory business, but government actions related to safety, health, and welfare of the electorate are never divorced from politics. Thus, while the setting of environmental, health, and safety standards has become routine to some degree, the quantitative decision models have not removed from the regulatory process the uncertainties of the political process. The analytic decision models are conceptually adequate, but in application they are vulnerable to many shortcomings in both the physical and the social sciences. These unfortunate facts of life have been best summarized by Graham, Raiffa, and Vaupel:

> The role of science and analysis in decision making is (and should be) limited for the following reasons:
>
> First, decisions about social problems—such as those involving risks—invariably entail some conflicts of interest among people. It is the rare case when a decision can be simultaneously the best for all parties concerned. Even in those rare cases when all people are made better off by a decision, some win more while others win less. . . .

---

[c]For example, Senator Byrd's (D-WV) influence on acid rain control legislation and Congressman Dingel's (D-MI) control over automobile emission control legislation.

Second, some policy problems that in principle are analyzable—that is, would respond to an intellectual resolution if they could be pursued long and painstakingly enough—are not, in fact, analyzable because they run beyond anyone's cognitive capacities or beyond society's store of information. . . .

Third, analysis can be done and is done by persons other than risk analysts. For example, public servants and business managers would, on some kinds of issues, be better off to conduct their own informal analysis of a risk problem, without any professional analysis, because they can draw on a fund of practical experience and can better cope with and respond to the realities of a particular organization.

Fourth, professional risk analysis, even when it is more competent than any other method of assessment or evaluation, is fallible and inconclusive.

Finally, professional risk analysis is expensive and time-consuming. It is simply impossible to subject every important aspect of a policy decision to professional analysis.[39]

The advancement of computer technology for accessing and applying information and portraying the many difficult regulatory trade-offs may help focus debate on real political issues instead of computational methodologies. This could mean an increase in government efficiency, so long as the policy analysts who develop the computer procedures assure that they are fully transparent in the sense of showing all assumptions and computations, and thoroughly documented so as to be subject to scrutiny of their peers.

References

1. Dupuit, Jules, "On the Management of Utility of Public Works," *International Economic Papers 2,* 1844.

2. Subcommittee on Benefits and Costs, Federal Inter-Agency River Basin Committee, "Proposed Practices for the Economic Analysis of River Basin Projects," May 1950.

3. Reagan, Ronald, "Executive Order 12291 of February 17, 1981," *Federal Register,* 46:33, February 19, 1981.

4. Gumbel, E.J., "Bortkiewicz, Ladislaus von," *International Encyclopedia of Statistics,* The Free Press, New York, 1978, p. 24.

5. Kendall, Maurice G., "Statistics: The History of Statistical Method," *International Encyclopedia of Statistics,* The Free Press, New York, 1978, p. 1095.

6. Pfeffer, I. and D. Klock, *Perspectives on Insurance,* Prentice-Hall, Englewood Cliffs, NJ, 1974.

7. Leinweber, David and Ray Squitieri, "Linking Uncertain Energy and Environmental Models," RAND Publications Series, Santa Monica, December 1980.

8. Reagan, Ronald, proposed legislation submitted to the Congress on Reorganization of Federal Energy Functions, The White House, May 24, 1982.

9. U.S. Department of Energy, *National Energy Policy Plan,* submitted to the Congress, July 1981.

10. House, P.W. and R.D. Shull, *Rush to Policy,* Transaction Books, New Brunswick, NJ, 1988, p. 112.

11. Hinish, James E., Jr., "Regulatory Reform: An Overview," *Mandate for Leadership: Policy Management in a Conservative*

Administration (C. Heatherly, ed.), The Heritage Foundation, Washington, 1981, p. 697.

12. Boggs, Danny J., "What the President Can Do by Executive Order," *Mandate for Leadership: Policy Management in a Conservative Administration* (C. Heatherly, ed.), The Heritage Foundation, Washington, 1981, p. 1077.

13. Reagan, Ronald, *op. cit.,*1981.

14. Bentkover, Judith D. et al., "Evaluation of the State of the Art in Benefits Assessment Methods for Public Policy Purposes," Report to the National Science Foundation by Arthur D. Little, Inc., Washington, December 1984.

15. Kolb, Jeffery A. and Joel D. Scheraga, "Discounting the Benefits and Costs of Environmental Regulations," *Journal of Policy Analysis and Management,* 9:3, Summer 1990, p. 381.

16. Kopp, Raymond J. and V. Kerry Smith, "Benefit Estimation Goes to Court: The Case of Natural Resource Damage Assessments," *Journal of Policy Analysis and Management,* 8:4, Fall 1989, p. 593.

17. Culhane, Paul H., H. Paul Friesma, and Janice A. Beecher, *Forecasts and Environmental Decisionmaking: The Content and Predictive Accuracy of Environmental Impact Statements,* Westview Press, Boulder, 1987.

18. "Air Quality Criteria for Particulate Matter," National Air Pollution Control Administration, Washington, January 1969.

19. Mazumdar, S., H. Schimmel, and I. Higgins, *Relation of Air Pollution to Mortality: An Exploration Using Daily Data for Fourteen London Winters, 1958–1972,* Electric Power Research Institute, Palo Alto, 1980.

20. Mathtech, Inc., "Benefits Analysis of Alternative National Ambient Air Quality Standards for Particulate Matter" (preliminary draft report, EPA Contract 68-02-3579), Washington, December 1981.

21. Brookshire, D., R. d'Arge, W. Schulze, and M. Thayer, *Methods Development for Assessing Tradeoffs in Environmental Management,* U.S. Environmental Protection Agency, EPA-600/6-79-0016, Washington, 1979.

22. Kelman, Steven, "Cost-Benefit Analysis: An Ethical Critique," *Regulation,* January/February 1981, p. 33.

23. "Revised Particulate Analysis Still Shows Benefits Increase with Stringency," *Inside EPA,* February 4, 1983, p. 2.

24. Environmental Protection Agency, "Revisions to the National Ambient Air Quality Standards for Particulate Matter," *Federal Register,* 40CFR50, Washington, July 1, 1987, p. 24634 ff.

25. op. cit., p. 24653.

26. op. cit., p. 24659.

27. King, Glen W. (ed.), *Statistical Abstract of the United States 1990,* U.S. Government Printing Office, Washington, 1990, p. 78 ff.

28. Covello, Vincent T., and Jeryl Mumpower, "Risk Analysis and Risk Management: A Historical Perspective," *Risk Evaluation and Risk Management,* Plenum Press, London, 1986, p. 519.

29. Lipton, Joshua, "Uncertainty and Risks from Ocean Dumping: Incorporating Bioconcentration Variability into a Risk Model," *ICET News,* 6:1, Cornell University, Spring 1990.

30. Merkhofer, M. W., et al., "Risk Assessment and Risk Assessment Methods: The State of the Art," Report to the National Science

Foundation by Charles River Associates and Applied Decision Analysis Inc., Washington, January 1985.

31. Camerer, Colin F. and Howard Kunreuther, "Decision Processes for Low Probability Events: Policy Implications," *Journal of Policy Analysis and Management,* 8:4, Fall 1989, p. 565.

32. Inhaber, H., *Energy Risk Assessment,* Gordon and Breach Science Publishers, New York, 1982.

33. Holdren, J., et al., "Risk of Renewable Energy Resources: A Critique of the Inhaber Report," *Energy and Resources Group Report ERG-79-3,* University of California at Berkeley, June 1979.

34. Evans, Leonard, et al., "Driving Versus Flying—Relative Risks," *Risk Analysis,* Summer 1990.

35. Herrington, John S., Secretary of Energy, "Energy Security: A Report to the President of the United States," Washington, March 1987.

36. Howard, R.A., J.E. Matheson, and D.W. North, "The Decision to Seed Hurricanes," *Science,* 176, December 1972.

37. Anthes, Richard A., *Tropical Cyclones: Their Evolution, Structure and Effects,* The American Meteorological Society, Boston, 1982, p. 119–130.

38. Merkhofer, M.W., "A Comparative Evaluation of Quantitative Decisionmaking Approaches," *Final Report to the National Science Foundation,* SRI International, April 1983.

39. Graham, John D., Howard Raiffa, and James W. Vaupel, "Science and Analysis: Roles in Risk and Decision Making," *Risk Evaluation and Management* (V. T. Covello, J. Menkes, and J. Mumpower, eds.), Plenum Press, New York, 1986, p. 503.

4.

"Reform '88": Personal Computers and The New Incrementalism

While striving to reduce the size of the federal work force early in his first term, President Reagan announced "Reform '88," an umbrella project designed to automate budgeting, payrolls, financial management, and project monitoring across the government. One goal, to place a personal computer on every federal manager's desk by 1988, amazed many managers, since the PC had been introduced only a couple of years before, and mostly for hobbyists and video-game addicts. But, in fact, the government came close to accomplishing that goal. The ratio of PCs to technical staff in the major science agencies like Defense, Energy, NIH, and the NSF was more than 1:1 by 1988. The Bush administration continued support of this modernization, and agency computer budgets became almost sacrosanct. The metamorphosis of policy analysis procedures in one of these agencies, the National Science Foundation, reveals how the procedures closely resemble the old "incremental" analyses that were abandoned in favor of the comprehensive approach.

The computer world is changing almost as fast as the advertisers claim. A graphic illustration of the staggering advances can be provided by an imaginary project to rebuild the SEAS model as a PC model. Much of the system design and programming code generated in SEAS development would have been unnecessary had current PC software been available. In today's PC terminology, SEAS was a series of interrelated spreadsheets. No matter how big the spreadsheet, the viewer can scroll around the screen and see any value. In the days of SEAS, such matrices were imagined, but could never be seen unless printed out on reams of 14-inch, fan-fold paper. They had to be represented and programmed with notations (e.g., A_ij, B_ij, $i = 1,2, . .m$; $j = 1,2, . . n$).

As described in Chapter 2, the heart of SEAS was an economic model that took forecasts of the future values of the components of GNP and, using an input-output model (a 185 x 185 array that defined how each sector of the economy related to each other in terms of intersectoral purchases), calculated the demand for goods and services. This matrix could easily be typed into spreadsheet software today, with all the cells completed in a couple of hours. As long as the values of the coefficients in the array were constant year after year, the forecasts of future demands would be merely the sum of the specified components of GNP. The more detailed these components, the more summation would have to be done to arrive at the value of a variable in the future. However, even these summations are a function of the desired output, and simple to set up on a PC spreadsheet.

With SEAS, calculation of the pollution generated by a given amount of economic activity was derived by the multiplication of the amount of demand forecast for each sector by the average pollution coefficient for that sector, repeated for each pollutant type as a matrix multiplication. The process iterated, depending on the number of pollutants of interest. A similar procedure was carried out to estimate the amount of pollution abatement, using sector specific pollution control coefficients. Today, all multiplication procedures could be done on the PC with a few keystrokes telling the spreadsheet software to multiply a given cell in one worksheet by a particular cell in another worksheet in a specified order.

In short, a comprehensive model like SEAS could be implemented on a modern PC, and some policy researchers have done just that. But for policy analysis in the 1990s, such an approach is no longer appropriate. Charles Lindblom's wisdom of the 1970s has been empirically demonstrated:

... one cannot be comprehensive, one cannot be complete, one cannot be completely broad for complex problems. The alternative ... is to be discriminating, selective, corner-cutting, tricky, cunning, strategic, and tactical. [We should] recognize that we must reach a decision before we have intellectually mastered the problem, and that we will begin to act long before all the facts are in.[1]

This statement was presented by Lindblom at a May 1973 National Conference on Managing the Environment, sponsored by the authors' program within the EPA. Lindblom's was the minority position at this conference, which was dominated by environmentalists and comprehensive analysts arguing that the earth should be considered as a closed system. Most of the audience lauded the conception and implementation of such a fully comprehensive analytical tool as SEAS. Comprehensive analysis is still the approach of choice in a conceptual sense, but it has been proven impractical many times over. On the other hand, incrementalism, sometimes called the "band-aid" approach, has proven adequate for many policy analyses and is truly cost-effective, especially since the advent of microcomputers.

The PC offers a new way of thinking about problems, more akin to the precomputer era than the technocratic approach of the 1970s. Analysts who began their careers with the mainframe computer have a hard time explaining to those who have always used PCs why it was so important to think through a problem completely before beginning to program. The difference in the technique engendered by the PC compared to that of the mainframe can best be characterized as a reduction in rigidity. In the mainframe days, once the system and file structure were designed, the model builders were frozen in this structure, their versatility constrained. They lived within the world they had created, their attempts to react to relevant new information hindered by the cumbersome framework defining that world.

The PC environment is totally different from that of the mainframe. There is no need to learn a complicated and rigid programming language, nor to be trained as a systems analyst in order to build a model. One merely learns the fundamentals of spreadsheet analysis (handling functions and data in columns and rows) and goes about constructing the model. Information or instructions are placed in cells in the spreadsheet, and the computer does all calculations automatically every time new data are entered. The results of the model construction can be seen instantly through the various graphics options integrated into each software package. Model builders get instant and constant feedback as they construct the algorithm. They can experiment and, because constructing the model is so easy, there is little penalty in wiping out false starts and beginning again. However, this major step forward in the development of computer models will not be the most important consideration for the policy analysis community in the years ahead.

One of the inefficiencies of electoral government comes from the loss of knowledge and experience when an election changes political leadership and management. Change brings fresh ideas and new vitality, but there is a lot to learn.

The slope of the learning curve differs by department and by individual. Sometimes it is very steep. In many old-line agencies where the mission and expectations are well defined, and where the bureaucracy has been in place for extended periods of time, the transition may not be so difficult, particularly if the new leadership is willing to make use of this bureaucracy. But, for many agencies and departments, the situation remains fluid for many months. Agency missions, scopes, and functions are largely defined by those in power.

After the inauguration, agency policy staffs are particularly susceptible to turnover because they have become so identified with the departing political regime that they are often asked to resign or are transferred to less sensitive (and less interesting) positions in the agency. Often this is done for show, a symbolic broom-sweeping, often fueled by the advocacy groups that felt disadvantaged by the previous administration. To the extent that the departing group have been analysts, as opposed to advocates, their knowledge and understanding could have been valuable to the new leadership. If the personalities must go due to perceived ideological beliefs or past associations, there is a need to develop some method to retain at least some of their neutral corporate knowledge.

With computer familiarity growing among professional government servants and the widespread use of sophisticated PC software, it may be possible to retain more corporate knowledge between administrations. It is possible to design systems that will retain not only the data bases of an agency but the ability to use the information effectively. Application, design, and development in the computer industry are moving in the direction of the people who are closer to the issue; programming is no longer the exclusive territory of specialists. By the year 2000, it is estimated, end users will be developing 80 percent of business and government applications. Continuing development in artificial intelligence and natural languages will make user interfaces still more accessible and programming tools more intelligent. In time, the end user will simply describe the relationship between data and transactions. We have come very far in capturing and using the analytic institutional memory needed for policy analysis.

CASPAR and the Expert System

The best management information systems have resulted from close cooperation and communication by the system users (the managers) and the system developers (the technicians). Systems designed solely by the technicians were computationally efficient, but managerially ineffective, i.e., they often didn't answer the managers' questions. On the other hand, systems developed solely by users were effective, accessing the right data and providing correct answers to management questions, but they were usually computationally inefficient, i.e., they cost more and took longer to respond than a system designed by computer professionals.

The technicians might understand that subsets of data need to be extracted from the master data base and assembled in some fashion to respond to policy questions. But should they not know what questions might be asked, they would have no appropriate criteria to guide their initial designs. The executives, on the other hand, might understand the questions, but know neither what relevant data were available, nor how to use them effectively to answer the questions. Since it is prohibitively expensive to have complete data sets in every possible subject area, some choices have to be made.

Such a system held the promise of taking some of the man-hours bite out of repetitive analytical tasks, familiar to bureaucracies, that had to be done from scratch every time, with extensive manual calculations often combined with guessed or remembered relationships. The authors constructed an expert system called CASPAR (for computer-aided science policy analysis and research) designed to craft responses to questions asked of NSF. The project motto was: "if you have to do it twice, make the computer do it the third time," a perhaps simplified expression of the information management potential of PC technology.

Designing and implementing automatic procedures does take time—but that time is continually shrinking before the technology. Figure 4-1 displays the evolution of the system from the 1970s' mainframe system to our current natural language system, showing the remarkable reduction in time from question to answer. Beginning at the bottom of the figure, we see data being gathered from many agencies by an individual dubbed a "librarian," often in hard copy form or in bulky reel-to-reel mainframe computer tapes. Next, the information was loaded into the mainframe computer by specialized "programmers" assisted by lower-level "keypunchers." It often took months to scan the incoming data to ensure that it was

Figure 4-1
The Technological Evolution
of Quantitative Policy Analysis

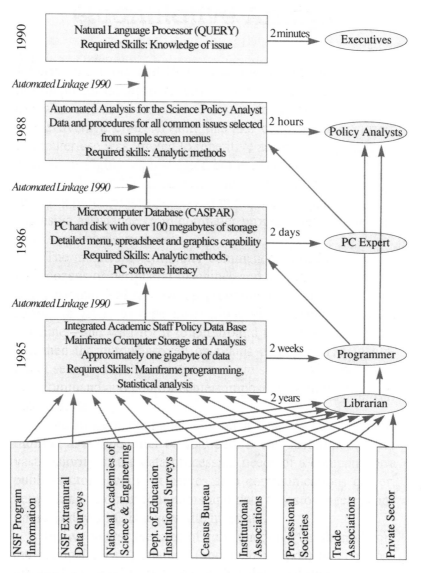

Standardization of data prior to incorporation requires extensive human knowledge.

free of errors, and that related data items collected by different agencies were calibrated and coordinated so they could be legitimately combined in analytical procedures. Once the mainframe data base was usable, summary data sets and analyses could be output to personal computers, where a specially trained PC operator conducted statistical analyses and prepared graphs, directed by the policy analyst who, often in the early 1980s, was not conversant with computers. Finally, after many months had passed, policy analysts selected the best set of information for presentation to senior policy officials.

Once the mainframe data base was assembled, sufficient resources were allocated to maintain and freshen it. Then the most commonly used fields of data were extracted and inserted into a user-friendly PC data base. Because the NSF's mission is the support of education and basic research at the nation's colleges and universities, the academic institution was chosen as the fundamental data record. The data base is simple in concept, containing one type of data on people and another on dollars. A third type of data is simply numbers, representing valuative scores such as quality evaluations, student performance, and number of scientific publications. The data come from four principal sources: NSF internal accounting organizations; traditional NSF surveys of other agencies, academic institutions, and industry conducted by the Science Resources Studies Division; the Department of Education (for comprehensive data on higher education); and the national academies, for special scientific personnel information.

The data base may be thought of as a ledger (spreadsheet), where the rows are institutions and each column is a separate variable describing science and engineering research aspects of the institution, such as research expenditures, graduate students, facilities expenditures. While simple in concept, the size is impressive. There are about 3,500 rows and currently about 150 columns, with plans for up to 200. With this idea in mind, we must now consider a large stack of these 3,500 by 150 ledgers, because NSF is concerned with not only where its money goes, but for what purpose, and how awards to each institution have changed over time. Thus, each cell in the original ledger can have a total value, a value for each of five coarse fields of science, for 24 fine fields of science, for a half-dozen different budget categories, and for all available years (currently about 30). Multiplying these ranges produces about 2 billion possible pieces of data. The first phase of the PC system could not handle this volume of data, but worked well with the number of institutions limited to 500 and the number of variables set at about 100. By 1990, the PC system, CASPAR, was operating at full scale. If the data contained in this system were to be stored in traditional printed reference manuals, it would require about 2,000 square feet of floor space (floor to ceiling).

This data could have been accessed by off-the-shelf data base software, but these tools, while easier to use than mainframe programming languages, still require reasonable symbolic skills to access appropriate data. Thus, a custom-designed data base that is completely "menu-driven" was chosen. That is, all variable choices appear on the computer screen, and the user simply moves the cursor to the appropriate variable names and presses the "Enter" key. CASPAR allows the user to build a spreadsheet that includes data items from several sources all in the same years and relates these to the categorical variables used as the crosswalk. Several simple algebraic calculations can be done on the data in the spreadsheet, and new rows or columns of data developed. The data can be ranked by a particular variable, and the spreadsheet shrunk to that portion of the data of particular interest. It can be viewed at this point, or printed as a spreadsheet.

By 1986, referring again to Figure 4-1, CASPAR could deliver quantitative responses to most policy questions within two days. By then, the policy analysts were computer-literate, particularly with spreadsheet statistical and graphic analysis, but in each case, the analyst had to select the appropriate analyses, select an appropriate graphic presentation, and implement these decisions through hundreds of keystrokes on the computer. To improve analysts' productivity, we began to automate complete analytical procedures, including graph preparation. Such statistical procedures as grouping, sorting, ranking, trending, correlation, regression, comparing, and contrasting were used so frequently that they were automated by "macro" programs, using a software control programming language built into the software package. With this automated analysis capability, when a request is received, the analyst extracts the appropriate data in spreadsheet form from CASPAR, then selects the appropriate spreadsheet macro program, and presses the "Enter" key. Within a few minutes, hard copy graphs are delivered, which the analyst then studies and uses to prepare a list of verbal highlights. By 1988, this process took two hours.

The final step in automation was interpreting the client's question and determining which variables, analytical processes, and graphic presentations were relevant in providing a response or a quantitative context for the issue. Addressing this challenge required moving into the new fields of artificial intelligence and natural language processing to enable the computer to understand a question keyed in English. Once the question is understood, a set of artificial intelligence algorithms decides which data fields within CASPAR are relevant, which analytic procedures are needed, and what graphs to draw. It then implements these choices and delivers the results to the screen.

This system, appropriately named "QUERY," allows users with no special knowledge of science policy or computer analysis to exploit this information base. The natural language processor frames the user's question so that the expert system can select, organize, and present data in such a way that the user can interpret the requested information. Instead of providing only one specific answer to a user's question, the computer-programmed "expert" provides the specific answer, as well as additional information that frames a broader context to the issue in question. If the user asks for the attributes of a particular variable (e.g., NSF funding to a state or its institutions), the system provides information sufficient to ensure that the question is answered and to enrich the response by placing the requested data in context. When the question is ambiguous, the system attempts to provide a response broad enough to ensure incorporation of the requisite answer. When the question is under-specified, defaults will be applied by the system, enabling the user to provide sufficient additional data to permit the computer to understand the question. This is all done in the spirit of making the natural language interface as useful as possible to those who have little patience or time for using traditional data base systems. Without training or any extensive understanding of the internal workings of the underlying science policy data base, almost anyone can quickly obtain answers to relevant science policy issues.

Although QUERY was always pushing the state of the art, that wasn't the principal goal. The objective was simply to accelerate the delivery of policy analyses to senior executives. A graphics package was developed to provide automatic presentation capability. The most satisfying feature of the system is that the technology now exists to allow senior agency officials to participate comfortably in the quantitative aspects of policy making in a completely interactive mode. Not only is it possible to carry out a sophisticated analysis quickly and get useful results, it is possible to update and enhance a briefing in response to such questions as "what would happen if ... ?"

QUERY was operational in 1990, and was far ahead of most government information systems in terms of capability, ease of use, and portability (although the USDA Agricultural Stabilization and Conservation Service was working on a similar system, but using a smaller data base and a mainframe computer).[2] It is built from off-the-shelf, relatively inexpensive components, common software packages, a modest amount of custom data base programming, and some original research in the field of artificial intelligence and natural language processing by division staff members.[3] The QUERY concept is easily adaptable to other federal agencies. It can be used on mainframe, minicomputer, or personal computer networks, and on portable computers with adequate storage and memory. QUERY enhances agency efficiency in two ways: it expands executives' ability to monitor agency performance and reduces the demand for data processing and analytic staff. During the development of the CASPAR/QUERY system, the Division of Policy Research and Analysis shrank in size from more than 30 staff members to under 15, while its output of useful analyses to policy officials grew by an order of magnitude. With the help of the personal computer, government productivity has vastly increased in this one small area.

At NSF, this system allows highly specific statistical analyses which were previously prohibited by cost, time, or system constraints. Some agencies already have executive information systems on PC networks, but these systems are mostly for current and summary information about the agency. At NSF, the QUERY system provides access to the entire agency data base as well as to data from several other agencies, comprising hundreds of variables for more than 3,500 higher education institutions, the Foundation's principal constituency.

As the technology of personal and portable computers and the skill of their users advance, the capabilities described here will continue to become more powerful and cost-effective. A system like the current QUERY could be installed in a few months at minimal cost. Thus the ultimate design is a generalized, transparent, comprehensive, and user-friendly system for the analyst, and a specific and equally friendly system for senior executives.

The New Incrementalism

The policy analysis group at the NSF has adopted what might be called modern incrementalism. Analyses begin with readily available data and straightforward relationships. Policy officials are rapidly informed of facts, constraints, and decision possibilities with simplified presentations. If these first-cut analyses cannot provide a clear picture, the policy staff dig deeper, expanding the data base where possible, and bringing in secondary considerations to clarify existing situations, determine causes of observed phenomena, and define policy options more precisely. If the second analysis is still not considered definitive, the iteration procedure continues until a satisfactory definition, a decision time, or a resource limit is reached. Thus, incrementalism proceeds cautiously from simple toward complex, while comprehensive modelling attempts to simulate an entire system and then sort out the portion at issue. The following example demonstrates the incremental process.

Following World War II, the U.S. experienced a "baby boom": the annual number of births grew 48 percent in 12 years and remained constant for another five years. Starting in 1962, however, the trend reversed: the annual number of births steadily declined until 1975, when births were 27 percent below the 1957 level. Annual births have subsequently increased, but are still 10 percent below the 1957 number. The average age of bachelor's degree graduates is 22 years. The steepest part of the decline of 22-year-olds occurs during the early 1990s, with the smallest number occurring around 1997 (see Figure 4-2). This "baby bust" generation precipitated a decline in the number of qualified students in higher education science and engineering curricula, and might then reduce the available number of technically trained entry-level employees in many different occupations over the next decade.

In the U.S. market economy, price adjustments will en-

Figure 4-2
Estimated U.S. Population of 22-Year-Olds

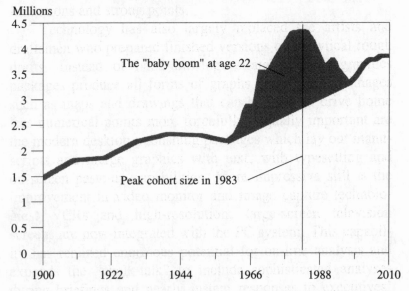

Source: U.S. Bureau of Census

Figure 4-3
U.S. Bachelor's Degree Participation

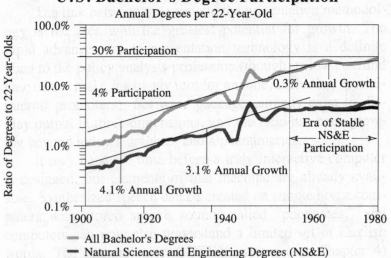

Source: D.L. Adkins, *The Great American Degree Machine*

courage a balancing of supply and demand for new scientists and engineers. College graduates in scarce fields can be expected to command increasingly higher salaries, until demand levels off as employers find ways to conduct business with fewer staff from those skill fields. As starting salaries rise, more young people will pursue those profitable fields, tempering the growth of salaries. Thus, supply and demand interact until some equilibrium is reached. The question is where this equilibrium will be, and how it will affect the technological competitiveness and the standard of living in the United States.

Labor markets do not respond instantly, and the market for college-trained individuals has a particularly sluggish response, since it takes a minimum of four years to obtain a bachelor's degree and about eight years more for a doctorate. As discussed below, annual production of bachelor's degrees in the combined subset of disciplines identified as "natural scientists and engineers" has shown only weak response to market forces over the past 30 years (although considerable complementary shifting among disciplines in the subset has occurred).

During the 1960s, the growing demand for scientists and engineers was easily met because of a growing population of college-age people and a growing number of Ph.D.s available to train more undergraduate students. In the 1990s, however, we face a declining number of college-aged citizens and a declining stock of university professors. Thus, even though theoretically the market should adjust to the changes, we have never before experienced such declines, and therefore cannot be sure what the market solution will be. Can we entice a larger fraction of our citizens to attend college, and a larger fraction of students to pursue natural science and engineering careers? Will the universities fill empty seats with foreign students? Will businesses turn to foreign sources for their research and development tasks, or will they recruit foreign-trained bachelor and doctoral scientists and engineers to work at U.S. facilities? How many lower-level scientist and engineer jobs will be eliminated by computers as they have been in the technician and clerical job markets? How much will salary premiums grow in these fields? It is impossible to answer any of these questions precisely, but application of simple PC analyses provided a good understanding of the situation which allowed federal officials to consider and debate various approaches to the problem.

The economics of the U.S. professional labor market are complex. Depending on the occupation, training can take from four to eight years, so there is a built-in lag in any type of supply response to shortages and rising salaries. It is difficult to switch majors in college after the second year, so students tend to complete the curriculum they chose before the third year. Thus, if the market has an oversupply of aerospace engineers and a shortage of chemists, a junior or senior college student in aerospace engineering would likely complete that course of study anyway. If incoming freshmen choose chemistry as a major because of current high salaries in that profession, by the time they graduate the demand may have dropped, with premium salaries being offered in another field. Similar response lags occur for students pursuing master's and doctoral degrees.

Moreover, many choose college curricula and professions for reasons other than economic. Another factor complicating economic analysis of the professional labor market is that many of us end up in jobs only partly related or often totally unrelated to the college degree we obtained. Some scientists and engineers end up as physicians, technicians, managers, executives, clergy, musicians, artists, or attorneys. Job definition and titles also add to the analysis complexities. According to the Bureau of Labor Statistics (BLS), a professor of chemistry is not a chemist, but a professor; an electronics engineer selling scientific equipment is a salesman, not an engineer; the director of a division of research engineers is a manager, not an engineer. And, the people assigned traditional physical science and engineering titles may not necessarily have a baccalaureate degree in that particular field. A chemist with a strong computer background may be hired as a computer scientist, a physicist with background in fluid flow may be hired as an aeronautical engineer, or a biologist with good writing skills may be employed as a technical editor or public relations specialist.

Matching up employment data with professional training data is possible only at aggregate levels. Thus, even though it is possible to design and develop a large, comprehensive, SEAS-type model of the employment in the entire economy by detailed sectors of business, the outputs of such a model are not much help in analyzing the production of science and engineering bachelor's degree attainment because of mismatches between data. In fact, such a model has been developed by Data Resources Incorporated and used by the NSF.[4,5] The model has been scaled to fit on a desktop computer, essentially monopolizing the machine's 50-megabyte hard disk capacity. But just as in 1975, complex, comprehensive economic models have so many simultaneous variables and so many assumptions to be made and calibrated, that a new scenario run on the model still takes several days of fine tuning, just as the SEAS model did in 1975. But, so many necessary assumptions[6] have little scientific or empirical basis that the model results are tenuous at best.

If modelling the world isn't practical, what then? The solution turned out to be a return to incrementalism, using the large quantities of data on college degree production and national demographics, combined with a few simple rules and simple economic models. First, the problem was narrowed to the scope of concern to the NSF: the production and utilization of new scientists and engineers. Using an incremental look at a subset of all higher education, ignoring the arts, humanities, and non-engineering professional disciplines as well as advanced degrees in law, medicine, and other fields outside of sciences and engineering. The analysis was then split into B.S. degree production and Ph.D. production, since the Foundation was interested in both issues and the factors affecting the two supplies are quite different.

The next focus was the national participation rates for B.S. degrees (the annual number of degrees granted divided by the number of people in the country of typical B.S. degree age [22 years]). Figure 4-3 shows this participation rate for all bachelor's and first professional degrees and for the subset of natural science and engineering (NS&E). The average annual growth rate of these participation fractions in the 20th century has been 4.8 percent for all degrees and 3.0 percent for NS&E B.S. degrees. That these rates have been steady for so many years is empirical evidence of some type of natural growth process. But most natural growth meets with upper boundaries at some point, and the question is whether this growth in higher education achievement will continue along the past growth curve or begin to stabilize or fall. As shown in Figure 4-3, even without recovering to the average growth line, if the long-term participation slope is extended from the most recent data, then by the year 2010, 65 percent of our population will be obtaining four-year college degrees, and 7 percent of the population would be getting NS&E B.S. degrees. Projecting only from the last 20 years yields much lower rates, i.e., less than 30 percent for all B.S. degrees, and 4 percent (no change) for NS&E excluding computer science.

The NS&E participation rate is particularly disconcerting; it has shown only modest growth during the past two decades and, following a recent spurt due principally to the popularity of the computer sciences, has begun a rather sharp drop. NS&E participation has been very stable regardless of starting salary changes (relative to mean starting salaries for all bachelor's degree graduates) over this period, which provided another factor for simplifying the analytical model: the production of NS&E B.S. degrees in the U.S. in recent times seems to have virtually no relation to economics and is almost entirely demographically driven. Further analysis of this phenomenon showed that the subfields within NS&E do show a notable response to economics, but that the NS&E fields have been complementary. Thus, the supply projection model offered the projection of 22-year-olds for the next 22 years, multiplied by a rather stable participation rate.

Because federal science policy officials were concerned about a possible shortage of scientists and engineers, some type of demand projection was needed. The Bureau of Labor Statistics does provide projections of various labor categories, including several science and engineering jobs, but, as discussed above, these values are at considerable odds with the number of degrees granted for comparable fields and years. What was needed was a projection of demand for people with natural science and engineering training, irrespective of where and how they were employed. Since there was no data base with this type of information, not only was there no good quantitative demand model, there was not even quantitative evidence of whether demand would go up or down. In the absence of a demand projection, the impact of declining production was demonstrated by comparing it to a constant rate of degree production. To dampen the recent computer science oscillations, a production level equal to the average production level of 1984 through 1986 was chosen.

The projected supply and production level are shown in Figure 4-4, along with several previous years of supply for context. The projected shortfall, the sum of the annual differences between the constant production level and the falling supply line, was 675,000 for the period 1986 through 2010. This graph, created from a simple six-column PC spreadsheet, became a factor in federal policy toward education of scientists and engineers. It was presented to congressional committees, the national academies, and professional groups,

Figure 4-4
Actual and Projected NS&E B.S. Degrees

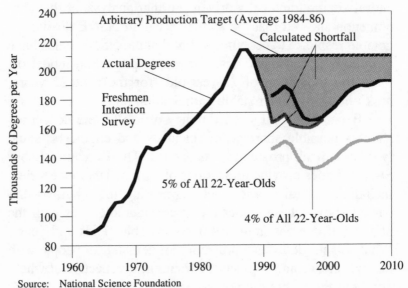

Source: National Science Foundation

Figure 4-5
Projected NS&E Ph.D. Degrees

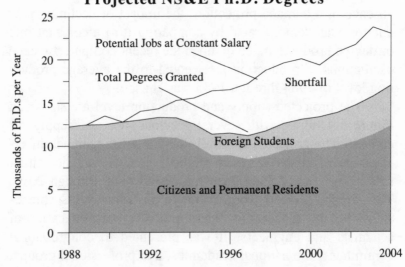

Source: National Science Foundation

and was requested by university administrators all over the country.

Many science policy officials were convinced that the market solution to the shortfall would be unsatisfactory. Reflecting on the high rate of attrition of the numbers of individuals interested in mathematics, science, and engineering activities from elementary school through Ph.D. degree, and growing evidence of declining mathematical and scientific capabilities of high school graduates, they decided that a change in the generic philosophy of teaching math and science was necessary. Attrition in these fields of interest claimed not only those people with limited quantitative skills, but also a large number with commendable skills. In addition to stemming the declining supply of baccalaureate graduates in NS&E, advancement of scientific literacy of the overall population was selected as a national objective.

The shortfall figure, 675,000, was quoted and debated in countless speeches and magazine articles. A number of critics believed participation would rapidly increase automatically or that other market mechanisms would obviate the shortfall problem, but most analysts saw the projection as inherently reasonable.

In the end, the result was simply the annual difference between a constant and the product of two numbers. Probably the most significant contribution of PC technology was to the discovery of the stable participation rate of the particular aggregation of disciplines called natural science and engineering. This was not a common aggregation, the standard categories being both larger and smaller. But the ease of calculating on the PC participation rates with many different combinations over many years of data provided the incentive for the research, and produced the remarkable discovery in a matter of hours. The only reference found which speculated on this phenomenon was a 1971 paper by Brode.[7] Availability of data and ease of computation allowed us to trace the participation rate back to 1900 to emphasize the plateau of recent decades.

The long-term population of 22-year-olds was also presented to emphasize the "baby boom" and "baby bust" effects. None of these tasks is theoretically complex in itself, but together or separately they involve sufficient computations that a policy analysis staff probably would not have attempted it in the days before PCs. If the exercise had been attempted in the "old days," the human resources requirements would have had to have been ten times as great to produce comparable material.

Describing the Ph.D. issue was more complex than the B.S. case, because data showed that the production of advanced degrees was indeed influenced by economics, among other things. Fortunately, the Ph.D. population is much smaller, and routine surveys of Ph.D. scientists, engineers, and researchers by various institutions provided sufficient data to implement a simplified market supply and demand model with variable prices. Although also implemented on a personal computer using spreadsheet software, this model was noticeably more complex than the B.S. model. First, Ph.D. production is constrained by the number of B.S. degrees produced, so the B.S. model became the basis for the Ph.D. model. Instead of using BLS occupational category definitions, other survey data provided estimates of Ph.D. scientists and engineers employed in industry, academic institutions, and other institutions, including government.

The demand model was based on the number of Ph.D.s hired by these three sectors to replace departing individuals and because of growth. Replacement needs were calculated based on survey data on the average age of Ph.D.s in the three sectors. Demand for expansion was linked to the annual rate of growth of research and development in the three sectors. A demand elasticity (decrease in demand relative to increase in salary) of 1.0 was assumed based on observed data for the last decade. The base supply of NS&E Ph.D.s is demographic, using a Ph.D./B.S. participation rate analogous to the concept employed in the B.S. supply model. But the actual rate rises or falls above this average value based on Ph.D.s' starting salaries. Observed supply elasticity (increase in Ph.D. graduates relative to increase in starting salaries) appeared to be about the same as demand elasticity (1.0) for U.S. citizens, but higher (1.5) for foreign students.

These data were used to construct a classic economic supply-demand model, where an equilibrium salary is found at which the supply equation equals the demand equation, each containing salary variables. Implementation of the model required many additional assumptions about how employers allocate their budgets and how starting salaries relate to average salaries of employed Ph.D.s, as well as R&D growth rates in the three sectors. In every case, however, at least anecdotal data were available to guide the assumptions. Figure 4-5 shows the results of one set of assumptions that was widely used by policy officials in conjunction with Figure 4-4. Here the shortfall was defined as the difference between the market solution and the demand that would have occurred if salaries had remained constant.

It took some tricky algebra and several man-days of highly experienced economists and policy analysts to develop the model, but in the end, it was a small incremental model relative to the large national economy input-output models like SEAS and the DRI model. It was a spreadsheet of about 100 columns and 100 rows, which required 15 input variables to run, used about 100 kilobytes memory, and produced results in less than five seconds. Compare this to the DRI model, which begins with a 1,000 by 1,000 matrix macroeconomic model, flows to a 92 by 92 input-output matrix, then to a 92 industry by 51 job occupations employment model with user-adjustable productivity variables for each occupation in each industry, and requires several days of calibration and fine-tuning each time a major change in assumptions is desired. The DRI model can be squeezed onto a large PC, but it is far from being an interactive model in a realistic time frame, and is so opaque to all but trained econometricians that it has never become a useful day-to-day policy tool.

Most federal agencies are saddled with a set of "perennial issues"—complaints from Congress, the press, or the electorate about the way the agency does business. These issues just won't go away, no matter which response the agency chooses. Besides always being behind on its enforcement schedules, EPA is routinely accused of placing priorities on the wrong medium (air, water, or land), on the wrong pollutant, the wrong area of the country, or the wrong type of environment (e.g., urban versus wilderness). The DOE must routinely defend allocation of its R&D budget among nuclear, solar, coal, oil, and gas fuels and energy conservation technologies. A favorite perennial issue at the NSF is the national geographic distribution of its grant awards to research universities.

An important member of Congress focusing on one of these perennial issues can tie up an entire agency policy staff for weeks. All it takes is a clever congressional staffer to ask the perennial question in a slightly different way, and then methodically nitpick the agency's responses. If the agency staff answer the charges subjectively, a cycle of conflicting perceptions can ensue, ending only when the agency head and the congressmen declare a truce or when the congressional staff get busy on some other issue or agency. The increase in analytical capability has helped analysts to reduce the time spent on these issues by showering them with cold, hard, facts. If policy analysts have the information and knowledge to portray their agency's programs from many different perspectives, they can avoid being directly drawn into the battle to defend policies.

NSF is the main federal supporter of basic research, awarding grants to individuals based on written proposals which are reviewed by committees of peer scientists. Most recipients are, therefore, professors or full-time researchers at the nation's leading research universities. The act establishing NSF was passed in 1950 after more than three years of debate over the proposed organizational structure and operational philosophy. A key issue in the debate was whether the Foundation's awards should be based solely on excellence (scholarly quality of the proposal and reputation of the proposer) or on some type of national "need" distribution formula like that used by the Department of Agriculture in funding research at land grant universities. The compromise reached was that funding would generally be based on excellence, but that NSF should "avoid undue concentration of such research and education." The phrase "undue concentration" was never officially defined, and so has been subject to various interpretations over the past 40 years.

The bulk of complaints about geographic concentration come from congressional delegations in states that receive the least funding. Figure 4-6 shows that the distribution of NSF's research awards for fiscal year 1988 was heavily concentrated in seven states. States at the lower end of the distribution might consider NSF funding unduly concentrated. Since NSF's principal criterion for funding research is "excellence," the Foundation created a program to build academic research capability in those states, called "EPSCOR" states (for Experimental Program to Stimulate Competitive Research; see Figure 4-6). The program was established in the mid-1970s to address complaints from these states, setting aside a few million dollars a year available by competition among only the EPSCOR states. The states were selected based on a certain formula of total R&D expenditures, federal R&D support, and NSF grant awards.

But where NSF funding is concentrated, is it unduly or unfairly so? NSF has dispersed the majority of its research funds according to the "excellence" standard, under which awards go to the best research proposals submitted by individual investigators. NSF routinely solicits audits of the peer review process and it has been found to operate as advertised. Could it be shown that the award distribution is reasonable and fair?

Using the data in Figure 4-6 as numerators, the task was to find denominators and put the state totals in various perspectives in which "fairness" can be judged. The first case is state population: because many federal programs are population-based, NSF's awards might be judged on a per capita basis. FY 1988 state award totals per capita are shown in Figure 4-7. This analysis might satisfy Wyoming, since it's now sixth in the nation. However, Massachusetts is still far out in front.

Because NSF awards go mostly to university professors, and research universities are not uniformly distributed about the country, NSF funds per research university might be a good measure of fairness. Thus, the denominator for Figure 4-8 is the number of research universities in each state. This perspective turns out to be useful, if the complaints are from Minnesota, Hawaii, or Alaska. But California is fourth, New York is only average, and Texas is way below two EPSCOR states.

NSF hypothesized that, since research universities are different sizes, maybe grants divided by the number of academic researchers in the state would help to define the ranking list a little better. The results of applying this new denominator are shown in Figure 4-9. This parameter was useful in that California and New York were brought down to near the average and several average states were elevated to the top. However, many EPSCOR states remained near the bottom, Massachusetts remained stubbornly in the top five, and Texas was still below average.

A last attempt in the denominator search provided a useful defense for complaints about the funding distribution. The new denominator attempted to measure excellence directly. It was related to a 1981 national peer review of the "scholarly

Figure 4-6
Distribution of NSF FY 1988 Awards by State

Academic Awards to Each State, Millions of Dollars

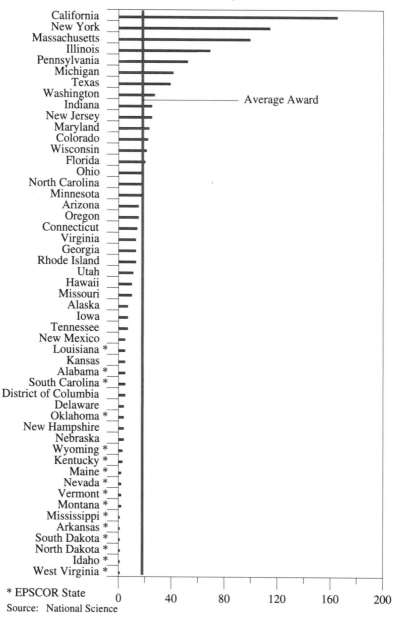

* EPSCOR State

Source: National Science

Figure 4-7
Distribution of NSF FY 1988 Awards
by State per Capita

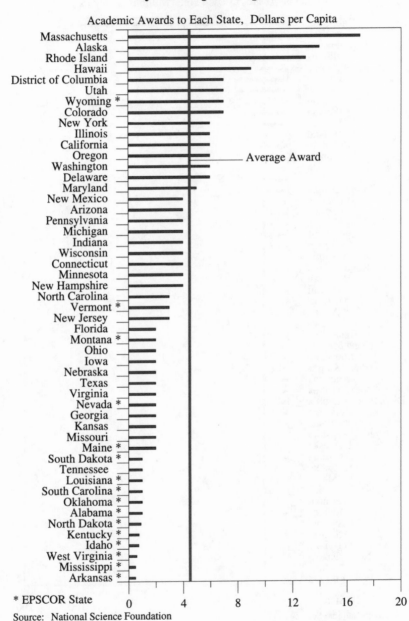

Academic Awards to Each State, Dollars per Capita

* EPSCOR State

Source: National Science Foundation

Figure 4-8
Distribution of NSF FY 1988 Awards
by State per University

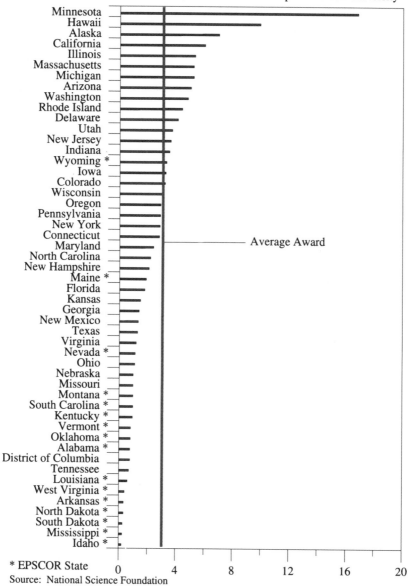

Academic Awards to Each State, Millions of Dollars per Research University

Minnesota
Hawaii
Alaska
California
Illinois
Massachusetts
Michigan
Arizona
Washington
Rhode Island
Delaware
Utah
New Jersey
Indiana
Wyoming *
Iowa
Colorado
Wisconsin
Oregon
Pennsylvania
New York
Connecticut
Maryland — Average Award
North Carolina
New Hampshire
Maine *
Florida
Kansas
Georgia
New Mexico
Texas
Virginia
Nevada *
Ohio
Nebraska
Missouri
Montana *
South Carolina *
Kentucky *
Vermont *
Oklahoma *
Alabama *
District of Columbia
Tennessee
Louisiana *
West Virginia *
Arkansas *
North Dakota *
South Dakota *
Mississippi *
Idaho *

0   4   8   12   16   20

* EPSCOR State
Source: National Science Foundation

Figure 4-9
Distribution of NSF FY 1988 Awards
by State per Researcher

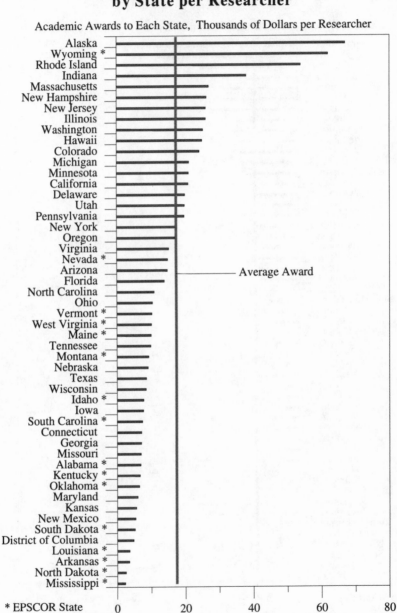

Academic Awards to Each State, Thousands of Dollars per Researcher

* EPSCOR State

Source: National Science Foundation

quality" of research university faculty by departments, conducted by the National Research Council (NRC). NSF claims to award grants to the best proposals received, and good faculties presumably submit good proposals, so the "number of high quality doctoral programs" in the state was used to normalize NSF's FY 1988 awards. Using the NRC scores (0–5 subjective peer rating), a high-quality department was defined as one that scored more than one standard deviation above the mean score for a given field of science. In the NRC evaluation, several states, including most of the EPSCOR states, lacked departments that met the criteria for "high quality." To circumvent the problem of dividing by "zero," it was assumed that each state must have at least "half" of a high-quality department; i.e., the denominator for states with no high-quality departments was 0.5.

This denominator produced results (see Figure 4-10) that moved most of the top-funded states to the bottom of the list (even Massachusetts was below average), and spreading the EPSCOR states across the list (three in the top 10). In this light, the lower-funded states were indeed doing well, considering how few good university faculties were in their state. Another complaint was that the same schools got the same proportion of NSF's budget every year by virtue of a cycle of improvement driven by their favorable funding by NSF.

This assertion was countered by a series of time trends of NSF funding by individual institutions grouped together in a three-dimensional graph like Figure 4-11. The universities in the figure are sorted according to the amount of NSF funding they got in 1971. If they continued to get the same proportion of NSF funds each year, the sorting would always be the same, and each institution's time trend would be the same shape, affected only by the total amount of funding NSF allocated to these 50 universities (Figure 4-12). This is not the case, however; considerable increases and decreases occur from year to year as shown in Figure 4-11. In fact, seven of the institutions shown on the axis are not among NSF's top 50 in 1988. Re-ranking the schools in any subsequent year would mix up the list extensively. Of course, MIT and Harvard never fall to twentieth place, but many institutions have shifted ranks by a dozen places or more, both up and down. This presentation is an excellent example of unsubstantiated political rhetoric laid to rest with an easily retrieved set of facts which would have been impractical to employ a few years ago.

In general, for any given issue, quantitative policy analysis is more incremental, or less comprehensive, than many of the earlier computer models. This is partly because PCs are not quite able to accommodate the large, comprehensive models of the previous era, but also because the transparency and simplicity of common statistical analyses performed on PCs for principal components (increments) of the issue (instead of all conceivable components) have made them very powerful tools for policy makers.

Analysis is more graphic, and therefore often more convincing and useful to the policy maker. Graphics give a better understanding of relative sizes of competing problems and budgets, and they clearly depict instability, periodicity, steep and shallow slopes, and discontinuities in time trends of data. Varying graph styles, colors, and layouts can pique a viewer's interest and draw attention to key facts during extended briefings.

Analysis is more rigorous, thanks largely to calculations so fast that procedures can be repeated many times, determining the sensitivity of the outcome to different causative factors, data accuracy, and required assumptions. Simple computer operator errors are much more detectable.

Of all of the changes that have come to policy analysis because of the advent of the PC, possibly the most enduring will be the introduction of the potential for ubiquitous policy analysis. The practice of data-driven policy analysis is no

Figure 4-10
Distribution of NSF FY 1988 Awards
by State per Doctoral Program

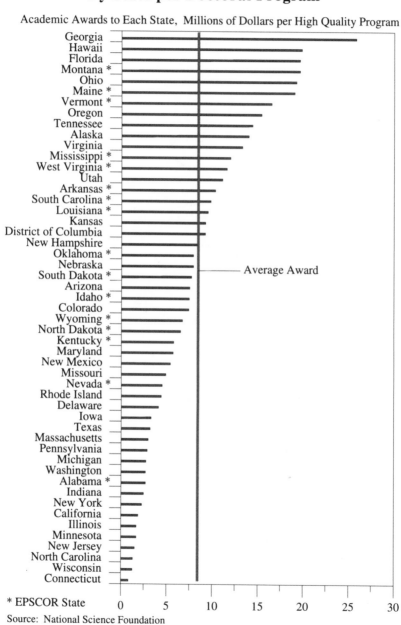

Academic Awards to Each State, Millions of Dollars per High Quality Program

* EPSCOR State

Source: National Science Foundation

Figure 4-11
NSF Annual Awards by Institution,
FY 1971 to FY 1988

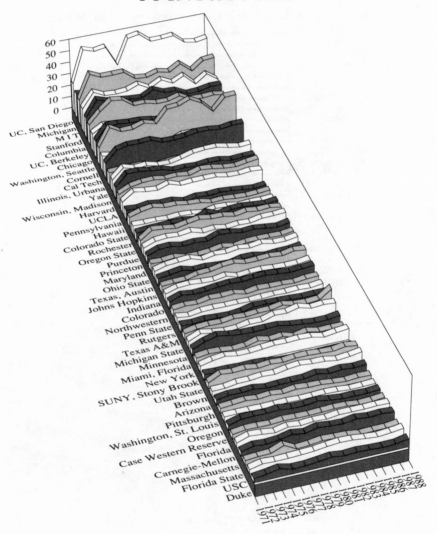

Millions of Constant 1988 Dollars, Sorted by 1971 Obligations

Source: National Science Foundation

Figure 4-12
NSF AWARDS: Annual Hypothetical
Noncompetitive Funding

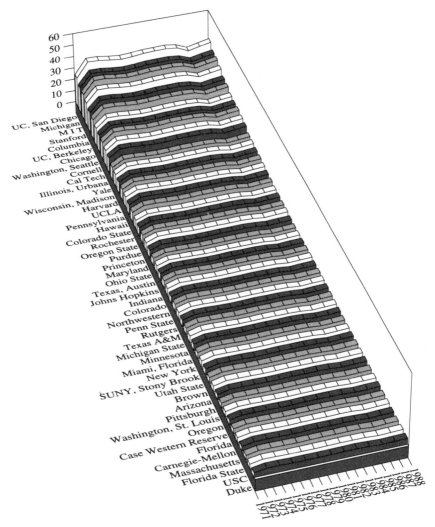

Millions of Constant 1988 Dollars, Sorted by 1971 Obligations,
1971 Shares Maintained Through 1988

Source: National Science Foundation

longer the monopoly of the few who have access to or can program a mainframe, or who are privy to a sophisticated analytic technique or possess a data base. Data and information are widely available and the PC permits very sophisticated analyses by almost anyone trained with some math and statistics, bringing into question anew the delineations of the policy analyst's role in the political process.

References

1. Lindblom, Charles E., "Incrementalism and Environmentalism," *Managing the Environment*, U.S. Environmental Protection Agency, U.S. Government Printing Office, Washington, November 1973.

2. Taft, Darryl, "ASCS Data System 'Converses' in Plain English," *Government Computer News*, 9:5, Washington, March 5, 1990, p. 34.

3. Lukes, Guy, Bryan Thompson, and Paul Werbos, "Expectation Driven Learning with an Associative Memory," *Proceedings of the International Joint Conference on Neural Networks*, Lawrence Erlbaum Assoc., Hillsdale, NJ, January 1990, p. I-521.

4. Vanski, Jean, "Projected Response of the Science, Engineering, and Technical Labor Market to Defense and Nondefense Needs: 1982–1987," *National Science Foundation Special Report* 84–304, Washington, January 1984.

5. National Science Board, *Science and Engineering Indicators— 1989*, U.S. Government Printing Office, Washington, December 1989, p. 74.

6. Data Resources, Inc., "Proposed Methods for Modeling the Academic Science and Engineering Labor Force Market," unpublished,

submitted to NSF Division of Science Resources Studies, January 18, 1989.

7. Brode, Wallace, "Manpower in Science and Engineering Based on a Saturation Model," *Science,* July 16, 1971.

5.

The Role of Quantitative Analysis

During the 1960s and 1970s, much was made of the specter of computers taking over government management. But the hardware and software were so costly, and often so perplexing to the average civil servant, that the coup never occurred. Computer use was limited to repetitive accounting tasks (e.g., payroll) or highly sophisticated but mechanical research work (e.g., satellite orbit mechanics, environmental quality analyses). If a problem was perceived to require computer analysis, extensive assistance from computer programmers and technicians was necessary.

The mainframe computer commanded a dedicated space with dozens of peripheral machines and a squad of operators. The customer had to develop programs and submit decks of cards—or later, to type instructions via a terminal into the machine—and wait for it to get around to processing his job, and then the output arrived on reams of paper. The institutional settings for the mainframes were sterile, with overtones of a command and control center: imposing, intimidating, and inaccessible.

The modern computer sits on a desk or lap and is as familiar as a typewriter or note pad. It can accommodate the vast majority of the data processing needs of a company or a public-sector agency. It serves as a communications center, networking to other computers and data bases over telephone lines. Today's PC is a versatile machine.

In five years, the size of full-function PCs shrank from the original to a "portable" (about 20 pounds) to "laptops" (about the size of a briefcase, with a flat, fold-down display, about 13 pounds and battery-powered), to the present "notebook" (8" x 11" x 1," weighing about four pounds and powered by batteries). These notebook computers are far superior in capability to the original PC.

The mainframe became easier to program with the advent of standardized programming languages that could be used on many different computers. But these languages required special vocabularies and highly structured procedures. Almost every application, from adding up a column of numbers to creating a complicated and sophisticated algorithm, had to be coded anew. Businesses sprang up everywhere selling codes for particular problems.

Today, because the market for computers is broad-based, substantial effort has been expended to make software useful for a wide range of users, not just for the analytically inclined. Instead of programming languages, the emphasis is on user packages: spreadsheets for accounting-type applications, communications facilitators, work and time organizers, word processors, graphics, and publications formatting, to name a few. Competition between vendors is not only over whose package can do the most, but whose is easiest to learn and perform.

The programming languages for customized procedures are much more efficient, effective, and forgiving than those of the 1960s. Controlling the software has been greatly simplified, with instructive graphics, ample "Help" screens, tutorials, and clearly written manuals. For those uncomfortable with a keyboard, many options are available, including touch-sensitive screens, cursor arrow keys, joysticks, mice, trackballs, and, soon, voice recognition for vocabularies of a few hundred words.

For repetitive tasks, the computer can be taught to copy the same keystrokes, recall them on command, and execute the desired sequences automatically. These automated sequences, termed "macros," can be quickly produced by anyone familiar with a particular software package, and experienced users can produce macros that maximize both speed and efficiency, making the solution to any repetitive procedure impressively fast. In short, the computer is designed and built for all comers, and professionals who understand the software and applications can push the general-purpose software packages to great lengths.

Nor will this be the ultimate stage of the computer evolution. The mainframe has grown to be a supercomputer, and the electronic chips now in the design stage promise PCs with ever-faster computation times and ever-expanding memory capacity. The software is likely to be equally impressive. Fast, easy data retrieval capabilities like CASPAR (see Chapter 4) will be available everywhere, and, with the growing improvement of artificial intelligence and the development of neural network theory, the environment will be very different and powerful indeed. In 1990, AT&T introduced computers that could understand callers' names and numbers, and give simple responses like "yes" and "no." Some stockbrokers and their major customers now transact purchases and sales with computer voice recognition systems.[1] Low-cost voice recognition systems also became available for PCs, which could be "trained" to perform one-word commands used in most software packages, like "PRINT, ZOOM, SAVE, MOVE, COPY, GRAPH," etc. It is only a matter of time that the keyboard, increasingly seen as an impediment, will be circumvented by computer systems driven by voice commands.

Data availability and manipulation capabilities have rapidly expanded over the past several decades. It used to be that few data were encoded, and the process was cumbersome. Paper tape or 3″ x 7″ cards with punched holes served as the input medium.[a] Maintaining precise order of the "deck" of cards was extremely important: the possibility of dropping a

---

[a]Federal Government checks and bonds were issued on these cards for many years, and were the source of the famous computer-age adage "Do not fold, spindle, or mutilate."

deck was a constant nightmare for data users. For many applications, the user had to present a set of program cards and a
set of data cards at the computer center to perform any analysis. Tape drives, teletype machines, and modems made the
job of capturing data a little easier. But there was still a long
way to go, and selling data sets was big business. The U.S.
Census was computer-automated by 1960, but that task required mainly sorting and averaging data.

As computer hardware improved, the use of data in the
policy process became more routine, and information became
a weapon in the adversarial process of public-sector decision
making. Every business, institution, and citizen was a potential target for government data requests. Every agency had to
collect its own data, and each unit in each agency had specialized needs of its own, requesting information from whomever
it pleased. Nothing was coordinated. Eventually, businesses
felt that the demands had gone too far, and Congress passed
the Paperwork Reduction Act. The executive branch established a unit in OMB to coordinate all federal data collection
efforts.

Now, every agency has a data "budget" consisting of the
number of "burden hours" (for filling out forms) it may place
upon survey targets. Every time data are requested from more
than 10 people, the agency must request approval from OMB.
Over the past decade, very few new surveys have been approved, and the amount of data requested in older periodic
surveys has been significantly reduced. The debate over the
value of survey data versus the burden on the survey respondent will undoubtably recur several times in the next few
decades.

The major tasks of policy analyses over the past decade
will continue to be needed in the future. These include data
definition, calibration, transformation, comparison, and standardization. Data on employment of scientists and engineers
in the nation are collected by the Bureau of the Census, the
Bureau of Labor Statistics, the Department of Education, the

NSF, the NRC, and many professional societies. Many cases of repetitive, duplicative, corroborative, or competitive data collection exercises could be cited, whether the subject be people, money, transportation, energy, or environmental quality. Rarely do policy analysts have even one data source of unquestionable quality. More often, they have insufficient data, data of questionable quality, or conflicting data.

In the development of the authors' data system (CAS-PAR, see Chapter 4), the largest single cost was for standardization of data that came from several different sources. It was a knowledge-intensive process not amenable to automation—in fact, it was not even possible to delegate much of the work to junior analysts or technicians. Experienced government statisticians were required for many hours to review the survey forms from many different collection agencies, and to match, map, and translate different definitions for the same general data element.

Whenever information on a specific issue is demanded, standardization of different data sources will be necessary, but there is little incentive for coordination between data collectors in subjects where the data is not contested. Thus, every time an issue arises for the first time, policy analysts may face time delays of months of data preparation before getting a clear picture of the issue, despite the advanced capabilities of their analytical tools. Reconciliation of similar or related data from different sources will remain a major task for policy analysts in the future.

Progress in computer applications will most likely decelerate, though the technology in sight often seems as staggering as the advances of the 1980s. But while the next two decades may not see the rate of growth in data collection and availability of the past two, there will, of course, be two more decades worth of data available to strengthen policy analyses. Increased data availability and enhanced data-handling tools will encourage greater use of quantitative analysis, but not necessarily at the political level.

The decade of the 1960s was one of rationalism in the realm of policy analysis, manifested as a belief that the analytic techniques applied in defense and business decisions could be transferred to the government at large. One group after another championed such techniques as offering the public sector the "best" solution to any specific problem. Allied to this was the belief that agencies should "plan" and that these plans ought to be "long-range." Forecasts of the future were developed and scenarios defined based on different sets of assumptions and policies, and agency policies and plans were studied in terms of these futures.

Since the computer had obvious potential as a tool to improve the decision-making process in the public and private sectors, all that remained was to create the software necessary to make it so. This task attracted competent professionals as well as a number of charlatans. Many new techniques and algorithms were developed. Many national economic models refined during this period are in widespread use today in the business and financial communities. "Optimization" became a popular buzz word. Optimization models would give you the "best" solution to a complex problem provided that all related phenomena could be described mathematically or in terms of dollar costs and benefits. Simulation models were adopted by most agencies. Some worked very well, such as NASA's satellite orbit computations; others, such as environmental quality or energy use projections, frequently failed.

The most extreme of the various techniques was systems dynamics, which provided an algorithmic solution of simultaneous partial differential equations that had been developed for mechanical and electrical systems. It was originally applied to military strategies, then industrial problems, then urban issues, and finally all others. At its pinnacle, its proponents claimed that it was the only way to address any issue facing the public sector, and in some areas it became a requirement to apply systems dynamics. After an initial flurry, however, the technique receded to its proper stature: just one of many methods.

Since then, both the intellectual climate and the character of the modeler have changed. No new analytic procedure has been introduced to policy analysis in years. Although new capabilities permit many more analyses faster with more data, the basic analytical techniques are the same as those used even before the comprehensive period. Some statistical techniques have been in use for a century or more. New computer concepts such as expert systems, artificial intelligence, and neural networks are in fact mathematical or algorithmic attempts to mimic the analytical talents of humans. Since analyses are so economical now, there is little incentive to construct large, generalized, comprehensive models to conserve resources by using the same model for many different issues and applications. Analytical tools are now selected based on how well they fit the issue and the available data. Rather than waiting months for output from a comprehensive analysis, executives prefer quick preliminary answers provided by simple models, followed by incremental enhancements of the analysis and more sophisticated answers. Thus, in essence, the present consensus has circled back to incrementalism, as defined by Lindblom in the 1960s.

In the early days of computer applications, gallons of ink were spilled arguing whether it was the job of programmers or the user to determine how they ought to analyze an issue. Regardless of particular winners or losers of those battles, the policy analyst, as a component of the user hierarchy, became the translator, the witness to the data lost by misinterpretation, irrelevence, or inscrutability. Today, the user and developer are often one and the same. Rather than consulting a programmer, the policy analyst merely selects the appropriate menu in a software package and follows its instructions. Thus, analysts are more immediately involved with the analyses, and more conversant with the full range of results. This arrangement tends to foster more responsible policy analysts, more relevant analyses, and greater understanding of their limitations and strong points.

Technology has also largely replaced the artists and draftsmen who prepared finished versions of analytical rough drafts. Instead of hand-drawing, straightforward graphics packages produce all forms of graphs and scores of images such as maps and drawings that can be used to drive home less numerical points more forcefully. Equally important are the modern desktop publishing packages which lay out manuscripts and merge graphics with text, with typesetting and on-screen paste-up capabilities. More impressive still is the improvement in video monitor and image capture technologies. VCRs and high-resolution, large-screen television screens are now integrated with the PC system. This capability has realized enormous potential for on-line analysis and expands the "chalk-talk" to include sophisticated analyses during briefings and nearly instant responses to executives' detailed questions. Several analysts can also have access to the same screen to make improvements or clarifications using a large shared data base and the latest in analytic techniques.

The link between the user and the presentation methodology is the area with the greatest potential for growth. The rapid advancement of presentation technology is a definite boon to the policy analysis profession (though its low cost and ease of use make it a handy tool for anyone, including special-interest promoters). Software packages already exist to display output in three dimensions, and the field has been growing beyond today's graphics and alphanumerics.

It may be some time before a truly interactive computer is designed, but elements of that machine are already available. Synthesized speech can be created on simple home computers with stored speech sounds called "phonemes," and computers can now also understand a limited set of English words. The authors' own QUERY system (see Chapter 4) understands many keyboarded English questions that relate to our special data base. This sector of the technology holds the promise of the user and the computer engaging in a form of dialogue limited only by the speed of the computer, its information base, and its artificial intelligence. Clashes between interest groups and analysts, among others, will be lit by computer animation, video conferences bringing executives and computer simulations face to face, and, of course, ever quicker and more sophisticated models to back up the power of the presentation with data.

The PC and the Future of the Error

Personal computers enable a single well-trained policy analyst with access to appropriate data to conduct in one day the kind of analyses that a decade ago would have consumed man-months of time of several professionals in various fields. Other than reduce the size of policy analysis staffs in both government and business, what does the new technology hold for the future of policy analysis? Will increased productivity be swallowed up by excess information, inadequate quality control, baffling computer bugs, a proliferation of "experts," and overzealous automation?

People make mistakes. Computers make mistakes. Computer software makes mistakes. Data can be wrong. Data, computers, and analyses can be used for unethical purposes. Sophisticated radar and computers helped the U.S. Navy launch a missile that destroyed a commercial airliner over the Persian Gulf. A computer on a newly designed airliner shut down both of its engines at 40,000 feet without asking the pilot. A computer error shut down the AT&T long-distance networks across the nation for an entire day, and a software error on a regional network blanketed the nation's capital and surrounding area in telephone silence for the better part of a business day. Omission of critical data on government weight specifications from an executive information system at Lockheed Aeronautical Systems Corporation may cost the company $300 million in redesign expenses.[2]

These mistakes can all be attributed to human design, testing, or other decision errors. In addition, computer hackers have disrupted business, financial, and administrative computations with security breaches and viruses, to say nothing of outright computer fraud, the sophistication of which clearly increases with the power of the technology. Could contaminated data be inserted into a system to advance special causes, and go undetected by objective analysts? Can computer calculations for policy analysis, especially if automated to the level described in Chapter 4, lead to similar catastrophic situations?

Provided that two very likely conditions endure, each ensuring a measure of human responsibility, the answer is probably not. So long as knowledgable humans are involved with the system, and the analytic models do not directly trigger some type of operational mechanism, with an effect such as that of program traders in the financial markets, the specter of computer-generated catastrophes will remain remote.

Policy decisions are made by people, not computers, and executives consider analysis as aids, rather than formulas for decisions. The results of analyses are digested by executives along with many other considerations. As long as executives and policy analysts are generally knowledgable about the issue at hand, they will have a range of expectations for the analytical results. The probability of a computer analysis leading to a major policy mistake is inversely proportional to the relevant knowledge of those involved in or affected by a decision. At the same time, the probability of a computer mistake being discovered is directly proportional to its deviation from expected values.

Professional analysts know the importance of carefully performed work and rigorous self-checking. Even when policy analyses are done against short deadlines, unlikely patterns are carefully watched for (the graphic capabilities of today's software are invaluable for this purpose) and the end results are necessarily checked for plausibility. But only knowledgable analysts or executives will spot anomalous phenomena or implausible analytic results. PC software analyses are subject to the same kind of human errors as are manual calculations—misplaced decimal points, transposed values, values copied from the wrong row, omitting a factor from an equation—as well as new software-specific kinds such as pressing the wrong function key, selecting from the wrong menu, recalling the wrong file, dividing by the wrong column in the spreadsheet, or selecting the wrong type of graph.

These kinds of errors can produce results such as graphs with a certain point inexplicably out of line with the others, in which case they are immediately evident. The same logic applies to deliberate fraud: an attempt to pollute a data base with values which produce strikingly unexpected results would prompt unusual scrutiny.

The reexamining of the genesis of unexpected results should prevent analysts from labeling a true result as false or a false result as true.[b] Should, however, the results be plausible, but based on misconceived conditions, the situation would be problematical and tantamount to the failure of policy analysis and the supporting intelligence and scientific sources. Many of our nation's and our government's major mistakes have been caused by this type of error. Government programs and regulations which have no economic market correction mechanism are particularly vulnerable to errors caused by an unexpected change or unnoticed elements in the status quo. Also, policies attempting to respond to wildly fluctuating systems such as markets or meteorology will always be subject to such errors. Detailed technical expertise in the subject field can help understand these oscillations, but will rarely improve their predictability.

---

[b]Respectively "Type 1" and "Type 2" errors in statistics terminology.

In the late 1960s, tall smokestacks were proposed as a solution to air pollutants from coal-fired power plants. State-of-the-art atmospheric dispersion mathematical models predicted that maximum pollutant concentrations in the area around a smokestack declined with the square of the stack height and, therefore, with 1,000-foot stacks, all pollutants would be diluted to insignificant levels before reaching any receptors.[3] Thus, under existing air quality regulations, many large coal-fired power plants were authorized, each using a tall stack for dispersion. In the 1980s, environmental scientists learned that juxtaposition of many tall stacks, combined with atmospheric circulation patterns and the chemistry of sulfates and nitrates, produced a significant amount of acid rain.[4]

National energy policy (especially petroleum policy) is a field where reasonably predictable resource economics are confounded by international politics. Free market economic principles tell us that as petroleum becomes more scarce, its price will rise, and as the price of petroleum rises, purchasers will seek alternative sources of energy. But the U.S. imports about a third of its petroleum, buying it in the "world" market. About a third of the world production of petroleum comes from the politically unstable Persian Gulf area. Unilateral decisions by these producers on production rates and prices can markedly affect overall world oil prices (Figure 5-1).

Analysts can calculate supplies, demands, and prices under many assumed scenarios of Persian Gulf political events, but the timing and severity of such events are unpredictable. Initiating the production of crude oil in other parts of the world is strongly dependant on anticipated world oil prices which are not precisely predictable. Thus, for national policy development, worst case scenarios are often chosen, which in retrospect appear nonsensical. In the late 1970s, many national energy policies were based on projections of monotonically increasing crude petroleum prices.[5] But from 1981 to 1986, oil prices dropped 75 percent,[6] due in part to the

Figure 5-1
**Average Quarterly World Price of Crude Petroleum
and Possible Extrapolations**

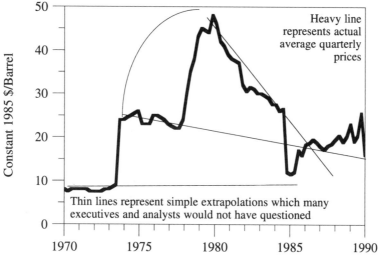

Sources: U.S. Energy Information Administration, 1989-90
    Extrapolations by the authors

collapse of the OPEC monopoly and expansion of supplies in other parts of the world.

Modern policy analysis offers no hope for avoiding such errors. They all resulted from lack of knowledge, where the future turned out not to be a projection of the past. Only continued research in the natural and social sciences can give us greater knowledge about phenomena that affect our physical and social environment. Optimism and pessimism also play roles in policy analyses. The tall-stack decision was based on a lack of understanding of the system. The energy policies were based on linear projection, not analysis. Where mistakes result from lack of relevant scientific and technical knowledge, our capacity to blunder will endure.

Countless competing interest groups are conducting mathematically accurate quantitative analyses of the same issue and reaching widely differing conclusions because their assumptions, guesses, intents, and purposes are different. The availability of low-cost computational capability combined with readily accessible data will probably exacerbate rather than ameliorate this situation. A few examples are presented below.

For the past few decades, the annual federal budget has been the focus of spirited debate between the President and Congress. The Gramm-Rudman-Hollings Act, aimed at deficit reduction, has sharpened this debate and provided a rigid procedure for its conduct. In brief, the Act specifies certain allowable deficit amounts each year. In developing the budget, the President (assisted by staff at OMB) must first calculate anticipated revenues, debt service interest costs, and entitlement expenditures before deciding how much discretionary spending should be included in the budget.

Calculating these factors requires guessing how fast the GNP will grow and what the government's borrowing rate will be next year. Staff analysts in the Congressional Budget Office (CBO) independently perform the same calculations as a check on the administration's projections. Predictably, they never agree, as the following table published in *The Washington Post* illustrates:

Key Assumptions in Estimating the FY 1991 Deficit

Item	OMB Estimate	CBO Estimate
Real GNP growth	3.3%	2.5%
3-mo Treasury bill rate	5.0%	7.2%
10-yr Treasury bond rate	6.8%	7.7%
Calculated deficit (billion dollars)	100	138

The congressional analysts predicted a deficit 38 percent higher than the administration's estimate. This is a difference big enough to justify different budget policies. The persistently divergent numbers, calculated on separate computer models by professional budget analysts, gave rise in the 1980s to the famed "rosy scenario" accusation, in which each branch of the government accuses the other of fabricating conditions to suit their ends.

Policy analysts are frequently prevented for political reasons from using most likely values for inputs to their computer models. Executives have sensitive political agendas and often wish to highlight only certain aspects of the issue. Calculating the effects of the desired policy under unfavorable assumptions might suggest too many frailties, providing fuel for the opponents' arguments against it. For example, one of the reasons the SEAS projections of future pollutant emissions and pollution control costs deviated noticeably from actual values (see Chapter 2) was that it was forbidden to forecast the most likely scenario: most pollution sources would be tardy in complying with the new EPA regulations, and would install less costly equipment than the "best practicable technology" that were simulated in our model. Consequently, actual emissions did not decline as quickly, and actual expenditures were not as high, as in our scenario. In a similar situation, at DOE in the 1970s, everyone was so worried about price increases that neither executives nor analysts considered scenarios in which the price of crude oil dropped. Thus, all our policy forecasts projected more coal, nuclear, and solar energy sources in the 1990s than actually occurred.

The urge to ignore certain scenarios or policy options will remain, but with the increasing ease with which alternate scenarios can be investigated, more scenarios will be investigated, either by government or outside analysts. This is a positive development for the long term. Expanded debate exposes more potential problems, promotes better definitions of and more proposed approaches to the problems, necessitates a better understanding of the will of the electorate, and, ultimately, it helps to provide better and more permanent solutions. As for bureaucratic efficiency in the short term, however, the outlook is for expanded and intensified debate consuming more time and resources for each issue that arises.

Global warming is clearly one of the more hotly contested issues of the 1990s for just these reasons. The latest methods of studying CO_2 concentration in the earth's atmosphere have produced widely divergent interpretations. The issue has been under study for many years[7], and it is clear that the average concentration of CO_2 has been steadily increasing since the beginning of record. However, determining the net effect of this increasing concentration on the earth's overall climate is an extremely complex task, even for the world's best environmental scientists. Environmental scientists, with extensive federal financial support, are attempting to assemble a comprehensive global climate model with 50 to 80 major variables representing physical, chemical, energy, biological, and human processes in the stratosphere, atmosphere, oceans, and land surfaces.[8]

Linking these many components together in a coherent mathematical model is a challenge far beyond the development of SEAS (see Chapter 2), and faces the threat of the same dilemma that SEAS ran up against: oversimplification and overgeneralization to the point of limited value. Projections of future conditions from early versions of such models vary widely, but the scientific consensus as of 1990 was that our earth is probably getting warmer, and that it may be warmer by an average of 3° or 4° Fahrenheit by the middle of the next century;[9] only a year earlier, estimates of average temperature rise were as high as 9° Fahrenheit, while as recently as the Bicentennial, several scientists were warning of the onset of a "new ice age."[10] Analytical results of this issue, as in the federal budget debate, are rarely politically neutral; the uncertainties and hence caution suggested by such diverse warming estimates are applauded by the fossil fuel interests, whereas the environmental lobby views this caution as stalling and fossil fuel favoritism.

Individual scientists and scientific disciplines are also prone to develop biases on issues influencing policy deliberations. Engineers or physical scientists often seek simple, mechanical solutions to complex problems. Moreover, the tendency of scientific advisors to speak out both as experts and as private citizens certainly will not diminish. The practicing policy analyst must be careful to sort the personal opinions from the facts and professional judgments provided by such experts. When business and personal fortunes are at stake, numerical analyses, no matter how precise, rarely change beliefs. In an issue as significant, long-term, complex, and uncertain as that of the global climate, there will always be room for questioning the data and analytical procedures, and both sides will continue to compete until a political solution is reached.

Contributing to the situation is the fact that anybody with a PC can be a policy analyst. Analytic proliferation will occur not only between opposing sides on policy issues, but also within executive agencies. This will make it more difficult for agency executives to choose strategies, because there will be many different "experts" with different types of advice. In the near future, when data bases are ubiquitous and everyone can produce a spreadsheet and a graph, the proliferation of free advice can only increase. Federal policy makers receive many letters, "studies," and suggestions every year. Most are ignored, but those from respected members of the community must be taken seriously and handled diplomatically.

The likely response to the plethora of experts is (as it was in the days of large-scale models) a call for independent judges and uniform standards. When several of the large-scale models (see Chapter 2) disagreed, executives sought federal data coordination and standardization, independent groups to validate models and techniques, and other remedies. Through these reforms, the practice of analysis evolved (see Chapter 3). Similar standardization and protocols may be a part of the future evolution of policy analysis, but because of the very feature, versatility, that makes the PC so valuable to policy analysis, the implementation of standards will be difficult.

The issue of the production of new scientists and engineers presented in Chapter 4 provides a good example of a such a disagreement within NSF. One position, supported by a simulation designed and implemented by the authors, was that the number of new natural science and engineering degrees earned annually by American citizens or permanent residents would most likely decline steadily in the 1990s. This would lead to a shortfall which could result in employment of less skilled people in NS&E jobs, increasing salaries, increasing automation, delaying retirements, and other types of market adjustments.[11] Another analysis focused on the number of graduates employed in jobs officially classified as scientist or engineer, according to BLS surveys. This analysis highlighted the small employment flow (8 percent leaving and 12 percent entering NS&E jobs), concluding that the economic impact of reduction in graduating scientists and engineers on the national economy would be small, if noticeable.[12]

Internal agency debates usually lead to better policy analyses. In many cases, the debate is between the statistical unit, responsible for data collection and statistical analyses, and the policy analysis or development group. In most agencies, these groups are separate and independent.[13] In theory, the statistical unit should be shielded from political pressures so it can compile the objective, statistically reliable information necessary to provide a sound basis for evaluation and management of federal programs and policies. The same theory would hold that the policy unit should not collect data because it might tend to support policies of the incumbent administration.

In practice, the separation is often blurred for many reasons, one of which is rooted in the interests and skills of the two groups. Statistical group members have ready access to the data and are often tempted to analyze it; the policy staff often collect some of their own data or use the statisticians' data in ways not condoned by the statisticians. The availability of the low-cost, massive computing power of the PC will no doubt heighten the competition between statisticians and policy analysts. While this may lead to management problems in the short term, the heightened involvement should provoke debate, ultimately producing better government policies.

The theoretical firewall between the statistical unit and political pressure could partially shield a policy analyst from political heat, but in practice, the situation is more complicated. When an executive is running hard to respond to the pressures of the White House, the Congress, and the electorate, the policy situation is best described as semi-organized chaos. Sometimes the urgency of an issue can be dulled by commissioning a study, but most issues must be resolved quickly. Decisions have to be made, and they will be made with or without rigorous analysis.

Agencies established for decades with defined missions, and structured over the years to respond to the expected demands of their constituencies and the Congress, may be less chaotic. Policy analysts in these agencies are rarely called upon to deal with true brushfires, and analyses are apt to be long and erudite compared to the shoot-from-the-hip kind in the more volatile agencies. The way policy issues are addressed is also influenced at the political level. A new appointee is often substantially ill equipped for the position: If the principal characteristic sought by the White House is ultimately political compatibility and the prospect's contacts are powerful, little other expertise may be required. Similarly, an appointee's leadership qualities have a strong bearing on an agency's analysis.

Many policy issues arise when a study begins to trouble the status-quo beneficiaries. One example of this came about during the early days of the energy crisis. The ERDA policy office was an amalgam of people from all disciplines and beliefs. One such individual was a maverick who believed his mission was to push for solar energy and energy conservation without restraint. He commissioned a study to determine whether a large state like California could meet its energy requirements with only existing sources, energy conservation, and new solar energy sources. The study was conducted by the University of California at Berkeley, assisted by two DOE national laboratories. When the study was in draft, it was brought back to Washington for "review"—not by scientists and technicians, but by Congress, the media, and the solar lobby. Questioning the results of the study at that time was politically unwise.

The authors' environmental policy shop became responsible for organizing an exhaustive review of this project for the new DOE, with which ERDA had recently been merged. A number of assumptions in the study were weak. The area needed by the solar collectors to supply electricity for the population already in place would have taken every roof top, every park, and a good portion of a nearby desert. The study was equally weak in the area of transportation. Given the area of several of the cities in the state, it was difficult to see how anything would replace the automobile energy source, gasoline. The study chose methanol produced from seaweed (kelp) farms for a liquid fuel source. It failed to calculate that adequate surface area for the kelp farms would require hundreds of square miles. To relate such a response to the ERDA draft required some relatively sophisticated analyses and a fair amount of political finesse.

The final report admitted to many of the problems associated with massive solar energy conversions.[14] A more thorough analysis, conducted after the solar rhetoric had subsided,[15] showed that solar energy technologies and energy conservation processes each had their own set of environmental, cultural, and economic effects on society, and that the "soft energy paths" had their share of problems.

Even the less colorful battles among policy analysts, interest groups, and each other illustrate the essential mechanical role human interaction plays in the policy-producing machinery. No matter how sophisticated the policy analysts' capability becomes, political or staff executives will not subjugate their policy staff to the machine, technological leaps notwithstanding. To the extent they consider an issue mundane or repetitive, they might turn to a machine much as they turn to a dictionary to find a definition. But it will be some time before they will believe that a machine can consider a sensitive policy question as reliably as an experienced human analyst. The job of analysts has always been to provide information, but frequently they have been expected to interact adversarily with their peers. In these situations, technical skills are not enough. Human interaction and oversight of quantitative computer analyses should preclude catastrophic policy mistakes because of computer errors, but computer analyses will probably be less successful in preventing human beings from making similar mistakes.

The authors were involved with three different government agencies while the profession of policy analysis was evolving, and have kept in contact with our peers in the Washington science policy community, both personally and by observing their performance in relevant policy debates, so the trends we have observed may be representative of the profession in general.

If better decisions are a function of better information, the executive of the future will make better decisions. The policy staff of the near future will all be PC-fluent and need a smaller analytical and support staff. Fewer people will be needed, but they will need new and more sophisticated skills. Managers of policy analysis offices will face difficult trade-offs between retraining and recruitment, between reliability and productivity, between humans and machines. Questions of size of the analytic capability, speed of access, user interface, and when and when not to use mainframe capabilities will be perpetual issues. But the likely steady advance of computer technology will transform the question from one of retaining productivity in the face of increasing demands, to one of producing better responses based on a larger volume of available information. The real cost of computer equipment will continue to drop, so acquisition should not be a major problem. Standardization of data bases requires extensive knowledge and judgment, however, and will represent expensive components of policy analysis.

There will be far more interaction and group participation among the many actors in the public policy process. Hence, the level of sophistication of analysis will continue to be at issue as will the sophistication of the presentation. The amount of common training, vocabulary, and understanding among executives and analysts is a key factor. Analytical documentation will be much easier, as each presentation can be electronically stored automatically, with its own data base, in a format typically familiar to anyone who wishes to use it or examine it at a later point.

The technology-driven shift in equipping and staffing agencies and the parallel shift in skills and roles suggest the twilight of the reign of the generalist. In the three eras outlined in Chapters 2, 3, and 4, generalist policy analysts were most successful. Regardless of the discipline of their training, if they developed skills in statistics, economics, mathematics, and political science, they were able to apply their skills readily to issues in such disparate areas as health, environment, energy, space, housing, transportation, resources, or defense. There were always plenty of experts in an agency to provide policy analysts with the necessary technical facts and principles.

The analysts provided the synthesis, sorting, comparing, analysis, editing, and exposition of the technical information. As more policy analysis procedures and data bases become standardized and automated, the role of the generalist in policy analysis may wane in deference to experts knowledgable in the data bases and the physical and social systems under study. These standards will, with the availability of the technology, in a sense level the playing field, stripping the generalists of their "expert" label. Academically expert analysts will be better able to distinguish between valid analyses and the superficial, inaccurate, or fraudulent ones submitted by the many new actors using the public data bases and "canned" policy analysis software.

Analysts will still need to be conversant with current policy analysis methods, so they understand what the automated processes are doing and what their relevance and reliability are. They will also have to be able to participate convincingly in debates about methodological assumptions such as social discount rates, market effects, risk projection models, and similar paradigms. In addition, they will need to have a good understanding of the political process and their own roles therein, but to be of most value, they will need to be, more than ever, experts in areas of their agency's responsibilities.

While remaining true to the adage that "some numbers beat no numbers every time," analysts and decision makers should see the quality of the numbers used in the policy process continue to improve. Technological advances will allow these improvements to be increasingly dynamic and responsive to the needs of the policy community. But what about the techniques and analytical procedures of the past? This history of analysis as it supported the federal policy process did not cover the field with glory. Many of the techniques could not be legitimately implemented because of lack of understanding and knowledge. Many of the methodologies and paradigms were brought into the policy arena well before there was information sophisticated enough to support them.

The capabilities provided in the PC era should reduce such occurrences, very gradually increasing the utility of cost-benefit, risk analysis, and other quantitative methods. Although these methods are sometimes quantitatively complicated, that has never been the constraint. The critical element in short supply has been valid information. If there is missing information and the analyst must rely on assumptions, the PC technology allows rapid reiterations of computations to ascertain the sensitivity of results to alternate assumptions. But nothing really makes up for bad or missing data, and the correction of this fault will be necessarily incremental and slow in coming.

A Pocket Guide to Quantification

More important, the government has adjusted to the use of sophisticated models and standardized enumeration and evaluation procedures. A significant group of professionals make their living at these activities, and government officials are accustomed to justifying their priorities in quantitative terms. Also, many important political figures have accepted these procedures and will be reluctant to abandon them without strong evidence of their irrelevance. As Milton Russell, former EPA Assistant Administrator for Policy, said recently:

> Without it you are doomed to regulating based on whim, uneducated opinion, or sheer public attention. That can impose very large costs on the economy, and do damn little good.[16]

Several examples of flaws in the use of mathematical analyses to resolve major policy issues have been reviewed in earlier chapters. There is a long list of subjective factors to consider when selecting analytical methods, but policy analysts, especially those in jobs which deal with a variety of issues, often need to make these choices on a daily basis. Drawing on that list, one can find some general "rules of thumb" that can be useful.

Table 5-1 provides a framework within which to assess the potential utility of mathematical analyses of a particular issue. However, because policy analysis is a complex art, there are no inviolable rules. In fact, use of this framework to help decide whether to quantify issues presents many of the same problems the table itself is intended to minimize: before the analysis is even begun, subjective factors are determining the weight to be given to each criterion, which indirectly represents a value judgment.

Nevertheless, it is useful to consider issues in this variety of contexts, since these are the contexts into which any analysis is likely to be received. The table represents the broad range of criteria which must be considered in deciding how much effort and what methods should be used in analyzing a public policy issue. Criteria range from moral, political, and emotional at the top to technicality and data availability at the bottom. The criteria are not completely exclusive, and any experienced analyst would present a slightly different list, based on personal experience.

The criteria are arranged so that issues more conducive to mathematical analyses are at the left. Thus, to make a quick decision on the desirability of quantification, simply choose the best description of your issue in each row. The greater the number of boxes checked on the left, the more likely mathematical analysis will provide useful insight. On the other hand, if any boxes in the far right-hand column apply, there is a strong indication that quantification should be avoided or used only for background understanding.

The debate over health insurance is one which might benefit from such an aid in deciding the utility of a mathematical approach. The question is whether all employers should provide health insurance. Legislative proposals included mandating the provision of health insurance, or charging those who don't provide insurance a "health tax" earmarked for a fund to support a federal health insurance program for employees of those firms. Following the criteria of Table 5-1, the issue can be broken down in this way:

Table 5-1
A Pocket Guide to Quantification

Criterion \ Suitability	High	Medium	Low	None	Negative
Morality	Amoral issues	Minor moral relevance	Moral issue to few	Moral issue to many	Clear moral issue
Political Principle	Apolitical issue	Weak implications	Political overtones	Major political position	Prime political position
Emotional Level	None	Special interest groups only	Headlines in tabloids	Headlines in established press	Catastrophic event
Statutory Constraint	Clearly required	Clearly implied	Allowed	Not mentioned	Prohibited
Level of Consensus	High	Two positions	Three positions	Five positions	No consensus
Number of Actors	One	Five	Ten	Twenty	Dozens
Decision Level	Staff	Manager	Third-level executive	Second-level executive	Chief Executive
Complexity of Issue	Few relevant factors	Many factors, most understood	Many factors, few understood	Conceptual understanding only	No understanding, hypotheses only
Current Knowledge	Extensive	Long-term observation	Several years of research completed	Early research underway	Anecdotes only
Technicality	Traditional physical systems	New physical systems	Physical/geographical issues	Physical/moral issues	Strictly legal issues
Available Data	Current, long-term, continuous, online	Long-term, intermittent	Recent data only	Anecdotal data only	None

- This is a moral issue to few people: most believe health insurance is important, but not a moral right;
- This issue falls in the low-to-moderate range of emotion-evoking content, because it doesn't involve an immediate threat to all small business employees—only a high cost to many who can't afford private insurance;
- A major obstacle to a successful and useful quantitative analysis of this issue is the fact that it is highly politicized, and in fact involves two fractious issues: the amount of regulation to be borne by small businesses, and the level of public sector involvement in a traditionally private sector field;
- There are no statutory constraints; indeed, this issue involves potential new legislation;
- The level of consensus on this issue has long been low, as most people agree that employers should provide health insurance plans, but many oppose mandating the provision of such benefits, either by the employer or by the federal government;
- This is a conceptually simple issue, with most of the debate centering on political principles, not the framing of the questions or the selection of the data;
- Issues with such high political profiles usually require high levels of leadership to marshall support for a program, and there is the threat of a presidential veto;
- Provision of health insurance is a relatively mechanical process, with established accounting principles, so the logistical consequences of any decision would not be prohibitive; and
- Extensive data exists on health expenditures, small business, and demographics in general, greatly facilitating quantitative techniques.

While the proposed activity can be reasonably well simulated with good cost estimates, cost is not the principal issue here. The issue is so heavily politicized, and divisively so, that the use of quantitative analyses would be of little to no value. Several other examples taken from current federal pol-

icy debate illustrate the utility of such an examination of issues considered for quantitative analysis. The following
sketches illustrate how some of the factors delineated in Figure 5-1 come into play:

- Gun controls: Quantitative analyses have been used in
  this debate, but are of little value. Data tend to show
  the futility of gun ban proposals,and the effort and
  expense required for various proposed gun purchaser
  qualification schemes. Despite these and other statistical conclusions, however, the principle debate remains
  centered on what are said to be Constitutional rights
  both to bear arms and to seek security.
- Global climate change: Quantitative data and analysis
  are certainly necessary to help understand this phenomenon, but these procedures will never decide for
  the nation or the world what to do about it. It is a moral
  issue to many, because it concerns the condition of the
  world we will bequeath to our progeny. Further, it is
  an emotionally charged issue involving sensational scenarios of new desert climates in some regions and rising ocean levels in others. But putting some of the
  more eye-catching scenarios aside, it is a very complex
  issue with many interacting factors, few of which are
  fully understood. Years of research have been completed, but additional necessary research is expensive
  because it involves gathering data on a worldwide basis
  and conducting simulations on the world's most sophisticated computers. As if these were not obstacles
  enough, the issue has strong international political implications, since most control strategies would have
  severe economic impacts on developing nations.
- Transportation vehicle safety standards: This is an area
  where quantitative analyses are very useful, with minor
  exceptions. Automobiles, trucks, trains, ships, and
  airplanes are technologies with which most citizens are
  familiar, and for which extensive data are available.
  The costs of any particular proposed standard are quite

easily and reliably calculated. The point at which the utility of models weakens, however, is the trade-off of the valuation of human lives. However, the number of lives saved by proposed alternatives can usually be estimated and compared with respective costs.

• Food and environmental contaminants: These are other areas where quantitative analyses can be helpful, but in certain cases, statutory constraints restrict their use. As discussed in Chapter 3, the "Delaney Clause" of the FDA requires that food have no detectable presence of compounds found to cause cancer in man or animal. This precludes the use of risk analysis to determine if exposure to a certain compound is, for example, more serious than exposure to certain natural carcinogens in foods. Similarly, EPA conducted a cost-benefit analysis in setting a primary ambient air quality standard, when the statute, reinforced by court tests, prohibited the consideration of costs in setting the standard. Had they used Table 5-1, they would have checked the prohibitive box in the "statutory constraint" row.

If proposed policy issues are considered in this format, analysts can provide an indication of the potential value of quantitative considerations to policy makers as a basis for a decision. This, in turn, gives the analysts a feeling for how much effort may be directed toward quantification. However, given their attraction to numerical results, they may prepare some quantitative evidence simply for the purposes of education and edification.

What this all points to is the importance of factors which are usually considered external, but, as they are the contexts in which an analysis is likely to be viewed, are actually integral to the effectiveness of an analytical endeavor. One of the authors' previous books, *The Art of Public Policy Analysis,* suggested that the sophisticated models available at that time weren't sufficient to deal with real policy issues. When the crunch came, it was not the analysis that was so important in most cases, but the political skills that escorted these models into the policy arena. Despite all the computing power available today, this premise is still true, and 20 years from now the key ingredient to successful policy analysis will still be the ability to design and present the information.

What this means to someone interested in policy analysis as a vocation is that the fundamental nature of the job will not change much from what it is today. By and large, practicing policy analysts did not plan such a career—they were drafted into this service from other disciplines based upon their understanding of the issues and of bureaucratic procedures and politics. However, they can just as easily be discharged, honorably or otherwise. Politics and personality play an important role in the public sector policy analysis game, where the bottom line is so very fuzzy. Good, even great, public servants are squeezed out to make room for friends, associates, or new faces, but the practice of policy analysis will prevail in the next two decades as the discrete profession it is today. The successful policy analysts will continue to be those who can create from available facts useful perspectives, and examine for flaws the analyses of the competition.

Just as today, the professional policy analyst will have to be versed in the techniques of the art, skillful in its practice, and knowledgable in the subject matter of his or her agency. A lack of understanding of the scientific principles involved in an issue could lead an analyst to a "plausible" finding that violates a fundamental principle of the subject area. Computer access to encyclopedic information may help in this regard, but will be no substitute for a good grounding in the sciences. Considering the increasingly multi-disciplinary substance of national public policy issues and the multitude of analytic methods, there will be a need for a team of analysts possessing not only generally interchangeable skills, but also complementary specialized backgrounds.

Government executives have always had consultants and

advisors whose role has been to respond to the question, "What happens if . . . ?" These services will continue to be needed in the future. What is uncertain is how these tasks will be performed. The changes, and there have been many, of the past four decdes followed the pattern of methodological choices being driven and often overshadowed by the power of the tools. These choices also influenced the development of the technology, but the human element has largely remained stable. Changes in the practice of policy analysis will in the future be as subtle and systemic as the shifting uses of technology to harvest expanding fields of qualified information.

References

1. Marion, Larry, "The Siren's Song of Voice Recognition," *Personal Workstation,* 2:3, March 1990, p.31.

2. Scheier, Robert L., "Lockheed Learns Costly Lesson in System Design," *PC Week,* 7:4, January 29, 1990, p. 1.

3. See for example, Gosline, C.A., L.L. Falk, and E.N. Helmers, "Stack Meteorology," Section 5.4 of *Air Pollution Handbook* (P. L. Magill, F. R. Holden, and C. Ackley, eds.), McGraw-Hill, New York, 1956.

4. GCA Corporation, *Acid Rain Information Book,* 2d ed., prepared for U.S. Department of Energy, National Technical Information Service, Washington, 1983.

5. The Secretary of Energy, *National Energy Plan II,* submitted to Congress, May 7, 1979.

6. Herrington, John S., Secretary of Energy, *Energy Security, A Report to the President of the United States,* U.S. Department of Energy, Washington, March 1987, p. 15.

7. Board on Atmospheric Sciences and Climate and the Committee on Global Change, Ozone Depletion, Greenhouse Gases, and Climate Change, *Proceedings of March 1988 Joint Symposium,* National Research Council, Washington, 1989.

8. Fisher, Arthur, "One Model to Fit All," *Mosaic,* Special "Global Change" Issue, 19:3/4, National Science Foundation, Washington, Fall/Winter 1988, p. 52.

9. Booth, William, "New Models Chill Some Predictions of Severely Overheated Earth," *The Washington Post,* 113:55, January 29, 1990, p. A3.

10. Interdepartmental Committee for Atmospheric Sciences, "Report of the Ad Hoc Panel on the Present Interglacial," August 1974, appendix to *The National Climate Program Act,* Hearings before the Subcommittee on the Environment and the Atmosphere, Committee on Science and Technology, U.S. House of Representatives, May 1976.

11. U.S. Congress, Hearings on the FY 1991 NSF budget, March 1990.

12. National Science Board, *Science and Engineering Indicators: 1989,* U.S. Government Printing Office, Washington, December 1989, p. 80.

13. Jones, Sidney L., "Staying on Top of the Numbers: How to Improve the Federal Statistics Program," *The Brookings Review,* Spring 1988, p. 35.

14. University of California, Berkeley, "Distributed Energy Systems in California's Future: Interim Report Volume I & II," prepared for U.S. Department of Energy, U.S. Government Printing Office, Washington, May 1978.

15. Mitre Corporation (with five national laboratories), "National Implications of High Solar and Biomass Growth," prepared for

U.S. Department of Energy, MTR 82W54, Washington, September 1982.

16. Taylor, Robert E., "Putting the Money Where the Math Is," *Government Executive,* 22:4, April 1990, p. 17.

Annotated Bibliography

"Experience must be our only guide. Logic may mislead us!"

Constitutional Convention Delegate John Dickinson

The debate over the value and appropriate use of quantitative analysis in the democratic policy process essentially pits those with experience in engineering and the mathematic, economic, and natural sciences against those with academic or practical experience in the realms of politics and the social sciences. The former favor greater reliance on quantitative methods, while the latter generally tend to believe quantitative methods are of limited value in the real world of politics. Like the range wars between cattle ranchers and sheep herders, the conflict between the social and physical scientists has been vigorous and often intractable, and will continue as long as the programs of each challenge those of the other or until some synthesis emerges. Further muddying an already unclear picture, there are others with special interests, such as environmentalists or industry lobbies, who participate at the margin from different and sometimes unpredictable angles.

We, the authors, find ourselves with one foot in each camp. Coming into the realm of public administration from backgrounds in quantitative disciplines, we were initially eager to use mathematical tools in policy analysis wherever possible, and contributed to some of the major efforts and larger models. Over time, however, our participation in the real world of policy development and politics has provided us many examples of situations or issues in which the application of quantitative techniques would be at least misleading if not absurd. Consequently, we now try to use quantitative methods when data are available, reasonably reliable, and clearly relevant to the issue at hand. But when these conditions do not apply, we believe it preferable for the policy process to run its course on the basis of politics and power, without the pretense of systematic analysis, lest imprecise analyses be manipulated for particular ends.

The following annotated bibliography illustrating landmarks of public policy analysis is highly selective, and may be found to represent more viewpoints from the side of the social scientists. We believe this aspect of the literature is not as well appreciated, while the academic literature abounds with articles favoring greater use of quantitative methods. The annotations are not intended to define a source's political views, but to place the works in the context of the wider debate on methodologies.

Brewer, Garry D., and Peter deLeon. *The Foundations of Policy Analysis*. Homewood, IL: The Dorsey Press, 1983. Qualitative discussions of policy issues illustrating the unsuitability of quantitative analysis, flavored by a strong opposition to the application of science and engineering principles to social and political problems.

de Neufville, Richard, and David H. Marks. *Systems Planning and Design: Case Studies in Modeling, Optimization, and Evaluation*. Englewood Cliffs: Prentice-Hall, 1974. Case studies chronicle of the rapid spread of quantitative methods from water resource programs into many other government programs, particularly transportation.

Dirickx, Yvo M., and L. Peter Jennergren. *Systems Analysis by Multilevel Methods, with Applications to Economics and Management*. New York: John Wiley & Sons, 1979. A presentation of approaches for optimizing production and transport problems in public and private sectors, this book provides useful tools for planning government expenditures, assuming governments ever become sufficiently coordinated to define that optimum.

Dorfman, Robert, Henry D. Jacoby, and Harold A. Thomas, Jr. *Models for Managing Regional Water Quality Systems*. Cambridge: Harvard University Press, 1972. Documentation of some of the classic quantitative management and planning technologies of the Harvard Water Program.

Dunn, William N. *Public Policy Analysis: An Introduction.* Englewood Cliffs: Prentice-Hall, 1981. Thorough, organized, and comprehensive, this methodical work covers many techniques of quantitative analysis, as well as a large selection of numerical methods. Chapter 2 includes a review of the use of expert advice by government executives over several hundred years. Dunn is a cautious and politically aware proponent of quantitative analysis.

Gass, Saul I., and Roger L. Sisson, eds. *A Guide to Models in Governmental Planning and Operations.* Washington, August 1974. EPA-commissioned handbook describing infrastructure simulation models utilized for air and water pollution issues, transportation, law enforcement, and energy management, among others.

Hoos, Ida R. *Systems Analysis in Public Policy: A Critique.* Berkeley: University of California Press, 1972. In this stinging evaluation, one of the first critics of quantitative methods reviews various applications of systems analysis and concludes that refinement and improvement of existing techniques leads only to "the perpetuation of the magic spell which promises a technology to solve social problems."

House, Peter W. *The Art of Public Policy Analysis.* Beverly Hills: Sage, 1982. Co-author House describes mathematical models developed under his own research program, and the events and situations which rendered many of them non-players in major policy debates.

————. *Trading Off Environment, Economics, and Energy: EPA's Strategic Environmental Assessment System.* Lexington: Lexington Books, 1977. Details the planning and implementation, successes and ultimate failure of the complex SEAS, developed under House at EPA.

House, Peter W., and Roger D. Shull. *Rush to Policy.* New Brunswick: Transaction Books, 1988. Authors House and Shull draw from their own experiences as federal policy analysts to detail the psychological, sociological, political, and environmental reasons for the failure of quantitative analyses to provide significant assistance in policy deliberations.

Janis, Irving L. *Crucial Decisions: Leadership in Policymaking and Crisis Management.* New York: The Free Press, 1989. Focusing on the executive, this book demonstrates the importance of clearly conceived and articulated goals, and logical, if not quantitative, reasoning in the decision-making process.

Jordan, John Matthew. *Technic and Ideology: The Engineering Ideal and American Political Culture, 1892–1934.* Ann Arbor: UMI Dissertation Services, 1989. An extensive review of the literature on the issue of technological control of the government, covering political philosophy from the turn of the century through the depths of the Great Depression and the Hoover Administration.

Keeney, Ralph L., and Howard Raiffa. *Decisions with Multiple Objectives.* New York: John Wiley & Sons, 1976. Documents efforts to use decision analysis to make appropriate decisions concerning very complex issues with several major objectives which are procedurally interdependent.

Kneese, Allen, and Charles L. Schulze. *Pollution, Prices, and Public Policy.* Washington: The Brookings Institution, 1975. Kneese spearheaded a move to tax pollution sources, a concept growing out of attempts to quantify the economic benefits of restored environmental quality.

Krutilla, John V., and Anthony C. Fisher. *The Economics of Natural Environments: Studies in the Evaluation of Commodity and Amenity Resources.* Baltimore: Johns Hopkins, 1975. A description of analyses studying the quantification of economic benefits resulting from restored environmental quality.

Levine, Charles H. and Peter M. Benda. *Expertise and Democratic Decisionmaking: A Reader.* Report to the Task Force on Science Policy, U.S. House of Representatives, December 1986. A special report prepared for the Committee on Science and Technology.

Lindblom, Charles E. "The Science of Muddling Through," *Public Administration Review,* 19, Spring 1959: p.77–88. One of the early critics of systems analysis, though Lindblom was anti-comprehensive rather than anti-quantitative.

Lynn, Laurence E., Jr., with Stephanie G. Gould. *Designing Public Policy: A Casebook on the Role of Policy Analysis.* Santa

Monica: Goodyear, 1980. Case studies demonstrating the use of analytical concepts, such as microeconomic and statistical inference, as well as illustrating the role of the policy analyst within the political and institutional context of public policy making.

Maas, Arthur, Hufschmidt, M.M., Dorfman, R., Thomas, H.A., Jr., Marglin, S.A., and Fair, G.M. *Design of Water-Resource Systems: New Techniques for Relating Economic Objectives, Engineering Analysis, and Governmental Planning*. Cambridge: Harvard University Press, 1962. Classic quantitative management and planning methodologies produced by the Harvard Water Project.

Magat, Wesley A., Alan J. Krupnick, and Winston Harrington. *Rules in the Making: A Statistical Analysis of Regulatory Agency Behavior*. Washington: Resources for the Future, 1986. An independent theoretical examination of the establishment of water quality standards at the EPA, illustrative of organizational and political constraints to the attainment of optimal public policies via quantitative analytical methodology.

Majone, Giandomenico, and Edward S. Quade, eds. *Pitfalls of Analysis*. Washington: John Wiley & Sons, 1980. A collection of cases illustrating mistakes made in the application of quantitative techniques.

McKean, Roland J. *Efficiency in Government Through Systems Analysis*. New York: John Wiley & Sons, 1958. Written in an era when quantitative analysis techniques were still largely confined to the military, this is an early and optimistic proposal for expanding the concepts to the civilian sector.

Meltsner, Arnold J. *Policy Analysts in the Bureaucracy*. Berkeley: University of California Press, 1976. Based on interviews with 116 practicing federal policy analysts during 1970 and 1971, this book strives to demonstrate interactions between political and bureaucratic considerations and analytical concerns.

Nagel, Stuart S. *Public Policy: Goals, Means, and Methods*. New York: St. Martin's Press, 1984. A prolific author in the defense of quantitative analysis, Nagel often offers interesting and impressive descriptions of social and antisocial behavior and the criminal justice process in structured, quantitative terms. Nagel is not shy about encouraging governments to run like machines.

Nagel, Stuart S., and William N. Dunn, eds. "Policy Analysis and Evaluation Concepts: Knowledge, Concepts, and Norms," *Contributions in Political Science,* No. 258, 1990. Recent evidence that the debate over methodology and application of quantitative analyses is becoming more knowledgable and respectful of the world of politics.

Palumbo, Dennis J., and Donald J. Calista. "Implementation and the Policy Process: Opening Up the Black Box," *Contributions in Political Science* No. 252, 1990. Another example of the current vitality of the debate over the uses and propriety of quantitative analyses.

Pareto, Vilfredo. *Manual of Political Economy.* Translated by Ann S. Schwier from original 1909 publication. New York: Augustus M. Kelley Publishers, 1971. The engineer, economist, and philosopher here introduced what is now known as the "Paretian optimum," a formulation of the concept of economic indifference and optimum resource allocation, as well as many other economic and sociological approaches still in use today, including general equilibrium analysis and the distribution of wealth.

Quade, E.S., and W.I. Boucher. *Systems Analysis and Policy Planning.* New York: American Elsevier, 1968. An overview of military applications of systems analysis techniques developed at the RAND Corporation, written by two RAND staff members.

Stokey, Edith, and Richard Zeckhauser. *A Primer for Policy Analysis.* New York: W.W. Norton & Co., 1978. In one of the more useful, clearly presented collections of quantitative methods for public policy analysis, two Harvard analysts offer extensive guidance on choosing simulation models

Trumbell, William N. "Judgements About Who Has Standing in Cost-Benefit Analysis." *Journal of Policy Analysis and Management,* Spring 1990, p. 201–218. A discussion of the players in cost-benefit considerations of quantitative analysis.

von Nuemann, John, and O. Morgenstern. *Theory of Games and Economic Behavior.* Princeton: Princeton University Press, 1947. The Nobel laureate mathematician provides a good background on the mathematics and statistics of economic behavior.

Whittington, Dale, and Duncan McRae, Jr. "Judgements About Who Has Standing in Cost-Benefit Analysis." *Journal of Policy*

Analysis and Management, Fall 1990, p. 536–547. More on the issue of determining whose costs and whose benefits should be counted by analysts and their models.

Wildavsky, Aaron. *The Politics of the Budgetary Process.* 2d ed. Boston: Little, Brown & Co., 1974. In this post mortem of the Program Planning and Budgeting System (PPBS) imposed by Executive Order on the executive branch's annual budget development process, Wildavsky describes the unavoidable failures of the system. The notion that bureaucratic politics hamper such efforts is countered by the observation that often the will of the electorate provides a similar, appropriate, and often fatal drag on the efficiency of formulaic policy analysis methods.

————. *Speaking Truth to Power: The Art and Craft of Policy Analysis.* Boston: Little, Brown & Co., 1977. A discussion of the human dimension of policy analysis, including the notion that many of the frailties which a systematic approach is designed to overcome actually continue to taint the implementation of the analytical system.

A Brief Biography of the Authors

Peter House and Roger Shull, although different in personality and background, have worked as colleagues on federal public policy analysis for the last fifteen years. Neither suffers the other easily, but early on they discovered that their divergent personalities and differing skills and approaches were highly complementary and productive in the policy analysis profession.

House was born and raised in Brooklyn and Shull is from rural central Michigan. Yet when they first joined the federal government, it was House who chose the Department of Agriculture, while Shull pursued industrial technology with the Atomic Energy Commission. House earned bachelor's and master's degrees in economics, and a Ph.D. in public administration from Cornell University. Shull has a B.S. in civil engineering, an M.S. in Sanitary Engineering, and a Ph.D. in environmental health engineering from The University of Texas at Austin. House studied the economics of land use, particularly the encroachment of urbanization on agricultural lands and the resulting economic issues. Shull's early specialization was the mathematical simulation of the effects of water pollutants on aquatic environments.

During the 1960s, House formed his own consulting firm, Environmetrics, Inc., which developed large regional gaming and simulation models in which policy researchers could play roles of politicians and public administrators faced with typical problems. Interpersonal negotiations were conducted as part of the game, and all decisions were entered into the computer model, which then calculated the new state of the region based on the policies selected. These models were used for research and training by federal and state agencies for several years.

At the same time, Shull, in the Department of the Interior's Federal Water Quality Agency, was studying resource economics and regional planning, and supervising a large extramural research program which developed and demonstrated quantitative methods for optimally planning and designing regional environmental quality management systems.

The Environmental Protection Agency was formed by President Nixon's Reorganization Plan in December 1970. House returned to the public sector as director of EPA's Environmental Studies Division, and Shull headed the Systems Analysis Branch in a related division. The Strategic Environmental Assessment System (SEAS, described in Chapter 2) was developed to the prototype stage by House's staff with extramural contract help. House and Shull first worked together on SEAS when EPA decided to use the system to prepare a national assessment of the cost of air and water pollution controls.

As a result of a major reorientation, reorganization, and downsizing of the EPA's research and development staff, many SEAS staffers moved on to other agencies or research outfits. House spent two years at the University of California at Berkeley, while Shull stayed behind at EPA to manage the winding down of SEAS. When the new Department of Energy was formed in 1977, House was chosen to head the Department's Office of Technology Impacts under the Carter administration. House recruited Shull to head the comprehensive assessments group, which was responsible for the maintenance and improvement of SEAS as a national assessment model particularly tuned to impacts of competing energy technologies.

House and Shull survived the heavy reduction in force brought on by the Reagan administration's subsequent efforts to abolish DOE, but when the opportunity arose, they moved to the National Science Foundation, where House is now Director of the Division of Policy Research and Analysis (PRA), and Shull is his deputy and chief analyst.